Harnessing Harmony

Harnessing Harmony

Music, Power, and Politics in the United States, 1788–1865

Billy Coleman

The University of North Carolina Press   CHAPEL HILL

© 2020 The University of North Carolina Press
All rights reserved
Set in Merope Basic by Westchester Publishing Services
Manufactured in the United States of America

The University of North Carolina Press has been a member
of the Green Press Initiative since 2003.

Names: Coleman, Billy, author.
Title: Harnessing harmony : music, power, and politics in the United States,
   1788–1865 / Billy Coleman.
Description: Chapel Hill : University of North Carolina Press, [2020] |
   Includes bibliographical references and index.
Identifiers: LCCN 2019054501 | ISBN 9781469658865 (cloth : alk. paper) |
   ISBN 9781469658872 (paperback : alk. paper) | ISBN 9781469658889 (ebook)
Subjects: LCSH: Music—Political aspects—United States—History—
   19th century. | Music—Political aspects—United States—History—
   18th century. | Political culture—United States—History. | Elite
   (Social sciences)—United States—History. | Conservatism—
   United States—History.
Classification: LCC ML3917.U6 C66 2020 | DDC 306.4/8420973—dc23
LC record available at https://lccn.loc.gov/2019054501

Cover illustrations: *Front, General Harrison's Log Cabin March and Quick Step*
(Baltimore: Samuel Carusi, 1840), priJLC_POL_002630, The Jay T. Last
Collection of Graphic Arts and Social History, Huntington Digital Library;
back, musicians marching, n.d., 7986.F.13, The Library Company of
Philadelphia, https://www.librarycompany.org.

A version of chapter 1 was published in a different form as "'The Music of a Well
Tun'd State': 'The Star Spangled Banner' and the Development of a Federalist
Musical Tradition," *Journal of the Early Republic* 35, no. 4 (2015): 599–629 (https://
doi.org/10.1353/jer.2015.0063).

For Kerrin and Clementine

Contents

Acknowledgments xi

Introduction 1

Prologue 13

CHAPTER ONE
"The Star-Spangled Banner" and the Development
of a Federalist Musical Tradition 21

CHAPTER TWO
Musical Organizations and the Politics of American Civil Society 48

CHAPTER THREE
Music and Respectability in Antebellum Electoral Politics 84

CHAPTER FOUR
Music and the Making of a Conservative Radical 112

Epilogue 158

Notes 165
Bibliography 209
Index 235

Illustrations and Table

ILLUSTRATIONS

J. Hopkinson, "Hail Columbia," 1798 38

Sketch of members of the Musical Fund Society
of Philadelphia, 1824 65

The Odeon Theatre, Boston, ca. 1838 73

Henry Russell, ca. 1838 85

General Harrison's Log Cabin March and Quick Step, 1840 91

"Six Patriotic Ballads," 1840 101

Musicians marching, n.d. 106

S. Willard Saxton's journal, 16 May 1848 115

S. Willard Saxton, 1864 116

"Jenny Lind and the Americans," *Punch*, 1850 127

"The Singing Girl," ca. 1840–80 147

TABLE

1.1 Comparison of George Washington's letter to Francis Hopkinson on 5 February 1789 with the second page of Charles Burney's *General History of Music* 29

Acknowledgments

The pages you are holding were written in apartments, houses, offices, libraries, and cafes in four different countries on three different continents. Each place a home made and left and made again. The themes of the book were first glimpsed as an undergraduate in Sydney, Australia. They took shape in London, England, were transformed in Columbia, Missouri, and were brought back together in Vancouver, British Columbia. At every stage—and in every place—I have benefited from the material, emotional, and intellectual investment of so many. It is hardly enough for me to offer a few brief words of recognition in return. But I will try.

Inspiring and generous scholars paved my path. At the University of New South Wales, Ian Tyrrell and Lisa Ford offered inimitable introductions to the historian's craft and, together with Julie Kalman (now at Monash University) and Mark Rolfe, encouraged my early attempts at figuring it out. Ariadne Vromen and Anika Gauja in the Department of Government at the University of Sydney modeled the meaning of mentorship at a crucial juncture, despite my not actually being their student. And at University College London, Axel Körner, Stephen Conway, and David Sim pushed me to link music, politics, and American history together in ways that mattered. Most importantly, Adam I. P. Smith (now at the University of Oxford) gave me the space—and the confidence—to ask big questions, to write about the past with heart, and to make my own way. For all sorts of reasons, the existence of this book is due to Adam's incisive, energetic, and steadfast championing of it.

The research was made possible thanks to the financial assistance of many institutions. A scholarship from the University of New South Wales underwrote an important and often overlooked stage of honors-level undergraduate research before University College London provided the means for making the larger project a reality. Anyone who has undertaken archival research in the United States from the United Kingdom knows that doing so amounts to no small expense. So it was my great fortune to receive travel grants from the BrANCH Peter J. Parish Memorial Fund, the Royal Historical Society, and University College London. And it was a privilege to benefit from an Andrew W. Mellon Foundation Fellowship at the Library Company of Philadelphia and Historical Society of Pennsylvania, a Lord Baltimore Fellowship at the Maryland Historical Society in Baltimore, and a Short-Term Resident Fellowship at the Newberry Library in Chicago. Finally, a semester spent at Yale University with Joanne Freeman and the Yale Early American Historians (YEAH) gave me invaluable access to a uniquely rich intellectual community as well as to the kinds of primary sources that could, and did, turn the book on its head.

All the funding in the world could have hardly made up for the resourcefulness, dedication, and hard work of archivists and librarians at the following institutions that I was lucky enough to utilize: the American Antiquarian Society, the American Philosophical Society, the Beinecke Rare Book and Manuscript Library, the Charleston Historical Society, the Chicago History Museum Resource Center, the Georgia Historical Society, the Harvard University Archives, the Historical Society of Pennsylvania, the Historical Society of Washington, DC, the Irving S. Gilmore Music Library at Yale University, the Kislak Center for Special Collections at the University of Pennsylvania, the Library Company of Philadelphia, the Library of Congress, the Maryland Historical Society, the Massachusetts Historical Society, the New Haven Museum Whitney Library, the New-York Historical Society, the Newberry Library, the New York Public Library, the Sterling Memorial Library Manuscripts and Archives Division, the University of Maryland Library Special Collections, and the Virginia Historical Society. The Missouri State Archives and the Massachusetts Historical Society also provided seamless and efficient remote-research services, and Lisa Francavilla at the Papers of Thomas Jefferson and Neal Millikan at the Adams Papers offered vital assistance in helping me unravel some tricky questions.

While traveling, I was aided by the exceptional kindness of friends and family. In particular, Nichole George in Boston and Jill Dancewicz in Chicago were both unduly kind in opening their homes to me for extended lengths of time. Participants at the Columbia University Seminar in Early American History and the Atlantic Seminar at Johns Hopkins University graciously greeted a bewildered traveler into their midst. And the intellectual camaraderie fostered among fellows at the Newberry Library in Chicago and the Library Company in Philadelphia made research there all the more rewarding. Special thanks also to Christian McWhirter and Jim Ashton, who both unreservedly shared their knowledge and enthusiasm for music and American history while I was in their vicinity. In London, the American History seminar series at the Institute of Historical Research brings together a collegial and supportive group of American historians that Americanists equal to anywhere in the world. There are far more people in London, and the United Kingdom more broadly, than I can mention, but Daniel Peart, Julia Mitchell, Jon Chandler, Erik Mathisen, Joanna Cohen, Richard Carwardine, Patrick Doyle, Alys Beverton, Mark Power Smith, Susan-Mary Grant, Andrew Heath, Nicholas Guyatt, and Camila Gatica Mizala all marked this project in many and various ways that collectively would take another book to detail.

A postdoctoral fellowship with the Kinder Institute on Constitutional Democracy at the University of Missouri enabled me to revise the manuscript in an atmosphere as stimulating and supportive as I could have imagined. Thanks especially to Jeffrey Pasley, Justin Dyer, Jay Sexton, Allison Smythe, and Thomas Kane for making my time there possible. It is rare to find an intellectual environment that blends scholarly encouragement, rigor, and sociability as effortlessly as the Kinder Institute, so thanks also to Karen Pasley, Armin Mattes (now at the University of Virginia), Caitlin Lawrence, Skye Montgomery (now at Durham University), David Golemboski (now at Augustana University), Lawrence Celani, Zach Dowdle (now at William Woods University), Bill Clark, Christa Dierksheide (now at the University of Virginia), Carli Conklin, Catherine Rymph, and Andrew Robertson for making me feel so welcome. Another postdoctoral fellowship in the Department of History at the University of British Columbia in Vancouver has allowed me to bring the book to completion from an incomparably picturesque perch. Leslie Paris and Eagle Glassheim have gone out of their way to promote my research and teaching, and I am grateful to colleagues at the top of Buchanan Tower for adding me to the fold, in particular, Michael Lanthier, Alisa Wade (now at California State University, Chico), Tristian Grunow (now at Yale University), Arlene Sindelar, Coll Thrush, Jocelyn Smith, Heidi Tworek, John Christopoulos, Michel Ducharme, Tina Loo, Brad Miller, and David Morton. As a newcomer, Bob McDonald never hesitated to extend the same wit, charm, and laughter to me that he had made a lifetime of sharing with everyone else.

Many friends and colleagues read and gave feedback on all or part of the manuscript: Adam Smith, Richard Carwardine, Joanne Freeman, Alisa Wade, Stephen Conway, Kirsten Wood, Daniel Peart, Jon Chandler, Axel Körner, David Sim, Erik Mathisen, Nicole Eustace, Scott Gac, Jeffrey Pasley, Skye Montgomery, Kevin Butterfield, Armin Mattes, and Jay Sexton. Portions profited immensely from a manuscript workshop at the Kinder Institute led by Johann Neem. And an early version of chapter 1, published previously in the Winter 2015 issue of the *Journal of the Early Republic*, indebts me to its editors and anonymous readers for their constructive criticisms and to the University of Pennsylvania Press and the Society for Historians of the Early American Republic for their permission to reproduce parts of it here. Three more anonymous readers for UNC Press also gave trenchant comments on the manuscript that clearly led to its improvement, Sophie Teed provided timely and thorough research assistance, and the deft guidance of Chuck Grench at UNC Press ensured a clear and sensible road to publication. Of course, the book could never have even been contemplated without the countless contributions of scholars who already enliven the fields of both early American political history and music. Hopefully my notes pay proper homage to their efforts, even (or especially) those with whom my work does not entirely agree. Naturally, responsibility for any errors of fact or interpretation remain stuck with me.

Two other constituencies deserve special mention. First, Toby Shain, my collaborator on the "book soundtrack" that accompanies *Harnessing Harmony*, has gone above and beyond in helping me turn this unusual idea into a reality. The soundtrack aims to re-create a number of the historical songs mentioned in this book in a contemporary style—as if the tunes could have plausibly been produced in the twenty-first century. It is free for anyone to stream or download and is accessible via a link on the UNC Press webpage for *Harnessing Harmony*. Toby has probably learned far more about nineteenth-century American music than he ever cared to, but I am incredibly grateful for his work. We hope the results will prove an interesting accompaniment to the text. Second, teaching is a joy of the job, and many of the students I have taught—especially those in my seminars Music and Politics in the United States or Early America in the 21st Century—may well see the impact of our discussions filtered onto these pages. The opportunity to explore American history with cohorts of smart and engaged students who care about the past and the world we live in is a privilege I can only hope continues, in one form or another.

The unconditional love and support of my parents, James and Carole Coleman, has made every possibility in my life appear possible and every challenge seem surmountable. And this book, yet again, is a result of the same boundless enthusiasm and practical assistance they have always given to me, time and again. But my deepest, most hopelessly inadequate thanks go to Kerrin Bell: the kind, funny, brilliant woman I get to share a life with. Academia has taken us farther around the world then we ever thought we would go. And surviving our geographic trajectory would have been a feat in itself were it not for starting a family at the same time. My daughter, Clementine, spares few thoughts for this book. But if a screen is on offer, one of her favorite characters is a girl named Luna who makes the "impossible possible." When she grows up, I hope this book will stand as evidence of just how much her mother has already made this happen for me.

8 August 2019
Vancouver, British Columbia

Harnessing Harmony

Introduction

On a warm Friday evening in July 1798, musical warfare broke out in New York City. Under the specter of the undeclared Quasi-War against France and following the recent passage of the Alien and Sedition Acts, a group of five young Federalist men enthused by the presence of President John Adams in their city took to the Battery to sing their favorite "Federal Song—'Hail Columbia.'" Their celebrations were cut short, however, when "a much larger number of boatmen and low fellows, from the wharves and docks," volleyed back a competing rendition of "the infamous French song 'Ça Ira.'" Violence followed, with President Adams's secretary, Samuel Malcolm, suffering the worst of it: being "gouged" and "seized by the throat" with such force that he might have died save for the assistance of his companions.[1] The next night, "several hundred" men sporting black cockades determined to avenge the previous night's insults by congregating near the Battery, where they "appointed officers" and "formed themselves in a military manner" all to—as one Federalist newspaper put it—"evince their disposition to support our government against the insolence, perfidy, ambition and rapacity of France." Outnumbered, the Democrats present were forced to endure their Federalist foes marching "round and round them repeatedly, singing Hail Columbia."[2]

Song clearly gave these early Americans an accessible and explosive medium through which to hash out their differences. But the lesson that Federalists took away went beyond the fact that music offered Americans of all sorts with a ready means of political expression. As the *New York Daily Advertiser* explained, the sight of a four-hundred-strong band of "Hail Columbia" singers was "pleasing to see" not because it highlighted political division or demonstrated political engagement but because it contained "a number of Sailors and Merchants walking arm-in-arm with the first Gentlemen of the place like a band of brothers."[3] Music's political contribution, in other words, was notched up as a positive because it did more to drown dissent than voice it and because it united unwieldy elements of society in common cause with their betters. By contrast, Republican papers complained of "the inordinate zeal of the patriotic young men . . . patrolling the streets in the evening, singing *Hail Columbia!*" "Their incessant serenades," as the Republican *Bee* of Connecticut put it, "insulted the citizens" and amounted to "riotous proceedings" that had required the "active exertions of the civil authority" to put down. And here—at the intersection of these two interpretations—lay the real politics of early American political music: not in the freedom or the capacity of a people to express themselves but in the power to determine what that expression meant.[4]

Music, then, was a ground of contestation—one in which "low fellows" were supposed to be as well equipped to participate as anyone else. Singing a song required neither wealth nor enfranchisement, necessitated no great amount of education, and lay within reach of even those who lacked the smallest measures of social standing. The songs of the enslaved and the sounds of slavery, for instance, have shown that the agency of enslaved people—as well as their sense of humanity—could be expressed in music even while under the circumstances of white control.[5] Women in the early republic used music not only to articulate their political opinions but also to protest their political status—as did one "Young Lady" in New York City whose song asserting "The Rights of Women" was set to the tune of "God Save the King."[6] And the poorer working-class men who countered Federalist chants of "Hail Columbia" with French tunes showed that they, too, knew something about how to exploit music as a medium for resistance. But just because music could be used to contest established power does not mean it was not also used to preserve it. And early Americans, as it turns out, were well versed in music's conservative potential.

Music, of course, remained an important communicator of bottom-up beliefs, attitudes, and political expressions—but this role in itself paints an incomplete picture of its place in early American political culture. For, if music truly were a medium through which different kinds of people were capable of coming together to struggle for power, then an accurate representation of its effects is unlikely to be limited to its more subversive, democratizing, or progressive purposes. Indeed, alongside the many radical uses to which music has been put over the course of American history stands an equally strong tradition of eliciting political effect from its comparably less disruptive qualities: from the sense of order and respectability music can project, from its power to unify Americans under a supposedly common set of principles, and from its capacity to remind Americans of the sacrifices of their forefathers. In this sense, patriotic music was no less political than protest music. And for early American elites—whether self-styled or otherwise—the accessibility of the form made the power to control it all the more alluring.

HARNESSING HARMONY TELLS the story of how these understandings of musical power were used to try and shape the development of a popular American political culture from the early national period to the Civil War. During a time of mass democratization and rapid social change, elites in particular looked to music to persuade Americans to rise above political and partisan conflict to instead create a more unified, ordered, and deferential society. And the existence of this conservative strain of musical thought and action is instructive. Why did Americans participate in politics? What did they understand that participation to mean? And how were their political values conveyed and contested other than through the vote? In response, I use music to highlight the power of elites not merely to organize the institutions of popular politics but also to define the culture of politics itself. By teasing out the relationship between elite power and "the people" through their uses of culture in politics, this book illustrates the extent to which the goal of a more harmonious union often stood at odds with the creation of a more democratic nation.

Historians have already done much to unravel the early American political landscape. We know the debates that Americans engaged in over policy and legislation. We know that a vibrant civil society occupied a nation of joiners in voluntary associations, which some people worried might become too powerful. We know that ideology, gender, race, and class all contributed in meaningful ways to the creation of political identities. And we know that partisanship was capable of both attracting and repelling Americans from the political arena. Musicologists have likewise brought us a long way toward recovering the origins and progress of music and its reception throughout the course of the new nation's earliest decades. Histories of sound and the senses have even begun to reveal to us what an early American world sounded and felt like. *Harnessing Harmony* builds on all these insights, but it is set apart by its desire to embed music into the larger narratives of early American political life—narratives that were animated by fundamental tensions over nationalism, patriotism, abolitionism, and slavery. In the face of resistance from various groups, elite Americans consistently and adaptively turned to music as a means of social control, and this is precisely what made the goal of harnessing harmony at once so difficult and so important.[7]

To illustrate how and why early Americans harnessed harmony, this book weaves together two key lines of inquiry, the first being research that has begun to probe the presence of music of early American life and politics and the second being work that combines aspects of early American culture, politics, and aesthetics to grapple with larger questions of power and authority. If we can conceive of the early American state as a "work of art" or the founding era as a "republic of taste," then surely there is something in the "science of sound," the connection between "music, harmony, and politics," or the "politics of popular song" capable of shedding new light on the links between intimate and institutional power before the Civil War.[8] It could hardly be otherwise because in an age before recorded sound, music, like politics, was almost necessarily a collective endeavor—an activity that could rarely, if ever, happen without effort or organization. And indeed, from our present vantage point, surrounded by music in almost every part of daily life, it can be difficult to imagine just how miraculous it could be to hear music in an earlier age. Indeed, the political presence of music during this period is revealing because its purpose cannot be explained away as a matter of course, as something people did from time to time without much thought. Music was instead always deliberate, and its connection to politics only ever came about through the conscious ideas and actions of particular individuals in particular places and points in time.

Music also taps into the profound and shifting emotional landscapes of early and antebellum American politics. Americans at the start of the nation inhabited a culture of sensibility that involved a range of ideas and practices aimed at bringing mind, body, and society together through sensations of sympathy and fellowship, and through bonds of affection. In this context, music was always capable of contributing to the American republican experiment less as a self-interested tool of emotional manipulation than as a public-spirited catalyst of true patriotic feeling.[9] By the mid-nineteenth century, however, as sensibility gave way to sentimentalism, new rationales for music's use in public life subtly took hold. Increasingly, music's public presence was justified as a moral corrective as opposed to an idealized blend of reason and feeling. Rhetorically, the shift could appear slight: music continued to be promoted throughout the early republic and antebellum periods as a force capable of combining the American people into a "harmonious whole" that could help the nation "proceed along the rugged path of life in sweet unison."[10] But nineteenth-century sentimentalists tended to underwrite these descriptions with a growing belief that music would inject a distinctive sense of private-sphere respectability into an otherwise corrupting, divisive, and masculine public political culture.[11]

The central players in *Harnessing Harmony* comprise the type of people who took the time to record their own ideas about music and politics. Remarkably, this group is in many ways quite large: few early American diarists fail to mention music at least once—a testament to how remarkable musical experiences really were. Yet it is also true that materials preserved in archives of historical societies and university libraries tend to chronicle the lives of the middle to upper class more so than their lower- or working-class colleagues. Paper and ink cost money, literacy was not universal, and the time to indulge in musical reflections would have been a luxury to many.[12] Nevertheless, a key aim of this book remains to help chip away at the assumption that historians must choose between writing political history from the perspective of either the elite or the street. Historians of early American political culture understand that the political practices of elites and nonelites were produced in tandem. But over the past fifteen years, their arguments have consistently downplayed the importance of top-down power in a conscious and laudable effort to resist the perpetuation of elite-centered narratives. This book, however, shows—via a populist medium like music—that American popular politics was not something that percolated up entirely from below, nor was it something that elites invited into being by mistake. Rather, through a musical lens, I emphasize how the practices of American popular politics were often designed consciously from above in the interests of serving, rather than challenging, established elite power.[13]

But what, exactly, does it mean to write a musically driven political history? Music in history is a topic that can strike many people as interesting but trivial—fun but insubstantial, a subject that, in the end, is more likely to reflect a past we already know than to tell us something new. However, the key to moving past these stereotypes is to acknowledge that music is already a familiar presence in early American politics—we know that patriotic and partisan songs enlivened political rallies, filled newspaper columns, and increasingly found their way into growing numbers of middle-class homes and parlors across the nation on the back of a rapidly growing and increasingly profitable sheet-music industry.[14] To recognize the connection requires no grand feats of reasoning or theoretical manipulation: music and politics in this period, observably and obviously, existed together. Consequently, the two questions that drive this work are straightforward to express, if not to answer: First, what motivated music's political use? And, second, how was its political function understood?

Addressing these questions directed me away from detailed analyses of music itself and toward sources that comment more directly on the political logic of its use and the impact of its presence. In fact, the types of materials that inform the ensuing chapters draw largely from the typical stock-in-trade of the political historian—correspondence, diaries, newspapers, and pamphlets. For many readers, the application of these sources to a musically orientated political project may seem unusual—and not without good reason. Until recently, it had often assumed that reconstructing a sense of what nineteenth-century people privately thought about their musical experiences was a practical impossibility. Mentions of music in archival sources are rarely catalogued, and more often than not, diarists or letter writers refer to music-related thoughts or events only in passing and with tantalizingly little contextual information. Use of these fleeting references often requires wide-ranging investigations into the lives and local contexts of little-known individuals and, in the case of more recognizable individuals, requires deep appreciation of the political context and cultures in which they operated. But such a task is by no means impossible.[15]

This book also makes use of what might appear to be more specialized materials like music periodicals, songbooks, songsters, manuals for musical instruction, and organizational records. Yet, in these sources—as with every other source—my focus is on using them to examine how Americans *thought* about music in relation to politics. I take greater interest, for example, in a short preface to a songster outlining the intended effects of its publication (which can then be compared with evidence of its reception at the time) than I do in analyzing the lyrics of that publication's songs or the melodies assigned to them. This is not a value judgment on the relative worth of one type of evidence over another. Rather, to show how American ideas about the power of music shaped the American political experience, I refer to the sources that speak closest to that goal—to what Americans perceived were the purposes and effects of music in political situations. Only rarely are lyrics so blunt or histories of a tune's melodic associations so prescient as to show exactly what a songwriter intended a song to achieve or to foretell with little doubt how its performance would affect listeners. At a time when early Americanists exhibit a thorough and nuanced appreciation for the political significance of everything from poetry to parades, clothing, and even mammoth balls of cheese, it is in some ways only fair to apply the same level of methodological rigor to music.[16] But fairness is just the beginning. Here an understanding of how Americans approached the place of music in politics points at the extent to which elitist ideals lay at the heart, and the origins, of American popular politics.

THE MOST COMMON CONTACT that early Americans had with music occurred in print. Newspapers went out of their way to convey the sounds and sensations of political gatherings to their readers—even to the point of visibly spacing out type in such a way as to indicate the rhythm of toasts and the responses of audiences to them, which often involved breaking into song.[17] As a result, notionally local events (and the contributions that music made to them) took on national significance as printed accounts of them spread across the country. And since early American print culture encompassed a wide variety of formats, it is likely that the same song, melody, or lyric could have meant very different things—even to the same person—depending on where one came across it. A well-known melody like "God Save the King" would have been imbued with a specific set of associations when published in a partisan newspaper that was not necessarily shared by versions of the same melody published as a broadside, in a songster, or as part of an almanac.[18] If the melody was sung out loud by a crowd at a parade, its significance would have been different again. So, while music was a medium that early Americans invested with specific meanings, so too were the various formats through which its lyrics and melodies circulated.

Beyond print, however, most of the music that early Americans heard was the music they made themselves—a task typically accomplished together with friends and family. To experience music, in other words, was to engage in a participatory sport.[19] In every instance, music had to be an activity people *did*, not a professional recording heard at the touch of a button. This meant that hearing music performed by other people was not rare, exactly, but it did tend to strike early Americans as a noteworthy surprise—one that drifted into their lives and would cause them to wonder (if not actively to seek to find out) what had compelled someone to go to the trouble of making it. Certainly, our modern-day assumption that it is possible to enjoy music by passively listening to the studio-perfected renditions of expert musicians would have been completely foreign to Americans of this period and perhaps might have even seemed a little dystopian. Music shed of its physicality or the risk that its performance might fail is not necessarily an improvement. Either way, the Americans in this book enjoyed far less music than we do today but were generally well experienced in what it meant—and what it felt like—to be a party to its creation.

The participatory nature of music did encourage many early Americans to talk as if music were an inescapable part of their lives. "Almost every young lady and gentleman from the children of the Judge, the banker, and the general, down to those of the constable, the huckster, and the drummer, can make a noise upon some instrument or other, and charm their friends, or split the ears of their neighbours," observed the *Mirror of Taste and Dramatic Censor* in 1810, adding facetiously that it is "on these grounds we take it for granted that we are a very musical people."[20] The author intended to criticize Americans for confusing the quantity of their music with its quality. Though for many the conflation would have made perfect sense. At a time when every musical experience always involved at least some degree of specialness, risk, and collective participation, its effects could easily feel magical. It united and divided, was powerful and malleable, and, depending on one's perspective, had the potential to celebrate or improve the American people and their politics.

THE CHAPTERS THAT FOLLOW traverse wide temporal and thematic terrains. And in treading a path that spans late eighteenth-century Federalist elites through to Confederate women, I make no serious claim to comprehensiveness along the way. The benefits of this wider time frame, however, easily outweigh its drawbacks if only because it enables an engagement with elements of change and continuity over time that would otherwise be impossible to appreciate. It is remarkable to find, for example, how similar certain conservative ideas about music's place in politics remained in the face of significant change—as partisan groupings rose and fell from prominence, as technologies and organizational practices evolved, and even when the political process failed altogether. Music, of course, is an adaptable tool, and the broad purview of this book allows for a clearer sense of music's ability to suit the specific needs of different users across time.

Substantively, the book is organized into four thematic chapters arranged according to the chronology of their temporal focus. Chapter 1 begins in the early republic with an account of the political lineage of "The Star-Spangled Banner" that ties its composition to the identification of a distinctively Federalist conception of music in early national American politics. "The Star-Spangled Banner" is usually considered in relation to the immediate story of its composition—that during the War of 1812, while in full view of battle, Francis Scott Key found the inspiration to write a truly enduring patriotic anthem. However, it is less well understood that Key's moment of patriotic inspiration occurred within a particular partisan context and that its composition built on a longer legacy of Federalist musical thought and action. By connecting Key and "The Star-Spangled Banner" to an older Federalist conception of music in politics, this chapter contributes to an elite turn in our understanding of early American political culture and suggests that Federalism may bear more responsibility for the rise of popular American political culture than commonly thought. Influenced by contemporaneous English debates, Federalists justified their top-down approach to popular patriotic music by appealing to music's capacity to moderate the temperament, to instill support in the nation's leaders, and to soothe rather than inflame factional differences—meaning that the composition of "The Star-Spangled Banner," in effect, represented a culmination of Federalists' efforts to use music as part of a political strategy to ensure that their elite values were reflected in national culture.[21]

Notwithstanding the apparent success of "The Star-Spangled Banner," the conclusion of the War of 1812 proved calamitous to the reputation and electoral viability of the Federalist Party. Already internally divided, northern Federalist leaders sealed their party's fate by gathering at the Hartford Convention to threaten disunion over their opposition to a conflict that ultimately provided Americans with a decisive moral victory. However, a younger generation of Federalists groomed on the values of public service and the natural-born right of their station to exert social influence were not as quick to abandon the principles of Federalism as they were its party label. With fewer opportunities to serve in public office, many Federalist-orientated young men turned to private associations to perpetuate an ongoing project of elite stewardship. Chapter 2, then, follows the influence of elite ideas about the role of music into the realm of early musical organizations and societies. Since the colonial period, members of American musical organizations had considered themselves purveyors of a public benefit. And their tendency to assume that Americans required close guidance to reach a more acceptable level of musical sophistication made them ideal partners for an aspiring class of socioeconomic elites who similarly sought to wield an improving influence over the public. Through a focus on the founding of two of the most influential early American musical organizations—the Musical Fund Society of Philadelphia and the Boston Academy of Music—this chapter, more than simply highlighting the scale and variety of early American civic society, argues that these organizations consciously sought to influence the relationship between civil society and the state by promoting a highly hierarchical vision of society, one in which the nation's success depended on respect for authority, subordination to an educated elite, and a willingness of the majority to accept their place in the greater chorus of the nation.[22]

Chapter 3 takes up the more familiar topic of music in antebellum elections. In doing so, I explore how the use of music in electoral politics during this period was born of the same conservative impulses that had earlier animated music's use by Federalists and their descendants in organized civil society. Using the famously musical presidential election of 1840 as a centerpiece, the chapter traces how Whigs drew from evangelical religion and reform to cast their campaign music as a respectable and refining influence over an otherwise unruly process of popular democracy. Indeed, for Whigs, the use of campaign songs was less about attracting voters to the polls than it was about reining in the dangers attendant to those who had already shown their willingness to participate. Accordingly, when Democrats criticized Whig campaign singing, they were not criticizing the idea of music in elections so much as they were highlighting the supposed hypocrisy of a party whose use of campaign songs betrayed, as Democrats saw it, a preference for improving the people rather than submitting to their will.[23]

Chapter 4 illustrates how elite conservative ideals about music could shape even its most radical uses. To do so, it explores the thus far unexamined early life of S. Willard Saxton. In the grand scheme of American history, Saxton was not an especially significant figure: he spent most of his time in the 1850s as a Boston-based itinerant printer—perennially mired in debt—frequenting concert halls and making small talk with girls he fancied. But Saxton's unusually large and evocative manuscript diary offers unparalleled insight into the mind of a reform-minded young man who harbored a deep love for music and who cultivated an ever-developing taste for politics. Saxton's relationship to music helped fuel his decision to cast a vote for the first time, to volunteer at the polls, to survive for a time as an avowed abolitionist in the South, and ultimately to interpret emancipation and Union victory as the realization of the better world that music had encouraged him to believe had always been coming.[24]

The book concludes with a brief epilogue that follows the story into the Civil War initially via Francis Scott Key's daughter Ellen Key Blunt, who extended her father's patriotic songwriting tradition by writing songs in support not of the Union but instead of the Confederacy.

ON 15 JULY 1852, New York's leading music periodical, the *Musical World and Times*, published two "spirited political songs"—one in support of the Whig Party's presidential candidate, General Winfield Scott, and another in support of the Democratic Party's presidential candidate, Franklin Pierce. Convinced that American politics would benefit from "a strong infusion of harmonious elements," the *Musical World* committed to print songs in support of both major parties for the duration of the election period and appealed to political newspaper editors to join it in "this great and beneficent work." By turning the "presidential contest [into] a war of melody—a harmonious strife"—editors Oliver Dyer and Richard Storrs Willis promised their readers nothing less than the preservation of American "liberties" and "the perpetuity of our glorious institutions for ever secured." Partisan songs—responsibly promoted—would become a genuine source of antiparty patriotism: "We don't care a demi-semiquaver which party beats," explained Dyer and Willis, who claimed to think as little of "one *regime* as the other." But if music had the power to "soothe the breast of a savage," they reasoned, one could "anticipate the most happy effects from its application to politicians." Accordingly, on news that "over *seventy* Members of Congress" subscribed to the *Musical World*, its editors conceded, "There is hope for this nation," now that they knew there was "Music in Congress."[25]

The suggestion that music had a positive role to play in presidential elections and in Congress upends easy assumptions about the role of music in early American political life. As Willis put it, "The effect" of music "upon our national counsellors must be softening—tranquilizing—refining—harmonizing"—a far cry from the Election Day soundtrack of raucous partisanship that typically characterizes song in early American politics.[26] Yet the *Musical World*'s conviction that music could elevate American politics above partisanship was but one reflection of a long-standing and widely held belief in the power of music to improve the well-being of the American republic and its citizens. From the moment ratification of the Constitution was assured, Americans thought seriously about how to use music to persuade their fellow citizens to become better, to unify with each other, to submit to the wisdom of the right leaders, and to follow the most correct course of action. However, these thoughts about music did not happen by accident, and attempts to put them into practice did not occur in the absence of context or agenda. Instead, the expectation that music would provide a natural defense against partisanship was a deliberate and recurring trope, one that routinely justified conservative values in a society that all too often appeared to be spinning out of control.

Purveyors of music in American public life regularly claimed that its influence would be uplifting, elevating, refining, that it would make American democracy a more appealing and respectable place. Music, in this sense, appeared a palatable way of encouraging Americans to live up to proper standards of respect, deference, and decorum. But again, these were never ideologically empty goals or assertions. And as such, the pages that follow gesture to both the aspirations and challenges that animated the creation of a popular republican democracy in the United States. From the moment a federal government was assured, conservative elites consistently pushed the idea that music in politics served a definition of the public interest that closely aligned with their own interest. Their efforts were not without effect. Music helped participants in a political culture averse to partisanship to make sense of the fact that they routinely engaged in partisan combat anyway; music made political participation appealing even to those who considered themselves above it; and music allowed at least one ordinary American to envision the possibility of a future that lived up to his ideals of truth and justice. Music could do all this and more because the medium had a message—one that elites went out of their way to help fashion. Tunes were accessible tools but only insofar as the logic behind their use was the product of people who wanted to control popular politics more than they wanted to facilitate it. This was as true for Americans approaching the Civil War as it was for those at the start of a new republic when a nascent Federalist administration took the first steps in a fraught negotiation over the proper relationship between the American people and their leaders.

Prologue

> WELCOME, mighty Chief! once more,
> Welcome to this grateful shore:
> Now no mercenary foe
> Aims again the fatal blow—
> Aims at thee the fatal blow.
>
> Virgins fair, and Matrons grave,
> Those thy conquering arms did save,
> Build for thee triumphal bowers.
> Strew, ye fair, his way with flowers—
> Strew your Hero's way with flowers.
>
> —verses sung to George Washington on his visit
> to Trenton, New Jersey, April 1789

Little affected George Washington like a song. When serenaded by the "young ladies" of Trenton, New Jersey, on the way to his first inauguration in New York, Washington claimed that the sound of their "gratulatory song" had helped produce such "exquisite sensations" within him that his memory of their efforts "will never be effaced." "The scene was truly grand," agreed a correspondent for the *Pennsylvania Packet*, "When his Excellency came opposite the little female band, he honored the ladies by stopping until the sonata was finished." As he did so, "universal silence prevailed—nothing was to be heard but the sweet notes of the songsters—and the mingled sentiments which crowded into the mind in the moments of solemn stillness during the song, bathed many cheeks in tears."[1] Across the new nation, newspaper readers were drawn to the tearful optics of Washington's sentimental exchanges, the grand triumphal arches erected in his honor, and the elaborate floral decorations adorning them. But the message to be drawn from the sonic sensations of these spectacles was just as clear: if harmony, and harmonious feeling, was to unite a disparate nation, then it would do so not just by legitimating the voice of a sovereign people but also by legitimating the right to rule of its best men and natural-born leaders.[2]

Both Washington and the women of Trenton went to such lengths because they knew forging a new nation required more than legally codifying its federal framework. Americans might have agreed on the importance of liberty and unity, but they disagreed on just about everything else. How powerful should the federal government really be? What would American values consist of? And who, exactly, were "the People" for whom the Constitution claimed to speak? Addressing these questions ostensibly enjoined Americans together in a common nation-building project. But the process was also divisive.[3] Americans, it turned out, had dramatically different, sometimes contradictory, ideas about the kind of nation they wanted the United States to become. Some, like Alexander Hamilton, envisioned a powerful urban-based commercial and military empire. Others, like Thomas Jefferson, imagined a "Yeoman's Republic" of self-sufficient agrarian landholders that would avoid the opulence, corruption, and decline they associated with Hamilton's more centralized plans. Powerful planters in the lower South dreamed of a republic buttressed specifically by the expansion of slavery and its profits, while a range of lower- to middle-class laborers, artisans, and immigrants, energized by radical elements of the Revolution, eagerly predicted the rise of an ever more democratic and egalitarian society.

At the heart of these conflicting visions—and the key to enabling any of them to come true—lay questions over the role of the state and its relationship to the people. And despite efforts made by the Constitution's framers to assuage party conflict, two loosely organized but ideologically coherent groups quickly coalesced around these issues, generally labeled Federalists and Republicans.[4] Both parties agreed that sovereignty ultimately lay with the people. However, Federalists reasoned that the state and its representatives, once subjected to valid elections, embodied the people's will. Especially at the national level, an elected leader, by virtue of being elected, spoke *for* the people and was both empowered and entrusted to act independently on their behalf. All of which meant that as far as Federalists were concerned, it was impossible to oppose the government without also opposing the people who created it—a conviction that rendered most efforts to influence the government outside of elections as illegitimate.[5]

Republicans felt that a more vigorous public sphere was required to ensure that the people's will was heard and respected. So, when Treasury Secretary Alexander Hamilton pushed through a suite of financial legislation aimed at consolidating the power of the federal government through the resumption of states' debts, a standard currency, and a national bank, a nascent Republican Party opposition emerged to claim that a minority clique of self-interested elites had hijacked the will of the people.[6] Organized informally around two leading critics of Hamilton's ideas, James Madison and Thomas Jefferson, Republicans countered the Federalists' goals of creating an urban-centered fiscal-military state by promoting an agrarian-based alternative instead predicated on local control and the extension of political rights to broader constituencies of white men. In doing so, Republicans justified their dissent on the grounds that citizens had an obligation to correct the course of leaders who failed to respect public opinion. Federalists, however, dismissed the very idea of Republican resistance as a dangerous attempt "to organize faction," to "give it an artificial and extraordinary force," and "to put, in the place of the delegated will of the nation the will of a party."[7] How, Federalists wondered, would the new nation ever survive if its people were not unified in support of their government?

From the start of Washington's first administration, then, the Federalists in charge of it emphasized the need for the nation to rally behind its governing elites. Because if the United States was to be ruled by consent, then it held to reason that responsibility for its success had to cut both ways. Leaders had an obligation to interpret and act on the common good (a duty Federalists understood to involve more independence of judgment than going along with whatever the majority wanted). But the people also had an obligation to defer to the wisdom of their elected representatives, even—or especially—when they happened to disagree with their policies. To utilize Alan Taylor's categories, Federalist and Republican leaders framed themselves as "fathers" and "friends" of the people, respectively.[8] And as fathers, Federalists felt it was only natural that elected men of superior wealth, intellect, and manners be entrusted to know what was best for the rest. If "general harmony" was to be "preserved," the high Federalist Jonathan Jackson explained, then this necessarily involved everyone "learning his proper place and keeping in it."[9] To that end, safeguarding social stability—through the maintenance of social unity, order, hierarchy, and deference—was critical to Federalists, who considered it the only way to ensure that a nation forged in revolutionary violence would avoid the fate of revolting against itself.

Federalists often expressed this conservatism in antidemocratic ways. "Liberty has never lasted long in a democracy; nor has it ever ended in anything better than despotism," Fisher Ames charged.[10] Because if left unchecked, Federalists had no doubt democracy would turn the natural order of society upside down. "There will be no End of it," John Adams complained: "Women will demand a Vote. Lads from 12 to 21 will think their Rights not enough attended to, and every Man, who has not a Farthing, will demand an equal Voice with any other in all Acts of State."[11] Although comparatively more receptive to the "informal" political participation of women and minorities than Republicans were, the prospect of an expanded franchise was worrying to Federalists, who had no interest in supporting a republic defined by its lowest common denominator as opposed to its highest ideals.[12] Even Federalists who claimed to celebrate the Constitution as the founding of "*a free democratic Government*" still felt that the nation's leading men had a duty to "school" their constituents in "sound policy and good government" as well as "urbanity and politeness."[13] To Federalists, it was the responsibility of the national government to set the "political tone" of the country. Those wishing to empower ignorance instead, Federalists argued, were tempting fate: "I have passed through one revolution," Benjamin Tallmadge warned his colleagues in Congress, "and most devoutly do I pray never to behold another."[14]

Nothing fanned Federalist fears more than the French Revolution. Initially, Americans were unanimous in interpreting French *liberté* as a glorious result of their own Revolution's "contagion of liberty." But once the French Revolution gave way to a bloody Reign of Terror, Federalists quickly perceived this violent trajectory as an alarming reminder of just how precarious the American republican experiment remained. Federalists were already prone to consider natural rights a fantasy: that without a government strong enough to secure social order, human beings would create societies ruled by force (at best) or by violent disorder (at worst). The French Revolution appeared to confirm their suspicions. In a chillingly short space of time, Federalists claimed, democracy had reduced French civilization to a horrifying state of barbarity. "The calamitous proceedings of the triumphant party in France," Noah Webster declared in 1794, "displayed a rancor of malice and cruelty, that reminds us of savages"—a truly freighting descent for a nation that had once been "unquestionably the most polite in the world."[15] If unrestrained freedom and liberty could bring uninhibited violence and chaos to France, then Federalists were confident that similar fates awaited those who were foolish enough to follow a similar path.[16] Far better, they reasoned, to model the American republic on the comparatively more sober example of Britain. In most cases, the Anglophilic urge in Federalist thinking drew from sincere respect for the British values and traditions they felt the American experiment should seek to perfect. But Republicans dismissed Federalist efforts to secure the revolutionary settlement through a revival of British commercial and cultural ties as a disingenuous step toward reanimating the forces of monarchical tyranny that the Revolution had been waged to defeat.[17]

Sometimes the threat of disorder was overwhelming. "Our days are made heavy with the pressure of anxiety, and our nights restless with visions of horror," Fisher Ames wrote in the wake of Thomas Jefferson's reelection to the presidency. "We listen to the clank of chains, and overhear the whispers of assassins. We mark the barbarous dissonance of mingled rage and triumph in the yell of an infatuated mob; we see the dismal glare of their burnings, and scent the loathsome steam of human victims offered in sacrifice."[18] The source of these alarming prophecies came from all directions: enslaved people might revolt, or maintaining their enslavement might dispose communities to violence; mobs might rise up against their elected leaders or against the laws of society itself; and congregations, if empowered to act on their own interpretations of God's will, would end up practicing barbaric blood-sacrifice rituals or even cannibalism.[19] For Federalists, then, social control was more than just a convenient tactic for shoring up political power—it was what made civilized societies free in the first place. And this is why Federalist leaders had no compunction telling the American people how they should live their lives: Federalists believed they naturally knew better and felt a duty to use their expertise to save Americans from themselves.

Republicans were not as quick to cast aside their Revolutionary ideals. "The liberty of the whole earth" rested on the success of the French Revolution, Jefferson declared, explaining that even though "innocent blood" had been spilled, he would have rather "seen half the earth desolated" than endure watching the cause of freedom fail. Jefferson emphasized that these "sentiments" in support of the French Revolution were not his alone but "really those of 99 in a hundred of our citizens."[20] And exaggeration notwithstanding, Jefferson was not entirely wrong. Long after news of the September Massacres hit the United States, Republicans of all classes continued to mark the victories and progress of the French republic by shouting the "The Marseillaise," sporting tricolored cockades, and staging elaborate celebratory feasts and processions. When a French diplomat, Edmond Genêt, arrived in the United States in 1793, his presence elicited not just huge crowds of American supporters but also the creation of a radical set of debating societies—called Democratic-Republican clubs—that called on the United States to align with France over Britain. Federalist leaders replied by denouncing Democratic-Republican clubs as an unelected, unconstituted, and illegitimate influence over the people and their government.[21]

To be sure, early American political parties were scarcely equivalents of the much more structured and organized party institutions we are familiar with today. At the time of the Founders, the significance of political parties lay not in their (relatively limited) capacity to ensure that certain candidates were elected to public office but in their ability to connect Americans from various places, social classes, professions, genders, ages, and races into likeminded communities of shared principles and passions.[22] Debate persists over the technicalities of when and where political parties first emerged in the United States as an organizational reality.[23] But party labels were meaningful to Americans right from the start. To those who wore a Federalist black cockade, its presence marked them as a patriotic Friend of Order, as opposed to a Republican tricolored cockade, which denoted its wearers as agents of Jacobin terror.[24] Fashion, in these ways, alongside songs, plays, and print culture provided an evocative and accessible canvas for men and women of all kinds to display patriotic and partisan allegiance.[25] But the distinctions they conveyed were more than just aesthetic. Federalists—wherever they were or whatever they did—tended to assume they possessed the talents, morals, and intelligence to justify power and authority, whereas those who disputed the natural basis of the Federalists' right to rule were generally Republicans; and it is a fact of circumstance and timing that Republicans were, at root, a party born in the spirit of opposition.[26]

When Federalists commenced the job of governing the American republic, they did so in the hope that they could make it both better and distinct from all that had come before it. To do so, unity was the precondition for achieving their postcolonial dreams. And this meant that in a country as large and diverse as the United States, the first order of business had to be fashioning a national identity and culture capable of bringing together an otherwise disparate population. The problem was that neither an American identity nor an American culture could be created from scratch. No one knew how an American president should act, what style of manners would be appropriate in an American republic, or, for that matter, what a distinctly American music would sound like. But so long as Americans agreed that monarchs were capable of commanding respect, that Old World court cultures were polite, and that Europeans produced music of high taste and refinement, then any effort to create alternatives had to compete against European standards of reference.[27]

None of this is to suggest that Americans were incapable of reinterpreting Old World measures of cultural excellence to suit their circumstances. That is exactly what a song like "Yankee Doodle" sought to do. Early British versions of the tune had poked fun at "Yankee" Americans by depicting them as a hilarious rabble of upstarts who did not know their place. Americans, however, happily adapted the song (and the insult that went with it) into a point of pride. They might not have conducted themselves with the proper airs or worn the right clothes, but Yankees were still capable of gloriously turning the tables on their betters when it mattered. Variants of the same trope continued to animate popular ballads throughout the early national period. During the War of 1812, for instance, Samuel Woodworth's ode to the rough-hewn "Hunters of Kentucky" famously cast American success against the British at the Battle of New Orleans as proof that the fighting spirit of common Kentuckian volunteers could upend the aggressions of a highly feted professional Old World foe. In these songs lay a more radical musical tradition than what Federalist elites, or later Whigs, were apt to exploit. Rather than improving the nation, tunes like "Yankee Doodle" and "Hunters of Kentucky" reveled in the image of boorish white Americans, labeled them a wellspring of American patriotism, and celebrated their capacity to exceed expectations.[28]

Yet music's close connection to elite culture and religion ensured the survival of less radical traditions as well. In the colonies, accessing and appreciating cultivated European music had always been an exclusive activity. In 1763, existing records document the presence of no more than about twelve to fifteen music teachers in total throughout all the colonies.[29] And the cost of procuring their services was high. One music teacher, a Scottish émigré in Philadelphia named James Bremner, offered musical instruction to "young ladies" and "young gentleman" at a rate of twenty schillings per month, on top of a forty-schilling entrance fee—which together made for an upfront cost of three pounds (or a sum roughly equal to the purchasing power of $550 today).[30] Certainly, to possess high-toned musical skill was a mark of distinction among colonial Americans, for whom cultured instruction, decent instruments, and sheet music were only available at a substantial price.[31]

Meanwhile, arguments against extending church congregations the freedom to sing as they pleased during worship were ascendant. A book of psalms—known as the "Bay Psalm Book"—had probably been the first book-length version of anything printed in the British American colonies.[32] However, American congregations soon tended to dispense with psalm books in favor of lining-out: a practice in which a single lead singer, usually a deacon or a minister, would voice each line of a psalm one at a time before the rest of the congregation repeated each line back to him by ear.[33] Advocates of lining-out—or "the Old Way," as it became called—reveled in the communal atmosphere of its call-and-response style. But critics worried that the practice permitted congregations to stray too far from the "Rules" of musical notation.[34] So, to improve devotional singing, they advocated for the adoption of Regular Singing instead, which meant teaching congregations to sing from notes on a page rather than by ear. Reformers hoped that by sticking to printed music, they could encourage the control, self-discipline, and standardization needed to praise God appropriately.

In turn, the musical literacy required to facilitate Regular Singing in church underwrote its presence at public spectacles and celebrations. And as a result, music—among other popular practices like toasts, effigies, marches, and tarring and feathering—contributed to Revolutionary-era celebratory politics in two unique ways. First, music possessed a closer association with sacred art and worship than most other popular political practices did.[35] Second, despite music's sacred overtones, its power to influence people derived from a more scientifically verifiable basis than faith itself. Music, the composer and tanner-by-trade William Billings helped suggest at the time, was at its core an organized set of vibrations that created involuntary physical sensations whenever it encountered a human body.[36] And because of this, music offered everyone—regardless of one's class, station, or education—access to the same harmonious sensations that united Americans in common bonds of feeling.[37] These popular theories about the physical properties of sound blended with religious associations to make music an ideal way for Americans to contribute to the virtuousness and respectability of the public events, principles, and celebrations they supported.

Against this backdrop, Federalists took their perceived role as stewards of the people seriously. If Americans were left to their own devices, Federalists did not assume that they would magically surpass the heights of civilization achieved in Europe. Instead, those who possessed greater talents, education, and intellect had a responsibility to teach the nation how to be great. In the process, a desire for the United States to both emulate and improve on Old World standards ensured that cultural contests were imbued with political consequence. Debating what music best befit the American post-Revolutionary moment—as with what theater, clothing, literature, furniture, paintings, or sport did the same—was to debate the substance of American nationalism. What values united a disparate, often fractious, people? What characteristics made American patriotism unique? Was it necessary for the majority of people to defer to the political and cultural expertise of others in deciding on their answers?[38] Given the stakes, it is hardly surprising that many Americans wanted to entrust the leadership of their republican experiment to the most experienced hands available. And once those people were in charge, the idea that music could forge a harmonious republic supplied the cause of conservative governance with an evocative and enduring political lodestar.

CHAPTER ONE

"The Star-Spangled Banner" and the Development of a Federalist Musical Tradition

The popular image of Francis Scott Key composing "The Star-Spangled Banner" is legendary. Overcome with patriotic inspiration while watching the bombardment of Fort McHenry from a British warship during the War of 1812, Key composed a set of verses describing the perilous scene he witnessed and his relief at finding that American defenses had withstood British attack: that the star-spangled banner still waved. The song and the tale of its creation continue to resonate. In the lead-up the two hundredth anniversary of "The Star-Spangled Banner," the aptly named Fort McHenry National Monument and Historic Shrine received the highest annual number of visits to the park in more than twenty-five years.[1] Five years later, the centerpiece of Fort McHenry's visitor experience remains the purpose-built theater space opened to mark the occasion. Here visitors are invited to stand alongside a bronze statue of Francis Scott Key to watch a short film reenactment of the battle that inspired his famous stanzas: to see what he saw, to feel what he felt. At the film's conclusion, the projection screen lifts to reveal a panoramic view of Fort McHenry itself, complete with a replica star-spangled banner occupying the same position as did the original when it moved Key to write what would become the nation's most enduring patriotic anthem. By the end of the film, as one park ranger explains, "you will feel that same emotion that Key did."[2] And the ranger is not far wrong. Key's wish was never to express his patriotism as part of a historically distinct experience; it was to project his particular patriotic ideals as a universal, timeless impulse. To this end, at least, few cultural artifacts from the early republic have proven more lasting and successful.[3]

The assumption of timeless patriotism raises questions: Why did music become a conspicuous part of early American politics? How were music's political uses justified? And what, exactly, would a young Federalist lawyer like Key have hoped to achieve by writing a patriotic song? Answers to these questions matter because the incorporation of music into early American politics was never inevitable. Instead, music's political presence was, in every instance, contingent on a host of individual decisions—to write, perform, and disseminate music—that were predicated on, if not determined by, political considerations. This chapter, then, explores music's political presence in the early American republic by tracing the development of a distinctively Federalist musical tradition and demonstrating its influence over Key's decision to compose "The Star-Spangled Banner." Recognition of this Federalist approach to musical power establishes a conceptual foundation for the book as a whole and points toward the elite origins of popular politics in the United States.[4]

THE HISTORY OF "The Star-Spangled Banner" goes deeper than what can be elicited through the familiar image of its creation or through the story of its success. By the time of its composition, Federalists had long been engaged in efforts to negotiate a place for music in America's early national political culture. Inspired by contemporary English debates about musical power in the ancient world, Federalist elites found a top-down approach to popular patriotic music that spoke to their hope of persuading (rather than compelling) the public to defer to the views of an elite-born class of Federalist leaders. Subsequently, a Federalist musical tradition emerged under the assumption that a popular medium could be placed in the service of elite ends.

Standard accounts of the creation of "The Star-Spangled Banner" that focus on an individual's single moment of patriotic inspiration tend to miss the broader political context in which a southern Federalist lawyer like Key operated and, in turn, tend to obscure his connection to a longer tradition of Federalists who had theorized and used music as part of a political strategy to define the nation on their terms.[5] This is not to suggest that "The Star-Spangled Banner" continues to possess Federalist associations or even that Americans interpreted the song as having Federalist associations during the War of 1812. It is, however, to suggest that the composition of "The Star-Spangled Banner" was motivated by a larger legacy of Federalist-orientated efforts to use music as a way of convincing the public to unify through common consent to government power. In short, "The Star-Spangled Banner" has a political history and one that can be simply stated: it was born of Federalism.

Although evidence of popular music in politics is typically depicted as a harbinger of democratization—a medium truly accessible to anyone with a voice, a melody, and a message—closer attention to the thinking that surrounded music's political presence from Ratification to the War of 1812 complicates this expectation. Indeed, the Federalist musical tradition fits uneasily with modern efforts to highlight music's subversive, democratic, or even deliberative powers. Instead, as Jacques Attali has emphasized, when it comes to music's social effects, the context of its production matters. At different points throughout history, Attali observed, music has been both emancipatory and hegemonic depending on the power structures that regulated its use; it is not inherently bound to be one or the other.[6] And while music did offer some scope for bottom-up participation in the early republic, it is equally important to recognize Federalism's role in ensuring that one of the most effective and overlooked legacies of music in this period was as a top-down means for elites to shape popular opinion, not vice versa.[7]

Recognition that the cultural power of Federalism went beyond its partisan dimensions has already allowed scholars to trace the influence of Federalist ideology beyond the limits of institutionalized party competition.[8] And to this end, the contribution of early American literary specialists has been salient. William C. Dowling, for instance, has argued that Federalism in the first decade of the nineteenth century "vanished from the political sphere to be reborn as a mode of literary expression." By turning away from politics in the decade after 1800, Dowling claims, literary-inclined Federalists were able to achieve the kind of cultural successes that eluded them while they conceived of their battles in more strictly political terms. From this perspective, "The Star-Spangled Banner" could well be considered the breakout success of the Federalists' supposedly conscious process of depoliticization. Alternately, however, its connection to a longer legacy of Federalist thought and action shows that this so-called retreat into a literary world—a shift that, in other iterations, is ironically simultaneous to a turn to popular culture—had actually been part of the Federalists' ideological universe all along. My focus on the Federalists' understanding of music's proper role in politics helps show that any distinction between a Federalist political culture and a popular political culture was always more permeable than Federalist rhetoric tended to imply.[9]

The most interesting thing about "The Star-Spangled Banner," restored to its initial context, is not the fact that it was successful. It is unraveling why a Federalist lawyer like Francis Scott Key thought writing it was a good idea in the first place. The point of this chapter, then, is not so much to explain the meaning or success of "The Star-Spangled Banner" as it is to reveal the political logic behind the production of a song that has gone on to become one of the most traditionalized, day-to-day, and routine conflations of culture and politics in American life. Doing so links Key into an intergenerational strain of elite Federalist thought, the elitism of which has to do less with an individual's wealth or access to capital than with one's habits of mind.[10] Elite Americans in the new republic valued the social stability that the cultivation of a national culture modeled on elite ideals promised to exert over an otherwise unwieldy body politic, and Federalists arguably had more skin in this game than anybody else.[11]

The Federalist Conception of Music in Politics

Federalists cared about music because they stood for more than their leading men, presidential candidates, and legislative agendas. The Federalist Party and its associated ideology—Federalism—also stood for a distinctive political culture, one that spoke to a unique combination of deeply entrenched religious, moral, and economic principles. At the heart of this Federalist mentality was a conviction that deference to an elite set of highly educated natural-born leaders was required to produce the kind of harmonious society they felt the Revolution had been fought to preserve. And with the goal of social harmony in mind, Federalists were quick to recognize that music could be a useful way of orchestrating support for Federalist values.

Francis Scott Key, a southern Federalist lawyer born into a prominent Federalist family, was one of many Federalists who had become interminably frustrated by the quality of politics practiced at the time he composed "The Star-Spangled Banner." As far as Key was concerned, partisan conflict alongside demagoguery and cheap sensationalism had limited the nation's capacity for good governance and obstructed its citizens from performing their true patriotic duties. Yet his antiparty sentiments also spoke to an older, decidedly Federalist orientation. Before Key, two generations of Federalists had similarly experienced moments when the politics seemed to vindicate their belief that the "common man" lacked wisdom enough to save the nation from itself. In response, many of them reflexively sought out the power of music to help right the course of a wayward nation. By doing so, they developed a distinctly Federalist ideal of music's place in politics—patriotic tunes written by elites for the masses in the name of top-down patriotism.

Of the nation's founding generation, John Adams stands as one of the most evocative articulators of the Federalist musical ideal. In March 1796, Adams had become so frustrated with debates over the Jay Treaty—a diplomatic agreement that effectively worked to ally the United States with Britain rather than France—that he wrote two letters, one to his wife, Abigail, and another to his son Charles, detailing how he longed to wield the persuasive powers of Amphion's harp over congressional debates and European politics.[12] "If I had this Instrument," Adams explained to his son, "I could compose the War of Kings in Europe, the War of Factions in France and the War of Seditions in England—and what is more pathetic to Us, the Contests in Congress and our wild States of Georgia [and] Kentucky &c."[13] From Adams's perspective, the political usefulness of music derived not from its capacity to inflame passions but instead from its ability to encourage a moderate temperament. The inspiration for this take on musical power came in large part from his reading of the English poet Alexander Pope. In letters to both Abigail and Charles, Adams transcribed a verse about the political power of music that Pope had authored in 1730 for an alternative version of his "Ode on St. Cecilia's Day":

> Amphion thus bade wild dissension cease,
> And Soften'd Mortals learn'd the Arts of Peace,
> Amphion taught contending Kings
> From various discords to create
> The Music of a well tun'd State:
> Nor Slack nor Stram the tender Strings,
> Those useful touches to impart,
> That Strike the Subjects answering heart,
> And the Soft Silent harmony that Springs
> From Sacred Union and consent of Things.[14]

The verse suggests that a legislator like Amphion, imbued with the eloquence of music, could harmonize the discord of dissenting voices, soften men to the "Arts of Peace," and govern a people who were unified in consenting to the judgment of their leaders. "Amphion and I have the same objects in view and the Same Employment," Adams explained to his son; however, he added, "I have not been able to do any Thing but by main force. He did all Things with his Harp."[15] Adams stretched the metaphor even further in his letter to Abigail: "An uncomplying World will not regard my Uncouth Discourses," he complained. "The Rocks in our H[ouse] of R[epresentatives] will not dance to my Lyre. They will not accord to a well tun'd State. They will not endure the Harmony that Springs from Sacred Union and consent of Things." Without the power of the Amphion's harp, Adams figured, all his best efforts to lead the nation in the right direction were doomed to fail. "I have been thirty years Singing and whistling among my Rocks," Adams explained to Abigail, "and not one would ever move without Money."[16] Adams here translates Pope's poetry into a distinctively Federalist idiom: while Pope is suggesting that European civilization has degenerated from a time when virtuous leaders like Amphion could persuade their people to adopt the correct course, Adams extrapolates that the progress of the new American republic is clearly

The Development of a Federalist Musical Tradition 25

bound to experience the same fate.[17] "Alas! I am not an Amphion," Adams concludes. But, he told his son, "I want his harp."[18]

Adams's dream that musical power could act as a means of social and political control was metaphorical, but it goes a long way to suggesting how and why political elites did use music in the first decades of the United States. Music was a means of popular mobilization, to be sure, but to Adams's mind, it was supposed to be an elite-driven mechanism. This understanding of music in public life derived from English writers like Pope, but it also made a good deal of practical sense. Elite gentlemen had often been behind the creation of popular political songs in the Revolutionary era because they had the time, wealth, and connections to publish and disseminate their efforts. In 1769, Adams attested to this top-down quality of popular music in the Revolutionary era when he applauded the effect of a group of men singing John Dickinson's "Liberty Song," describing it as an exercise in "cultivating the Sensations of Freedom." Such songs, Adams explained, "tinge the Minds of the People, they impregnate them with the sentiments of Liberty. They render the People fond of their Leaders in the Cause, and averse and bitter against all opposers."[19] In 1796, when Adams invoked Amphion's lyre to his wife and son, he clearly longed for some way of recapturing the same unity in purpose and respect for leadership that he had witnessed Revolutionary songs engender. The Jay Treaty debate had shown Adams that sensible governance was eroding under the weight of factional interests. And musical power appeared an effective means of convincing people to forgo partisanship and rally behind the wisdom of the nation's leaders.[20]

Among Adams's Federalist Party colleagues, at least, his take on musical power was far from unique. Indeed, some of the earliest foundations of the Federalist musical ideal are detectable in a series of letters exchanged between Francis Hopkinson and George Washington between December 1788 and April 1789. Written in a unique moment of political flux when ratification of the Constitution was assured but before Washington had assumed the presidency, the correspondence mulled over the question of how music should be incorporated into American public life. And like Adams's reading of Pope, at the foundation of both men's positions on musical power was a close appreciation of contemporary English debates surrounding the quality of music in ancient Greece and an awareness of the ancient prediction that civilization inevitably progresses westward over time.[21]

On 1 December 1788, Francis Hopkinson wrote to Washington to present him with a book of songs, which at least five weeks earlier he had composed and dedicated conspicuously in honor of "HIS EXCELLENCY GEORGE

WASHINGTON, ESQUIRE."[22] Unsure of how Washington would respond to the dedication, Hopkinson had avoided telling the president-apparent about the project until after it was fully completed. Hopkinson's reticence derived largely from the unprecedented nature of his actions. In December 1788, the question of whether the rulers of an American republic were to be the type of leaders who had songs written in their honor had never been addressed. And like other accoutrements of American national political culture at that point in time—clothing, ceremonial titles, handshakes, or representative pay—the place of music was uncertain. In Europe, the most common patrons of music and the arts had been monarchs and aristocrats, which meant that if music had been dedicated to anyone apart from God, then it was typically a king, a queen, or some other titled patrician. Washington, in short, had reason to hesitate before agreeing to assist Hopkinson in an endeavor that might cause his reputation to be associated with a trapping of monarchical privilege.[23] Hopkinson, by contrast, had reason to be hopeful: so long as Washington did not dismiss his songs "too severely," he figured, then "others may be encouraged . . . and the Arts in succession will take root and flourish amongst us."[24] As president, Hopkinson assumed that Washington's position and influence over the American people uniquely enabled him to inspire the kind of artistic excellence the new nation needed to prove itself in the eyes of the world.

Washington's response to Hopkinson's musical dedication was a long time in coming—poor weather had delayed the mails—and characteristically equivocal when it came. His reply opened with a sweeping allusion to what was then a fashionable debate over the power of music in antiquity. "We are told of the amazing powers of musick in ancient times," Washington explained, "but the stories of its effects are so surprising that we are not obliged to believe them." Instead, Washington rationalized that the only way that the extraordinary tales of musical power in the ancient world could be believed was if "they had been founded upon better authority than Poetic assertion—for the Poets of old . . . were strangely addicted to the marvelous."[25] Ancient poets had indeed attributed musical power to everything from war to good health.[26] Somewhat facetiously, then, Washington explained that the quality of Hopkinson's compositions only helped to confirm his suspicions of such stories. If ancient music "could sooth the ferocity of wild beasts—could draw the trees & the stones after them—and could even charm the powers of Hell by their musick," Washington quipped to Hopkinson, "I am sure that your productions would have had at least virtue enough in them . . . to soften the Ice of the Delaware & Potomack."[27]

The Development of a Federalist Musical Tradition 27

Although the tone of Washington's reply was positive, he concluded not to lend his endorsement to Hopkinson's collection of music, preferring more circumspectly to attest to the reputation of its author instead. Washington had his tongue in his cheek, but participants in the debate over music's power in the ancient world generally invested more into their arguments than simply whether or not one was prone to believe fantastical stories.

The key reason why debates about ancient music history were fashionable during the late eighteenth century—apart from the fanciful stories—was because the larger issues that its discussion provoked were evocative of philosophical dilemmas that went to the heart of intellectual life in an Age of Enlightenment.[28] Arguments over the nature and quality of music in antiquity were, in effect, proxies for debates over the desirability of modernity itself and whether its rise signaled the overall progress or decline of human civilization. And Washington, despite his witticisms, was thoroughly aware of this: "If I before *doubted* the truth of" the ancients' stories "with respect to the power of musick, I am now fully convinced of their falsity," Washington told Hopkinson, "because I would not, for the honor of my Country, allow that we are left by the Ancients at an *immeasurable* distance in everything."[29] As a patriot, Washington claimed, he was averse to the idea that American music could be so "immeasurably" inferior to ancient music that it was impossible to compare them. If music had ever really been capable of a feat like softening rocks, then his logic probably deduced that the definition of music was more likely to have changed than the quality of music was. But Washington, by alluding to such a debate, showed he was aware that music had been ascribed incredible powers, and he was aware of the possibility that such understandings of music could change over time. More important, his familiarity with these arguments suggests that he could have conceived of how a person's understanding of musical power could influence one's perspective on the world and the trajectory of human civilization.

That Washington thought at all about the power of ancient music was a result of contemporary English debates on the topic. And the nucleus of such debates, as they stood in 1789, centered on one of the larger coincidences in the history of musical scholarship, which was that two Englishmen had separately produced what each thought would be the first comprehensive history of music in the English language at almost exactly the same time. In 1776, Charles Burney published the first volume of his five-volume tome *A General History of Music, from the Earliest Ages to the Present Period* (1776–89), only to find that another man, Sir John Hawkins, four months later published all five volumes of his similarly titled *A General History of the*

TABLE 1.1 Comparison of George Washington's 5 February 1789 letter to Francis Hopkinson with the second page of Charles Burney's *General History of Music*

Washington	Burney
"We are told of the amazing powers of musick in ancient times; but the stories of its effects are so surprising that we are not obliged to believe them."	"It is difficult to believe implicitly every pompous description given us by the ancients of the powers of their music."
"Should the tide of prejudice not flow in favour of it [Hopkinson's songs] (and so various are the tastes, opinions & whims of men, that even the sanction of Divinity does not ensure universal concurrence), what alass! can I do to support it?"	"The opinions of mankind seldom agree, concerning the most common and obvious things; and consequently will be still less likely to coincide about others, that are [like music] reducible to no standard of truth or excellence, but are subject to the lawless controul of every individual who shall think fit to condemn them."

Source: Quotations on the left-hand side are extracted from George Washington to Francis Hopkinson, 5 February 1789, FO, https://founders.archives.gov/documents/Washington/05-01-02-0208. Quotations on the right-hand side are extracted from Burney, *General History of Music*, 1:2.

Science and Practice of Music (1776). The two men became quick rivals, although Burney proved the more combative personality and ultimately derived more success from his work during his lifetime.[30] Washington never specifically claimed to have read Burney, Hawkins, or any other literary work about music for that matter. But the passages about music in Washington's letter to Hopkinson correspond so closely to passages in the first few pages of Burney's *History of Music* that it is hard to deny his general familiarity with the text. Two side-by-side comparisons drawn from the same page of Burney's work demonstrate the remarkable similarity between Washington's sentiments and Burney's writing (see table 1.1). If Washington had not been a close reader of Burney's *History of Music* then at the very least he had scanned its pages or conversed with others around him who had. It was precisely the inability to control or predict musical interpretations alluded to in the second comparison above that became key to the logic behind Washington's equivocal encouragement of Hopkinson's songs.

Francis Hopkinson's deeper interest in musical affairs encouraged him to engage more critically with Burney's *History of Music* than Washington had done. In 1784, Hopkinson intimated at some of his objections in a letter to Thomas Jefferson, in which he mentioned, "I have read *Burney* on Music which is really a very learned Work, but as I cannot subscribe to all his Doctrine, have made some Remarks as I went thro'."[31] It is unclear precisely what about Burney's doctrine Hopkinson took issue with, but his earlier support for instrumental music in church demonstrates that, unlike Washington, Hopkinson was inclined to admit to some aspects of music's power. Indeed, the title page of a popular pamphlet, often misattributed to Hopkinson, *The Lawfulness, Excellency, and Advantage of Instrumental Musick in the Public Worship of God*, featured a popular quotation from William Congreve's *The Mourning Bride* (1697), which specifically invoked some of the more miraculous effects that ancient poets had associated with the music of Orpheus:

Musick has Charms to sooth the Savage Breast,
To soften Rocks, and bend the knotted Oak.

The pamphlet itself argued for a greater use of instrumental music across every Christian denomination in Philadelphia. And in the process, it conceived of music as if it were an active agent in human affairs—an "expedient" that could "allay these Animosities, which break us into different Factions and Interests," and that could "excite the whole Nation" because of humankind's unique capacity to subject music to harmonic analyses that render it "subservient to the Use and Operation of his noblest Powers!"[32] So whereas Washington had understood music's effects to operate primarily through people's interpretations of it, supporters of Hopkinson's position on the introduction of instrumental music into public worship claimed that its effects came more directly from the intentions of those who created it or who had decided on its use in a particular situation or for a particular purpose. The conjunction of these two opinions formed the basis of what would later become a recurring Federalist strategy for manipulating public opinion and public affairs. Music, whether in and of itself or via the effects of its interpretation, was understood to be capable of producing powerful and desirable real-world results.

The distinctiveness of this emerging Federalist musical tradition was perceptible even in its earliest stages. On the same day that Hopkinson sent a copy of his book of songs to Washington, he sent another to Thomas Jefferson, whose correspondence cast Hopkinson's musical efforts in a decidedly different light. Hopkinson's dedication to Washington had emphasized the civic logic behind his music—that the songs might contribute to the "Universally avowed wish" that the "Glory of America will rise conspicuous under a Government designed by the *Will*, and an Administration founded in the *Hearts* of THE PEOPLE."[33] And the private letter Hopkinson sent to Washington to accompany his songs focused almost entirely on his decision to publicly dedicate his book of songs to the incoming president.[34] However, when it came to Jefferson, Hopkinson downplayed every aspect of his work that could be interpreted as public, political, or even patriotic. Instead, Hopkinson's songs were couched to Jefferson exclusively in terms of personal enjoyment and family-centered recreation. "I have amused *myself* with composing six easy and simple Songs for the Harpsichord," Hopkinson advised Jefferson.[35] And once the full collection was completed, he asked that Jefferson accept a copy on behalf of his daughter in the hope that "it may be to her Taste."[36]

But public issues were never far from the surface. Hopkinson, at the time, was engaged in a vigorous and highly public show of support for the Constitution and its ratification.[37] And the delivery of his songs to Jefferson was intended, at least in part, as an opportunity to vet his Virginian colleague's loyalty to the proposed federal system. "You have been often dish'd up to me as a strong Antifederalist, which is almost equivalent to what a Tory was in the Days of the War," Hopkinson wrote to Jefferson directly after discussing his songs. "For what Reason" these accusations were made, "I know not," Hopkinson hedged, "but I don't believe it and I have utterly denied the Insinuation."[38] Jefferson took the bait. After acknowledging receipt of Hopkinson's tunes—and relating an anecdote about how one so affected his daughter Maria that it left her "all in tears"—Jefferson's reply to Hopkinson shifted into a self-described "egotistical dissertation" on the evils of party that remains his first written comment about partisanship on record. Jefferson assured Hopkinson that he was in favor of the Constitution but that he differed with the Federalists' program on a range of issues from his support of a bill of rights to the perennial reeligibility of the president. "If I could not go to heaven but with a party," Jefferson memorably declared, "I would not go there at all."[39]

Jefferson's response suggests he considered the issues at play in Hopkinson's correspondence more as matters of principle than policy. And to this end, the musical context of the letter was important. When Hopkinson presented his book of songs to Jefferson, he attempted to cloak his political concerns under the guise of family interest and private life—an approach, however, that allowed Jefferson the opportunity to reply to Hopkinson's political concerns in kind, not as a politician or a diplomat but as a father with a family that appreciated the "pathos" of Hopkinson's musical compositions.[40] Striking this posture spoke to the fact that Jefferson did see music as a valuable nation-building tool, one that he hoped would help fashion a class of public men capable of injecting the qualities of a harmonious family life into the new nation's political life.[41] But using music to fashion a better class of public men is different from using it to improve everyone else. In a nation wary of elitist plots, cabals, threats, conspiracies—and ultimately wary of the very idea of elite power itself—Jefferson found music politically attractive precisely because its association with the private sphere appeared to cast an elevating influence over the country's leading men, not just their followers.[42]

The oppositional roots of the Republican Party also help account for why its leaders appeared less drawn to the idea of engaging the public through music than Federalists did. Whereas Federalist elites who controlled the government clearly stood to gain from the supposedly unifying, socially refining, and patriotically uplifting effects of music, Republican elites—as the first group to oppose a federal administration—inherited a more politically complex position. Republicans had to find ways of criticizing elected representatives without necessarily criticizing the people or the government they represented. And their attempt to do so by forging a sense of patriotic opposition did not obviously stand to benefit from promoting odes written explicitly in honor of the president. Conversely, the prospect of an elite gentleman openly writing songs in support of a nonelected figure or oppositional cause would have been incongruous with his social standing in a political culture that universally derided the influence of faction and parties. So, although Jefferson could intuitively perceive how music made by Republican supporters could burnish his reputation, the role of music in Republican politics never threatened to become a two-way street.

The Development of the Federalist Musical Ideal in Early National Political Culture

As differences between political factions hardened during the 1790s, the Federalist conception of music's public utility, articulated by Adams and debated by Hopkinson and Washington, was consolidated by a younger generation of Federalists who came of age at the turn of the nineteenth century. This new generation of Federalists looked back to the Revolutionary era as a high-water mark of American patriotism, seeing both the sacrifices of the revolutionary generation and the inspirational role of music. And they began the perpetuation a Federalist musical tradition that in one instance, at least, was passed down literally from father to son.

When Joseph Hopkinson, Francis's son, finished writing the song "Hail Columbia" in 1798, he also wrote to Washington to submit it for approval—a gesture made deliberately in keeping with his late father's precedent. Joseph Hopkinson, by then already a staunch and successful Federalist lawyer, advised Washington that he had written "Hail Columbia" to honor the patriotism of his forefathers and to boost public support in their government. "It is my fervent prayer," Hopkinson told Washington, "that your Countrymen may never lose sight of your great example, or be ungrateful to your incalculable Services." More than this, Hopkinson confided to Washington, "I trust that we that are young will keep in view the constancy, the courage and the invincible patriotism of our fathers, and prove ourselves worthy of the rich inheritance they have atchieved for us."[43] "Hail Columbia," in other words, was presented to Washington as a device for reminding Americans of their *true* patriotism and of their forefathers' original devotion to an independent American nation.

Hopkinson principally blamed partisanship for what he perceived to be a decline in the strength of American patriotism. When Hopkinson wrote "Hail Columbia," in April 1798, the Adams administration had just released the details of the XYZ Affair, which exposed how French agents had effectively demanded a £50,000 bribe in return for allowing American envoys the opportunity to negotiate a diplomatic peace with France.[44] The effect on American domestic politics was explosive. Since the Jay Treaty debates, tensions had continued to grow between Republicans, who supported an alignment with republican France in their post-Revolutionary conflict with Britain, and Federalists, who had supported establishing closer ties with Britain at the expense of America's relationship with France. Once the details of the XYZ Affair were made public, however, general opinion shifted dramatically in favor of the Federalist position. But the whole episode left Hopkinson with a foreboding sense that factionalism was destroying the republic and that bickering over whether to align with Britain or France had trumped the idea of actually pursuing America's best interests. Whatever happened, Hopkinson wondered, to Washington's more virtuous and sensible goal of neutrality? Hence, Hopkinson later explained of "Hail Columbia" that "the object of the author was to get up an *American spirit* which should be independent of, and above the interests, passions and policy of both belligerents, and look and feel exclusively for our honour and rights."[45]

To be sure, Hopkinson's concerns about the effects of partisanship were not entirely unfounded. By 1798, Federalists had become more conspicuously participatory in their politics than ever before—a development that helped to foster an unheralded level of partisan hostility driven by the question of whether to continue supporting the French after their Revolution turned violent.[46] Out of doors, men donning the black cockades of Federalism ran Republicans with French tricolor cockades off the streets, while in theaters, Federalists replaced Republican calls for French-associated tunes like "Ça Ira" or "La Marseillaise" with British-associated melodies like "God Save the King."[47] Driving these surface-level contests were fundamental disagreements over the comparative value of order and liberty, the relative danger of British monarchy or French republican tyranny, and the very desirability of democracy itself—all divisions that had been brought into sharp relief by the French Revolution. It may well have been no coincidence that Hopkinson chose to address his letter to Washington about "Hail Columbia" on the same day that reports emerged of a young Federalist mob that, fresh from delivering a mass address to President Adams, had proceeded to ransack the home of a Republican newspaper editor, Benjamin Franklin Bache—a personality who had already become one of the fiercest and most prominent critics of "Hail Columbia."[48]

Within this context, it is unsurprising to find that Hopkinson's conception of real American patriotism derived from a distinctly Federalist point of view. What the younger generation of post-Revolutionary Americans had lost, according to Hopkinson, was someone—or something—that could "once more . . . bind us in the irrefragable bonds of firmness & unanimity." In Hopkinson's estimation, the popularity of a song like "Hail Columbia" was a sign that Americans were finally starting to think like Americans again. As Hopkinson put it to Washington, indications of the popularity of "Hail Columbia" are "pleasing and convincing testimonies of the great change that has taken place in the *american* mind, when american tunes and american sentiments have driven off those execrable french murder shouts—which not long since tortured our ears in all places of public amusement, and in every lane and alley in the United States."[49] "Hail Columbia" was obviously patriotic, Hopkinson observed, because it was written by a native American, was set to the tune of "The President's March" (which had first been played at Washington's inaugural), and featured lyrics that claimed allegiance to nation over faction. However, his condemnation of murderous French melodies (popular with Republicans), the inference that Americans were lacking in unity, not liberty, and even the nerve to suggest that a Federalist-favored tune like "The President's March" was broadly patriotic all point to a far stronger Federalist mindset than Hopkinson was either aware of or willing to admit.[50]

Republicans, for their part, perceived and denounced the Federalist character of "Hail Columbia" almost immediately. The song's most outspoken critic was Bache, editor of the pugnacious Republican *Aurora*. Within two days of the debut of "Hail Columbia," Bache ravaged it as a manipulative partisan stunt: "On Wednesday evening," Bache reported, "the admirers of British tyranny, again assembled" at the New Theatre in Philadelphia, "in consequence of the managers having announced . . . that there would be given a *Patriotic song* to the tune of the President's March." Bache's italics on "Patriotic song" were heavy with sarcasm—for not two sentences earlier, he had called out the Federalists for showing up to the theater "in full triumph" and demanding the orchestra play "the President's March and other aristocratic tunes." In attendance at the debut of "Hail Columbia," Bache continued, was not a house of Americans but one full of "all the British merchants, British agents, and many of our Congress tories [who] attended to do honour to the occasion." The unveiling of the song itself only solidified Bache's dim view of the proceedings: "When the wished for song came,—which contained, amidst the most ridiculous bombast, the vilest adulation to the Anglo-Monarchical Party, and the two Presidents, the extacy of the party knew no bounds, they encored, they shouted . . . and in the fury of their exultation threatened to throwover, or otherwise, ill treat every person who did not join heartily in the applause. The rapture of the moment was as great as if . . . John Adams had been proclaimed king of America." "For what reason the managers presume to offend a great body of citizens of Philadelphia by devoting their theatre to party purposes," Bache concluded, "we are at a loss to determine."[51] Later Bache continued his campaign against "Hail Columbia" after the passage of the Alien and Sedition Acts, arguing that "a man must sing Hail Columbia and wear a black cockade, or he is called by them a disorganizer, a Jacobin," even though many, Bache claimed, "see in [the Federalists'] favourite song more of idolatry than of patriotism."[52] According to Republicans like Bache, the entire premise of "Hail Columbia" being anything other than a partisan ploy was little more than cynical Federalist Party posturing.

Republicans also ridiculed the news that Joseph Hopkinson may have obtained a lucrative political appointment on the back of his songwriting success. Within a few weeks of the first printing of "Hail Columbia," Hopkinson accepted a presidentially appointed job as an Indian commissioner, empowered specifically to negotiate a treaty between Oneida peoples and the federal government. And Republicans could not help pointing out how ridiculous the appointment made him and the government appear. The *Aurora* summed up its take on the issue with economy, remarking that Hopkinson must have "written his song to some tune—that's clear."[53] Privately, Jefferson expressed an even more cutting take on the appointment: Hopkinson was "a youth of about 22 or 23," he complained, "and has no other merit than extreme toryism, & having made a poor song to the tune of the President's march."[54] If ever there was to be incontrovertible evidence that "Hail Columbia" was a Federalist ruse, then Hopkinson's conspicuously timed career advancement was more than enough proof for Republican partisans.

Federalists, to be sure, roundly rejected Republican criticisms of "Hail Columbia." John Fenno's *Gazette of the United States*, the Federalist rival to the *Aurora*, even went to the trouble of offering its readers a line-by-line rebuke of Bache's entire description of the song's premiere. According to Federalists, "Hail Columbia" was a song that rose above party, a line of argument that equally worked in praise of the song as it did in depicting more critical assessments of it as petty partisanship. The song was now "before the public," Federalist publications pointed out, "and they will see there is not throughout a single allusion to any party or to any party principle or question." That Bache and the Republicans could contemplate interpreting a song that celebrates *"our country and liberties, without reproach to any foreign nation"*—a song that honors America's Revolutionary forefathers and that "contains a fervent wish of unanimity, or a cordial and brotherly coalition of all good men of all parties"—through the lens of party politics only showed how beholden Republicans really were to their own factional interests. Republican responses to "Hail Columbia," argued Fenno's *Gazette*, indicate that the cause of American unity "strike[s] the pangs of hell through Bache and his associations in French corruption."[55] William Cobbett in the *Porcupine's Gazette* made a similar point, noting somewhat more soberly that it was a stretch for Bache to charge that the song was in praise of England when "it abounds in *Eulogies on the men, who planned and effected the American Revolution!*"[56]

Clearly, the lyrics of "Hail Columbia" did not speak for themselves. Where Federalists saw (or feigned) patriotism, Republicans saw (or claimed) partisanship. The clarity of the divide derived, to a degree, from the fact that Hopkinson's lyrics were a thinly veiled, but nonetheless blatant, expression of Federalist goals and ideology. Like many Federalists, Hopkinson sought a society unified in its respect for elected leaders, and he offered "Hail Columbia" as a means to this end. Certainly, the chorus of "Hail Columbia" does not mince words in projecting American unity as a precondition for American liberty:

> Firm, united let us be,
> Rallying round our liberty,
> As a band of brothers join'd,
> Peace and safety we shall find.

Meanwhile, the song's verses offer praise not just to the "immortal patriots" of the Revolutionary generation "who fought and bled in freedom's cause" or to "Washington's great name," which should "ring through the world with loud applause," but also to the current "chief who now commands." The lyrics do not mention President John Adams by name. But his image was prominently displayed in early sheet-music printings of the tune, and it is not hard to imagine why a Republican opponent might interpret the following verse about the president as hagiographic:

> Behold the Chief who now commands,
> Once more to serve his Country stands.
>   The rock on which the storm will beat,
>   The rock on which the storm will beat,
> But arm'd in virtue, firm, and true,
> His hopes are fix'd on Heav'n and you—
>   When hope was sinking in dismay,
>   When glooms obscur'd Columbia's day,
>   His steady mind, from changes free,
>   Resolved on death or liberty—
>   Firm—united &c.[57]

Hopkinson's later claim that both parties immediately favored "Hail Columbia" is demonstrably untrue, but this was, nevertheless, exactly how Federalists framed its reception from the moment of its appearance. Federalists had never really considered Republican Party opposition to their government to be legitimate, and from their perspective, the popular reception of "Hail Columbia" reaffirmed the Federalist belief that Americans would eventually unite in support of their leadership once the public was wise enough to judge them properly. As the *Gazette of the United States* boasted of a later rendition of "Hail Columbia" performed in the presence of the president, "The National Songs [were] met with unbounded applause [and] 'Firm—united—let us be' was the universal sentiment" in a theater that "witnessed the joyful return

Benjamin Carr's 1798 sheet-music edition of Joseph Hopkinson's "Hail Columbia, the Favorite New Federal Song" featuring an image of President John Adams. Library of Congress, Music Division.

of American feelings and sentiments, . . . [for] the spirit of America is aroused—Let its enemies beware."[58] Republicans, by contrast, saw Federalist efforts to promote such songs as evidence of an aristocratic conspiracy.

Despite the demonstrable passion for music displayed by some Republican leaders—Jefferson himself being a prime case in point—few, if any, left a record of having thought deeply about the role of music in public affairs, even after their victory in the election of 1800.[59] It is possible, therefore, that Republican elites conceived of music in politics in similar terms to Federalists. That said, the evidence from their songwriting followers suggests otherwise. Michael Fortune, for instance—an immigrant storekeeper and lottery agent—who wrote a version of "Jefferson and Liberty" in 1801 to celebrate the Fourth of July, articulated a conspicuously principled set of motivations for doing so: "The popular Song has sometimes produced greater effects than the sublimer flights of Poetry," Fortune explained in a letter to President Jefferson, and "it is the duty of every good Citizen to support a wise and virtuous Administration, by conciliating the minds of the people." It is "the Province of the Poet," Fortune continued, "to promote Union by Means of harmony."[60] Later, in 1809, when Louis Dubois—a little-known clarinetist and music master from Charleston, South Carolina—composed a march in honor of James Madison's inauguration, he too felt compelled to justify his actions on the grounds of doing duty to a higher patriotic purpose. "It is only a march," Dubois told Madison, "but in the scale of society, [he] who pay[s] his Share of talents and usefulness to the common good, has done his duty; as the head of this Enlightened Republic, I hope, you will see my work in that light."[61] Francis Hopkinson or John Adams could hardly have put the sentiment any better but for one crucial difference: Fortune and Dubois both turned the top-down Federalist premise on its head, placing the onus on the citizenry instead of its leaders to use music as a way of ensuring that "sentiments of concord and union" safeguard "the fruits of liberty" from becoming "poisonous." From Fortune's and Dubois's perspective, patriotic music translated into a legitimate bottom-up expression, one that bound "the minds of freemen" together in support of an administration that respected their liberty—a subtle but important contrast to a Federalist musical tradition that in form as well as content emphasized consent to power by deferential submission.[62]

Elite Republicans were by no means averse to using or appreciating political music. A Republican campaign song, "Jefferson and Liberty," for example, was the first item Jefferson thought to include in a collection of literary scrapbooks he compiled during his presidency.[63] Moreover, the inclusion of other unattributed Republican tunes into these scrapbooks, like "The People's Friend," an "Ode Inscribed to the 4th of July, 1805," and a "Song" sung "by a society of the friends of the people in Philadelphia," all point to Jefferson's tendency, as president, to promote popular patriotic music as a useful medium for highlighting his personal connection with the American people.[64] Indeed, leading Republican men rarely put their name to popular songs written in support of either Jefferson or his party. More typical was an "Ode to Liberty" for the Fourth of July in 1808, which was composed by a shipmaster named Elihu Doty,[65] or a "Patriotic Song" to the tune of "Anacreon in Heaven" for the Fourth of July written by William Ray, a financially insecure poet and veteran of the First Barbary War.[66] Comparably more elite Republican songwriters like the Harvard-educated Charles Pinckney Sumner or the Brown College graduate Benjamin Gleason do appear by name in Jefferson's scrapbooks, but since Jefferson often liked to place works for and against his policies side by side, his collection actually ends up identifying more elite Federalist songwriters than Republicans.[67]

Both Republican and Federalist elites shared a respect for the nationalizing capabilities of patriotic music, but their assumptions about how music was best placed to produce them differed.[68] In 1814, for instance, the Massachusetts Federalist Isaiah Thomas justified his now famously large collection of early American broadside ballads—many of which supported Republican policies—as a way of documenting what was "in vogue with the Vulgar."[69] Unlike Jefferson, whose scrapbooks had used music to connect the president more closely to the class of people who produced them, Thomas's description explicitly distanced the collector from the contents of his collection. Equally, elite Republicans who anonymously published popular political songs tended to do so more as a way of celebrating the wisdom of the people than of improving it. Rembrandt Peale and Peter S. Du Ponceau, for example, two upper-class Republicans suspected to have authored the lyrics of popular unattributed Republican songs—"The People's Friend" and "Jefferson's March," respectively—each did so explicitly to mark Jefferson's inauguration day in 1801.[70] In these instances, therefore, the musical goals of Republican elites aimed less at correcting the nation's political trajectory than at commemorating an event that vindicated their purported faith in the people's judgment.[71]

Some Federalist commentators did specifically warn against the dangers of using music in ways that might encourage, rather than restrain, the effects of democracy. An 1807 columnist from the *Berkshire Reporter* of Massachusetts declared, for example, that an emerging preference for the "*Festival*

Songs of democracy" at religious services—which he distinguished largely by the use of fiddles rather than a church organ—was a sure-fire indication that "democracy" was "undermining the solid foundations of our holy religion" and that at this rate it would continue to "eradicat[e] every principle of order and regularity that can make society happy." For this Federalist scribe, the perceived attempt to use music to cater to the lowest common denominator was a "symptom of derangement" that pointed to a world in which the destruction of natural hierarchies had already led to chaotic and confusing circumstances.[72] Importantly, however, the column did not argue that music itself was unsuited to public life. A church organ, the columnist suggested, was perfectly capable of communicating the appropriately deferential relationship that should exist between worshipers and their God. Fiddles, by contrast, turned this properly top-down relationship on its head. And in this logic, Federalists could both attack their opponent's music as dangerous and laud their own as a correctly patriotic way of voicing respect for societal order.

"The Star-Spangled Banner": Delivering on a Federalist Ideal

During the War of 1812, it should not be surprising to find that another Federalist lawyer would also use music in his effort to combat yet another political crisis. Francis Scott Key wrote "The Star-Spangled Banner" only after becoming increasingly convinced over the course of the war that a stronger and more unified sense of American patriotism needed to be inculcated in the public for it to accurately judge the common good. According to Key, factionalism and partisanship had drawn the United States into an unnecessary war and inhibited the country's ability to repulse foreign aggressors thereafter. As with "Hail Columbia," then, the patriotism of "The Star-Spangled Banner" was explicitly intended as an antidote to partisanship, one that also conveniently helped steer the public toward seeing the conflict from a perspective that resonated with Key's own elite southern Federalist point of view.

Key himself revealed little about what influenced his decision to write "The Star-Spangled Banner," but his political reflections at the time chiefly concerned the deleterious influence of parties, the importance of patriotism, and the need for a restored sense of American unity. Key had attributed the War of 1812 to partisan intransigence and predicted, in language flush with Anglican revivalism, that the suffering caused by the war might result in some good if it forced the country to reevaluate its partisan addictions.[73] Accordingly, over the course of the war, Key repeatedly advocated plans for establishing an antiparty newspaper. Just how nonpartisan Key really intended this antiparty paper to be was unclear, however. "I should like to see a fair honest paper opposing the administration & disclaiming Party established here," Key explained to his longtime correspondent John Randolph six months before he composed "The Star-Spangled Banner," adding, "I wish somebody from your state"—Virginia—"would re-animate the spirit of 76 & take this ground."[74] An antiparty newspaper with the avowed purpose of opposing the Republican administration is hardly the model of nonpartisanship one might have assumed Key had in mind. But this potentially paradoxical position in fact helps reveal the presence of a Federalist-orientated worldview in Key's political understanding. Americans "must become better," Key had told Randolph, and now he intended to educate the public on the proper duties of being a republican citizen.[75]

Even after the bombardment of Fort McHenry, Key remained adamant that the threat of partisanship loomed large. "I fear little from the war in comparison with other mischiefs which I think threaten us," Key reiterated in justification of his antiparty newspaper two months after "The Star-Spangled Banner" was written. And the largest threat now was northern Federalists. "These yankees are sad fellows," Key said of his northern counterparts. "I believe they will revolt from the Union & consult their selfishness & the personal ambition of their leaders at the expense of every feeling of patriotism & even of party spirit."[76] From the moment Key heard that British soldiers had plundered American property on their way to Washington, DC, his southern Federalism had broken with his Federalist colleagues in New England who persisted in protesting the war in line with their economic dependence on British trade. For Key, the only explanation for northerners' continued opposition to the war was that they had abandoned the true cause of patriotism and unity for the sake of lesser interests. Northern antiwar agitators, Key argued, "say they are oppressed," but "so are we all—& in Maryland & Virginia far more than they are."[77] From Key's perspective, it seemed that wartime pressures had actually managed to make things worse, exacerbating factional divisions between Americans rather than giving them cause to come together as he had hoped. Key wanted a return to the "spirit of '76" and felt that without it, a lack of American unity would remain the nation's biggest threat. In the process, Key had no trouble convincing himself that his antiparty measures could be used as a means for delegitimizing those with whom he disagreed, such as northern Federalists.

That Key was working through issues associated with antipartisanship immediately before and after he wrote "The Star-Spangled Banner" speaks to the partisan context of his musical efforts. When Key wrote "The Star-Spangled Banner," he intended it to be a patriotic anthem, but the patriotism Key expressed around the time of its composition was more particular than universal. Key believed national unity was important, but he also had a specific vision for how that American unity was supposed to look: the best way to ensure American liberty was to band together; to argue for one's particular interests was by definition a detriment to the public good—all of which underlines the fact that "The Star-Spangled Banner" did not emerge out of a single moment of patriotic vision. For Key, the song was instead one part of a larger effort to unite Americans around his own way of thinking—for the country to rise above party in order to recognize the wisdom of a southern Federalist point of view. Key was by no means unique in his adoption of a partisan antipartisan political strategy, but his use of musical meter to convey it links him to a long line of Federalists who had considered music an especially desirable way of influencing political debate by ameliorating rather than exacerbating factional conflict.

To be clear, the political intent of "The Star-Spangled Banner" is not wholly apparent in its lyrics or melody. The lyrics themselves simply describe Key's eyewitness account of the American defense of Fort McHenry in straightforward but evocatively patriotic language. The song lauds the United States as "the land of the free, and the home of the brave" and contrasts this with the British, whose military reliance on the "hireling and slave" is meant to suggest that their cause lacked the purity and justice needed to attract the honest support of "freemen."[78] Meanwhile, the melody Key chose, "To Anacreon in Heaven," was widely known and was no stranger to being used by both Federalists and Republicans. At the time, the most prominent politically associated iteration of the tune was yet another song by a Federalist lawyer: Robert Treat Paine Jr.'s "Adams and Liberty."[79] But Republicans had also used "To Anacreon in Heaven" as the basis for everything from an 1803 version of "Jefferson and Liberty" to an 1813 printing of a song called "Jefferson's Election," as well as various other odes celebrating the Fourth of July (which was then a predominantly Republican-orientated holiday).[80] Certainly, one of the most effective ways to write a popular song during this period was to match it to a familiar melody, and "To Anacreon in Heaven" was no exception to this rule.[81] Yet to take the lyrics and melody of "The Star-Spangled Banner" at face value and conclude that its purpose was to be benignly and broadly patriotic is to overlook the politics of patriotism itself. Americans could agree that patriotism was a virtue, but the substance of what that patriotism represented was deeply divisive. In the end, Key's decision to write "a patriotic song" was of a piece with his assumption that a "nonpartisan" newspaper would convince Americans to see the wisdom of his own perspective.[82]

Unlike "Hail Columbia," however, when "The Star-Spangled Banner" spread across the country, it met with hardly a word of criticism. As Americans celebrated the defense of Fort McHenry and read the news of the victory alongside Key's tune describing what it was like to witness the event, no one stopped to question the patriotism of Key's song or his motives. Instead, as the Washington, DC, schoolgirl Julia Hieronymus Tevis later recalled, when she and her friends finally got a chance to hear "The Star-Spangled Banner," "everyone's patriotism was at full tide." Tevis continued her remembrance of the song by noting its reception in terms that Key, even at his most optimistic, might not have let himself hope for: "The powerful effect produced by this soul-stirring song," Tevis explained, "was not owing to any particular merit in the composition, but to the recollection of something noble in the character of a young and heroic nation successfully struggling against the invasion of a mighty people for life, freedom, and domestic happiness."[83] For Tevis, at least, the song really did work to remind her of the value of American independence, freedom, and liberty, as well as the importance of fighting to maintain these privileges. In newspapers contemporary to the song's release, it is hard to find a single negative word attributed to it. When in the months immediately following the song's composition Key was granted a presidential appointment to assist with the settlement of Native land claims, not one critic emerged to begrudge his capacity to leverage songwriting success into a plum political position.[84] A Federalist anthem had never met with such widespread success and acceptance.

Yet reasons for the success of "The Star-Spangled Banner" during the War of 1812 were largely circumstantial. Key's tune was distinguished from predecessors like "Hail Columbia" chiefly by its intimate relationship with the successful defense of the United States against an external military aggressor on home soil. Moreover, by the end of 1814, Key's increasingly fervent support for the war, in opposition to his Federalist colleagues in New England, allowed for his southern Federalist position to connect with the sentiments of Republicans who had supported the idea of war all along. Details regarding the manner of the song's initial distribution also add to the uniqueness of the situation. As a Federalist lawyer of some repute, Key might have had difficulty procuring a printer for his song in Baltimore (a city that had recently been the site of violent anti-Federalist riots) had he not benefited from the assistance of his brother-in-law and former Republican congressman Judge Joseph Hopper Nicholson, who is believed to have organized the original publication of "The Star-Spangled Banner" on Key's behalf.[85] Indeed, given the depth of partisan feeling in Baltimore, it is not surprising to find that the first printing of "The Star-Spangled Banner" issued in that city attributed the tune to an anonymous "gentleman" rather than a well-known Federalist lawyer or that the first publication to indicate Key's authorship of the song was the *Frederick-Town Herald*—the local organ of Key's boyhood home town.[86]

Aside from contextual factors, however, "The Star-Spangled Banner" also had the benefit of appearing long after Federalist elites first began to employ music to influence the patriotic affairs that mattered to them. And by the War of 1812, superficial elements of the Federalist musical tradition were common to the musical politics of both Republicans and Federalists. To this end, Republican prowar songs during the War of 1812 were just as likely to make patriotic appeals to unity in honor of the revolutionary generation as were Federalist songs like "The Star-Spangled Banner."[87] The logic of music's suitability to the expression of a nostalgia-fueled American patriotism was perhaps expressed most eloquently by Zachariah Gardner Whitman, who in 1808 delivered an address on music to Boston's Harmonick Club that made a rousing appeal for Americans to use music to help restore the "political concord" that had been lost since the time of Washington: "While the goddess of liberty stands weeping over the sufferings of her beloved country, let us awake the powers of Musick to assuage her grief," Whitman declared. "Let us attune our instruments to that *harmonious political concord*, which shall dry up her tears, and make her again own us her delightful and worthy children. May the genius of *political harmony* strike the lyre, and may the tune be WASHINGTON'S *March*; then shall America rejoice, and the mild sway of wisdom's laws restore that *golden age*, with permanent peace, happiness, and immortal renown, from which, having 'waxed *rich* and *wanton*,' we have so *basely fallen*."[88] Given Key's frustrations with party politics and his concerns about patriotism, it is hard to imagine that Key's motivations for writing "The Star-Spangled Banner" did not reflect the sentiments in Whitman's address. Yet Key was not interested in simply expressing *his* patriotism; Key's aim was always to persuade. The nearly unanimous positive reaction to "The Star-Spangled Banner" was enabled by timing and circumstance, to be sure, but it also delivered on a long-held and distinctly Federalist ideal of using music to unite the nation in support of its elite leaders, to achieve liberty through unity.[89]

In 1857, when Roger B. Taney compiled *Poems of the Late Francis S. Key*, he decided to conclude it not with a poem but with a journalized account of an 1834 speech supposedly given by Francis Scott Key at a "Political Meeting" of Democratic partisans. In it, Key is reported to have explained that while witnessing the defense of Fort McHenry, his "heart spoke" to him and asked, "Does not such a country, and such defenders of their country, deserve a song?" Simultaneous with this question, "came an inspiration not to be resisted"—a genius that inhabited Key for the purpose of producing "The Star-Spangled Banner." Therefore, if the piece is due any "praise," Key was said to have concluded, then let it be directed "not to the writer, but to the inspirers of the song."[90] Such romanticized stories of why Key wrote "The Star-Spangled Banner" have obvious appeal, but they naturally say little of the partisan political context in which Key operated or the Federalist political culture in which he was versed.

By the time Francis Scott Key wrote "The Star-Spangled Banner," he had access to a legacy of patriotic music writing, much of which had been composed by young Federalist elites just like himself. And this meant that it seemed only natural for Key to think of using music to educate the public in the particular type of patriotic feelings he thought they should possess. However, in doing so, the story of *how* Key wrote "The Star-Spangled Banner"—as a witness to an inspiring American military victory against a foreign aggressor—all but eclipsed the Federalist lineage of its composition, bestowing the song instead with an air of sublime patriotism. Federalist party leaders, like John Adams during the Jay Treaty debates, had long dreamt of being able to use musical power as a means of political persuasion and social control, and now Key's particular circumstances during the War of 1812 allowed him to succeed in writing an indisputably patriotic song when the results of others using the same formula had been mixed. That one man's irresistible rush of patriotic emotion was considered motivation enough for the composition of "The Star-Spangled Banner" speaks well enough to the wartime context in which the song was written. That such an explanation was unquestioningly accepted for the next two hundred years speaks instead to the enduring legacy of Federalism and its culture.

THE SIGNIFICANCE OF recovering the Federalist lineage of "The Star-Spangled Banner" is not to trivialize the song by placing the locus of its power at the level of routine party politics. Instead, it is to reveal that Federalist elites in fact devoted a substantial amount of intellectual resources to understanding the political impact of music and that the resonance of the Federalist conception of music that this effort produced helped justify the composition and dissemination of patriotic songs for generations. For Federalist elites, their use of music was less a cynical nod to Republican popular politics or a retreat from politics altogether than it was a ready-made means for fostering precisely the kind of political culture they interpreted the Revolutionary generation to have envisioned in the first place, one in which elite values shaped American values. Ultimately, then, populism and elitism were never mutually exclusive aspects of Federalist conservatism. And the original political context of "The Star-Spangled Banner" suggests that elites themselves may bear more responsibility for the rise of a popular American political culture than commonly thought.

CHAPTER TWO
Musical Organizations and the Politics of American Civil Society

In mid-December 1822, John K. Kane, a young Philadelphian lawyer, received some encouraging reports from his contacts in the Pennsylvania state legislature. Over the past two years, Kane and his associates in the Musical Fund Society of Philadelphia had been engaged in an intermittent but determined campaign to obtain a charter of incorporation for their association. It had not gone smoothly. The society's first petition to the Pennsylvania legislature for an act of incorporation had been rejected, and its present effort continued to face *"considerable resistance"* in the state's House of Representatives before it would have to prevail against "strong opposition" in the Senate.[1] Meanwhile, the enmity that the bill was producing among legislators was obvious. "The bill to incorporate the Musical Fund society . . . excited some warmth in the house," one observer relayed to the *Philadelphia Democratic Press*. In response to "Mr. Powell of Montgomery declaring that he could not understand the bill, Mr. Holgate of Philadelphia went over it by sections, explaining each section as he passed it, and concluded by saying, 'I hope the gentleman now understands it.'—'Powell—I cannot.' 'Holgate—Then you cannot understand English.'"[2] James Clark, another principal opponent of the Musical Fund Society's bill was said to have "ridiculed the idea of giving a charter to a set of idle musicians" at some length on the floor of the legislature.[3] Yet despite these challenges, Kane's correspondents reassured him that all their "zeal shall be exerted" on the society's behalf.[4] "I have not a doubt," Daniel Groves reported to Kane from the state capitol in Harrisburg, that "you will have the liberty of fiddling & singing, in a short time according to Law."[5]

The ferocity of the debate over whether to incorporate the Musical Fund Society of Philadelphia between 1820 and 1823 is not immediately intelligible to the contemporary mind. Why would a musical society care so much about obtaining a charter from the state legislature? And why, in turn, would some members of the state legislature so staunchly oppose the society's efforts? At first glance, existing literature does not appear to provide much assistance. Work concerning civil society and voluntary associations affords scant attention to musical organizations, which, when mentioned at all, are usually summoned up to flesh out the sheer scope and variety of early American associational life.[6] Conversely, studies pertaining to American musical culture in the early nineteenth century have done surprisingly little to connect the rise of musical organizations to the larger web of voluntary associations that emerged during the early national period.[7] However, American musical culture was by no means an isolated subsection of American civic life. Rather, like early American literary societies, art societies, theatrical associations, or even sporting clubs, to understand musical organizations in the United States requires that we take seriously their claims to have interpreted the provision of music as an inherently *public* good and to consider the implications of their efforts in this light.[8] Musical organizations, I argue, were significant in the largest sense because their efforts to reform American public life contributed directly to wider disagreements over the proper relationship between civil society and the state.

EARLY AMERICAN MUSICAL ORGANIZATIONS—societies, clubs, academies, and so on—encompassed an incredibly broad range of associational structures and engaged in an even wider variety of activities. Music-related associations spanned sacred and secular groups; operated according to formal and informal governance structures; were in some cases education focused and in others devoted to organizing professional concert performances; enforced homogeneous and heterogeneous membership eligibility standards; were led by professional musicians, amateurs or both; and inhabited the entire spectrum between being of purely local significance and exerting nationwide influence. Every individual musical organization, moreover, was likely to involve a unique selection of attributes from all the above. Yet, eclectic as they were, early American musical organizations shared the same fundamental goal: that of working to help cultivate a higher taste and skill for music in the United States. And they all went about doing so—unlike other important forms of early American musical infrastructure like theater companies or artist troupes—under the guise of nonprofit enterprise.

Central to the development of a shared purpose among American music societies was a burgeoning homegrown American music press that bound musical associations together in a common print culture. "It is to the establishment of these nurseries," explained the country's first music-specific periodical in June 1822 of musical societies, "that we are to expect the dissemination of taste for the practice of this delightful art."[9] In fact, specialist music periodicals like Boston's *Euterpeiad, or Musical Intelligencer* (established in 1820) or New York's *Lyre, or New-York Musical Journal* (established in 1824) largely claimed to be working toward the same beneficent purposes as the musical societies they reported on—"to diffuse a general knowledge of this pleasing Science" in order to "render some service to the Public."[10] And to this end, journalizing the progress and activities of musical societies was an important and recognized function of the American music press. "One object of the Lyre," its editor, James H. Swindells, made plain in 1824, "is to make mention of all respectable musical societies in the Union."[11] Through soliciting profiles and communications from a dizzying array of musical societies, the columns of American music periodicals connected a growing number of musically interested Americans from across all parts of the nation into one like-minded community.[12]

By the same token, the attention that music journalists lavished on early American musical organizations also burnished the idea that musical organizations offered members a civically engaged refuge from political discord. Part of the reason for this was that even the music critics who penned some of the most strident criticisms of musical societies tended to be genuinely supportive of their aims and hopeful of their eventual success. As one anonymous but self-described "grumbletonian" explained in 1825, the purpose of his or her highly unfavorable reporting of a series of New York Philharmonic Society concerts was actually to encourage the directors of that society in their "zealous perseverance in [a] right and successful course."[13] So while American music critics subjected the quality of music produced in America to close scrutiny, musically interested Americans rarely questioned the assumption that private musical societies were a laudable way for Americans to organize and produce music for the benefit of the public. Proponents of musical organizations, for their part, justified their activities on the basis that they fulfilled an obvious and intrinsic public good. However, to project music's public value under the cover of civil society was never an apolitical endeavor. Musical organizations in the United States could not seclude themselves from the vicissitudes of public life just because their most organized and vocal supporters believed that their goals allowed them to transcend political divisions. And neither could opponents of musical organizations in the United States easily exclude musical groups from public life on the grounds that their existence was irrelevant or detrimental to the public interest.

By concentrating on the founding of two key early American musical organizations—the Musical Fund Society of Philadelphia (established in 1820) and the Boston Academy of Music (established in 1833)—this chapter explores the elitism that underpinned their creation and shows how their decisions to contribute to the public good through music reflected deeply conservative conceptions of how American society should function. Admittedly, the Musical Fund Society of Philadelphia and the Boston Academy of Music were by no means typical of American musical societies more broadly. Both institutions cultivated significant national reputations and attracted unusually large concentrations of power and influence among their membership. But while these characteristics set them apart from most other comparable organizations, they also transformed what might have been two distinctive approaches to musical organization into widely followed templates, emulated by other groups of various sizes and in various places throughout the country.[14] The Musical Fund Society of Philadelphia and the Boston Academy of Music amplified a preexisting tradition of American musical organizations conceived for the purposes of providing a public benefit by tailoring an elite Federalist ideal of music in politics to an expanding world of American civic associations. The results thrust musical organizations into the heart of highly politicized debates over the public influence of private associations and signaled the persistence of Federalist ideology long after the demise of its political party.

The Origins of American Musical Organizations

By 1820, musical organizations—broadly defined—had long been an important component of early American musical life. This would probably have been true, to some degree, if only for the fact that making music oftentimes requires substantial organization. But in many ways, the shape that early American musical organizing actually took was imported from European, specifically British, precedents. Indeed, during the eighteenth century, most of the earliest known American musical institutions are best understood as but one variety of the roughly twenty-five thousand voluntary associations and clubs that had sprung into being throughout the English-speaking world.[15] By the mid-nineteenth century, an unprecedented number of associations were assembling in capital cities and provincial centers across all parts of the British Isles to organize fashionable subscription concerts, for choral singing, to join singing clubs, or to raise money in support of "decayed musicians."[16] And British Americans keen to replicate the cultural sophistication of their British counterparts had been quick to encourage the creation of a semiprivate salon concert culture of their own through organizations like Charleston's St. Cecilia Society—established in 1766 in imitation of the upper-class musical societies then flourishing in Britain—or by patronizing the attempts of foreign musicians to get up their own exclusive series of subscription concerts.[17] Many of these immigrant musicians had worked closely with prestigious musical organizations in the Old World and brought these experiences to bear on the American subscription concerts they initiated. The influence of the Edinburgh Musical Society, for example, is observable in late eighteenth-century Philadelphia by way of the programs, concert arrangements, and repertoires used by the Scottish musicians who pioneered much of Philadelphia's early concert life.[18]

Less conspicuously wealthy British Americans also congregated to make music, usually under the auspices of singing schools held seasonally by itinerant singing masters or in conjunction with a local church. Singing schools were initially intended as a way of improving the quality of psalm singing during worship, but their scope and popularity expanded significantly over the course of the eighteenth century as a result of the Great Awakening, incipient urbanization, and, later, increasing communications with Europe. Boston's first singing school probably started in 1714, and notably, by 1722, singing schools benefited from the promotion of at least one Boston-based advocacy group—the Society for Promoting Regular Singing in the Worship of God.[19] Although singing schools were predominantly a New England phenomenon, their adoption and influence were by no means limited to the Northeast. Charleston had singing schools as early as 1730, Philadelphia by 1753, and New York by 1754—eventually, in 1844, the *Sacred Harp* tune book, published in Georgia, would become the standard bearer of this old-style singing-school tradition, by then already out of fashion in New England.[20]

Singing schools were run by self-taught singing masters who instructed classes of generally young scholars through the basics of musical literacy and vocal skill. The goal, ostensibly, was to facilitate Regular Singing in church— congregations that sung psalms according to printed notes on a page as opposed to the then traditional practice of lining out by ear. In practice, the cocurricular attractions of attending singing school (it being one of the few socially accepted mixed-sex forums available to young people outside the home) contributed more than a little to the popular success of the institution. Moreover, the repertoires of music taught to singing-school students quickly expanded beyond psalms alone—a development that would do much to deepen the religious connotations of secular-based musical activity thereafter.[21] By the Revolution, singing school was commonly known to instruct scholars in hymn singing, secular glees, and patriotic pieces in addition to the psalms. Samuel Adams, who kept up a secondary avocation as a singing master, for example, was derided by his Tory opponents for "instituting singing Societies of Mechanicks" that specialized in "inculcating Sedition."[22]

Nevertheless, if singing schools by the time of the Revolution had developed into something of a uniquely American custom, it was one that had firm roots in a British psalm-singing tradition and that had expanded in the shadow of a larger British-based associational world.[23]

Together, both elite salon concerts and mainstream singing schools provided a fertile foundation for antebellum American musical organizations. On the one hand, immigrant musicians catering to elite European-based tastes encouraged musical appreciation for the sake of fashionable consumption. On the other, successful singing schools often inspired students to take an ongoing interest in music making that led in many cases to the formation of local singing societies.[24] By the late eighteenth century, it is clear that many of America's early musical societies had been established by amateurs who were fresh from a season of singing school and keen to publicly attempt larger, more difficult, and more fashionable pieces of music—often for patriotic purposes and with an eye to European tastes. In this sense, musical organizations in early America—even in their incipient forms—had always been publicly orientated societies, at least to the extent that they proposed to enable the nation to live up to ever-higher cultural and religious standards of practice.[25]

The progression from singing-school participation to formalized musical organizations is illustrated through the account of one young Bostonian's role in the founding of the Boston Independent Musical Society. In 1788, Nathan Webb worked as a teaching assistant at the North Writing School in Boston.[26] Webb eventually grew up to have a long, if relatively undistinguished, career in various public offices including a term in the Massachusetts House of Representatives, but when he started a diary in his early twenties, he was still aspiring to such a life.[27] Initially, Webb described his musical participation as a matter-of-fact affair. "Went to our singing school about 7 o'clock," as one characteristic passage goes, "made out tolerably well."[28] The routine nature of Webb's participation in organized musical events meant he rarely felt the need to add much commentary to their occurrence. At most, Webb would mention that he had accompanied a particular lady to and from a singing (as they were called), list the tunes sung, or add that he had attended a singing despite very cold weather.[29] But beginning in November 1788, Webb's diary indicates an uptick in his attendance at singing school and meetings of the New North Singing Society.[30] By January 1789, Webb was conversing with his friends about the idea of "entering into a Society for performing Vocal musick for pastime," and the plan was soon put into action.[31] Webb spent a good portion of his spare time in February 1789 drafting the articles of a constitution to establish the Independent Musical Society, which met for the first time at the end of the month, when its members elected Webb its founding clerk and treasurer.[32]

With the Independent Musical Society, Webb mixed music, socializing, networking, and patriotism together in one venture. The group was ostensibly a private club limited to thirty-five male singers and twelve female singers, but they did not keep to themselves, taking to the streets to perform regularly at civic occasions around Boston.[33] Of the male members, most worked as schoolteachers, including all three of the elected officers. Female membership was contentious. After what Webb describes as "a desultory debate with respect to the manner of admitting Female members," a special nine-member committee was formed "to hunt up" some ladies, only to be abandoned a week later after failing to find more than six who were willing to join.[34] But for an upwardly mobile twenty-one-year-old teaching assistant like Webb, the chance to preside as clerk and treasurer over this combination of colleagues, mentors, and sociable ladies was an exciting opportunity.

The Independent Musical Society was also different from the musical groups Webb had previously been involved in. Unlike singing schools, the Independent Musical Society had no specific religious affiliation and instead performed in public spaces and at public events — often singing odes tailored to patriotic activities. Appropriately perhaps, the Independent Musical Society gave its first public performance on 4 July 1789, at Boston's Independence Day celebrations. In contrast to the simpler fare sung at Webb's singing school or at the New North Singing Society, the Independent Musical Society marked Independence Day with "an Anthem by Mr. Handell [sic], & an Hallelujah Chorus by Doct. Rogerson" as well as "an ode adapted to the occasion."[35] In October 1789, the society performed in public again, this time to "mark the arrival of THE PRESIDENT at the TRIUMPHAL ARCH, in Boston." There they sang another song composed for the event—"Ode to Columbia's Favorite Son"—which called for all present to "in full chorus burst the song / And shout the deeds of Washington!"[36] Three days later, the society was due to reprise its celebratory ode, along with a selection of other pieces, "in presence of the PRESIDENT of the United States" at a concert to be given at Boston's Stone Chapel.[37] On the day of the concert, however, many of the musicians slated to perform fell ill in an influenza outbreak, which led organizers to postpone the musical program. Washington, not so easily deterred, showed up to his concert anyway and received "several pieces," which, according to the *Massachusetts Centinel*, "merited and received applause."[38] Webb, then, was one of the usually faceless individuals who made the effort to sing songs about the political excitements in their lives. He did so in part because the start of a new federal government was exciting but also because singing school had primed him to consider music an apt way of expressing patriotism and contributing to public life.

Groups like the Independent Musical Society were at the forefront of a growing phenomenon. By 1800, formally organized musical societies similar to the Independent Musical Society could be found all along the East Coast from New England to Georgia.[39] Getting a sense of exactly how many musical organizations existed at any one time is difficult, but their numbers were considerable. By 1818, according to one contemporary estimate, the New Hampshire state legislature alone had chartered a total of twenty-seven musical societies.[40] While varied in their focus, all were in the business of advocating the use of music to help improve American public life. In 1801, for instance, a "Music Society" instituted in Morristown, New Jersey, requested the assistance of all in Morristown "who are acquainted with the rules of singing" to join it in the cause of "promoting vocal music" on the grounds that the cultivation of music "forms an important link in the chains of causes by which nations are civilised, and made happy."[41] In 1808, Z. G. Whitman similarly promoted the effects of musical organizations with reference to their public benefit in an address to the Boston Harmonick Club: "The effect which Musick has had on society, by tending to civilization, is incalculably great," Whitman reasoned, "its nature being to purify and refine the tender, while it polishes the rough passions of the soul."[42] In 1810, the Handel Society of Dartmouth College and the Middlesex Musical Society of Massachusetts proposed a joint concert in Concord, New Hampshire, for the purpose of "introducing into public worship, genuine and serious music"—a goal the *New Hampshire Patriot* lauded over "the 'unmeaning and frivolous airs' of American authors, who," they determined, "present nothing like [a] 'concert of sweet sounds'—nothing like the spirit of true devotion."[43] Invariably, these organizations and their supporters had more interest in encouraging Americans to live up to European standards of musical excellence than in defining American alternatives to them.

At an organizational level, most early American musical organizations shared the same basic structures adopted by other types of American civic organizations. Typically, formalized music societies were governed according to a constitution that set out its objects, operating procedures, and activities along with the rights and obligations of membership—all in very close detail. There were rules about who could be members, different classifications of membership, official lists of members, minutes of meetings, numerous committees, officers, boards of directors, voting procedures, financial arrangements, and procedures for changing the rules when necessary. In principle, musical societies were organized no differently from Bible societies, fire-prevention societies, mutual-protection societies, or library societies—and more often than not, amateur members of musical organizations were active in some selection of those other forms of civic organization as well. Broadly speaking, though, the formal organization of American musical societies, like much of the rest of the American associational world, was largely in keeping with the traditions set by the British musical societies that many initially had sought to resemble.[44]

Musical societies, then, were neither ad hoc affairs conducted on a whim for purely pleasurable purposes nor private affairs conducted away from the public eye. Instead, musical organizations and those who populated them were involved in conscious efforts to frame their activities as positive contributions to America's burgeoning civic and associational life. Part of the reason for their public-facing orientation was historical: at least since colonial clergymen decided to institute singing schools to improve the quality of church music, organizations convened for the purposes of making music in the United States had generally considered their efforts to involve the provision of a public good in one way or another. However, with a new generation of Federalist elites coming of age to find their electoral prospects wanting, the orientation of at least some musical organizations began to take on a more discernibly political hue. By centralizing musical authority and expertise in corporate-style structures and by seeking to educate the public in what kind of music was best for them to support, these musical organizations saw it as their duty to ensure that American musical progress occurred under close supervision.[45]

Elitist Conservatism in Early American Musical Organizations

Musical associations in the United States were not Federalist in any explicit sense, but their stated motives—the kind of impact they aimed to exert over the public—aligned with an elitist sensibility that was attractive to people with Federalist inclinations. These were organizations led by individuals who were convinced that a poor level of musical taste in the United States reflected a larger moral malaise that inhibited the country from reaching its full potential. And, in fact, musical organizations did often justify their existence on the grounds that a population that failed to patronize good music could hardly be trusted to make the right decisions in other areas of public life either. The political debates that surrounded musical societies, however, derived not from a prejudice against music itself but from partisan schisms over the assumption that private institutions deserved to have significant influence over American public life. Musical organizations were primed to become part of these debates because the elitist mindset of their members tended to support the idea that when it came to music, at least, Americans could not be trusted to make the right decisions without the expert guidance of those who know better.

Orations delivered to early American musical societies do much to illustrate their elitist agendas. In 1809, for instance, Solomon Kidder Livermore explained to the Middlesex Musical Society that "liberty" had endangered American society by giving too much "latitude to vice and folly." Pretenders of all kinds, Livermore alleged, had been given free rein to dupe a public now fully empowered to act on whatever ideas seemed persuasive regardless of whether they were right or correct. "The quack politician," Livermore told the Middlesex Musical Society, "mounts an exhausted cask, and intoxicates a gaping auditory by harangues more stale, than the dregs of his rostrum," just like "clans of quack musicians have for a long time infested the community" with tunes "wont to be vociferated by bacchanalians, or whined in dire historical ditties."[46] For Livermore, however, the answer to such problems lay for the most part with societies just like the one he was addressing. The Middlesex Musical Society was "engaged in a glorious cause," Livermore contended, one that had "restored order and beauty to the garden lately incumbured by briars and thorns and loathsome weeds." And, according to Livermore, through "refinement of taste and soundness of judgment," the members of the Middlesex Musical Society had already done much to help "preserve the fruits of the valley from depredation [and], to guard the beds of spices from rude feet of interlopers."[47] Caleb Emerson similarly understood the mission of musical organizations to be one of projecting an elevating influence over the public. "The object of MUSICAL SOCIETIES," Emerson articulated for the Handellian Musical Society in Amherst, New Hampshire, was "to cultivate the knowledge of this excellent art—to collect and introduce in practice the best productions—to acquire and diffuse a correct taste—and to enjoy the refined pleasures of melody and harmony." Emerson further advised that from the members of musical societies is "expected that correctness of taste and performance, which will entitle them to respect and imitation."[48]

Such top-down sentiments were representative of most American musical organizations and endured remarkably well over time regardless of geographic location. In 1821, the Union Harmonic Society in Charleston, South Carolina, for instance—which was said to have been established "in imitation of similar associations in our Northern Cities"—was told that its efforts to improve sacred music were "not only essential to the interests of religious exercise, but to the general taste and refinement of a nation."[49] And this was the case, explained the South Carolinian orator, because the "the powers of music" contribute with singular directness "to national strength and political security."[50] The next year, in Providence, Rhode Island, the Psallonian Society was similarly congratulated by a visiting speaker for having cultivated "correct" music in a country plagued with the "ranting melodies and doleful ditties" of American "tune makers [who], in general, knew no more about the laws of harmony than the peckers of a mill-stone knew about Italian sculpture."[51] In 1835, a "meeting of citizens favorable to the establishment of a 'Musical Fund Society' on the plan of those in London, New York and Philadelphia" took place in Cincinnati, Ohio, for the purpose of "refining and improving taste and execution, by comparison, imitation, or emulation."[52] Likewise, in 1848, a committee that was formed to establish the Hallowell Musical Institute in Maine did so on the basis that "the low state of musical education in this place demands that measures be adopted to create a higher public interest in the subject, and to afford the means of a higher musical cultivation." If citizens wished to encourage the institute "without being subjected to the anxieties, perplexities and disappointments of a singer's life," the editors of the *Maine Cultivator and Hallowell Gazette* suggested, then monetary donations were the best way of getting involved.[53] By 1850, the Worcester Mozart Society in Massachusetts could establish itself by alluding to a long-practiced "custom" of organizing musical societies in order to "practice . . . the higher branches of vocal music for mutual improvement and the cultivation of a correct musical taste."[54]

The elitist orientation of American musical organizations did not always sit easily with their rapid expansion in number. If musical organizations were about consolidating musical talent in a community and enabling the public to emulate the best and highest taste in music, then it made little sense for there to be many more than one musical society in any one place. The logic was not lost on contemporaries. In 1835, for example, the New York–based *American Musical Journal* concluded an overview of that city's musical societies by criticizing the increasing number and influence of so-called minor musical associations. "There is in our city talent sufficient, when concentrated and properly guided, to produce performances on a scale of splendor to which we are as yet strangers," explained the *American Musical Journal* editor. "But it is quite evident, that if our amateurs are split up into small parties, none of them can accomplish anything worthy of notice." And for this New York music editor, the very idea that many smaller independent musical societies could produce a better result than a small number of larger societies was injurious to both the musical community and the American public at large: "Is it not morally certain that these minor associations not only do not, but cannot, do any thing that in a musical point of view can be considered credible?" And "are they not an injury to the musical character of the city by their imperfect performances, and by preventing that concentration of talent which is so desirable!"[55] A decade earlier, the editors of the *Western Recorder* in Utica, New York, had made the same point less confrontationally: "Musical societies of a disconnected and independent character . . . have sometimes done much good," the editors explained; however, "it must be acknowledged that they have at other times been attended with consequences of the opposite nature."[56] Later, Samuel A. Eliot, as president of the Boston Academy of Music, would refuse to lend members of the academy's orchestra to assist the performance of another Boston musical society on the grounds that in the field of instrumental music, "competition cannot be useful, & indeed can only be mutually destructive."[57]

The first organization to embody the centralizing aesthetic of early American musical societies was the Boston Handel and Haydn Society. Established in March 1815 and incorporated in February 1816, the Boston Handel and Haydn Society was soon a recognized leader of American musical taste and performance. The reason for its influence had a lot to do with the reputed quality of its concerts, but it also reflected the fact that the predominantly middle-class socioeconomic makeup of the organization belied a genuinely elitist agenda. Like many of the American musical societies already in existence by 1815, the Boston Handel and Haydn Society was formed "for the purpose of improving the style of performing sacred musick, and introducing into more general use, the works of HANDEL, HAYDN, and other eminent composers."[58] And not unusually, these goals were again brought about by a conviction that the improvement of music in the United States should be considered an intrinsic public good. "While in our country almost every institution, political, civil, and moral, has advanced with rapid steps," explained the preamble to the Handel and Haydn Society's founding constitution, "the admirers of musick find their beloved science far from exciting the feelings, or exercising the powers, to which it is accustomed in the old world." And the poor state of American music was worrisome, the society claimed, because by neglecting music, the nation was missing out on the influence of "a science, which has done much towards subduing the ferocious passions of man, and giving innocent pleasure to society."[59]

Once established, the Boston Handel and Haydn Society immediately began recruiting the best of the city's musical talent into its ranks. As a contributor to the *Columbian Centinel* described its initial course of action, "The Handel and Haydn Society will combine and select members from the choirs of the several congregations gathered in this metropolis, and will extend to gentlemen properly qualified from towns in the vicinity."[60] In bringing together the best musical talent of the city, the correspondent explained, the society would enable the public to experience the music of Europe's most eminent composers more regularly and at a higher standard than ever before. Accordingly, the "gentlemen" who founded the society felt it was "necessary . . . to act with caution and circumspection in the admission of members to the Society, as well as in the election of its officers."[61] The constitution and bylaws of the society stipulated that a unanimous vote was required to secure membership, and later studies have shown that the selection process, which was supposed to evaluate the quality of an applicant's voice, evinced a decided prejudice against working-class applicants.[62]

However, it was the reach of the Boston Handel and Haydn Society's publications that was most instrumental to the scope of its influence. In particular, the breakout success of *The Boston Handel and Haydn Society Collection of Church Music* equated the name of the society with the broader popularization of European musical tastes that it helped encourage. The society's collection of church music succeeded in shaping the ambitions of musical organizations all over the country principally by framing the correct performance of sacred works by European masters as both a worthy and achievable aim for amateur American vocalists.[63] And the profits generated by this gambit were immense. First published in 1822, *The Boston Handel and Haydn Society Collection of Church Music* had sold well in excess of fifty thousand copies by the time of its final reprint in 1858. Income from these sales soon accounted for 50 percent of the Handel and Haydn Society's entire revenue stream while eventually paying its editor, Lowell Mason, a total of $12,000 over a nineteen-year period—a sum roughly equivalent to an income value today of over $6 million.[64] It was the first time that a musical venture in the United States produced a significant monetary return and was the result of a single publication becoming the nation's common source of accessible *and* respectable music.

Nonetheless, Lowell Mason initially harbored notably poor expectations of how the public would receive his work. "My object is to have the book become popular," Mason explained to the music-journal editor John Rowe Parker, but, he added, "I fear musical taste is not yet sufficiently advanced to appreciate [it]." Mason believed that Americans had the capacity to improve their musical tastes but also felt that close guidance was required for them to do so. And while Mason was happy to declare his forthcoming book worthy of supplanting rival publications that no longer "deserve public patronage," he did not trust that the public was yet capable of recognizing the superiority of his work or the "modern principles" of harmony on which it was based.[65] Mason was not one to readily pronounce his political opinions, but a few decades later, he did articulate a deep-seated conservative political philosophy that paralleled his generally low estimation of American musical capacities. Writing to a correspondent in 1861, Mason admitted that while "incapable of judging what is best" himself, he had "for many years doubted the success of our republican institutions," which were, in his opinion, far "too democratic" for a country where "there is not intelligence enough among the people to sustain universal suffrage."[66]

Of course, Mason's political paternalism was not necessarily representative of everyone involved in the leadership and expansion of early musical organizations. But his perspective closely resonates with similar sentiments articulated in the speeches given to a range of other early American musical organizations across the country. Moreover, the leadership positions Mason held within the Boston musical community would suggest that a substantial proportion of the musical community admired his particular way of encouraging a more correct American taste for music. By 1845, Mason had been president of the Boston Handel and Haydn Society, helped establish the Boston Academy of Music, assisted a successful movement to incorporate music in the curriculum of Boston's public schools, and served as superintendent of music in Boston schools—all while regularly touring the country to instruct music teachers in the skills of their trade (and selling them his books in the process). Mason and the Boston Handel and Haydn Society showed that Americans could be persuaded to defer to the tastes and expertise of a higher authority. And it did not take long for men more politically orientated than Mason to recognize the attraction of enlisting institutions for the promotion of American musical life into their efforts to maintain control over the trajectory of American society.

Federalism and Cultural Control in the Founding of the Musical Fund Society of Philadelphia

The founders of the Musical Fund Society of Philadelphia took the conservative elitism already embedded in American musical organizations a step further by integrating the goals of a musical organization directly into a broader Federalist-orientated project of elite cultural stewardship. During the so-called era of good feelings that followed the War of 1812, Federalist elites—who had long doubted the decision-making skills of a public that was less educated, refined, and technically capable than themselves—turned to a range of private associations to maintain their influence in the face of declining electoral prospects. For Federalists, private organizations with public purposes represented an ideal opportunity for serving a common good that was free from the politics and partisanship of government. As such, Federalists considered themselves and their civil institutions uniquely capable of advocating for what was right rather than what was popular.[67] The Musical Fund Society of Philadelphia was designed in the spirit of this broader Federalist effort and sought to better the quality of American public life through guardianship and control of its artistic culture.

The stated purpose of the Musical Fund Society of Philadelphia was twofold: to form a fund for "the relief and support of decayed musicians and their families" and to promote "the cultivation of skill and diffusion of taste in music."[68] The approach was closely modeled on British institutions like the Royal Society of Musicians and the New Musical Fund in London, which similarly orchestrated financial support for the well-being of "decayed musicians" and arranged cultured concerts for the benefit of the public and contributing members.[69] Typically, professional musician membership in these organizations involved the payment of an annual subscription fee in addition to an ongoing obligation to appear in the society's public performances. In return, musical fund societies would effectively agree to provide income protection insurance for participating musician members and their families. In the case of the Musical Fund Society of Philadelphia, professional members who found themselves unable to work were entitled to apply for a five-dollar weekly allowance from the fund, or in the event of death, their widow could apply for a three-dollar allowance plus an extra one-dollar per child. The fund in Philadelphia would also provide up to five-dollars' worth of medical aid per week, sourced in most cases from one of two physicians annually elected to serve on the society's board.[70] Fees for amateur (nonmusician) members were equivalent to those paid by professional members but provided only complimentary access to Musical Fund concerts and practices, not relief funds. Unlike British musical fund societies, however, the Musical Fund Society of Philadelphia did not officially consider itself a charity, instead emphasizing in its constitution the "mutual benefit" its members provided one another in a joint effort toward advancing the art of music in their city.[71] In other words, this was an organization that saw itself as a means for bringing Americans of all classes and politics together in support of a common good that benefited the public at large.

The identities of those who organized the Musical Fund Society of Philadelphia were closely connected to that city's Federalist establishment. In 1824, four of the six candidates named on the Federalist ticket for election to the Pennsylvania State Assembly from the city of Philadelphia were also prominent members of the Musical Fund Society.[72] Among them was John K. Kane, a young Federalist lawyer and founding secretary of the Musical Fund who had recently finished studying for the bar under the guidance of Joseph Hopkinson; two other young lawyers described in campaigning materials as "good speakers, liberal politicians, and amiable companions"; and William Lehman, an older Federalist lawyer who possessed "experience, judgment and a character of moderation and impartiality which should render him a universal favorite." In usual Federalist style, it was the "solid merits" and "qualifications" of all four of these candidates, rather than their political views, that made them fit for "public service."[73]

Key members of the Musical Fund Society were also connected to a range of other Federalist-orientated civil society institutions. John K. Kane, for example, in addition to serving the Musical Fund Society at various times as president, vice president, and secretary, also held leadership positions in the American Philosophical Society, the Philadelphia Academy of Fine Arts, the Institution for the Instruction of the Blind, and the Law Association of Philadelphia, among others. Such institutional crossover was common for Philadelphian Federalists. Within the first thirty years of the Musical Fund Society, for instance, it shared twenty-four of its directors and eight of its officers with the Philadelphia Academy of Fine Arts.[74] Indeed, all these societies that Kane was associated with were part of a broader constellation of Philadelphian institutions—ranging from professional legal associations to scientific assemblies, the University of Pennsylvania, and the Historical Society of Pennsylvania—that Lee Schreiber and others have linked to Federalist attempts to shape the city's public life through the institutionalization of cultural and professional power.[75] To be sure, individual Musical Fund Society members did not all identify as Federalists. However, most who did not, like Peter Stephen Du Ponceau or founding vice president Dr. Robert M. Patterson, were representative of a genteel Republican faction that after the War of 1812 came to find they shared more common ground with Federalist elites than they did with the less educated and more socially radical leaders of their own party.[76]

The goals of a broader Federalist civic project were also central to the fund's origin story, as told in the later recollections of the group's founding members. As John K. Kane remembered it, the "germ" of the Musical Fund had been an exclusive "Quartette party" club that met every Saturday to listen to works by Haydn and Mozart and to "boggle over Beethoven" before retiring to "eat crackers and cheese, and drink porter or homeopathic doses of sloppy hot punch." The group was composed of around "fifteen or eighteen" Philadelphian gentlemen—"the elite of the time," as Kane described them—who sought not simply to have a good time but to escape the poor taste and decorum that they felt characterized Philadelphia's music scene. At even the best concerts, Kane complained, Philadelphian audiences paid hardly any attention to the music at all. Instead, "the ladies chatted and laughed in ancient tea-party fashion, and gentlemen stood upon the benches with their hats on, or walked around the room to exchange compliments and retail the last joke."[77] From Kane's perspective, examples of crude audience behavior were illustrative of an American public that lacked the ability to discern, support, or even respect what was good for them. And to this end, Kane and his companions devised the Musical Fund Society of Philadelphia to help members of the public benefit from the wisdom and cultural sophistication of their betters.

Accordingly, Kane's proudest personal achievement concerning the Musical Fund Society had little to do with music itself. "I was . . . the first committeeman," Kane boasted in his autobiography, "who dared the suggestion, and carried it out, that gentlemen should be uncovered [hatless] and seated, and ladies silent, while the music was going on," adding, "I was laughed at for imagining such a reform, but one night perfected it without a police officer."[78] For a young Federalist lawyer like Kane, there were few clearer victories to be had than arranging the public's orderly compliance to a higher cultural standard. Kane's friend and fellow Musical Fund officer Robert M. Patterson was similarly preoccupied with the behavior of American music audiences. In a note probably intended for Kane, Patterson categorized American concertgoers into seven detailed types, nearly all of which were incapable of fully appreciating high-quality music. Some audience members, Patterson observed, simply had "no musical ear, and . . . cannot feel plea-

Sketch of members of the Musical Fund Society of Philadelphia, 1824. Unknown artist. The Library Company of Philadelphia, www.librarycompany.org.

sure," while others seemed intent on missing out on any of music's most profound effects by focusing exclusively on either "the most delicate little melodies" and the "sweetest tone" or the "deepest science" and "most abstruse modulation" of harmony. Perhaps most frustrating of all to Patterson were "people of an apt ear," who "perhaps also know a little of music, can sing a good song among their friends and on Sundays," and who therefore seemed to think that they "know every thing and are as capable of judging Haydn or Beethoven as the best critic of the day."[79] For someone who served for twenty-six years as president or vice president of a music society that aimed to disseminate a public taste in music, Patterson was curiously committed to the idea that all Americans were *not* equally suited to the task of enjoying and disseminating musical pleasure.[80]

Patterson did, however, have faith in two special classes of music listeners. For one, there were some individuals who knew a great deal about music but who also possessed the "amiableness of disposition" to share their thoughts on the subject "in a candid but kind manner" based on "solid judgment and sound argument" that enabled them to rise above "the clamorous assertions of an ill natured or would-be critic." Equally, there were also "persons perhaps with very little knowledge of music" who could still be useful listeners so long as they "possess by nature a fine ear, a great love of the concord of sweet sounds, and above all 'musical feeling.'" Despite their lack of knowledge, the audience members in this latter category were in the "astonishing circumstance" of naturally being "so gifted" that they could "sit with unwearied delight to listen to music even of the highest class." To Patterson, these two categories together represented the essential minority of concertgoers who formed "the very marrow of every musical audience," which, by extension, also made them "the marrow of Society at large for amicable demeanor & correct conduct."[81] In some ways, then, Patterson saw concerts to function as a civilizing space where audiences learned and displayed the kind of refined sensibilities that he and his colleagues in the Musical Fund Society most valued. However, in other ways, Patterson's take on American concertgoers also reinforced an essentially hierarchical conception of society wherein some classes of people were naturally better suited to contributing their talents to the common good than others were.

To organize the Musical Fund, Kane and his amateur associates set out to gather up "the better sort" of Philadelphia's musicians to help aid their endeavor. And initially at least, the Philadelphian musical community was eager to get involved.[82] The committee for framing the Musical Fund's constitution was composed of Kane and Patterson alongside three of Philadelphia's leading musicians: Benjamin Carr, Charles Hupfelt, and Benjamin Cross. A short time later, at the society's first election of officers, the same three musicians all accepted positions as managers of the fund, directors of music, or both, alongside a who's-who list of Philadelphia's other most established musical personalities.[83] However, for these musicians, the Musical Fund Society was less an opportunity for uplifting society's tastes than it was a chance for elevating the status of their profession. "It is highly necessary to stir the public mind into respect for musical people," Benjamin Carr wrote to a correspondent in explanation of his decision to become involved in the Musical Fund.[84] Privately, in fact, Carr remained skeptical that the Musical Fund Society would live up to its promise. When the music-journal editor John Rowe Parker requested a description of the newly formed Musical Fund Society for his publication, the *Euterpeiad*, Carr could not bring himself to pen the kind of column he knew was expected. "In my own mind I look upon" the Musical Fund Society "as a mere experiment," Carr explained to Parker, before providing him with a description written instead by an "amateur member" of the society whose perspective on the institution was far more "sanguine" than his own.[85]

The public notice about the Musical Fund Society of Philadelphia published in the *Euterpeiad* placed a heavy emphasis on the society's commitment to refining public taste over its commitment to assisting distressed musicians, declaring explicitly that improvement of the "musical character and feeling" of the country was "perhaps the first object" of its regard. And to this end, the evidence of the Musical Fund's success was myriad. Due to the society's influence, the columnist claimed, in Philadelphia, "concerts are now numerously and respectably attended," to the extent that "music of an elevated and refined character now constitutes one of the ordinary recreations of the evening circles." Even the city's "*fashionables*" and the "*loungers*" had allegedly learned to observe the proper rites of "stillness" and "silence" because of the Musical Fund's efforts. Finally, in a not-so-subtle allusion to the Musical Fund's contribution to a larger civic project, the notice concludes that the successes of the Musical Fund Society should serve as a model for "the extension of similar means to the other arts."[86] Certainly, for this Musical Fund member, the most significant achievements of the society had not hinged on the quality of music it provided or the respect it engendered for musicians—a fact that Carr was presumably less proud to convey to the world than his amateur colleague was.

Republicans, for their part, were closely attuned to Federalist attempts to use private organizations like the Musical Fund Society of Philadelphia as a means of exerting public influence. And it was for this reason that Kane and his associates in the Musical Fund Society encountered such determined resistance to their application for a charter of incorporation. In the early 1820s, elite proponents of civil society like those involved in the Musical Fund sought charters for a variety of practical reasons—an incorporated society was entitled to hold capital and property in its own name, to assume rights of perpetual succession, and to carry on legal proceedings—but above all, public charters were sought because they conferred public legitimacy onto the objectives of private organizations.[87] And this is particularly true in the case of the Musical Fund Society of Philadelphia, which could have chosen to bypass the legislative approval process altogether by incorporating less ambitiously as a "literary, charitable, or . . . religious" association under the general incorporation act of 1791.[88] Republicans, however, were uncomfortable with the idea of allowing too many private organizations to benefit from the special privileges of a separate legal entity, meaning that the Republican anticorporationist concern, in its largest iteration, reflected a long-held Jeffersonian belief that the spread of voluntary organizations was dangerous to the cause of American liberty. Corporations either encouraged the nation's wealth to become concentrated in private entities beholden to the particular purpose of their charter in perpetuity or allowed a disproportionate share of the public's wealth to fall into the hands of the few privileged elites who could exert influence over civil society.

By 1820, the Supreme Court's decision in *Dartmouth v. Woodward* (1819)—handed down just a year before the Musical Fund Society of Philadelphia began seeking its charter—had raised the stakes of these anticorporationist arguments. In *Dartmouth*, the Federalist majority bench had ruled that the state had no right to alter the charters of private corporations, claiming a corporation should be treated as "an artificial being," endowed with the right to operate in society in support of its chartered objectives as if it were a natural person. The *Dartmouth* decision had far-reaching implications, but in the short term, one of these was to encourage many people to question the wisdom of bestowing unprecedentedly broad rights of incorporation on any and all who requested them.[89] And in this context, musical societies wishing to incorporate could be particularly vulnerable to Republican opposition. In Massachusetts, for example, when the Republican governor Levi Lincoln Jr. wanted to show that not every association was deserving of a charter, he chose to demonstrate this by vetoing a legislatively approved bill to incorporate the Salem Mozart Association.[90] Opponents of the Musical Fund Society of Philadelphia's charter followed what had become a typical Republican line of argument, framing their challenge in terms of the bill's "inutility"—that to incorporate a musical society would be of no practical use or purpose to the public.[91] If even the Musical Fund Society of Philadelphia was deserving of a state-sponsored charter, its opponents asked, then just who exactly was not?[92]

In the case of the Musical Fund Society of Philadelphia, the "country members" of the Pennsylvania House of Representatives—from whom opposition to its charter principally derived—were not wrong to be wary.[93] The Musical Fund Society *was* one of many associations in early nineteenth-century Philadelphia founded by an insular group of young, predominantly Federalist-orientated professionals in pursuit of an ambitious extramusical agenda. And their sense that the Musical Fund served a public purpose was inescapably connected to their own conception of what the public actually needed. At the heart of the Musical Fund Society of Philadelphia was one of the nation's earliest formal partnerships between social, economic, and cultural capital that was nothing if not a strategic bargain. Through this organization, an aspiring set of elite young gentlemen promised to safeguard from financial ruin "the better sort from among the Musicians of Philadelphia" in exchange for control over the very definition of how Americans were meant to enjoy culture in the first place.[94] Whether purposeful or not, the novelty of the Musical Fund Society of Philadelphia as an organization was its ability to align the economic power and social influence of an elite class of politically exiled natural-born leaders with a community of status-starved musicians who had already been trying to correct American musical tastes for decades. It was a coalition that rested on an uneasy conflation of social, cultural, and political objectives that became a blueprint of sorts for an even more influential breed of American musical organization soon epitomized by the Boston Academy of Music.

Whigs and Social Hierarchy in the Boston Academy of Music

At the establishment of the Boston Academy of Music in 1833, it—like every other musical endeavor in Boston to that point—had not been a particularly elitist concern. Economic and social leaders in Boston, presumably influenced by their Puritan heritage, had been conspicuously slow to adopt music into their cultural repertoire compared to urban elites in other cities like New York and Philadelphia. Even the Boston Handel and Haydn Society had been primarily a middle-class organization of self-styled cultural elites whose success came without the assistance of Boston's "first families."[95] But once elites did take an interest in the Boston Academy of Music, its leadership quickly adapted the organization to help support a Federalist-inspired hierarchical vision of American democracy and to effect political change from outside the political system.

Broadly speaking, the structure and purpose of the Boston Academy of Music again evolved from European precedents. In Britain, the "academy" label had long been popular with artistic and musical groups that focused on the promotion of Continental influences—this was notably the case, for instance, with the Academy of Painting (1711) and the Academy of Vocal Music (1768).[96] Similarly, the Boston-based American Academy of Sciences (1780) purportedly chose its name "out of deference" to French artistic traditions in light of that country's contribution to the American Revolutionary War.[97] By the 1830s, however, the American musical community had become enamored by another Continental innovation: public music education. The sentiment—propagated almost single-handedly by Lowell Mason—was that Europeans appreciated music more than Americans did simply because they had easier access to better music teachers. As a music teacher himself, this was a fairly self-serving argument for Mason to make, but it was influential nonetheless. In Germany and Switzerland, the first annual report of the Boston Academy of Music explained, their citizens' knowledge of music ensured that its use would "elevat[e] their hearts above the objects of sens[ory pleasure]" and fill their entertainments "with social and moral songs, in place of noise, and riot, and gambling." In these Continental countries, as the Boston Academy of Music put it, the incorporation of music into their public-school curriculum had helped make music into an art form that was truly *"the property of the people."*[98]

Originally, then, the Boston Academy of Music was founded by a cross-section of individuals roughly analogous to those who had formed the Handel and Haydn Society—namely, middle-class Congregational evangelicals with a penchant for improving church music.[99] The comparable member profile of the two organizations was probably a result of the fact that their initial goals were not especially different—each existed primarily to improve sacred music, and both organized public concerts and lectures in order to do so. The Academy of Music focused comparatively more than the Handel and Haydn Society on delivering a large-scale music-education program, but otherwise their fundamental purpose was largely the same. In 1835, nine members of the Academy of Music also maintained memberships with the Handel and Haydn Society.[100] And though Lowell Mason's precise role in the founding of the academy is not certain, he was invested enough in its success to resign the presidency of the Handel and Haydn Society to become the academy's first professor of music.

However, similarities between the Academy of Music and the Handel and Haydn Society did not prevent the academy's founders from promoting their project as a unique addition to American associational life. As the Academy of Music's second annual report pointed out, its "plan and organization" as well as its "object" made it "essentially different to any other institution which is known to have been established in this country." Unlike other groups, the academy boasted that it had no professional category of membership, that it did not exist for the "improvement" of its own members, and that the association was explicitly "not designed to be limited in the sphere of its operations and influence." Instead, the academy worked toward two unapologetically public goals: "to raise music to the place it deserves to hold in the estimation of the community" and "to make it a branch of common education."[101] The plan for doing so, effectively, was to provide music education as a means to its own end. The logic here was simple but circular: Americans failed to appreciate music because they had never been taught to understand it properly, and without a proper understanding of music, Americans would never recognize its value as a branch of public education; therefore, the academy would teach music to Americans so they could understand it, see the wisdom of adding it to the public-school curriculum, and thereby enjoy the societal benefits that derived from its general appreciation and respect.[102]

The early success of the academy's educational program was unprecedented. In its first year, the academy taught vocal music to over fifteen hundred pupils, immediately needing to employ a second professor just to meet demand. During its second year, the academy expanded further to provide instruction to seventeen hundred pupils (five hundred of whom at this time were adults) in addition to over five hundred more who were taught in private schools whose headmasters could be talked into the "experiments."[103] In the same year, the academy organized two public exhibition concerts of juvenile singers to showcase the effectiveness of its musical instruction alongside training an amateur academy choir to "perform acceptably some of the most approved compositions of the greatest masters."[104] Also in its second year, the academy published the first edition of the *Manual of the Boston Academy of Music* (1834), a book mostly composed of unattributed translations from a German guide for teaching vocal music that Lowell Mason recast into America's most popular template for musical instruction.[105] The academy's program, then, was ambitious, but it was also confined primarily to vocal music and restricted almost entirely to sacred music. Its charter, which had been procured without fuss from the Massachusetts legislature in 1833, specified that the academy was incorporated "for the purpose of promoting education in the science and practice of music," and in its own capricious way, this remained the measure of what the academy's activities sought to accomplish during its first two years.[106]

In the academy's third year, however, an injection of elite support substantially altered its ideological underpinnings. The figurehead of this shift was Samuel Atkins Eliot, whose election as president of the academy in 1835 was as surprising as it was consequential. Previous to becoming president, Eliot maintained at best a tenuous connection to Boston's musical community, and there is little evidence to suggest that he cared particularly much about music in private either.[107] This was a man who spent an entire three-year tour of European cultural centers after graduating from Harvard without mentioning music even once in any of his letters back home.[108] Although the academy's rationale for Eliot's election is unknown, it is impossible to imagine that members who supported his nomination were unaware of Eliot's wealth or connections. Kin ties related Eliot to almost all of Boston's most prominent political families, and his public-service career by 1835 had already included a stint as alderman on the Boston City Council, membership of the Boston School Committee, and a seat in the Massachusetts House of Representatives. Eliot's economic wealth is perhaps even harder to overstate than his sociopolitical connections: in 1846, the total value of Eliot's (largely inherited) estate was $300,000, an amount that outsized Lowell Mason's net worth by more than seven to one and that was forty-six times greater than the net worth of Boston's third-wealthiest musician, George Webb.[109]

Eliot's election as president of the academy makes sense to the extent that its members recognized the public orientation of their objectives. The goal of incorporating music into Boston's public-school curriculum was, in truth, a matter of public policy that groups like the Academy of Music could only realistically have hoped to achieve by bridging the gap between civic society and state power. And in this context, the benefits of a leader with the means and political skill to attract support from outside the organization had to have been obvious. As for Eliot, once he became president, his record of attracting external support for the academy was exemplary. Within a year of accepting the post, Eliot had raised $4,000 to renovate the dilapidated Federal Street Theatre and turn it into the academy's own high-end music hall—renamed the Odeon. Significantly, most of the funds attracted for this purpose came from a selection of Boston society's wealthiest patrons, none of whom had ever before financially supported a musical endeavor. Of the larger

The Odeon Theatre, Boston, ca. 1838. From Abel Bowen, *Bowen's Picture of Boston; or, The Citizen's and Stranger's Guide to the Metropolis of Massachusetts, and Its Environs*, 3rd ed. (Boston: Otis, Broaders, 1838), 188. Library of Congress, Prints and Photographs Division.

$100 category donations given to the academy's renovation fund, only one of them, aside from Eliot, came from a member of the academy; the rest came predominantly from individuals with vast fortunes who were not otherwise affiliated with the organization.[110]

However, it is notable that many of the individuals who contributed financially to the Academy of Music's renovations in 1835 were connected to an 1826 "Circular" that had earlier advocated but failed to attract elite patronage of a "Society for the promotion of a taste for Music and the encouragement of the progress of this Science in this City."[111] The circular itself, penned by Eliot's brother William, basically proposed to establish a Boston-based version of the Musical Fund Society of Philadelphia that would sponsor a series of tasteful public concerts and create a fund to support the families of the musicians who took part in them.[112] The printed version of the document was signed by nine Federalist-associated individuals who, like their counterparts in Philadelphia, were generally active in a range of other civil society institutions at the time.[113] Later, in 1835, three signers of the 1826 circular would also donate $100 to the Academy of Music's Odeon project alongside three more donors who were directly related to three of its other signers.[114] The aim of the circular had been not simply "to promote the cultivation of the Science of Music" but also "to advance the growth and diffusion of an *enlightened* taste in this department of the Fine Arts"—an object especially important in Boston, where the signers claimed that an absence of elite patronage had made musical taste into a rare commodity.[115] In light of William Eliot's sudden passing from a fever in 1829, scholars have speculated that Samuel A. Eliot saw his leadership of the Academy of Music as an opportunity for realizing the vision that his brother had articulated in his 1826 circular.[116] If so, Eliot's vision of musical organization was entirely resonant with the same Federalist impulse that had animated the signers of that earlier document.

In a larger sense, Eliot's presidency of the Boston Academy of Music transformed the organization into the same kind of formal alliance between socioeconomic power and cultural capital that had characterized the Musical Fund Society of Philadelphia from its inception. And the very fact that this transformation was allowed—even encouraged—by all who were a party to it reflects just how compatible the ideals of middle-class musical reformers and the ideals of a certain class of conservative Boston elites really were. Both groups saw cultural stewardship as an act of public duty and recognized that each other's contributions could amplify their own. However, these similarities in purpose concealed significantly different ideological motives. Whereas Boston's middle-class purveyors of musical taste had assumed that their efforts would help them to transcend class divisions as well as exercise their moral duty as citizens, their elite counterparts were investing in the same project to emphasize the virtues of *maintaining* social hierarchy. In this sense, the Academy of Music represented an uneasy alliance between the ideological remnants of Federalism and a newer aspirational constituency of middle-class reformers.

The academy's union between the descendants of Boston's elite Federalist gentry and a rising group of Boston's middle-class evangelicals reflected two specific contextual forces. For one, the Federalist Party in Massachusetts had remained a viable electoral concern for much longer than it had in other states. Bostonians elected a Federalist mayor as late as 1829 (the last time an avowed Federalist won a race for high office anywhere in the country), and until 1830, Federalists technically still controlled the Massachusetts Senate.[117] So when the Boston Academy of Music was established in 1833, the full political collapse of the Federalist Party was still a relatively recent phenomenon. Meanwhile, the other force at play was that the associational world Federalist elites had traditionally retreated into was no longer their own to exploit. By the 1830s, the fervor of the Second Great Awakening had produced an explosion of middle-class benevolent organizations that catered more to a middle-class need for self-definition than to an elitist desire for social control.[118] To adopt Johann Neem's categories, in the moment that Eliot took over the Boston Academy of Music, the organization became an instance wherein the "elite public sphere" and the "grassroots public sphere" overlapped in the service of a common project.[119]

That Eliot personally saw the Boston Academy of Music as a means for promoting his own elitist conception of music's political purpose—one reminiscent of an outdated Federalist style—is clear. As president of the academy, Eliot fashioned himself into one of the nation's most prolific antebellum exponents of writing on music, and he did so in the midst of serving three consecutive terms as mayor of Boston (1837–39) as well as spells in the Massachusetts House of Representatives (1834–37), Senate (1843–44), and US Congress (1850–51).[120] Politically, Eliot had followed a well-trodden path in New England from the Federalist Party to an elite conservative faction of the Whig Party (via the National Republicans) and in the process came to see music as the perfect vehicle for educating society in the correct organization of republican democracy.[121]

Ideologically, the key agenda that Eliot pursued with the Boston Academy of Music was an attempt to prevent Americans from succumbing to the dangers of an unchecked popular democracy. In an 1841 article about music that Eliot anonymously published in the *North American Review*, he complained that in the United States "every man is so apt to entertain the idea that he is born with a genius for any thing he may choose to undertake" that "now even respect for the opinions or reasonings of the ablest and best of our contemporaries is quite behind the spirit of the age."[122] And for Eliot, the problem with encouraging this newly emboldened ideal of a "self-made man" was that it diminished the public's proper respect for authority: "the time has already arrived," Eliot protested, "when the attempt of one portion of society to restrain another to any degree beyond its own convenience, is universally considered unconstitutional." From Eliot's perspective, the social and political disorder born of the nation's collective lack of deference was contaminating the heart of every power relation in society: "States nullify, whenever it suits their pleasure; towns comply with State requisitions, if convenient; individuals obey town laws, if they find it for their interest; children obey their parents when it is not more desirable that the parents should obey them; teachers are at the mercy of their pupils, and master and servant is a relationship no longer known to exist." "Everyone, in short," Eliot continued, "places himself on his reserved, natural right of rebellion; and the constitution itself is made to maintain the most self-destructive doctrines." Disunion was the only endpoint to popular democracy that Eliot could imagine. And therefore, Eliot considered it "providential" that music remained the "one pursuit of an attractive character, which cannot be thus inverted; in which learners must submit to teachers, the less advanced must yield to those who are more so, and where everyone must take his appropriate place, and not seize upon another for which his natural and acquired powers do not fit him."[123]

Eliot valued music education quite literally as a means of mitigating the threat of civic and political disorder and of instilling instead a greater respect for the virtues of a hierarchical power structure. Given, as he put it, that "the bass cannot sing soprano, nor can the bassoon play the violin part," Eliot reasoned that participation in music emphasized the unique contribution of every station in life to the fulfillment of societal goals. "One voice or one instrument [cannot] say to another, 'I have no need of thee,'" Eliot explained. "All are wanted, and so long as they will submit to be governed at once by nature and by the rules of art, all are indispensable to the production of great effects." Equally, an appreciation of music and how it is made would also show how easily disorder results from failing to carry out the role to which one is assigned: "the moment that disobedience or carelessness is suffered to prevail, the charm is broken, music takes her flight, and the air is filled with 'wild confusion's dreadful noise.'" Eliot called for anyone with a "just value for the peace and order of society" to join with him in promoting "the study of that art, which will do more than all other studies to impress on the minds of youth the importance, the necessity of discipline, order, and subordination in the affairs of this world."[124] If, as Eliot claimed, the Boston Academy of Music was leading the nation toward "a *musical revolution*" then, politically speaking, the only radical thing about it was the depth of its conservatism.[125]

It is unlikely that the middle-class evangelicals who initially elected Eliot president of the Boston Academy of Music would have agreed with this political ideology. They did, however, share Eliot's interest in musical education and the value he placed on the discipline that musical study could provide. Organizations loosely affiliated with the Evangelical United Front or the Benevolent Empire—be they Bible societies, tract societies, temperance societies, prison-reform societies, or, in this case, a sacred-music society—typically aimed at helping Americans find redemption through at least some measure of self-discipline.[126] And in this sense, it was characteristic of the evangelical founders of the academy to make the introduction of music into public schools one of their original objectives and to partner with someone like Eliot in order to achieve it. Once president, however, Eliot quickly moved to secularize the institution: removing the academy's previous emphasis on sacred music, all but disbanding its amateur vocal chorus, and forming in its place what would become one of the nation's most highly regarded all-professional instrumental orchestras.[127] While Eliot did not exactly pursue objects that went beyond the bounds of the organization's charter, he clearly tailored the activities of the academy to suit his more elitist secular-Unitarian agenda.

And it worked. In 1838, the Boston Academy of Music did successfully introduce music into Boston's public schools under Eliot's leadership. But the two-year campaign took longer than expected, and Eliot's personal possession of significant political power was central to its success. In 1836, Eliot's first effort to petition the Boston School Committee to introduce music into the public schools on behalf of the academy was virtually ignored. However, once Eliot became mayor of Boston in 1837, he automatically also became the chairman of the School Committee and could reappoint the subcommittee tasked with considering the academy's petition to be filled with individuals he knew were supportive of the academy's project.[128] Within a few months, Eliot's new subcommittee submitted such a sparklingly positive recommendation in support of the Academy of Music's petition that its report became a de facto manifesto for proponents of musical education all over the country.[129] The School Committee chaired by Eliot unanimously accepted the subcommittee's recommendation and resolved that the Academy of Music be placed in charge of an experiment to introduce music into four of Boston's public schools, which would be delivered in consultation with a special subcommittee of the School Committee on which Eliot also placed himself.[130] The School Committee's request that the Boston City Common Council appropriate funds for the experiment was referred to its committee on Public Instruction, which, as per normal procedure, invited members from the Board of Aldermen to join in its deliberations—Eliot chaired the Board of

Aldermen, too.[131] In the end, however, despite Eliot's appointing himself and other members of the Academy of Music to the Common Council's joint committee in time for the final vote, he still failed to convince a majority of that body to commit public funds to the academy's project.[132]

The objections made to the Academy of Music's first plan for introducing music into Boston's public schools take some teasing out to fully appreciate. Only one local criticism was published directly in response to the plan, which came from a member of the School Committee who was absent at the time the measure got passed onto the Common Council. The absent committee member, the newspaper editor Nathan Hale, complained that music's introduction into state schools was simply a poor policy, one that would distract students from more important studies and that would compel children with no talent for music to waste their time learning it.[133] It is unclear just how prevalent Hale's attitude to music education was, but it certainly was not one that many antebellum Americans bothered to put in print very often.[134] The existence of contemporary debate on this topic is typically inferred from the large number of pieces written *in favor* of musical education as well as their defensive tone.[135] But the paucity of substantive replies that these arguments actually generated makes it hard to avoid the conclusion that many of the supposedly staunch opponents of music education in antebellum America were really just the straw-men constructions of its proponents, assembled from the very real debates of an older generation.[136]

Another principal objection to the Academy of Music's plan might well have been its cost. However, Eliot's official report on the deliberations of the Common Council's joint committee was at pains to emphasize that the group's lack of agreement had arisen *even though* "no great sum of money was asked for by" the proposal's "friends, amounting to only $110 for each school."[137] Eliot may have been self-serving here, but he was not lying about the amount requested or being particularly disingenuous in his suggestion that the funds requested did not amount to all that much in the context of Boston's public-school budget.[138] Nonetheless, cost did become a significant factor in retrospect because when Eliot and the School Committee later reformulated their plan, they did so in a way that allowed them to bypass the Common Council altogether—by making it cost nothing to deliver. Lowell Mason had recently returned from a tour of Europe and had offered to teach music in Boston's public schools for a year without charge to help facilitate the experiment, which enabled Eliot and the School Committee to propose a scaled-down version of the project under their own auspices as a no-cost program.[139] In a practical sense, then, lowering the cost of the project was instrumental to getting the academy's experiment off the ground but only because Eliot recognized that a free version of the plan avoided any need for government approval or public discussion.

Smaller changes in the School Committee's revised plan also reveal a deeper set of political objections to the academy's project that relate less to the issue of music in public schools than to the power that Eliot and the Academy of Music appeared to be wielding over the process. Eliot and the School Committee's reformulated proposal, for instance, voluntarily transferred the responsibility for implementing their program to introduce music into public schools away from the Academy of Music and placed it instead in an individual—Lowell Mason.[140] Eliot also quietly chose not to join the special committee of the School Committee that was formed to superintend the delivery of Mason's program.[141] Practically speaking, these changes made little difference—Mason was a member of the Academy of Music, and Eliot was still ultimately responsible for overseeing his work—but as a symbolic gesture, they demonstrate that concerns over the influence of private interests in public life animated at least part of the opposition to the introduction of music education in Boston.

Such reservations were not misplaced. As in the Musical Fund Society of Philadelphia, the Boston Academy of Music's effort to get music instruction into public schools *was* also part of a larger partisan-based attempt to influence public culture through civil society institutions. In April 1837, Massachusetts governor Edward Everett controversially proposed to appoint an independent "board of commissioners" to investigate the condition of Boston's public schools and in doing so turned the issue of public schooling into a partisan battleground. For Massachusetts Whigs like Everett, the ensuing creation of a Massachusetts Board of Education was meant as a way of counteracting President Andrew Jackson's so-called spoils system by empowering independent experts to help guide government policy. However, nine of the ten men Everett appointed to serve on the Massachusetts Board of Education ended up being Whigs, including its secretary, Horace Mann, who became the board's chief public advocate and spokesperson. As such, Democrats were quick to be suspicious of Whig educational reformers and considered their use of supposedly independent experts, nonpartisan regulatory boards, and nonprofit institutions as a transparently political attempt to use the power of the state to embed Whig Party values into the public-school curriculum.[142]

Incidentally, the Common Council would fail to agree on whether to fund the Academy of Music's plan to introduce music into public schools six months after the establishment of the Board of Education—a moment when partisan frictions over the Board of Education were very much front of mind. And it is not difficult to consider how the political maneuvering of a Whig mayor like Eliot might have looked from the perspective of his partisan opponents. As mayor, Eliot had convinced a School Committee of his own appointees to accept a petition he had written himself on behalf of an organization he led. Then, in accepting that petition, Eliot, acting as chairman of the School Committee, proposed that his organization be placed in charge of a public program to be overseen by a subcommittee of School Committee members that he was also on—meaning Eliot would effectively supervise himself. And if all that were not enough, Eliot then put himself and other Academy of Music members onto the joint committee that voted to decide whether their own organization would get public funds. It is little wonder that some of the other members of this Common Council joint committee might have had reservations about funding the Academy of Music's proposal.

In other words, it was logical for Democrats opposed to the Board of Education to also oppose the Academy of Music's program for public music education. On a procedural level, Eliot had done his best to ensure that the experiments of musical experts received state sanction by evading as far as possible any public debate over the wisdom of their ideas. Similarly, on a policy level, there was conflict. Members of the Board of Education did not shy away from testifying to the virtues of a public-school music education. Horace Mann, for example, in a widely copied extract from his eighth annual report of the Board of Education, defended the inclusion of vocal music in the public-school curriculum on the grounds that "harmony of sound produces harmony of feeling," before claiming that in the presence of music, "enemies are at peace; rivals forget their contests, partisans lay aside their weapons; and the bosoms that harbored acrimonious or vindictive feelings over which time seemed to have no power, are softened into kindness."[143] Music helped to unify society, Mann insisted, and on that basis, he concluded that it would be wrong to "deny homage to an art that can make men brethren, even for an hour!" Eliot and his colleagues in the Academy of Music could hardly have disagreed and accordingly held Mann's preference to promote an "inductive system of teaching" in high regard.[144] Democrats, on the other hand, considered the whole program an elitist plot, one that allowed a distant cabal of privileged experts to control public education policy rather than the people or their representatives.

As the president of the Boston Academy of Music, Eliot similarly tried to frame the civic importance of this organization in terms of enabling Americans to rise above partisan predilections. It was through such organizations of civil society, Eliot believed, that an "active sympathy" was generated across all levels of American society, leading to a more unified American polity "knit together by feelings and interests intertwining in every direction."[145] In terms that drew from his earlier orchestral analogy, Eliot explained that the successful operation of benevolent institutions in Boston illustrated how in the United States, "no one can say to any other, — 'You are not wanted; we can do without you'" because the rise of civic benevolence proved that there was a "mutual dependence" at the heart of American life that separated it from the more antagonistic class divides of the Old World.[146] Elite-led civil society associations like the Boston Academy of Music, which selflessly enabled Americans of all stations to live "better" lives, were to Eliot's mind the nurseries of American civic virtue — the producers of the "habits" that "set us perfectly free."[147]

In this sense, the Boston Academy of Music, like the Musical Fund Society of Philadelphia before it, was intimately bound up in an ongoing dispute over the role and influence of private associations in public life. With Eliot as president, the academy's objectives combined the musical goals of evangelical reformers and the political goals of elite philanthropists without needing to reconcile their differences in motivation along the way. And this is precisely what Eliot had hoped for all along: a community brought together through mutual interest where everyone knew one's role and played one's part. Leaders led (Eliot), teachers taught (Mason), and musicians performed (a professional orchestra). A Federalist impulse was responsible for animating Eliot's conservative Whig ideology as well as for his sense that music was an effective vehicle for furthering its influence. However, the achievements of the academy derived less from the persuasiveness of any political ideology than from the organization's more practical ability to leverage civic influence into political power.

The Academy of Music was able to pull together elites of every variety — cultural, social, political, and economic — to advance a public project under the auspices of civil society. All its participants, whether middle-class musicians or elite patrons, shared a common conviction that the American public was incapable of judging the common good in the absence of expert guidance. Together, through the Academy of Music, they were remarkably effective at marshaling the resources required to achieve their objectives without actually having to demonstrate that the public agreed with them. And this, in a nutshell, was the point of Whig efforts to connect civic society to public life: if the state's political institutions rewarded party loyalty more than the right person and rewarded party ideology more than the right policy, then fashioning a new role for independent organizations and experts promised to balance this equation. As such, the Academy of Music fulfilled a political function as much as a musical one and exploited the public value of civic space to do so.

THE MUSICAL FUND SOCIETY OF PHILADELPHIA and the Boston Academy of Music brought together powerful combinations of economic wealth, social status, and cultural capital. And by considering these organizations through the prism of the interlinking interests they promoted, it becomes plain that early nineteenth-century efforts to cultivate American music were not simply about altruism or artistic devotion. Both these organizations used music to support a fundamentally conservative and hierarchical vision of how American society should be run and unsurprisingly faced substantial political opposition as a result. In the case of the Musical Fund Society of Philadelphia, its struggle to procure a charter of incorporation highlights that a significant number of Pennsylvanian legislators were reticent to bestow public legitimacy on a private organization whose members sought to refine public taste through cultural stewardship. Later, the Boston Academy of Music made use of the publicly elected positions of its officers to finesse the introduction of music into Boston's public-school curriculum, despite its failure to procure financial support from Boston City's Common Council. In each instance, these organizations linked to a larger Federalist (and later Whig) attempt to use their influence over civil society institutions to restore a respect for social hierarchy that could protect American democracy from its excesses.

American musical organizations had always possessed an element of public purpose. Whether for worship or fashion, colonial singing schools and urbane music societies had each sought to enable British Americans to live up to higher standards of cultural sophistication and produce a more enlightened populace in the process. However, by the latter stages of the early national period, two of the most organized efforts to uplift American society by refining its taste in music had become thoroughly politicized. Part of the reason for this was that early proponents of music in America had always approached the promotion of music from a culturally elitist perspective. The basic rationale of most American musical organizations—whether consciously political or not—was that Americans were not only unwilling but also unable to cultivate a good taste for music without the determined assistance of those who knew what was best for them. And this top-down take on promoting music in the United States proved especially enticing to a certain set of conservative socioeconomic and political elites who had turned to civil society institutions to exert public influence in the wake of the Federalist Party's electoral demise. In a democratizing society, the elite inheritors of Federalist ideology still distrusted the wisdom of the "common man" and found in the musical community a concentration of individuals and organizations who were largely apt to agree.

CHAPTER THREE

Music and Respectability in Antebellum Electoral Politics

On 12 March 1840, George Templeton Strong, then a fresh-faced lawyer on Wall Street, decided to throw his "law [work] to the dogs" for the evening to go see Henry Russell sing at Niblo's Gardens.[1] Russell, a wildly popular English vocalist, was well known for being a contentious character, but this particular performance had been engineered for controversy. Not unlike modern celebrities, Russell had a knack for promoting himself by way of promoting a cause, and amid an unprecedentedly carnivalesque presidential election campaign, the Whig Party had emerged as his latest cause célèbre. Newspaper notices anticipating Russell's show at Niblo's all highlighted his intention to use it as a platform for introducing New York audiences to "The National Whig Song"—a recently composed campaign tune Russell was adapting into a signature piece of his own.[2] And according to Strong's account, the tune's reception at Niblo's did not disappoint. "The National Whig Song" "was first met by hisses, bahs, and penny trumpets from a miserable minority of [Democrat] Locofocos," Strong told his diary, "but this opposition, though received again and again, was always overwhelmed utterly by thunderous applause; and it ended with . . . three cheers for Harrison," the Whig presidential candidate. Strong recognized that Russell's Whig song was an "unmitigated humbug," but he could not help recording the rousing effect that its performance had on him. "Hurrah for the Whigs! Harrison forever!!!" Strong exclaimed, followed by a loose attempt at transcribing a slice of the song that still reverberated in his mind:

> For though he took the of-fi-ces
> He never took the spoils!!!
> Row de, dow dow de, dow dow de, dow!³

Others viewed Russell's use of campaign music with less enthusiasm. The theater's proprietor, William Niblo, was convinced that Russell's "National Whig Song" had caused a "row" and reneged entirely on his offer to reengage Russell for a second performance, citing that a reprise of the tune was sure to cause another disturbance.[4] When pressed, Niblo maintained that his saloon was a place that attracted the "numerous company of respectable

Henry Russell (Philadelphia: P. S. Duval's Lith. Press, ca. 1838). Library of Congress, Prints and Photographs Division.

ladies" and that as he considered it "strictly speaking, *a place of amusement*," he felt it his duty to "avoid letting it for anything of a partisan or political character."[5] As naive or calculated as Niblo's decision-making might have been, resolving to ban Whig Party songs from a public theater was an unlikely way of avoiding politics altogether.

Russell, for his part, had no intention of allowing Niblo's actions to be the last word on the issue and soon fed details of the dispute through to New York's Whig Party press.[6] Predictably, the furor surrounding Russell's right to sing Whig tunes as advertised took on a life of its own. "Has it, then, really come to this!" exclaimed a widely copied piece in the *New York Courier*. "May not the *Whigs* have such songs sung to them as they think proper, without the . . . threat of riot" from Democrats? Whig papers further alleged that Niblo had acted at the behest of the Democratic *Evening Post* editor William C. Bryant and insisted that their freedom of expression should not be restricted for the sake of a few quarrelsome Democrats.[7] Bryant strenuously denied any conspiracy with Niblo and chastised the Whig papers for reporting "the conversations of individuals on random hearsay, and making them the basis of personal attacks." "We merely asked Mr. Niblo why he allowed party songs to be sung in his saloon," Bryant clarified, and later expressed his "satisfaction that a place destined for the general amusement of the public was not to be turned into a political conventicle."[8] The Whig papers, Bryant charged, had knowingly blown the whole episode out of proportion.

News of Russell's willingness to mix partisan politics into a public concert elicited a slew of animated attacks and defenses throughout the country. The *Alexandria Gazette* in Virginia, for example, argued, "Mr. R. is, in our view, pursuing a very silly course" with his use of political song in New York, adding, "we can conceive of nothing in such very bad taste, as political allusions in assemblies composed of all political parties."[9] Similarly, the *North American* in Philadelphia, although Whiggish in politics, judged that Russell's "admirable vocal powers might be devoted to a better cause than party politics."[10] The *Ohio State Journal*, by contrast, copied a paragraph from the *New York Express* claiming instead that Russell and the Whigs were "taking just [and] proper means to add the power of song to the power of politics" and that Democratic attempts to "smother" Russell's tune only emphasized why "all the world must go to hear it."[11] The editors of the *Connecticut Courant* went the furthest in their praises and after having heard Russell sing "The National Whig Song" advised their readers that "the Whigs of Connecticut could not do a better thing for the advancement of the good cause, than to engage Mr. Russell to sing this song in the various cities and large towns in your State until after the election."[12]

Yet while newspaper editors traded opinions, the singer at the center of the debate went about making the most of the publicity. Within a few months, Russell was getting up entire "Whig Concerts" and reportedly delivering them "to the admiration and delight of the brilliant multitude of bright eyed young Whigesses" who filled his houses.[13] By the end of the election, Russell's popularity among Whigs had risen to such heights that even one of his most dedicated detractors had to admit that this degrading "experiment" in party singing had—from Russell's perspective at least—"succeeded to his heart's content."[14]

THE PRESENCE OF music in election campaigns is now so commonplace that Russell's exploits almost take on an air of inevitability. Of course, opportunistic performers would exploit partisan politics for their own gain. Of course, politicians and political managers would exploit popular melodies and popular personalities. And, of course, political opponents would, in turn, criticize the propriety of each other's cultural appropriations. None of these insights would appear to be at odds with most people's general understanding of how politics works. Antebellum Americans, however, did not share the assumption that music was either a natural or necessary part of achieving political change. For better or worse, the use of music in the 1840 presidential election tended to strike contemporaries as a genuinely innovative addition to American political practice. Despite its many precedents, music as a means of blatant political persuasion suddenly seemed *new*, and in this sense, the idea of using music as a political tactic was hardly obvious.

Whether technically new or not, the introduction of new electoral tactics rarely occurs without justification. However, the reasons antebellum Americans had for involving music in their efforts to support presidential candidates have not received much consideration. Instead, musical evidence in political contexts typically helps draw one of two conclusions: that antebellum Americans were either unusually engaged in politics or that the quality of that engagement was unusually superficial. These polarized interpretations of music's political presence exist concurrently because antebellum Americans engaged in almost exactly the same arguments. There was no agreement—then as now—on whether singing a party-political song should be a legitimate form of political expression. Debates that mirror the terms of their source material are bound to struggle with circularity at one point or another, and arguments over the popular nature of antebellum political participation in the United States have not escaped this problem.[15]

This chapter suggests that coming to grips with how Americans conceived of the power and purpose of music as an agent of political change can help us to better understand—rather than judge—antebellum political participation on the basis of its social and cultural connections. What exactly was the point of a campaign song before the Civil War? Why did some Americans choose to write or sing them? And why did others criticize their choice to do so? To this end, it is important to recognize that political uses of music during the antebellum period were not always intended to encourage political participation.[16] Instead, the seemingly sudden injection of music into antebellum elections was in many ways a conservative reaction to the expanded political nation that had already come into being during or before Andrew Jackson's presidency.[17] Music in this context was more about providing a respectable outlet for the public's political passions than it was about generating political interest in the first place. At a time when Americans were struggling to reconcile the rise of mass democracy with the maintenance of social order and the preservation of national unity, music appeared a uniquely accessible way of making the practice of popular politics palatable for those who were wary of its excesses. The arguments that ensued over its use pivoted less on the quality of political engagement it produced than on the desirability of popular democracy itself.

Unraveling the Significance of Music in 1840s Electoral Politics

Usually the presence of Whig Party electoral hoopla—like rallies, log cabin raisings, and songs—is explained as evidence of the fact that by the 1840 presidential election Whigs had finally become organized enough to give the Democrats a taste of their own medicine. Democrats had pioneered mass political organizing techniques during the Jacksonian period, and the rise of populist Whig campaigning, particularly in 1840, has been depicted as a capitulation to the effectiveness of a style of politics that Whig partisans had tended to think was beneath them. Songs, however, complicate this picture. Whigs were attracted to political music in 1840 not because they wanted to copy or appropriate Democratic campaigning tactics for political effect but because Whigs thought music was a respectable way of helping them to conduct a popular campaign. Not every trick of Whig electioneering had to be poached from the Democratic toolkit. Indeed, the alleged newness of Whig music in 1840 belied its direct lineal relationship to a Federalist musical tradition that had long been comfortable with music as a means of popular persuasion—a connection that Democratic opponents were only too happy to point out. Singing, in sum, would enable Whigs to celebrate the virtues of the "common man" without having to become common in the process.

Of course, the American Whig Party was by no means unique or even particularly original in drawing a link between music, morals, and public utility. During the mid-nineteenth century, ancient ideas about music's capacity to exert a controlling and refining influence over an otherwise unwieldy public had become truisms among a growing population of middle-class reformers across both sides of the Atlantic. Dave Russell, for example, explained that popular music in Victorian England was controlled predominantly by those who used it to "destroy the potentially 'dangerous' elements within working-class culture and to create a respectable, self-reliant, collaborationist working class."[18] In England, the sheer scale of the Chartist Movement during 1838 and 1839 had demonstrated the political power of the working class, and this had led some English elites to respond—at least in part—with efforts to teach workers to improve themselves by learning how to sing national songs, hymns, and glees more correctly.[19] In both Britain and the

United States, music was already part and parcel of temperance reform and evangelical revivalism, and soon it would become equally important to the antislavery movement. Generally speaking, participants in nineteenth-century reform of any kind were apt to find no better "rational recreation" with which to support their cause than music.[20]

However, election music in the 1840s is rarely, if ever, explicitly considered as a product of the reformist context from which it emerged. Part of the reason for this is that despite the wealth of scholarship that exists to show how porous the dividing lines between religion, reform, and politics could be before the Civil War, there remains a desire—whether natural or otherwise—to uphold a sense of separation between these spheres that did not always exist. One of the Whigs' primary slogans for the 1840 election was "Harrison and Reform," and the campaign itself has been characterized correctly as an exercise in "redeeming the nation" or of "political revivalism."[21] Yet when it comes to accounting for the use of campaign music in 1840, scholars often seem to think it satisfactory to note that earlier examples of Americans singing in election campaigns exist and that its antebellum popularity resulted from the expansion of the franchise and the establishment of a competitive two-party system.[22] The problem with this explanation, however, is that it tends to imply that music in popular politics is somehow natural or unavoidable, and it downplays the possibility that American election singing took inspiration from anything other than its own political context and precedent.[23]

In fact, the emergence of music in antebellum American elections was much less a way of acquiescing to the necessity of populist politics than it was an effort to meet the genteel aspirations of a growing middle class. By 1840, failing to possess significant wealth was no longer an impediment to enjoying at least some of the trappings of an elite lifestyle. The mass production of pianos, for instance, transformed what had been an item of almost unbridled extravagance into a cherished focal point of middle-class domestic life, one that symbolized its owner's ascension to polite culture and that attested to the owner's appreciation of the hard work needed to play the instrument properly.[24] Music—much like Wedgewood china, good manners, or houses with parlors—was a way in which middle-class Americans could claim ownership of a cultivated life.[25] Whigs envisioned that their music, once incorporated into election campaigns, would help attract the attention of precisely those individuals who sought respectability in their private lives by giving them an appropriate opportunity for demonstrating their capacity to display it in public.[26]

Accordingly, issues of class and refinement dominated the notoriously musical canvass of the 1840 presidential election. When in the midst of a severe and prolonged economic depression a Democratic newspaper mocked the Whig presidential nominee's old age by claiming he would be content to retire to a log cabin with a barrel of hard cider, the Whigs were quick to counter by extolling the virtues of these well-known standard-bearers of rough living.[27] Harrison's supposed affinity for log cabins and taste for hard cider were lauded as proof that "he is a man of substance, not of show—plain in his dress and manners; a practical farmer; works with his own hands, and treats every honest man as his equal."[28] Old Tippecanoe—as Harrison was affectionately known from his military exploits at the Battle of Tippecanoe—was in reality anything but a common man of the people, having served as a general, territorial governor, congressman, and United States senator after being born into a prominent Virginian family.[29] However, Harrison's man-of-the-people image still proved a sharp contrast to the incumbent Democratic opponent, Martin Van Buren, whom Whigs tarred with responsibility for causing the depression as well as for failing to help the nation out of it all while indulging a passion for expensive champagne in the White House.[30] The Whigs' messaging gave a sense of respectability to plain-living inhabitants of log cabins, but it stopped short of conflating their humble values with the refinement of polite society. Harrison may have appreciated a log cabin, but once he was ensconced inside one, Whigs tended to suggest that he spent more time immersed in scholarly tomes than working his land or relaxing with a glass of hard cider.[31] As Richard Bushman has rightly observed, "The Whigs solved the problem of class in 1840 by projecting an egalitarian political society while preserving inequality in culture and so in private life."[32]

Music in elections worked for Whigs on the basis that it was thought to cast an elevating influence over scenes otherwise populated by honest but admittedly rather rugged log-cabin dwellers and hard-cider drinkers. And given that Whigs in the 1840 election also encouraged white women to take on a more prominently partisan role than ever before, it was important that the environments these women were invited into boasted at least some redeeming features.[33] In this respect, evangelical revivalism had a formative influence on the Whigs' brand of morally orientated electioneering. The American evangelical movement had from its beginning utilized the ritual power of hymnody to enhance religious experience and as part of a "self-conscious strategy to promote the success of conversion."[34] And singing political hymns at party rallies was neither in form nor substance all that different from singing religious hymns at a revival meeting. The immediate

General Harrison's Log Cabin March and Quick Step (Baltimore: Samuel Carusi, 1840). priJLC_POL_002630, The Jay T. Last Collection of Graphic Arts and Social History, Huntington Digital Library.

object of the words may have changed, but the melodies were often familiar; and the inherent desire to will a better world into existence was fundamental to music's use across both religion and politics.[35] Indeed, since music was otherwise most often experienced at home or in church, its presence at a political event was likely to remind participants of what it felt like to be in those places.[36]

Although political music and singing were not the exclusive provenance of the Whig Party during the 1840s, the Whigs *were* the political party to develop the strongest reputation for its use—and not without good reason. The Whigs had more songs than Democrats, were more proactive about singing them, and openly celebrated their effect more often. Numerically, at least, the difference between the amount of music created by the two parties is striking: the most comprehensive bibliography of American presidential campaign songsters to date catalogues a total of twenty-five Whig songsters from 1840, as opposed to just one from the Democrats.[37] And significantly, the songs Whigs produced, like "Tippecanoe and Tyler, Too," were popular enough to live on in the collective memory of contemporaries decades after the election was over. Certainly, late nineteenth-century chroniclers of the 1840 election spared little thought for Democratic songs when they reminisced about how in 1840 "for the first time in our land the power of song was invoked to aid a Presidential candidate."[38] For Democrats, the obvious reaction to Whig singing might have been to respond in kind, and to some extent, they did: Democrats excelled at parodying Whig songs as well as writing mock Whig songs from the point of view of Whig voters who had lost their mental faculties.[39] But Democrats largely chose to combat Whig music through criticism and derision rather than imitation. As one contemptuous Democrat explained it, the Whigs' passion for singing seemed to have rendered them incapable of "embrac[ing] truth" in any other way.[40] In turn, my focus on investigating the Whigs' approach to music in elections reflects a difference in tactics between the two major parties that did not go unnoticed at the time.

The Purpose, Sources, and Critics of Whig Campaign Music in 1840

"A new political danger has lately arisen which we confess gives us some anxiety," warned the *New York Evening Post* in June 1840, referring to what another New York paper had already dubbed a "New Auxiliary in the Electioneering Field."[41] The object of their joint concern—Whig campaign singing—was quickly becoming one of the more remarkable aspects of the 1840 presidential election, and Democrats found its popularity both worrying and ridiculous. Whigs had amassed "stores of ballads," the *Evening Post* alleged: "glees and catches are ready to be thrown into the camp like hand grenades [and] whig poets are at work like armourers and gunsmiths, fabricating election rhymes." Apparently, Democrats concluded, the Whigs' "plan is to exterminate us chromatically, to cut us to pieces with A sharp and lay us prostrate with G flat, to hunt us down with fugues, overrun us with choruses, and bring in Harrison by a grand diapason"—the widest margin possible. The effect of all this Whig singing might have been amusing, but it also seemed suspiciously bereft of substance. "We could meet the whigs on the field of argument and beat them without effort," the *Evening Post* complained. "But when they lay down the weapons of argument and attack us with musical notes, what can we do?"[42]

Much like Democratic critics, Whig commentators in 1840 also tended to approach political music as if it were akin to a new technology. James Gordon Bennett—who endorsed the Whigs' presidential candidate, William

Henry Harrison—could rattle off a potted history of political song ranging from the ancient Greeks through to Andrew Jackson while in the same breath characterize 1840 American campaign songs as a "new" phenomenon.[43] And Bennett was not alone. Most Americans knew music had been used throughout history to achieve political effect. But these precedents had yet to coalesce into any kind of shared sense of when, how, or what made music's presence appropriate in an American political context. As a result, Democrats in 1840 could accuse Whig music of bringing "a new political danger" on the nation, and Whigs could take credit for inspiring a new breed of patriotic song.[44]

Whigs, of course, were not blind to precedent and often highlighted the uplifting qualities of their electoral music by linking it back to a classical legacy of songs that had elevated other peoples and nations at key moments throughout history. Polybius, Whigs pointed out, had attributed the "hospitality and humanity" of the Arcadians to their emphasis on teaching children to sing patriotic hymns and had attributed the "savage manners" and "wickedness" of the Cynaethans to their neglect of music.[45] Whig writers similarly recalled Plutarch's description of the patriotic songs of Sparta, "which could rouse the soul, and impel it in an enthusiastic manner to action" by praising "heroes that had died for Sparta, or else of expressions of detestation for such wretches as had declined the opportunity."[46] Notably, Plutarch had also written of poet-musicians in Sparta who—not unlike Orpheus—had produced odes that led people of "many persuasions to obedience and unanimity," that "softened insensibly the manners of the audience, drew them off the animosities which then prevailed, and united them in zeal for excellence and virtue."[47] Music, Whig supporters proudly noted, had animated Trojans, Normans, and Highlanders and also contributed its share to the outcome of the American Revolution. "Almost every race and class of people have their songs," concluded the *Madisonian*, and now "the appearance of Gen. Harrison as a candidate for popular suffrage" had bestowed Americans with "precisely that kind of patriotic fervor and enthusiasm" that had given shape to some of the most storied music of human history.[48]

Whig songs, in this sense, were less of a promotion for the Whig cause than a living testament to the fact that it was worthy of true devotion. And this is why Whigs took so much pride in the musical character of their campaign: to them, the irresistibility of their songs was proof that their candidate and their cause resonated with Americans at a deeper level than politics. A popular Whig anecdote, first published in the *Pittsburgh Daily American*, told of three "hardy rough-skins, from the pine knots up the Allegany," whose "wild unpractised ears [were] arrested by the sound of a piano" during a walk through town. On investigation, they found the source of this "'first-rate'" music was a young girl who, it turned out, could "play nothing but Harrison tunes." All three of the men were Whigs who supported Harrison, so they took great delight in the performance; but the enjoyment they felt also got one of the men to thinking:

> "If Jim only heard that, do you think that he would vote for [the Democratic candidate] Mr. Van Buren?" . . . "Who is Jim?" said our heroine. "He is a comrade of ours, and a Loco Foco, but I think if he heard that song, it would turn him." "Go fetch him," said she, no way daunted, and the three started off, and directly returned with their stubborn and incredulous comrade. The young lady had now her ambition roused, and the young men being seated, she played and sang some of the most lively patriotic Harrison airs, while Jim himself had to join in the chorus, thanked the lady, and said he was no longer a Van Buren man, but would go the "whole figure" for Tippecanoe from this [day] out. They all departed, highly pleased.[49]

Whether the story is true is less important than its ability to showcase how comfortable Whigs could be with the idea that a few of their songs might sway their opponents. Key to this sense of Whig musical pride, however, was not a cynical take on how easy it was to manipulate Democrats but rather an evangelical-like conviction that their political adversaries need only glimpse a more honest vision of the truth to be converted to the right course.

To Whigs, it was no surprise to find that the Democrats lagged behind them in the production of songs. "There is no music in the name of Martin Van Buren," the *Cleveland Daily Herald* matter-of-factly observed, because "no great deeds of his are known to be celebrated in popular verse."[50] The *Daily National Intelligencer* likewise indulged its readers in an elaborate story about a Democratic scribe in the West who was "said to have attempted, on the urgent solicitation of his political friends, to compose some *Van Buren melodies*" but eventually had to give it up, "frankly confessing that he could not find a single incident in Mr. Van Buren's whole life which the muse would tolerate."[51] Given that Harrison melodies invariably found "an echo in the American bosom which thunder cannot silence," the *Albany Evening Journal* was left to smugly admit that it felt only "half fair" to see the effect of a Democratic band of music spoiled, seemingly without effort, by "a constant 'Hurra for Old Tip.'"[52]

Whigs, moreover, specifically produced election music with the intention of casting an elevating influence over their supporters. The compilers of *The Log Cabin Minstrel: or, Tippecanoe Songster*, for instance, wrote that in assembling the collection, they consulted with "several gentlemen of unquestionable taste and judgment, who have, in the very kindest manner, favored us with their productions," and added that they would like to "remind the Log Cabin boys of the land, — that they should always endeavor to preserve *harmony* in their ranks, remembering that *discord* assists our opponents, to the injury of ourselves."[53] Similarly, the editors of *Harrison Melodies* claimed to "owe" its readers "no apology for the undertaking, and no explanation of its object," given that the "number, variety, patriotic spirit and intrinsic poetical merit of these productions" have "been for some time sensibly felt at our 'Whig gatherings.'"[54] In Columbus, Ohio, the editors of *The Harrison Log Cabin Song Book* contended that no citizen could reasonably deny the refining influence of Tippecanoe songs, for "who cannot enjoy a good song? Who cannot join in one with heart and voice in joyful response?" The answer, of course, was only mean-spirited Democrats: "Every body is singing" log-cabin songs, the editors claimed, "and every body but the sour and crabbed Locofocos is delighted with their simplicity and spirit." When it came to the honest expression and healthy cultivation of patriotic feeling, Whigs contended that there was no better influence than their own tunes.[55]

At the same time, the compilers of Whig songsters also went to great lengths to frame their songs as authentic specimens of popular expression, even though songbooks, or songsters, were an inherently awkward medium for this message. Songs themselves might have been believably positioned as products of divine inspiration, but the process of selecting the best of them and publishing them together as a collection less easily adheres to the idea of a truly organic grassroots expression. One way that Whigs got around this issue was to depersonalize the work that went into producing their songsters. *The Log Cabin Minstrel*, for example, was attributed to "a member of the Roxbury Democratic Whig Association" and dedicated to the "Log Cabin Boys of the United States." The anonymous editor then explained that "the object of arranging this work is to present to the advocates, and supporters of that uncorrupted and incorruptible patriot, WILLIAM HENRY HARRISON — the People's candidate for the Presidency — a variety of patriotic and sentimental Songs that have been called forth from the talented of our land."[56] As such, Whig songsters ran a fine line between the presentation and dissemination of Whig songs *for* the people and the promotion of songs written genuinely *by* the people.

Some songsters were better than others at handling the task of providing Americans with access to the kind of musical expression that supposedly came to them naturally. The compilers of *The Log Cabin and Hard Cider Melodies*, for example, went out of their way to correct a then-oft-quoted phrase by the Scottish writer Andrew Fletcher of Saltoun (1653–1716), who had famously professed, "Let me make the Songs of a People, and I care not who shall make their Laws." According to these Whig editors, Fletcher was right to observe music's power, but he was wrong to suppose that "the Songs of a People may be *made*," when, in fact, "they flow spontaneously from its free, unshackled spirit."[57] As another New York songster put it, "The feelings of an oppressed people aroused to a full sense of their wrongs, and determined to redress them, find their appropriate expression in the language of song," and since "the people of this country are now in such a position, . . . their triumphal songs and joyous symphonies at once strike terror into the hearts of their opponents, and cheer and invigorate their own" supporters. Equally, however, the editors of the latter songster—revealingly titled *Songs for the People*—were quick to judge that Whig songs had been inadequate for the task at hand. The people's songs contained "many beautiful melodies," the editors confessed, but still "they want [in] that transition 'from grave to gay, from lively to severe,' so necessary to please all tastes and suit all occasions."[58] If Whig singing was to have its full effect, then a discerning hand was required to package and disseminate its output. Songsters provided this service and while doing so claimed to be able to fashion the true spirit of the people into something that could improve it at the same time.

Whig newspapers tended to receive Whig musical publications as its authors intended. The *Centinel of Freedom* in New Jersey welcomed the publication of *Songs for the People* by advertising that many of the songs within it "possess decided and peculiar merit as poems" and that "all of them breathe the loftiest, home-bred patriotism."[59] In Massachusetts, the editor of the *Nantucket Inquirer* emphasized how the recently issued *Harrison Melodies* songster "contains a great number of these popular songs, adapted to familiar airs, with which our political atmosphere is now ringing, as in one grand chorus of the people," before boasting of how the "rich and humorous effusions of Whig songsters and ballad writers" had brought together "the polished poet of the classic retreat" with the "humbler but equally patriotic and ardent lyricist of the far-off prairie and forest."[60] A few days later, when Isaac N. Whitting presented the *Ohio State Journal* with copies of the "National Whig Song" and the "Harrison Song," readers were advised that the tunes would be a "rich treat" not for Whigs, exactly, but for "lovers of good music, and especially those who feel the glowings of that patriotic spirit which now pervades the country."[61] Clearly, Whigs wished to make supporting their party into a broadly patriotic endeavor, and in this sense, music was key to showing how a belief in improving the nation and its people contributed to, rather than detracted from, the sum total of their patriotism.

There was a degree of truth to the Whigs' claim that their songs emerged naturally from the minds of the people. Making music a prominent part of the Whigs' 1840 election campaign was not—as Democratic criticisms would imply—a top-down initiative that Whig supporters carried out on orders from their national party leaders.[62] During the 1840 election, Whig Party politicos did exert significant influence over what was an unprecedentedly centralized campaign structure, coordinated nationally through a high-powered executive committee in Washington.[63] However, there is no direct evidence to suggest that these political managers took any practical interest in the musical aspects of their campaign.[64] Thurlow Weed, the recognized ringleader of the Whigs' national party organization, actually managed to cultivate a reputation for being *against* his party's political use of music (though he later denied this in his autobiography).[65] In fact, the most that can be said definitively of 1840 Whig campaign managers at the national level in regard to music was that they did nothing to stop Whig songs achieving prominence in the narrative of the campaign they helped organize.

Horace Greeley, in the absence of any evidence to the contrary, has become the individual Whig operative most associated with the institutional support of Whig music during the 1840 campaign. Robert G. Gunderson, for example, argued that Greeley "did more than anyone else to set the campaign to music," and few have found any reason to contest this assertion.[66] Certainly, Greeley as editor of the *Log Cabin* helmed the only newspaper at the time that went to the trouble of including full versions of campaign songs in every issue—words as well as printed music. The expense of printing musical type in an otherwise cheap campaign paper would have been significant, but Greeley was apparently convinced that the extra subscribers whom the songs attracted outweighed the costs of printing them.[67] Greeley was also keen to plug collections of Whig tunes in his paper when he received them: of the *Log Cabin Song Book*, Greeley enthused that "the bare sight of it is enough to give a Federal office-holder a touch of hydrophobia," and he appealed to all "friends of Old Tip" to "call or send in for half a dozen [copies] of them!"[68] But although Greeley might have supported Whig campaign songs more than most newspaper editors did, there is nothing to show that

Greeley actively solicited Whig music, organized its performance, or wrote about it at any length in his private correspondence.[69]

Where, then, did 1840 Whig campaign music come from if not from Whig political leaders? The answer to this question first lies in recognizing that Whig culture was not restricted to an exclusive set of Whig Party elites. Instead, like Federalists before them, the political culture of the Whigs encompassed far more than a political party, and it appealed to its supporters as such.[70] Whigs were people who believed that progress required planning, that moral duties trumped political rights, and that there was an interdependent unity to society that was easy to lose sight of in the pursuit of one's own interests.[71] In this context, it turns out that Whig songwriters were for the most part not lackeys to their party's political establishment but rather professional individuals who often held middling or locally prominent positions in civil society. And they were dedicated—like most other Whigs—both to self-improvement and to individuals' capacity to improve the world around them.

Alexander Coffman Ross, who wrote what became the 1840 campaign's theme song, "Tippecanoe and Tyler, Too," is an illustrative case in point. An Ohioan based in Zanesville, Ross was a jeweler by trade and a businessman wealthy enough to indulge in an incredibly wide range of extracurricular activities. Ross established the first company to install gas lighting in Zanesville, was a founding member and patron of the Zanesville Athenaeum library, and served as the town's express office mail agent. Meanwhile, an interest in scientific pursuits led to Ross becoming probably the first American to produce evidence of a working daguerreotype machine outside of New York City and to becoming the town's first electric-telegraph operator. If all this were not enough, Ross was also a skilled taxidermist, watercolor painter, and musician who had sung in the church choir from boyhood and as an adult was regularly "in demand on occasions requiring the services of an entertaining vocalist."[72] So although Ross may not have been a politician or a personality who attracted national attention, he was plainly one of the leading members of his community, even if some of his exploits might have been exaggerated over time. When the 1840 election began, Ross added the Zanesville Tippecanoe Club and its glee-club subsidiary to his list of organizational memberships and was said to have written "Tippecanoe and Tyler, Too" in order to provide for the "wild outburst of feeling demanded by the [Tippecanoe Club] meetings."[73]

The profiles of other individuals who attributed their names to Whig campaign songs are analogous to Ross, if only more lawyerly by orientation.

Thomas Power—who widely advertised his authorship of the "Harrison Song"—was a lawyer by profession, a retired but long-serving recording grand secretary of the Massachusetts Masonic Lodge, and a Whig orator reputable enough to give the featured address at the city of Boston's 1840 Fourth of July celebrations.[74] The writer of the "National Whig Song," William Hayden, was another Whig lawyer from Boston who sat on the Massachusetts Whig State Central Committee.[75] Alfred B. Street, again a lawyer and poet who was later appointed state librarian of New York, contributed an ode published in the *Tippecanoe Songbook* that was initially sung by a choir at the Democratic Whig young men's Fourth of July service in New York City.[76] And J. A. Andrew was yet another "young sprig of the law" who wrote tunes for Harrison in 1840 before taking on secretary duties for the Water Union of the Fourth Ward in Boston, serving as an appointed legal representative of the Massachusetts Society for the Abolition of Capital Punishment, and delivering orations before young men's Whig associations.[77]

To be sure, it was relatively uncommon for campaign songs to be printed alongside the name of the individual who wrote them. Most tunes give no indication of their provenance at all or are attributed in some cases to an unidentified "member" of a particular Tippecanoe Club.[78] On the one hand, the lack of attribution was a transparent tactic for ensuring that Whig campaign songs took on an air of popular authenticity. On the other, the practice was also a way of conforming to some of the subtleties of nineteenth-century amateur literary culture. Indeed, campaign songs were not unique in their tendency to lack authorial attribution: newspaper columns, poems, and pamphlets all often appeared in print anonymously or under pseudonyms. Yet, for interested parties, the identities of these authors tended to be more of an open secret than a complete mystery. Earlier in 1809, for instance, Daniel Mulford—a New Jersey–born Yale graduate who had traveled to Savannah for his health—contextualized the place of early nineteenth-century amateur song better than most when asking his younger brother Levi to include more hometown gossip in his letters: "Tell me who dies, gets married, makes good bargains, changes situations, grows religious, gets drunk, turns printer, writes two-penny-ballads & gets blackguarded for it in Mann's Paper &c &c."[79] As someone who had dabbled in crafting his own political songs only a few years earlier, Mulford spoke from experience.[80]

Anonymous authorship, then, did not necessarily prevent songwriters from becoming known in their community or from receiving a sense of recognition for their work. And this raises the question: Who exactly were these unheralded songwriters and Tippecanoe Club members who took it upon themselves to write Whig campaign songs? Evidence to answer this question is thin; but clues do exist, and they suggest that the type of people who had the inclination to compose campaign songs almost always possessed a certain level of local fame within their community. John Maxim, for example, was a contributor to *Songs for the People*, identified unusually both by name and profession as a "laborer" from Carver, Massachusetts. But, actually, Maxim was best known among his peers as a "celebrated local wit and writer."[81] Maxim did work by day as a molder at the local foundry, but he also maintained a significant civic presence in town, regularly contributing topical rhymes to the local papers, serving as clerk for the First Universalist Society in Carver, and working as the agent for local subscriptions to the *Christian Telescope and Universality Miscellany* and the *Barre Gazette*.[82] In 1840, when the Whigs ceremoniously erected a log cabin nearby at Wareham, Massachusetts, newspaper accounts of the event acknowledged Maxim—by way of his literary pseudonym "Bemis"—as one the "worthies of note" from Carver in attendance. And Maxim, under his own name, was active in his area as a vocalist capable of adding special interest to events with "appropriate songs, prepared for the occasion."[83] In local lore, Maxim would eclipse his status as a laborer to go down as one of Carver's most colorful inhabitants, remembered in posterity as the "bard of Huckleberry Corner."[84] Again, like Ross, within the context of his community, Maxim was a significant personality.

Songs written by unidentified members of Tippecanoe Clubs are the other most common category of authorial attribution contributing to the impression that campaign songs were products of direct grassroots expression. Tippecanoe Clubs, however, need to be recognized more as an outgrowth of a preexisting Whig-centered civil society than as whimsically organized or ramshackle get-togethers. These clubs were highly hierarchical organizations that involved the adoption of constitutions, the election or appointment of officers, and the formation of committees with recorded minutes, lists of members, and notices of meetings and proceedings delivered for publication in appropriate newspapers.[85] This is not to say that Tippecanoe Clubs were not venues for revelry, but it is to say that what revelry took place did so within the same structured confines as other mainstays of antebellum civil society, such as musical organizations, fire companies, and even temperance societies. And like most civic associations, Tippecanoe Clubs were framed explicitly as sources of both personal and societal uplift.[86]

That said, Tippecanoe Clubs were important instigators of the production and dissemination of Whig campaign music. Not only did these clubs provide a regular venue for the singing of Whig campaign songs, but in doing

"Six Patriotic Ballads respectfully dedicated to the Tippecanoe Associations."
New York: Thomas Birch, 1840. Lester S. Levy Collection of Sheet Music,
Sheridan Libraries, Johns Hopkins University.

so, they also provided the demand required to support the commercial publication of Whig tunes, either together as songsters or separately as sheet music. But given the hierarchical orientation of these organizations, it is unlikely that songs attributed to their members happened upon wider publication by accident—either members were sufficiently wealthy and well connected to have their own tunes published, or fellow members were capable of doing so on someone else's behalf. It is clear, for example, that a handsome collection of "Six Patriotic Ballads" dedicated to the Tippecanoe Associations of the Union and "partly written and arranged by a member of the Fifth Ward Club" was not the work of your average laborer. In this collection, homespun titles such as "Good Hard Cider," "Buckeye Song," "Tip's Invitation to Loco," and "Log Cabin" all betray the finery of craftsmanship on display in lavish lithographs by Nathaniel Currier and in the high-quality print work provided by Thomas Birch, one of New York City's leading music publishers.[87] In reality, it was a collection of tunes that looked more suited to a drawing room than a bar room, and that was precisely the point. "Our friends all over the Country who have music in their souls and don't mean to smother it there will be apt to find these Songs very much to their liking," Greeley's *Log Cabin* testified, because this collection of songs represented the ideal of what Whig campaign music was meant to be all about—making participation in the Whigs' popular political cause appear honest, elevating, and respectable.[88]

Whig Campaign Music in Everyday Life

Justifications for Whig campaign music had a tangible influence over how Americans experienced its presence. And the diary of a man named Joseph Sill provides one of the best examples of just how successful Whig music could be at making popular political participation appear honest, inviting, and respectable. Sill, in many ways, was the archetypal person that Whig campaign music was designed to influence. Born in Carlisle, England, Sill migrated to Philadelphia in 1819 at eighteen years of age with borrowed money and the promise of a job on his arrival that never materialized.[89] But after procuring a "humble clerkship" to pay his debts, Sill quickly ingratiated himself into a distinguished community of English merchants centered on the First Unitarian Church of Philadelphia, which included the likes of John Vaughan and the painter Thomas Sully—both of whom, incidentally, were active members of the Musical Fund Society of Philadelphia among other civic institutions.[90] In 1827, Sill and his wife opened a gentlemen's haberdashery store on Chestnut Street, directly opposite the State House, and by 1840, this had grown into a flourishing business, profitable enough for Sill to pay off the $22,500 purchase of his house and store with just a two-year mortgage.[91] Meanwhile, Sill became closely involved with charitable and artistic institutions, particularly the Society of the Sons of St. George, which gave assistance to impoverished British artisans in Philadelphia.

As a merchant who felt he had made his own way in the world, Sill was dedicated to the concept of cultivating an image of respectability.[92] And music had an important part to play in this process. In 1837, Sill favorably recounted a sermon he had attended by the conservative Unitarian minister Orville Dewey, who explained "that the habits of Men of business"—like Sill—"were generally very loose," because "the desire to gain was so great as to induce them too frequently to depart from strict rectitude of conduct." Communities of traders, Dewey emphasized, must together "guard against" impropriety "with all their might," and in doing so, "the great aids to guard men of business from it, were religion, and education, & the cultivation of a proper taste for the Arts, for Music, & the other refined pleasures of life."[93] Earlier, in 1832, Sill had attested not only to the "degree of harmony & sublimity in the human voice" but also to his belief that when the human voice unites "with the utterance of appropriate ideas and thoughts, and the beautiful contour and expressiveness of the countenance, it possesses a power of communicating melody, that cannot be equall'd by any inferior means."[94] Accordingly, Sill cherished time spent singing hymns with his children in the hope that the practice would prove "a beneficial influence upon their future lives."[95] And in the evenings, Sill frequently patronized the Musical Fund Hall to take in a variety of musical concerts.[96]

Sill's views on the spectacle of partisan politics could not have been in starker contrast to his ideas on music. And from Sill's home directly across the street from the State House, few had a better view of American political theatrics in action. Unsurprisingly, there were moments during the 1840 presidential election campaign that made Sill's home environment very "unpleasant." "We have the advantage or disadvantage of hearing all the news," Sill explained, and of "having our ears stunn'd with the vociferations and din attending the meetings of both" political parties. Even from the back room of his home, Sill complained, "the noise" of a Democratic rally "falls like . . . an Avalanche upon me." Yet Sill felt more than just inconvenienced by the partisan hullabaloo surrounding his house. "I dislike these party meetings excessively," Sill declared; "they display the very worst side of Human Nature—Men, who in the private walks of life, are moderate and full of

Truth, appear at these convocations full of the wildest passions, and can only see through one narrow medium—they are no longer even gentlemanly in their words or actions, but often coarse & vulgar in speech, and riotous and disorderly in behavior." On attending a Whig meeting the night before, Sill had been "grieved to see & hear a Man," whom he had "always thought upright and respectable," discredit himself entirely by addressing the meeting in a manner that "neither spoke well for his head or heart" and that was "unworthy of him in every sense."[97] For Sill, party political campaign meetings—whether Whig or Democrat—were inherently dangerous to one's reputation as a respectable person.

Sill had good reason to believe that political activity promoted poor behavior. Partisan mobs and election riots were rife in antebellum American politics, to the extent that one commentator in New Orleans likened Election Days to "a hell's holiday of drunkenness and perjury and bludgeons."[98] And in Philadelphia in particular, the combined threat and reality of violence, rioting, and mob action haunted almost every variety of public display.[99] The ubiquity of political violence in Philadelphia took a toll on Sill, who detested not just the riots themselves but also that the type of people who engaged in them could get away with leveraging disorder into political influence. On news that William Lloyd Garrison had been attacked by an antiabolitionist mob in Boston and paraded through the streets by the neck, Sill cast aside his own reservations about abolitionism to rail against the influence of public violence. Garrison's treatment seemed to Sill "a savage instance . . . of the brutality of the mob" and showed how frighteningly easy it was for "the passions of Men" to reign "triumphant over their reason!"[100] During the 1840 election, Sill was obsessively attentive in his diary to any hint of a disturbance at the polls or public gatherings in town, and oftentimes his wariness proved prescient.[101]

Nonetheless, in the middle of the 1840 campaign, Sill suddenly began to write about "great gatherings of people in the streets" with an air of excitement rather than trepidation. Sill described the "occasional Furniture Car rolling quickly thro' the Street, fill'd with *Musicians*," alongside "Workmen preparing the Polls" and "putting up the fixtures for Transparencies," while "Flaunting Flags are hung across the Streets" and "Politicians are hurrying about with their party Tickets" in preparation "for the coming political struggle."[102] Compared to his previous descriptions of political scenes populated with orators risking their reputations for the sake of partisan politics, this description of political life is almost fantastically positive. Sill instead underlines how valuable the democratic process was to Philadelphians who went out of their way to turn Election Day into an enjoyable event. And, notably, of course, the presence of musicians is quite literally emphasized in the process. The trend continued four years later.

In October 1844, during the Whigs' presidential campaign for Henry Clay, Sill cheerfully reported that a "Great Whig Convention" held in Philadelphia had produced "a wild enthusiasm" that "seems to pervade all ranks of life." The excitements began early in the morning when "Delegations from the Counties adjoining [Philadelphia] came pouring in . . . accompanied with Banners, Music, Trades at work &c." followed by "all the Clay Clubs in the City with their devices & colours . . . and the air was fill'd with the sound of Drums, Trumpets &c." The effect of the procession on Sill and his family was stirring in all the right ways: "It was agreed between us," Sill noted, "that we had never seen before in any procession, such a respectable body of men, as march'd along in this Convention; or so much real good humour and enthusiasm as was apparent both in the procession; and amongst the thousand[s] of gay spectators that lin'd the entire way."[103] Whenever it seemed Sill wanted to paint a positive description of a popular partisan event, music tended to feature conspicuously in his account of it. And in the context of what we know of how Whigs framed the purpose of election music, as well as Sill's belief in the refining influence of music and the deleterious influence of partisan politics, his passing emphasis on music and musicians starts to make a deeper kind of sense than coincidence.

Sill was not alone. In 1848, James Kendall Lee left his home in Richmond, Virginia, to study for the law at Princeton, but he quickly found distraction in election excitements.[104] A fervent Whig, Lee also had an incredibly positive take on the democratic process, but what made him particularly pleased was the orderly and respectable behavior exhibited by Americans at the polls. "Without noise without confusion each man boldly throws in his vote for the man of his choice," Lee observed of Election Day in 1848, "and though party animosity is high, the laws of his country are respected."[105] One could infer from Lee's short and upbeat description that music was simply not part of his Election Day experience, but this was probably not the case. Loosely inserted into this particular spot of the diary is a clipping about Francis Scott Key's tune "The Star-Spangled Banner"—that "beautiful and patriotic song," which, the article asserts, "maintains its primacy as a national anthem."[106] If Lee was to keep a memento from an election that he felt had passed in exemplary fashion, it makes perfect sense for this to have taken the form of a song often held up as a unifying celebration of American patriotism.

A year later, in 1849, another young man, named Nathan Beekley, moved to Philadelphia from Norristown, Pennsylvania, to take up work as a clerk.

Musicians marching, n.d. 7986.F.13. The Library Company of Philadelphia, www.librarycompany.org.

Beekley, like many of his age and situation, cared deeply about cultivating an image of respectability, and as such, he detested every moment spent among "rowdies"—whether in the street, in concert halls, or anywhere else.[107] So, when that year's Election Day came, Beekley was both impressed with the spirit in which it was conducted and wary of the passions that it produced. "This is the great Election day, and quite an exciting scene it is to be sure," Beekley recounted in his diary.[108] But he was not about to take any chances. "To keep out of broils," Beekley explained, "I went to the opera again this evening," and the next day, he watched despondently as the city once more became "the theatre of a dreadful riot."[109] The significance of Beekley's case may seem counterintuitive, but it represents a logical extension of what Whigs had always intended music to achieve. For Beekley, music really did allow him the ability to appreciate the value of American democracy as well as the ability to escape from the vicissitudes of practicing it at the same time.

Despite lacking any significant power or wealth, Beekley still considered himself better than those who inhabited the common fray of popular politics and he used his musical engagement to express this to himself and to others.

The Democratic Response to Whig Campaign Singing

Democrats, for their part, were merciless in their criticisms of all this feel-good Whig singing. If the Whigs really valued the people's opinion, Democrats charged, then they would be far more interested in following it than pretending to elevate it. "While the Whigs profess much friendship for the people," explained the *Hartford Times*, "their modes of electioneering furnish irrefragable evidence of the contemptuous estimate they place upon the popular intelligence."[110] And Whig songs were foremost among offenders. "By their glee-clubs and other kindred appliances," the Whigs "have endeavored to debase the minds of the people," insisted the *Albany Argus*, which was thoroughly unconvinced of the authenticity ascribed to the "'high minded' songsters" to which Whig glee clubs claimed to "have devoted their *best* energies." For Democrats, it beggared belief why a melody like the "Little Pig's Tail," which would be considered "vulgar" in any other context, was suddenly so patriotic and elevating when matched to the words of "Tippecanoe and Tyler, Too."[111] And once the *North American Review* confirmed that "the aid of music was invoked, not in vain, in our own late elections," the *Norfolk Democrat* could not resist pointing out that the "divine art of music" that the *Review* referred to had included such "beautiful specimens" as,

> We'll go for Harrison, therefore
> *Without a why or a wherefore,* —
> And him we will hurra for,
> Hurra! Hurra!! Hurra!!![112]

Democrats professed to see through the Whigs' attempt to frame their campaign songs as expressions of pure patriotism and tried to recast the practice instead as a humbug, a ploy that improved the practice of popular democracy only for those who distrusted it anyway.

For Democrats, there was no doubt about whether the production of Whig music was a top-down process. "The log hut—cider drinking—song singing—federal whiggery of the present day is the same old blue-light federalism which attempted to impose on the people by pretending to assume Washington's principles in 1812," argued the *Pittsfield Sun*.[113] And the fact that the Whigs in 1840 appeared "determined to sing [Harrison] into the

Presidency" rather than plainly communicate their principles seemed fair evidence that the threat of "modern federalism" was still as strong as ever.[114] Indeed, every time the Whigs boasted that "all party feeling lost itself in the rich flow of music" at one of their events, Democrats only became more convinced that the Whigs were refusing to honestly engage with the people on matters of substance. In Hartford, for instance, local elements of the Democratic press were incredulous at news that Joseph Hoxie, a celebrated Whig orator and vocalist, was soon scheduled to sing in their town: "Who is this Mr. Hoxie, this itinerant ballad monger, who comes among the descendants of the pilgrims, the intelligent people of Connecticut, to influence their political belief, and convince their understandings with Tippecanoe songs?"[115] Surely, if Hoxie and his Whig colleagues actually had any respect for the people, the same paper contended, they would take care to address them with "the open and frank demeanor which distinguishes the democratic freeman."[116] From the Democrats' perspective, Whig campaign music only spoke the language of the people insofar as it exposed just how low an estimation Whigs had of the people's capacity to responsibly contribute to the democratic process.

Attempts by Democrats to link Whig music to Federalism were part of a larger effort to paint Whigs as reincarnations of the same Federalist traitors who had plotted against American interests at the Hartford Convention. Typically, these efforts are now dismissed as the politically driven falsehoods that they were: Whigs did not, as the Democrats alleged, primarily fund their campaign with British gold.[117] However, when it came to music, there was more to the Democrats' critique of Whig singing than blatant political opportunism. And a column published in the *Ohio Statesman* in June 1840 describing Whig music as a "new mode of disseminating Federal principles" helps show just how on point some Democratic satires of Whig music could be. "It is *music* that is to do the business for . . . whiggery," mocked the *Ohio Statesman*, because according to the Whigs, "'soft and harmonious sounds' have a 'wonderful *controlling* influence over the PASSIONS and *actions* of the human species.'" What is more, the column continued, Whigs now realized that "even the BRUTE CREATION have many times been *captivated* and charmed by [music's] influence." Consequently, Democrats explained, the Whigs in their natural-born wisdom have decided that "therefore 'the exercises of this society shall consist in singing patriotic songs, *such as are calculated to aid* the ELECTION of W. H. HARRISON to the PRESIDENCY of the UNITED STATES!!!!!'" To drive the point home, the column concluded by accentuating just how little respect the supposed party of respectability actually had for the people: "Come up then, all ye 'BRUTES' of creation . . . Buzzards and 'coons, owls and asses, must all be *charmed* into support of old Tip by these *musical choristers!*"[118]

The *Ohio Statesman* was not the only Democratic organ to make these types of arguments against Whig music. When the *Albany Argus* reported on Henry Russell's Whig concerts in Boston, it explained how "it seems that the federalists, not content with the 'Harrison melodies,' and the 'log cabin' music divertissements, have employed the itinerant Russell to get up 'whig concerts,' for the benefit of the *reserved* gentlemen of North Bend [Harrison's place of residence]."[119] Earlier in the same month, the *New York Evening Post* charged that "two divisions of the whig party are united in the determination to destroy the democrats with music"—first, those respectable ladies and gentlemen of the "drawing room" and, second, the indecorous mobs of the "tap room." "While the one set trill their Tippecanoe ballads to the air of *di tanti palpili*," the *Evening Post* explained, "the other thunders them out to the tune of *come let us all be folly*."[120] Finally, the *New Hampshire Patriot and State Gazette*, not wanting to let Whigs get away with using religious melodies for their campaign songs, wrote with faux resignation that such blasphemy had become the predictable fare of a Whig Party that insists on claiming for itself "all the intelligence, talent, religion and decency in the community."[121]

Yet, regardless of how discerning Democratic criticisms may have been, they did little to dissuade Americans from singing in election campaigns on the basis that songs elevated their political experience. Whigs won the 1840 election on the back of what is still the third-highest voter turnout in American electoral history and in the process showed more clearly than ever that making music political could help make politics seem respectable. The appeal of their musical logic far eclipsed the 1840 election itself and remained embedded in the foundation of partisan justifications for music's electoral use at least through to the end of Reconstruction.

In 1844, Whig songsters like *The National Clay Minstrel* put forward carbon copies of the arguments used to support Whig music four years earlier. Here Whig music was again depicted as the "life blood" of an ancient and universal patriotic tradition spanning back to the ancient Spartans and as an altogether honest and improving influence. "Why the Loco Focos should complain of poetry and music wedded to and inspiring patriotism, we cannot understand," explained the editor's preface, "unless it be that they are opposed to all which is calculated to elevate, refine and harmonize the mass."[122] In 1848, a musical compilation in support of the Free Soil Party declared that "Music has ever been the handmaid of Liberty," and now that "thousands of hearts" are prepared "to stand or fall for the Right and the True, the emotions thus awakened gush forth . . . naturally in song."[123] In 1852, the *Albany Evening Journal* advertised the Whigs' *Scott and Graham Songster* as being suited to "all who are anxious for a harmonious campaign."[124] And in 1856, the Republicans' *Jessie Songster*, compiled in support of John C. Frémont and his wife, Jessie Benton Frémont, was touted as a respectable collection "worthy" of its compiler, Edward D. Howard—a local Ohioan lawyer—for featuring tunes "of a stirring character, suited to the state of our cause," and for ensuring that "good sense is nowhere omitted."[125] By 1860, it was possible for the editor of the *Republican Campaign Songster*, William H. Burleigh, to claim that "Song had been recognized as a legitimate political power, scarcely secondary in influence to that of the Speech itself [at] giving an impulse and a glow to masses of men."[126] To those who might have suggested that political songs were trivial, Burleigh confidently retorted, "Nothing is trivial that finds a response in the great heart of humanity, and stirs it with hope, or fills it with energy, or lifts it up with aspiration, as the influences of the moon control the tidal currents of the sea."[127]

Even after the Civil War, the sense that music made American election campaigns a more uplifting and inclusive experience remained a popular trope. During the 1868 election, the *Western Musical World* and the *Song Messenger of the Northwest* both came out firmly in support of the candidacy of Ulysses S. Grant and encouraged every Grant Club in the country to take advantage of songs written for their use. "Men and women singers," declared the *Song Messenger*, "you have a part to perform in the campaign now opening, second, hardly, to voting itself." So "form yourselves into singing clubs for campaign work," urged the two music periodicals, and "select the music which breathes the truest spirit of freedom, liberality and justice; attend every meeting where by your presence and your songs may aid the good work."[128] For, as the *Song Messenger* had reasoned two years earlier, "throughout all the vicissitudes of the late gigantic rebellion, as in all other political upheavings, music supplied the cause of right with an enthusiasm, an overwhelming impetus, that contributed largely to its triumph." When properly conceived and executed, music was nothing short of a "moral force," and the longevity of the Whig conception of music in politics suggests its purpose had purchase.[129]

MUSIC, THEN, HAD a deliberate role to play in antebellum electoral politics, and Whigs especially went to great lengths to promote its use and rationalize its function. As such, the intent behind campaign music was not so much to indiscriminately attract attention as it was to frame political participation into a more respectable endeavor. Whigs interpreted music as having a conservative effect on political affairs—one that tended to encourage order, safeguard propriety, and connect to the population's truest and most unifying patriotic sentiments. In the context of elections in which most all white men could vote, women were making their own partisan contributions felt, and violence and humbug nonetheless remained, music helped many Americans justify their participation in a perceivably chaotic popular political system simply by convincing them that they could transcend it. Yet the success of the Whigs' effort to deploy music in this manner was by no means uniform. Campaign music lay at the heart of a deep-seated conflict over the wisdom of popular democracy and the freedom with which it should be practiced in the United States, but its use in the 1840s should be seen less as an acceptance of common-denominator politics than as a means for mitigating its influence.

CHAPTER FOUR

Music and the Making of a Conservative Radical

In May 1848, S. Willard Saxton was out of work and facing the beginnings of an existential crisis. Eighteen years old and a printer by trade, Saxton had lived in Boston for six months but was struggling with his transition to urban life. "In a hot and dusty city with nothing to do; not even a home where I can go to [for] sympathy and encouragement," Saxton complained, "I sometimes feel as though I ha[ve] no friends, and that I am alone in this wide, cheerless world." Alongside repeated spells of unemployment, the combination of loneliness and homesickness was nearly too much to bear: "it makes me almost sick of life," he confided to his diary, "and wonder what I was put here for." However, like many urban bachelors struggling to make ends meet in America's larger mid-nineteenth-century cities, Saxton found respite in an increasingly accessible and commercialized music culture. That evening, Saxton was "delighted" to find that one of his closest friends, Louise Kleinstrup, "happened to be in the right mood" for music, and he was soon treated to a night of her and her friend Anna singing and playing on the piano. The music produced a lift in Saxton's spirits that left him marveling at just how powerful music really was. "'Tis said that 'music hath charms to soothe the savage breast,'" Saxton recalled, and he could understand why: "There is more eloquence in the sweet strains of music than any word I ever heard. . . . It is the outpouring of the soul itself, and I *love* it better than anything."[1]

Saxton's self-confessed "love" of music was more than the rhetorical flourish of a young diarist. Like most music lovers—past or present—Saxton understood his passion for music to involve something more profound than a simple urge to indulge in moments of idle amusement. As Saxton saw it, music could uplift people emotionally, spiritually, and materially. Its presence could attract, persuade, enliven, calm, or otherwise alter the frame of mind of its listeners. In short, music could *do* things. And for Saxton, the experience of music operating as an active agent in human affairs was a thrilling thought. What Saxton could imagine, in his most optimistic moments, was the possibility of a more musical world—one in which deeper truths could find expression and where social and political relations were honest, harmonious, and just. It sounds utopian—and, in truth, it was—but the fact that listening to music really did encourage Saxton to contribute his part toward making the world live up to these goals shows the extent to which his faith in progress and improvement went hand in hand with his faith in musical power. In Saxton's political imagination, if the mark of civilization was progress then its engine looked a lot like music.[2]

Historians and musicologists can analyze the content of antebellum music periodicals and the various speeches delivered before musical societies and artistic institutions.[3] But what of their effect? How might a young urban bachelor have internalized the ideas about music that he was presented with, and how might they have shaped his ideas about political life and democracy? The diary of S. Willard Saxton goes a long way toward suggesting at least one set of answers to these questions. My focus on Saxton is not meant to highlight his importance or representativeness per se.[4] Saxton did not deliver addresses to learned musical societies, author essays for music periodicals, or play music professionally; but he did hear such lectures, read such essays, and attend many professional performances. The significance of Saxton's relationship with music rests in the fact that it exists on an individual level in a recoverable form. Indeed, the evidence from Saxton's diary suggests that the way in which he thought about music is not wholly attributable to what cultural elites told him to think about music. Saxton's reception—not just of music but also of contemporary theories of musical power—was filtered through individual experience and shaped by his own evolving standards of judgment. Yet, at the same time, Saxton's conception of musical power was not entirely of his own making: its roots are traceable, and recovering them reveals the extent to which elite conservative ideals about music could shape even its most radical uses.[5]

Saxton, Music, and His Diary

Saxton never aspired to be a musician, but he devoted an unusually large amount of time and effort to musical interests. In one "ever-to-be-remembered" concert season over the winter of 1852–53, he attended ninety-two musical performances in eight months—an average of nearly three a week—in addition to time spent enjoying music privately in parlors with his friends.[6] Saxton's precarious financial circumstances should have prevented such regular attendance at musical performances, but he was adept at finding ways to access music on the cheap. Saxton convinced newspaper editors whom he worked with to give him free press passes to shows or, failing that, tried to talk his way into performances on the basis of his association with a newspaper anyway.[7] Sometimes, Saxton would simply loiter out front of a theater in the hope of claiming unused tickets or of taking the seat of a patron who left early.[8] Eventually, his most effective strategy was to score evening work in theaters as an usher and doorman—a position that gave Saxton plenty of access to performances while also enabling him to "pass in" his friends for free and make a small second income at the same time. However, when funds were on hand, Saxton was only too willing to pay for his access to music. In November 1850, soon after being let go from a job working in the print office for the *Boston Telegraph*, Saxton determined on making two purchases before he ran out of money again: first, he bought himself a new pair of trousers, and second, he subscribed for tickets to the upcoming 1850–51 season of Boston Musical Fund Society concerts.[9]

If few young men were as enamored with music as Saxton was, then even fewer documented their daily lives as diligently. Saxton's diary contains at least a page or two for most every day of his life from 1847 to 1927—a remarkable record and a testament in itself to the author's unflagging capacity for self-discipline (and longevity).[10] The stated purpose of the journal evolved over time. Initially, Saxton claimed to have been motivated to compose the diary simply "to look back occasionally, and think over the joys and sorrows of [his] past life."[11] However, within a few years, his diary writing began to take on a higher purpose than nostalgia. "Though it will never be of any use to the world, it is a source of pleasure to me, and oftentimes of profit," Saxton explained of his journal, "for we must learn wisdom by experience, & my experience I intend to put down as faithfully as I can, so that I can learn a lesson therefrom in time of need."[12] While in earlier years Saxton insisted that the diary aimed to be a complete and truthful record of his life, by the end of the Civil War he could acknowledge that being truthful was not the same as being comprehensive. "You cannot report anything, unless I so choose," Saxton wrote to his diary, "so you are unable to let out the secrets . . . & divulge any of my horrible wicked deeds." Nonetheless, Saxton maintained, "though you cannot tell all, I will try to have you speak truth when you say anything."[13]

Saxton often chastised himself for failing to use his diary to record a more interesting, accurate, and full account of his life. Yet such self-abasing professions were themselves reflections of the fact that Saxton's journal was never intended to be an entirely private document.[14] It was common for mid-nineteenth-century diaries to be shared among close family and friends, and Saxton did so regularly. But, more than this, Saxton also labored under a belief that an individual's worth—whatever may be one's place in history—would ultimately be judged on the basis of one's "inward life," by which he

Example of an entry from S. Willard Saxton's journal, showing his careful penmanship. In the second column from the right, as part of his entry for 16 May 1848, he underlines his "love" for music. The volumes that Saxton used for his journal varied in shape and size over time, but his hand remained remarkably consistent. Rufus and S. Willard Saxton Papers (MS 431), Manuscripts and Archives Division, Sterling Memorial Library, Yale University.

Photograph of S. Willard Saxton (1829–1933) in 1864. Photographer C. Seaver Jr. Courtesy of Pocumtuck Valley Memorial Association, Memorial Hall Museum, Deerfield, Massachusetts.

meant "his conduct in the social circle, in the friendly relations of life, [and] by his thoughts expressed at home or to himself." Public deeds alone were an inadequate measure of character. Once someone has "yielded up the ghost, & gone to a higher sphere of action," Saxton rationalized, it would be "his true character" and not his actions that will either be "condemned or pointed to as an example worthy of being followed."[15] The arc of one's inner story was something Saxton saw to be firmly within his own control, and it was a story he enjoyed crafting.[16]

Born in Deerfield, Massachusetts, in 1829, S. Willard Saxton was the son of a radical Unitarian preacher, Jonathan Ashley Saxton, who had been an early and vocal supporter of women's rights, antislavery, and temperance.

Despite being a Harvard graduate, Saxton's father did little with his law degree and did even less to ensure that his children got a similar education. In place of college, Saxton's father had hoped to persuade his elder son, Rufus Saxton, to join George Ripley's utopian experiment at Brook Farm, where he expected Rufus might acquire a trade and learn how people could better join in community with one another.[17] Rufus, however, envisioned a different trajectory for his future and accepted an appointment to study at West Point instead. But Willard, for his part, gladly took up residence at Brook Farm, where he soaked up the principles of Fourierist Associationalism and learned his trade in the printing workshop of the community's newspaper: the *Harbinger*. The circumstances of growing up in a highly educated family that placed little value on the traditional trappings and opportunities of privilege gave the younger Saxton the skills to record a highly articulate account of mid-nineteenth-century life from the margins of New England's cultural and intellectual elite.

Saxton began his diary at Brook Farm in 1847 in the middle of that community's dissolution. And for the next decade, the diary follows Saxton's life as a journeyman printer, winning and losing jobs on the vagaries of market demand. Boston became Saxton's spiritual home, but the search for regular work took him all over the country, from urban and regional Massachusetts to New York, Washington, DC, Ohio, Tennessee, Indiana, Georgia, and South Carolina. In every instance, holding down a job became all the harder once the Boston printer's union blacklisted him for having accepted work at under union wages during their strike. Saxton's struggles to find steady employment made the payment of debt a constant problem, one that eventually landed him in debtor's prison in 1860 (less than a month after his wife to be, Mary Grant, accepted his marriage proposal).[18] Determined to escape the physical and financial vicissitudes of work in a print shop, Saxton took on odd jobs canvassing for multiple political parties during the 1860 election before throwing his lot into a failed attempt to get up a newspaper and candy store of his own. Saxton considered enlisting as a soldier in the Union army during the Civil War but instead traveled to Port Royal, where he served as his brother's aide-de-camp before transitioning into a situation at the Freedmen's Bureau at the end of hostilities.[19] Although historians have never made sustained use of Saxton's diary before, the depth of detail and cultural orientation of its first twenty years offer a unique entry point into mid-nineteenth-century life that this chapter uses to reveal the place of music within the broader constellation of a young man's political understanding.[20]

John S. Dwight and the Foundations of Saxton's Musical Appreciation

Late on a Friday evening in November 1849, Saxton's financial problems were coming to a head. With two dollars in his pocket and a landlord insisting that his nine-dollar bill for board be paid by morning, he was almost out of options. The Boston Printer's Protective Union was on strike and offered up to six dollars of relief to members in need, a helpful amount but one that still left Saxton a dollar short. Saxton was all too aware of his predicament: "I am out of work, I am in debt, I have more debts constantly increasing, no prospect of anything to do at present, and no friend on whom I can call for aid." As he readied himself for sleep, Saxton sought in vain to find a silver lining. "I must make an effort here *immediately*," Saxton determined, "or leave the city and seek my fortune (if there is any for me) in other parts."[21]

That night, at half past two in the morning, the sound of music roused Saxton from bed. But far from being annoyed at the interruption or notching it up to more bad luck, Saxton could not have been more pleased: "What is there more delightful than to be awoke from sleep in the dead of night by a band of fine music," Saxton enthused. The experience, he continued, "was exquisite and soul-stirring, . . . and I certainly think I never was so charmed with any music as I was with that." The only frustration Saxton had with the band was "that they did not play but [more than] one tune": "for the effect of it upon me is very delightful."[22] This response to late-night serenades was not out of the ordinary for Saxton. In July 1850, when a visiting military company from New York struck up some airs at two in the morning, Saxton wrote that he "stood at the window about half an hour, perfectly enchanted with the beautiful music as it rose upon the midnight air." The music he heard "was indeed refreshing," Saxton recounted, "and for my share of the pleasure I am *vastly* grateful."[23] Such a reaction certainly speaks to Saxton's unquestionable affinity for music (and to the relative rarity of its occurrence even in a city like Boston). But it also poses some intriguing questions: Why would a journeyman printer like Saxton value music so highly as to make him "*vastly* grateful" to hear it? Why did he articulate its "effect" on him as "delightful" and "enchanting" rather than an amusing distraction from his troubles? And what made music both a "soul-stirring" force and a "refreshing" influence?

As individuals go, the question of how a young man like Saxton came to hold such ideas about music is unusually answerable. Saxton had neither the money nor the time to publish his thoughts on music, but his diary provided a more than adequate outlet for recording his views. Moreover, his experiences as a youth at Brook Farm highlight his personal connection to one of the key figures in mid-nineteenth-century American musical life, John S. Dwight, who *did* publish an uncommonly large amount of his thoughts on music. Dwight gave Saxton his first ticket to an oratorio concert and contributed dozens of pieces of music criticism to the *Harbinger* that Saxton no doubt would have read and in many cases would have even typeset himself.[24] Later, Dwight employed Saxton to assist in printing the first few numbers of his *Journal of Music*, invited Saxton to celebrate his wedding, and intermittently continued to procure Saxton tickets to musical events that he would not otherwise have been able to afford.[25] As such, Dwight remained an esteemed presence in Saxton's journal for decades after Brook Farm's dissolution—so much so that when working in the West, few activities made Saxton feel closer to home than perusing Dwight's latest musical reviews.[26] It is easy to hypothesize that Dwight shaped the foundations of Saxton's musical understanding, and, as we shall see, it is an assumption that rings true.

Understanding Dwight's Fourierism is key to understanding both Dwight's vision of music and how someone like Saxton could come to conceive of it as a politically active agent in human society.[27] Fourierism was a social-reform philosophy based on the writings of a Frenchman, Charles Fourier (1772–1837), who sought to remedy the injustices of industrial capitalism by proposing a scientific system of social relations organized through small cooperative communities. Just as Isaac Newton had discovered the physical laws of the universe, Fourier believed he had discovered a corresponding set of social laws in which a basic set of twelve fundamental human passions combined with a total of 810 different personality types to govern the outcome of all human relations. Fourier figuratively explained that the twelve human passions had emerged as branches from a singular "passional tree," the trunk of which represented the principle of "unityism"—a harmonious fusion of all the passions that when ordered properly produced what he referred to as a state of "universal fellow feeling." In a bewildering array of detail and pseudoscientific obfuscation, Fourier set out exactly how communities of precisely 1,620 people (called Phalansteries) could be arranged to make labor and industry more meaningful and efficient via a system of communal production and free-form social arrangements that he claimed would satisfy the full range of human passions.[28]

Fourierism was imported to the United States by Albert Brisbane, a young dilettante from upstate New York who had converted to Fourierism during an extended study tour through Europe. Largely due to Brisbane's exertions on behalf of the cause—which included everything from recruiting the influence of Horace Greeley and his *New York Tribune*, publishing original English translations and commentary of Fourier's works in the United States, and establishing American-based Fourierite periodicals—American Fourierism would come to represent an intriguing mix of foreign and domestic influences. American adherents, for example, quickly abandoned the most controversial aspects of Fourier's writings (which incidentally most of his French followers had renounced by the 1840s as well) in a conscious attempt to free themselves from the burden of dealing with Fourier's truly revolutionary ideas about free love and sexual relations as well as his fantastical predictions of a future in which humans grew tails and oceans turned to lemonade. Even more cannily, American Fourierists placed a higher emphasis than their French counterparts on Fourierist theory as a practical and scalable solution to their nation's ills. Party politics, American Fourierists maintained, had created a system of governance more interested in solving its own superficial political problems than in offering viable solutions to the nation's systemic societal problems. And in the aftermath of the economic chaos wrought by the Panic of 1837, the effects of societal deficiencies had become all too obvious. Association, American Fourierists argued, was simply a plan in which workers from all classes could better their lot by pooling their minds and hearts together rather than struggling to make ends meet on their own.[29]

By the time George Ripley's Brook Farm was converted into the nation's first officially recognized model phalanx, Dwight was already an important musical personality in Boston. And by simultaneously taking up leadership positions at Brook Farm as well as writing music criticism for the *Dial* and establishing the Harvard Musical Association, Dwight was uniquely positioned to capitalize on the musical resonances of Fourier's theories. Fourier, for instance, intended his twelve basic passions to be representative of the twelve notes in a musical scale, arranged his 810 identified personality types onto a keyboard-scale diagram, allocated dedicated spaces in his model phalanx plans to facilitate musical practice and performance, and ultimately sought to achieve a harmony of social organization that he felt humans had only ever managed to achieve previously through music. "An opera house is as necessary to a Phalanx . . . as its plows and its herds," Fourier explained, because "it also serves to educate children and to shape them in the ways of material harmony." By this, Fourier meant that with music one learns "to subordinate himself in every movement to unitary conventions [and] general harmonies."[30] Brisbane, too, was sensitive to the role of music in Fourierism and in 1844 dedicated six months to studying the science and practice of musical harmony in Paris. "It is a fact, though perhaps not fully appreciated, that man has realized *harmony* in but one department of his mental activity,—the musical," Brisbane later explained, claiming that his lessons in music were "a study to which [he] had given insufficient attention."[31] The broad connection between music and the goals of Fourierist Associationalism would have undoubtedly been clear to Dwight because the practical usefulness of music was built into the very structure of Fourierist philosophy itself.

The clearest articulation of Dwight's intertwining of musical criticism with Fourierist Associationalism came in his introduction to the "Musical Review" column of the *Harbinger*. Here Dwight situated the rise and trajectory of music in the United States firmly within the context of Associationalist idealism and set out an agenda for his music journalism that exclusively revolved around considering music in this utopian light. The column began by placing American musical progress within a broader frame of societal reform: "Among the hopeful movements of the day," Dwight declared, "there is a Musical Movement in this country."[32] According to Dwight, music in America constituted a "movement" because by speaking the language of pure sentiment, music had the capacity to join all Americans in expressing the common feeling that underlay their surface differences. "If it be true," Dwight explained, "that Humanity is now on the verge, nay in the midst of a grand onward movement; that society is inspired, not with dreams merely, but with most earnest, energetic strivings after the realization of a Divine Order, (strange . . . and conflicting as may be the forms which that inspiration often takes), then there is a great significance in this growing interest now felt in music."[33] Whereas speech was a product of the mind that produced "doctrines" and "distinctions," music was a product of "feeling" and "sentiment" that produced "a constant tendency to Unity." Dwight therefore interpreted the growing popularity of art music in America as an indication that Americans were subconsciously beginning to come to grips with the feelings that bound them together and the grand purpose to which the culmination of their efforts would eventually be put: "Whenever the life of a people is deep," Dwight wrote, "whenever broad and universal sentiments absorb and harmonize the petty egotisms and discords of men; whenever humanity is at all inspired with a consciousness of its great Destiny; whenever Love gives the tone to the feelings, the thoughts, and the activity of an age; whenever a hundred Reforms, all springing from so deep a source, all tend, in the very antagonism of their one-sidedness, in the very bigotry of their earnestness, to one grand thought and aim, the Unity of the race; in short, whenever there is a Movement, then, too, as by a law of Correspondence, there should be a new development of the passion and the art of music."[34] Musical appreciation, then, was the outward manifestation of an inward impulse that promised to both articulate and inspire the unity of the American people and of humanity as a whole. Importantly, it was an interpretation communicated clearly within the logic of Fourierist Associationalism, wherein "laws of correspondence" govern a people who are connected at a metaphysical level, regardless of their differences, by the foundational principle of "unity."

However, for Dwight, the rise of music in America was also indicative of a shift toward a more transcendental sense of religiosity. Or, as Dwight described it in the *Harbinger*, "we propose to treat . . . Music, as the language of that deeper experience in which all men are most nearly ONE; the language of those central fires, great heaven-born Passions of the soul, which prompt to holy ties of Love, of Friendship, of Family, of Social Order, which through these blissful foretastes of union steadily invite and draw us on to everlasting Unity with God." As far as Dwight was concerned, distinctions between sacred and secular music were meaningless. Instead, the spiritual import of music was less about the words to which it was put or the themes to which it was associated than the extent to which it tapped into a deeper current of feeling that connects the world together in a single unspeakable truth—God. To dictate the meaning of God's truth in a language other than music would be impossible, Dwight claimed, even though not all music in this respect was equal: Music meant merely to "amuse" does not stir the "passions of the soul" like a piece of music meant to articulate a "most religious outpouring of [a] composer's life" does. Yet, apart from the fact that Dwight felt that the more openly interpretive nature of instrumental music spoke most deeply to the greatest number of people, he maintained in the *Harbinger* that any genre of music theoretically had the capacity to engage the unifying passions so long as its composer was possessed of the genius required to express it. So, to the extent that sufficiently "deep and earnest" music offered listeners a direct connection to the unifying force of the universe, music produced a literally religious experience.[35]

Dwight concluded his first column in the *Harbinger* by combining the utopian convictions of Associationalism together with Fourier's observations about music's educational potential to address a more distinctive set of American circumstances. "Ever grateful let us be to music," Dwight advised readers living through times in which "there seemed almost no sincerity, no faith, no earnestness; . . . when every thought of the Ideal was damped by the triumphant sneers . . . and [when] the whole framework of society gave the lie to the voice of the preacher and of the heart." For music—which Dwight claimed his Puritan "elders" wrongfully dismissed as a "wayward, impracticable enthusiasm" and a "besetting sin of indulgence"—was now emerging as "our initiation into the great hopes of the Future, haunting us with a faith most irresistible though indistinct, that better days shall come, that the real destiny of Man is Unity and Harmony, and that the Law of Necessity must yield at length to the holier Law of Attraction,—of Liberty and Love."[36] Becoming musical, according to Dwight, was an essential step in the progress of the nation.[37]

By 1847, however, as fervor for Associationalism waned and the Brook Farm community prepared to disband, Dwight had already become impatient at the slow realization of his musical predictions. In a review of Franz Lachner's *Sinfonia Passionata*, Dwight marveled at how in this work "the whole soul is addressed, and is called out, with an integral force of feeling." Yet it seemed equally clear to Dwight that the lesser "little titillating pleasure of . . . music for *a*-musment" continued to remain as popular as ever. "Alas! when will the whole life of this people be so great and full, that music of the grander order alone will satisfy it?" Dwight complained. "Great music speaks now to our rarer, purer aspirations, and of course demands too much of those whose superficial lives are seldom or never troubled by such heavenly visitors." Dwight had not lost faith—"the time must come when what now speaks to the earnest few . . . will become as necessary to daily life of all"—but he could not help but be disappointed in the continued failure of Americans to appreciate the "difference between brilliant and fantastic overtures and songs and solos, or what is called popular music, and a great symphony, or oratorio, or organ-fugue."[38] It is tempting to interpret Dwight's writings on music during this period as being primarily concerned with the cultivation of an American taste for good music and high culture. However, taste was only part of the equation: what is also at play here is a conviction that the development of American musical life was itself a harbinger, one that was intimately bound up with his utopian Associationalist belief in the notion of "a better time coming." The musicality of the world was, in fact, the measure and the goal of its advancement toward a more harmonious order. And this was to be a central, if not the determining, aspect of how Saxton related to music throughout his bachelorhood.

Saxton regularly articulated his devotion to the principles of Association throughout the early years of his journal. On expressing his regret at the conclusion of the Brook Farm community, Saxton declared, "I shall keep in as close connection with the blessed work of Association as circumstances will permit, and do all I can to help forward the great cause; a cause in which many great and good men are spending their lives to help forward."[39] A visit to the Boston Navy Yard a few days earlier had made Saxton yearn for the day when instruments of warfare no longer marred the nation's coastline. "What a horrible state of society there is now," Saxton wrote, before assuring himself that "there's a better time coming" because of the "great and glorious work [of] Association."[40] After leaving Brook Farm, Saxton frequently attended Associationalist meetings and celebrations in Boston, especially annual celebrations of Fourier's birthday. "This is the anniversary of the birth of the immortal prophet," Saxton reported in 1851, "who came into this world to teach people to see the enormous wrongs that at present day exist in society, and to lay the foundation of a new order of things." Four years after leaving Brook Farm, Saxton claimed to still be as devoted to Association as ever, even if he reasoned that its progress would be slower than he had expected: "The ideal life, as unfolded by Charles Fourier . . . is to be, I confidently believe, but it cannot be forced upon the people at once. It has got to grow slowly, and meet with great discouragements and opposition, like every great work. Association is making a gradual change, and all the great reforms of the day are heading to that one point." "Brook Farm failed," Saxton admitted, "but we learned a good lesson thereby" and "will yet show the world that it is not all a 'folly and impracticability.'"[41] Saxton's predictions did not materialize. But even in 1859, when Saxton nostalgically noted that the anniversary of Fourier's birthday had passed by unmarked, that the "little band are scattered," and that "most of them have changed in their views," he could still convey a clear sense of Association's enduring effect on him: "the memory of those charmed evenings will ever remain fresh," Saxton explained, "for music, poetry, and all the fine arts contributed to their sanctification."[42]

Saxton would likewise always respect, if not defer to, Dwight's authority on musical matters. There were at least two reasons for this: first, Saxton simply did not have the time or money to see and hear all the music he wished to, and second, with limited experience, Saxton took a few years to develop confidence in the validity of his own aesthetic judgment. In January 1851, Saxton noted that his friend Jennie Clarke had enjoyed seeing the English soprano Anna Bishop at Boston's Tremont Temple.[43] Although Saxton had never seen Bishop perform, nor did he expect to "in consequence of a lack of funds," he explained he "should like to very much" not just because "she is quite celebrated" but also because since "John Dwight likes her very much," he supposed that "she is a fine artist."[44] A few days following, after Saxton transcribed a significant portion of Dwight's review of Beethoven's *Pastoral*

Symphony into his diary, he rationalized his musical interests by clarifying, "though I do not pretend to be a critic . . . I find by attending these concerts my taste for the true kind of music is constantly improving."[45] Again in 1850, Saxton complained, "such poor individuals as myself could not think of attending" a performance of the Havana Opera Company, "for the cheapest seats were half a dollar." Nonetheless, he remarked, they must have been "a superior company no doubt" for "John Dwight says there is nothing like it short of London or Paris."[46] Even as late as 1858, there were moments when Saxton enjoyed a concert so much that he felt incapable of describing the experience without Dwight's linguistic expertise. Saxton enthused of Mendelssohn's "Song of Praise," "I cannot speak—Mr. Dwight will [have to] do it for me."[47] Over time, however, Saxton did develop a clearer sense of his own musical values, which grew symbiotically with an emerging interest in political affairs.

How Loving Music Led Saxton to Cast His First Vote

The 1850–52 American concert tour of Jenny Lind was a transformative experience for Saxton.[48] Like thousands of Americans, Saxton was overcome with anticipation from the moment news came of the Swedish Nightingale's arrival in New York. "The 'Jenny Lind' mania is carrying everything before it," Saxton testified. "The papers are 'all about Jenny Lind,' the '*Northern Queen of song*,' as John S. Dwight calls her."[49] Saxton devoured reportage of Lind's tour and wrote at length in his diary about every facet of Lind's trip, from the thrillingly high prices of first-ticket auctions to her accommodations, profits, performance venues, and especially her donations to various charitable causes.[50] While Dwight had encouraged Saxton to understand his musical engagement within a utopian framework of nationalistic social reform, Lind's tour would demonstrate that linking these musical ideals to real-world actions amplified their positive effects—a realization that would help convince this radically minded young man of both the wisdom and necessity of exercising his franchise.

Once Lind arrived in Boston, Saxton was determined to get "a fair look at her," even though he feared that "the chance of hearing her, for . . . *poor boys*" like himself, "will be small."[51] Over the next month, Saxton's diary is replete with accounts of his efforts to witness whatever aspect of the Lind spectacle he could. Saxton cheered along with "the curious multitude" that gathered to see Lind disembark in Boston, applauded her appearances on the balcony of her hotel room, stayed out until two in the morning for the chance to hear her serenaded by the Boston Musical Fund Society, stole through a private house to eavesdrop on one of her performances from the top of a nearby shed, tried (without success) to procure work as an usher for her shows, and on several occasions loitered outside the theater with friends to listen to snippets of her voice.[52] Yet the culmination of all these half successes—managing to either see or hear Lind but not both—only drove home just how much Saxton wanted the complete experience.[53]

When Lind's last two Boston shows were moved from the Tremont Temple to the larger Fitchburg Railroad Depot, Saxton figured that this was his "last chance" and resolved to purchase tickets.[54] The more spacious venue had enabled Lind's managers to reduce their cheapest tickets from $3.00 to $1.00, a price Saxton could manage in a week when he earned the "excellent" sum of $9.50.[55] But the notoriously riotous performance he witnessed there proved disappointing.[56] Saxton could not get close enough to the stage to see Lind's face, was frustrated by unbearably hot conditions, and was distracted by unruly crowd behavior: "The mob made so much disturbance that the first overture was not heard at all," Saxton complained, and "the tumult had put me in a most unfavorable state of mind and nerves to enjoy" the performance. Still, to Saxton's eyes, Lind herself could do no wrong: "when the lovely Queen of Song made her appearance upon the stage, the hootings and yells of the excited mob ceased, and all was calm again," Saxton recalled, adding, "It was beautiful to see the influence she had to still such an excited crowd."[57] From Saxton's perspective, Lind, during her visit to Boston, had "endeared herself to the hearts of every body, and brought happiness to thousands," whereas her American audiences had shown themselves in need of some reform.[58] The extent to which such fundamentally conservative ideals about musical power informed Saxton's enthusiasm for Lind is important to emphasize. To the mind of a young man enamored with utopian dreams of societal change, Lind's greatness did not lay in firing up the passions of a crowd; it lay in calming the mob and stilling disorder.

Dwight's influence shaped and fueled Saxton's admiration of Lind even before her arrival to the United States.[59] "Hers is the genius to which we look to interpret to us the mystical and higher passions, as expressed in music," Dwight told *Harbinger* readers in an 1847 review of songs that claimed to be associated with Lind but that he felt were not "worthy of her divine power."[60] Later, Dwight's first reviews of Lind's American performances clearly added to Saxton's own excitement: "John Dwight has been in N.Y. attending the concerts, and I have read one of his criticisms, which was very fine," Saxton noted. "He is so delighted that he cannot criticize her; not enough can be said

"Jenny Lind and the Americans. From our own Reporters. Coronation of Jenny the First—Queen of the Americans," *Punch, or the London Charivari* 19 (5 October 1850): 146. Reproduced with permission of Punch Ltd., www.punch.co.uk.

in her praise."61 When Lind eventually returned to the Northern states for a run of farewell shows in the spring of 1852, Saxton was both jealous of Dwight's access to the star and admiring of his capacity to describe the concert experience:

> She [Lind] has been giving her three last concerts in America in New York, & Mr. Dwight & Mary [Dwight's wife] have been there through the whole, enjoying as much as is possible for mortal beings to enjoy, for they have not only *heard* her in public, but have been *with* her, & enjoyed her in private. He has written home to his paper the accounts of the concerts, & those of the last two are the most beautiful & enthusiastic of anything I ever read of his. . . . One can almost imagine that he were in reality face to face with the divine artist, surrounded by the thousands of sad & joyous faces, listening to her sweet farewell notes.62

To Dwight, "Lind Mania" in the United States showed that once Americans had heard real music, they would instinctively appreciate its uplifting,

Music and the Making of a Conservative Radical

soul-inspiring qualities. "Think of *seven thousand* faces, lit with sad enthusiasm," Dwight wrote of the farewell concert, "turned all to one focus, to greet and enjoy, for the last time . . . the presence and the almost more than mortal music, of a woman who, in eighteen months, by the mere divine right of goodness and of a matchless voice . . . has established a sort of moral and ideal empire in the hearts of this whole people, rude and cultivated."[63] And in this, at least, Saxton largely agreed: "The world acknowledges the well-deserved reputation of the 'queen of song,' of *music*, the divinest, the most beautiful, the most life-giving art God has bestowed upon his unworthy and almost ungrateful children," Saxton enthused after seeing Lind sing in 1851. "I am happy that I have heard thee, and I wish all the world could have the same pleasure."[64]

Of course, not everyone joined in the supposedly universal acclaim that Dwight or Saxton attributed to Lind. Some privately confided their disapproval to their diaries. Mrs. Joel J. Baily, for instance, the wife of a Philadelphian wholesale and retail hosiery merchant, was at a loss to explain the excitement generated by Jenny Lind's arrival in New York: "how foolish it is to make such a fuss with a public singer," Baily protested; "really the people are crazy."[65] Others mocked the general enthusiasm for Lind in letters to newspaper editors. Sebastian Pips, an apothecary and self-described "victim to the Jenny Lind Mania," wrote to the *Boston Evening Transcript* to take issue with everything from the price of the tickets to the degeneracy of the crowds and the seemingly endless supply of Lind paraphernalia that tempted his family: "I trust the departure of the Nightingale will relieve us, who are not Lind-mad," Pips wrote, "from the tedious rehearsal of her sayings and doings, and the turgid praises of her beauty, wit, and skill, with which we are now constantly overwhelmed."[66] Certainly, one Washington correspondent was unconvinced by the preponderance of positive reviews, claiming to be "egregiously disappointed" by Lind once he found her singing in fact to be not "the warbling of an angel" but instead "only the voice of a woman."[67] In the end, though, naysayers struggled to take much away from the efforts of a reported twenty-six journalists employed full-time by Lind's management to "puff" her shows across the country.[68]

For Saxton, however, Lind's tour helped crystallize his sense of why Americans needed reform and how to achieve it. Dwight had provided Saxton with an unusually sophisticated, albeit idiosyncratic, understanding of musical power, one that Saxton now began to direct toward the more immediate concerns and circumstances of his life. What this meant, in practice, was Saxton's adoption of a less abstract and more individualistic take on music's political power. The key factors in Saxton's transition were repeated disappointment at the poor behavior of Boston crowds in and outside Lind's performances; Lind's apparent capacity to use music to bestow order on otherwise-unruly audiences; the extension of Lind's musical effects through her conspicuous program of charitable giving, particularly in light of Saxton's own precarious financial situation; and, importantly, the passage of the Fugitive Slave Law, which occurred concurrently to Lind's first visit to Boston. What Lind's tour emphasized to Saxton was that moral and spiritual uplift could profitably intertwine with material uplift—a realization that led him to engage in ever more formalized forms of political participation.

Before Lind made an appearance in his diary, Saxton, always self-aware, was keen to present himself as a protopolitical citizen. "My time has not yet come," Saxton maintained on Election Day eve in 1848. "I do not enter into the strife of political life, but calmly watch the progress of affairs, and hope for the best."[69] Just as Saxton did not "pretend to be a critic" of music when he began to participate in Boston's concert scene, neither did he claim to possess any political opinions worthy of note when he reached adulthood.[70] Once Saxton left Brook Farm and settled in Boston, however, it is clear that he soon took an interest in a variety of civic activities—attending not just concerts and Associationalist gatherings but also temperance celebrations, public lectures, meetings in sympathy with the French Revolution, and, before long, antislavery events as well.[71] Saxton, nevertheless, reveals little of his own reaction to the issues raised at these events, instead recording the fullness of crowds, the intensity of their applause, and, in turn, whether or not he found the events generally "interesting." And interest, of course, does not necessarily beget opinion.

On occasion, Saxton was prone to explicitly downplay his engagement in matters of substance or complexity. Referring to his church attendance, for example, Saxton admitted, "I go there as much to hear the singing as anything. . . . Mr. [William Henry] Channing is often so meta-physical that I cannot understand him."[72] But even with the few issues that Saxton does articulate a position on at this time—his opposition to the Mexican-American War and his preference for the Free Soil Party—he makes sure to keep himself at a remove from the action. In 1848, Saxton rejected the premise propagated by the political press that "every man, as a Christian, [must] vote for their candidate, as though their lives depended on their one vote," while simultaneously professing that if he did vote, he would grudgingly do so in favor of the Free Soil Party even though he did not much care for its candidate, Martin Van Buren.[73] Such logic may be the reasoning of a politically interested person but not necessarily of one who saw all that much value in political participation. Similarly, in the case of the Mexican-American War, Saxton seemingly sways between watching a grand procession in honor of two fallen soldiers—"two brave heroes who fought, bled, and died, for their country," Saxton explained—and condemning the whole endeavor as "an indelible stain upon our country's honor."[74] Here what might appear to be a nuanced take on the war was instead a reflection of the classic patriotic antiwar sentiment that Whigs, Brook Farmers, and other antiwar agitators had professed to all along.[75] Indeed, Saxton remained far more comfortable transcribing other people's views on the Mexican-American War than he did articulating his own.[76]

Lind's concerts and Saxton's interpretation of how her music influenced listeners encouraged him to sharpen his political views. As Peter Buckley has explained, one of the most significant aspects of Lind's tour was its capacity to create a distinctive "public" of its own, and in this way, Lind brought Saxton face-to-face with a confronting vision of the American people.[77] In September 1850, for instance, Saxton described having gone to Bowdoin Square to see Lind serenaded by the Boston Musical Fund Society only to find that "the crowd acted so they [the serenaders] could do nothing"—even with police assistance, the musicians could not secure a safe space to perform and had to abandon their effort. "The mob—for such it was"—Saxton clarified, "was the most disgraceful assembly Boston has seen for many a day." But the fact that this kind of riotous behavior occurred in honor of a foreign personage like Lind had made it all the worse. "Boston boys ought to be ashamed of themselves," Saxton figured, for "Jenny cannot give them much credit for to-night's proceedings."[78] The next day, Saxton could not help but assume that Lind's feelings about the previous night must have echoed his own: "It was a long time before the 'watch' could clear the square," Saxton explained, "but they finally succeeded, and Jenny was allowed to sleep in peace, not very well satisfied, I am sure, with the evening's entertainment."[79]

As Saxton described it, a disorderly American public met Lind at almost every turn. "The crowd was so rude" at the Boston Mechanic's Fair, for example, that Lind was "obliged to retreat" from her scheduled appearance, "much to her disappointment."[80] A rabble-rousing throng outside her first concert in Boston was so full of "boys and rowdies" who "seemed determined to make as much noise as possible, by yelling and screaming at every thing that went by, and every thing that happened" that the police were required to quell them.[81] Saxton's own experience of seeing Lind sing at the Fitchburg Depot had been punctuated by "the hootings and yells of the excited mob" in the theater.[82] Yet, according to Saxton, Lind and her music had the capacity to reform all these people: "What magic spell dost thou use most beauteous queen, that will draw such crowds even to outside walls where thy voice can just be heard, a spell that will calm the most turbulent rioters, and throw the canopy of peace and quiet over the scenes of wrangling and blasphemy." Unsurprisingly, the spell Saxton referred to was music—or, as he put it, "the most life-giving art God has bestowed upon his unworthy and almost ungrateful children."[83] This was not the talk of a young man led into an infatuation with Lind purely because of Barnum-style humbug and puffery. Saxton had long been versed in the idea that music, order, and reform shared an intimate and interrelated connection. So, when Saxton saw Lind to have uplifted "rioting" and "blasphemous" Americans through the "spell" of her music, what he also saw was Dwight's Fourier-influenced theory of musical power translated into practice: Lind's concerts showed Saxton the power of musical appreciation at work and in doing so signaled hope for the rise of a better, fairer, and more just American future.

With these higher justifications of his musical appreciation confirmed, Saxton proceeded to revel in the scope of music's power and to imagine the pleasure that Lind must derive from possessing it. "Though thou art subjected to many irksome scenes and have troubles we know not of," Saxton rationalized, "how much happiness must be thine to be able to dispense so many blessings upon every side."[84] The notion that possessing musical power not only could make other people feel better but also served to make its provider happy held considerable sway over Saxton. When Lind returned to Boston in the spring of 1851, Saxton marveled at the impact of her performance on her audience alongside the wonderful impact that this must have had on Lind herself: "Great and glorious Jenny Lind, art thou half conscious of the happiness thou sendest home to ten thousands of hearts and homes. If you are, what delight you must take in being able to spread so much joy throughout the world. I have heard the glorious queen of song, and enjoyed her with my whole soul, and long shall I remember this night."[85] Earlier, in November 1850, Saxton had similarly longed for music's power after returning home from a concert by a popular Scottish ballad singer, William Dempster.[86] "He has a fine voice, and sings a certain class of songs with great effect," Saxton reported, and "I think I would be very happy if I had as good a voice as his, for then I would be able to add much to the happiness of others."[87] Saxton, however, would soon enough resign himself to the reality that he would never have the money to "study music" to the level that would allow him to "be able to make others as happy as music" made him.[88]

The key to Saxton's belief in music's emotional generosity was a combination of personal experience with how music made him feel—regardless of its genre—and Dwight's more metaphysical and elitist construction of music's purpose in the United States. "Music does make me happy," Saxton admitted; "at the moment there is an unusually fine organ in the street playing some familiar polkas, & other airs, and there is a pleasure in listening even to that." Whether listening to an organ grinder, a popular balladeer like Dempster, or one of Beethoven's symphonies, Saxton explained, good music would always have good effects on people because "our souls are attuned to harmony, and however simple they are, wherever they are heard, sweet sounds will send a joyous thrill through one's senses."[89] By contrast, in January 1850, while stewing over his inability to afford to take his sister to see a performance of the Boston Philharmonic Society, Saxton dreamt of how his "days of fortune will come sometime" when he would be able to "visit such places as are congenial to [his] taste, and be able also to make many others happy who are much lower, in the world's view of the case, than [himself], in the scale of humanity."[90] To this end, music was important because it was also the most accessible way for individuals to access higher and more refined avenues of thought and experience, making the gift of music—as well as its appreciation—something that Saxton invested much value in giving.

After experiencing Lind's concerts, Saxton's newfound emphasis on music's ability to make people happy contributed to a subtle divergence between Saxton's conception of musical power and Dwight's more elaborate theoretical constructs. Musical power, Saxton recognized, resided more than anything in the simple fact that it could make people *feel* better. And it is this relatively straightforward insight that underpinned Saxton's assertion that Lind wielded "a mighty influence" both "among kings and queens in their palaces, and the poor in their wretched dwellings."[91] Humanity, as Dwight had pointed out to Saxton, was connected at a level far deeper than any class distinction, and the attraction of Lind as an artist was partly in her capacity to use music as a way of exploiting that connection, to unify her audiences by tapping into the vein of universal fellow feeling that held the key to social harmony. But Saxton also saw Lind as a powerful force for good on a more basic individual level: *she* made the members of her audience feel good about themselves, no matter who they were or where they came from. Of course, this was not necessarily true—Lind demonstrably did not make everyone in her audiences feel better about themselves—but it was an important reason why Saxton, given his perennially poor financial circumstances, felt such a close bond with Lind: a rich, foreign singer who had succeeded in becoming one of America's first genuine celebrities.

Lind's reform-minded program of charitable giving did the most to solidify Saxton's emotional connection to the star's personality. On hearing that the $10,000 profit Lind made at her New York concerts would be distributed to various charitable societies, Saxton wrote at length in admiration of her remarkable "benevolence." Like a modern-day Robin Hood, Saxton wrote, "she receives this money from the rich, who would seldom think of giving a penny to assist in any benevolent project, and gives it to those who need it." Reports of Lind's charity were central to Saxton's estimation of her character: "true and beautiful goodness as in her can never go unrewarded," Saxton mused. And it was this generosity of spirit that Saxton would invariably hear in her voice and read into her appearance.[92] After catching a glimpse of Lind as she exited the Tremont Theatre in Boston, Saxton wrote of how he witnessed "her countenance beaming with benevolence and love."[93] There were, ultimately, "a thousand examples of her benevolence" that could be pointed to, Saxton claimed, and he was convinced that in Lind he had found something of a kindred spirit.[94] "I wish Jenny Lind knew my circumstances, & my *worthiness* for her charity," Saxton told his diary; if only he were to meet Lind, she would recognize and reward the goodness of his heart.[95]

To be sure, Saxton's hope that Lind would somehow manage to bear witness to his heart's "worthiness" was not necessarily as far-fetched as it sounds. Because this is exactly what appeared to happen to his friend Louise Kleinstrup. Saxton had met Kleinstrup at Brook Farm and had struck up an especially close, if not romantic, connection with her while living in Boston.[96] In July 1850, however, as Saxton was walking Kleinstrup home from a leisurely stroll through Boston Common, he was concerned to see her coughing up blood and spent the next day trying to convince friends and family to attend to her health. "I wish I could do something" for her, Saxton explained, "but though the heart is willing, the purse faileth."[97] By the time of Lind's tour, Kleinstrup's condition had deteriorated, and it was clear that she had contracted tuberculosis. However, owing to her father's long and unsuccessful trip to California in search of gold, Kleinstrup's family had little means to provide her with the medical attention she needed.[98] Lind somehow caught wind of Kleinstrup's situation, and after her show at the Fitchburg Depot, she conspicuously slipped a $100 bill into Kleinstrup's hand. The generosity of the gesture might have been too much for Saxton had he not come to expect such kindness from Lind. "I suppose this is only one of a thousand instances of her disinterested benevolence," Saxton repeated in response to the news of her gift: "How much happiness it must be to her to think of the joy and peace she will bring to the homes of many a destitute family. Her reward will be great both in this life and in the life to come. I am rejoiced that Louise has had such a privilege as she has, and more, that Jenny has so bountifully opened her heart towards her, for she is truly deserving of it, and I know it will do good."[99] In this instance, Saxton's prediction that Lind's goodwill would inspire more of the same in others also came to pass. An account of Lind's generosity to Louise Kleinstrup that ran in the Boston-based Associationalist newspaper the *Chronotype* so engaged the "sympathies" of one anonymous reader that the person sent the editor another $50 note to have added to "Jenny's $100."[100]

The official disbursement of funds from Lind's Boston charity concert—a day following news of her gift to Kleinstrup—signified the public culmination of her charitable actions in that city. Saxton followed reports of the proceedings closely. In total, Saxton wrote, "$7,225 . . . has been distributed among the various benevolent societies," of which Saxton was particularly "glad to see that $225 was given to Charles & John M. Spear, the prisoner's friends, to aid them in their good, and benevolent labors." But Saxton was less interested in the details themselves than in reflecting on the spirit he imagined must have been behind them. "What an angel of mercy Jenny Lind is," Saxton enthused, for how else could he describe someone who caused "the dark and almost impenetrable clouds of adversity to disperse" to be replaced with "the bright and genial sun of hope, which will light up the faded check of youth, and give old age the blessedness of peace." Lind's musical prowess had become a practical but effective tool for promoting the benevolence of Lind's character. Saxton, for his part, understood that the main attraction at a Jenny Lind concert was Lind herself, over and above the music. "Jenny is truly a *great* woman, not only for her wonderful voice," Saxton declared, "but for those numerous virtues that are always an ornament to their possessor. She is a beautiful Christian, and . . . she takes the money from the rich, and disperses it freely to the unfortunate."[101] Lind's attraction, then, was the quality of her character, which revealed itself in all sorts of ways, one of which was through her music.

The experience of Lind's music and generosity along with the public's reception to both had profound and politicizing implications for Saxton. Music, if anything, would become an even larger obsession, but so too would a range of civic and political causes. Lind helped facilitate this expansion of Saxton's political interests because in appreciating the quality of her character, Saxton came to infer that *action* was far more important than he had thought.

Indeed, after Lind's tour, Saxton reserved some of his harshest criticisms for those who he felt were either afraid or unable to commit to the causes they claimed to believe in. Saxton, for instance, would get particularly frustrated when discussing political issues with his brother Rufus, who being a military man was "bound to support the government & country right or wrong." To make matters worse, Rufus insisted on advising his younger brother against his "fanaticism" and in favor of Daniel Webster, who was, according to Rufus, "the greatest, most eloquent man of the present or any past ages" who had done more than any politician to help defend the law and Constitution of the country.[102] By this point, however, Saxton saw little wisdom in the approach of the nation's great compromiser. Of Webster, Saxton complained, "Debauchery has ruined his physical strength, & his apostasy to the cause of liberty has caused his political death." Because of Webster's vacillations over slavery, Saxton claimed, the "People do not love him, nor will they trust him, as they once would."[103] Saxton's observation of Webster's political trajectory may not have been quite as generalizable as he suggests, but it certainly represented his own point of view. Music and musical appreciation remained important to Saxton, but they now would occupy a position alongside other, more formal and directed ways of participating in the issues of the day. And in this sense, musical appreciation became the gateway to Saxton's political life.

Almost as soon as Lind's tour left Boston, Saxton began to engage in formal forms of political participation for the first time. Whereas in 1848 Saxton had dismissed his own capacity to enter into political affairs, by the end of 1850 the cause of Free Soil politics and anti–Fugitive Slave Law agitation had already ushered him into the mechanics of the nation's political system. "The Jenny Lind excitement is dying away somewhat," Saxton observed on 17 October 1850, and within a month's time, he was attempting to cast his "maiden vote for the cause of Liberty and humanity."[104] As Saxton had never paid a tax, he was "not allowed the privilege" of casting a vote his first time round, but he was clearly well enough versed in the intricacies of Boston politics to demonstrate the value he placed on formal participation: "There is great rejoicing in the Free Soil party on account of the recent election," Saxton reported to his diary soon after Boston's local Election Day in 1850: "There is a much larger majority against [George N.] Briggs than ever before, and of course [he] is not elected Governor by the people. The Free Soilers and Democrats having united, formed a coalition, so that there will be a majority of Free Soilers and coalition in the House. [George S.] Boutwell, democrat, will probably be elected Governor, & it [is] hoped that Charles Sumner will be sent to Congress."[105] A few months later, in January 1851, Saxton kept his diary abreast of election news as attention turned to whether Charles Sumner would be sent to the Senate as per the terms of the Massachusetts Free Soil–Democratic coalition.[106] Saxton's perspective on the matter and his admiration for Sumner's willingness to abide by his stated principles was clear. Should Sumner go to Washington, Saxton declared, "the halls of Congress will ring [with] the eloquence of a *man* . . . who will not be flattered into subserving to a slaveocracy or a cottonocracy as some of our northern men have been."[107]

Congress had passed the Fugitive Slave Law during Lind's first visit to Boston, and Saxton rabidly opposed it. The bill stipulated that Northern states would no longer be able to provide a safe refuge for fugitives from slavery whose owners desired their return, and he predicted that Northern sentiment against the law would make it unenforceable in Boston. "I trust that it never will be said that a brother man was taken from *our* midst, and carried into hopeless bondage again," Saxton declared. "I think the human bloodhounds will not *dare* come here, for if they do, they will get the worst of it." Yet even an ostensibly backward step like this fit into Saxton's utopian belief in humanity's progress: "Though it is a most inhuman law," Saxton reasoned, "it may result in good, and make a revolution in the operation of things in this country, especially in regard to slavery."[108] Consequently, Saxton's accounts of Lind's tour were interspersed with accounts of his attendance at Free Soil meetings and news of high-profile fugitive-slave cases. Before Lind had left Boston, Saxton had already heard the likes of Frederick Douglass, Charles Francis Adams, Wendell Phillips, and Theodore Parker all speak against the Fugitive Slave Law.[109] The confluence of Lind's tour together with the Fugitive Slave Law instilled Saxton with the determination to act on his convictions and provided a timely cause for their application.

IN NOVEMBER 1851, Saxton had paid his taxes and was fully prepared to cast a vote in that year's Massachusetts gubernatorial elections. "I went down to the polls this morning early, cast my first vote, and for the Free Soil candidates," Saxton explained, "not with the expectation of electing them, but believing those men the best representatives of our party, and capable of calling forth the largest number of votes, to defeat the election of [Whig candidate] Mr. Winthrop." What is more, in 1851, Saxton also committed to the unenviable task of canvassing Election Day polls on behalf of the Free Soilers. "I then took my stand to distribute votes, which I continued to do till one o'clock," Saxton added. "It was rather tiresome work, especially as such a small portion of the voters were willing to vote our ticket."[110] When the 1852 presidential election came around, the value Saxton placed on participating in it was clearer than ever. "Now is the time for all true friends of humanity to act, for another election is drawing near," Saxton declared in July 1852. "Both the Whig & Democratic parties have bowed in the dust, to serve the *slave* power," but, Saxton explained, "the Free Soilers, Abolitionists, Free Democracy, or whatever they may be called, *will 'agitate'* and . . . they wish to ask," Saxton emphasized, *"What are you going to do about it?"*[111]

Saxton's newfound stridency did not come at the expense of his devotion for music—in fact, it was precisely during the 1852 election that Saxton was also enjoying what would later become his fabled, "ever-to-be-remembered" Boston concert season (in October and November of 1852 alone, he attended twenty-six concerts, practically one for every other day).[112] Earlier, in 1851, after his first day of volunteering at the polls, Saxton had retired home to play a few tunes on his borrowed flute and to play for his friend Jenny what he thought was a rendition of Beethoven's "Spirit Waltz" on the piano. "It is soothing in its influence, and touches the purer, finer sentiments within," Saxton said of the "Spirit Waltz," "and gives a better expression than words can do of what the soul would express."[113] Both formal political participation and music had become important parts of Saxton's efforts to improve himself and the world around him. And no matter how radical Saxton's goals may have been, music helped ensure that the impetus behind them appeared, to him at least, both conservative and respectable.

The Hutchinson Family Singers and the Political Resonances of Loving Music

In November 1851, with Election Day over, Saxton resolved to give up his "loved and happy" life in Boston to search for more stable employment in New York City.[114] However, the bigger city would present him with disappointingly few solid opportunities. Saxton took on every scrap of work he could find but in the two weeks before 10 January 1852 had earned just $1.74—an amount so low that he could only console himself with the thought that in the future it would hardly be possible to make less.[115] Yet New York still offered Saxton much by way of music. And Saxton, true to form, remained far more adept at getting into concert halls than he was at getting himself into a steady job.

Given his lack of funds, Saxton enjoyed a remarkable selection of New York's musical fare. Whether it was the "far-famed" Christy's Minstrels—their "harmony beautiful and affecting, but their comic is side-splitting"—the renowned pianist Richard Hoffman in the "parlor-like" surroundings of Niblo's concert rooms, or the blockbuster performances of the Irish superstar soprano Catherine Hayes at Metropolitan Hall, Saxton was at the ready to accept invitations to hear music "in a twinkling."[116] Indeed, in most every case, Saxton's concert attendance appears to have been underwritten by the generosity of friends with whom he had worked or boarded. Attending all these shows was a significant improvement over having to "read the programmes without the funds to buy a ticket," but it was not until Saxton saw the Hutchinson Family Singers that he truly began to have the kind of musical experiences he had grown to cherish most.[117] "A song the Hutchinson family have sung to-night went home to my very soul," Saxton enthused in January 1852; "[it has] thrown a ray of warmth around [me] that I have not felt for weeks." "It made me happy" to hear them, Saxton explained, "and it seemed as though it were worth a week of pain to experience the delight I did there."[118] Saxton's enjoyment of the Hutchinson Family Singers' concerts far eclipsed anything else he had seen in New York, and the reasons for this had as much to do with their politics as their music.

In the mid-1840s, the Hutchinson Family Singers had emerged from rural New Hampshire to become one of the nation's most well-known musical acts. Celebrated for their homegrown vocal harmonies, they also unabashedly used their music to advocate temperance and abolitionism to audiences around the country as well as in Europe. And they achieved considerable success by doing so. One of the Hutchinsons' most noted compositions was a song called "Get Off the Track!," which was penned in 1844 after they were mortified to find that President John Tyler—an enslaver—could invite them to sing at the White House only to have his proslavery friends simply appreciate their music without bothering to take issue with its antislavery sentiment. In response, "Get Off the Track!" was published explicitly as "a song for emancipation, sung by THE HUTCHINSONS" at a time when their popularity was such that they could command sums upward of $1,000 from a single performance.[119] If ever there was an antebellum musical act with the courage of their convictions, the Hutchinsons were it—far more so than Jenny Lind would prove to be.[120]

The Hutchinson family first came into Saxton's orbit at Brook Farm. Even though Saxton had not yet joined the community at the time of the Hutchinsons' most widely documented visit there in 1843, he claimed that one of the group's members, Abby Hutchinson, recognized him from Brook Farm when he saw her in New York.[121] This may have been wishful thinking on Saxton's part, but the idea that members of the Hutchinson Family Singers might have returned to Brook Farm after their initial visit is not hard to fathom in light of their determined attempts to adapt aspects of Brook Farm's communitarian practices into their own family's farming and financial arrangements.[122] Either way, the Hutchinson Family Singers and Saxton shared communitarian predilections, reformist ideals, and a devotion to the power of musical expression. On moving to Boston, Saxton's diary documented his attendance at several Hutchinson Family Singers concerts in 1848, which he enjoyed but described in little detail. "I attended the concert of the Hutchinson Family, and was very much pleased," Saxton reported in January 1848. "It is certainly a rich treat to hear them; there is none like them, and I hope this will not be their last one."[123] A little over a week later, he used a free editor's ticket to see their second concert and was "more pleased than before."[124] Yet, as much as Saxton appreciated the Hutchinson Family Singers in 1848, his reaction to them then was subdued in comparison to his account of seeing them in New York a few years later.

Saxton's increasing attachment to the Hutchinson Family Singers stands in stark contrast to the established narrative arc of the group's fading fortunes throughout the 1850s. In 1849, Abby Hutchinson, the much-adored female member of the Hutchinsons, wed her longtime admirer, Ludlow Patton, and left the group—an absence that, in Frederick Douglass's phrase, cast "a lonely aspect" over the remaining three brothers.[125] By 1853, the trio were earning roughly a tenth as much per show than they had done during the height of their success. And their internal quarreling would soon become so fierce that the brothers chose to divide into separate "tribes" of the Hutchinson Family Singers rather than continue to sing together.[126] Within the context of Saxton's personal trajectory, however, *his* excitement over the Hutchinsons in 1852 makes a lot of sense. Music, in one way or another, had been sharpening and shaping Saxton's political beliefs ever since his days at Brook Farm, and his newfound level of appreciation for the Hutchinson Family Singers became the high point that the connection between music and politics would reach in his political imagination.

In early 1852, Saxton—fresh from his first experiences of Jenny Lind and his involvement in Free Soil politics and newly arrived in a large and unfamiliar city—was primed to appreciate the Hutchinson Family Singers for more than just their music. "What a beautiful atmosphere pervades this whole house to-night," Saxton wrote early in January 1852, "for the 'Hutchinson Family' have been here, and filled it not only with their sweet melody, but left the salutary influence of their noble souls, which pervades every benevolent heart."[127] For Saxton, it was the remarkable quality of the Hutchinsons' "true and honest souls" that impressed him as much as the musical talents that gave their souls expression.[128] After one of the group's New York performances, Saxton retired to his boarding house to find that the Hutchinsons were singing and socializing in an adjoining parlor. "I was not invited in, and could only enjoy the sound through the wall," Saxton lamented. But before long, "the folding doors were thrown open," and he was given the special pleasure of hearing the "nest of brothers" sing *with* their sister, Abby, who had by then retired from the public stage. Even more special, however, was the chance to personally connect with people whom he considered champions of a common cause. When Asa Hutchinson, the bass singer, took Saxton's hand "in his cordial grasp, and said 'good night brother,'" Saxton recounted, "I wished every moment of his life would be as happy as those few moments were to me."[129] As with Lind, quality of music and pureness of character again went hand-in-hand.

A few days later, Saxton left New York City for Washington, DC, hoping that the nation's capital might hold the possibility of a more agreeable work situation. Initially, Saxton was enthralled by the "stately magnificence" of Washington: "I am at last in this far-famed land, which I have ever before known only in dreams," Saxton reported as he reveled in his first chance to witness "those who compose the wisdom of the nation" in Congress as they "met to legislate for the good of the whole people."[130] But life in a Southern city fueled by government business, animated by politics, and mired in the practice of slavery did not resonate well with Saxton's sensibilities. "Dissipation, & all kinds of vulgarity & profanity are universal, almost, & never not even in New York have I seen so much of it as here," Saxton complained, noting that "from all accounts . . . the members of Congress, many of them, are the most prominent in all this debauchery."[131] Though surprised to find that in his estimation "thousands of the slaves are happier here than the free negroes at the north," his firsthand experience of slavery only emphasized to him how dehumanizing the institution really was. He said of the enslaved people he saw, "[They] are not owners of their own souls, are kept in entire ignorance, taught to fear & obey us as their superiors, have no minds of their own & however agreeable may be their fortunes, let me never say that such a state of things is right."[132] When Saxton read that the Hutchinson Family Singers were planning to give "one or two concerts" in Washington, he expressed his anticipation: "It will be like meeting brothers among a set of savages to see them here, & what a 'heaven-high' feast of music will I have."[133]

The enthusiasm in Saxton's descriptions of the Hutchinson Family Singers in Washington is unmistakable. "How beautiful it was this evening, when my feelings have been in such a state of turbulence and grief all day," Saxton wrote in reference to a string of recent troubles including the death of his friend Louise Kleinstrup (succumbed to tuberculosis) and the loss of his latest job on account of the Boston Printer's Union, "to sit down and listen to the sweet, home-like, soul-inspiring, heart-touching music of the Hutchinson family." It is true, of course, that a significant part of the Hutchinsons' appeal for Saxton was their capacity to provide him with a meaningful way of escaping the travails of his daily life. As Saxton more plainly put it, when watching the Hutchinsons, "for a moment I would forget the darkness that had again obscured my path, & I was happy." And Saxton continued in a similar vein at some length: "I wish I could always be as happy as when listening to the outpourings of those honest, kind-hearted, and harmonious spirits. I wanted to throw my arms around each one, and 'thank them with my tears' for the joy, the rich joy they had given at least *one* heart. . . . I met John [Hutchinson] in the street this morning, & it was good to feel the grasp of that honest hand, for I spoke to him, & he gave me a ticket."[134] More than this, however, was that to Saxton the Hutchinsons also represented a group of individuals who had succeeded by advocating a set of values and political beliefs that accorded closely to his own. Revealingly, as Saxton described it, the chance to see the Hutchinson Family Singers perform in Washington was an opportunity to indulge in a "feast of reason" as well as a "feast of the soul, too."[135] In a city populated with some of the nation's most accomplished orators (whom Saxton made a habit of watching from a seat in the reporter's gallery of the Senate), it is notable that the only "feast of reason" he claimed to have witnessed there was delivered by the Hutchinson Family Singers.[136]

To understand how music contributed to Saxton's conservative-minded desire for radical change, it is helpful to compare his reception to the Hutchinson Family Singers in Washington and New York to a potentially similar set of experiences he had with Senator Charles Sumner of Massachusetts during the same period. As with the Hutchinsons, Saxton had originally become an admirer of Sumner—his character as well as his performative capacities as an orator—back in Boston. The first time Saxton heard Sumner speak at a Free Soil meeting in November 1850, he exclaimed that Sumner gave "the most eloquent and interesting speech it was ever [his] good fortune to hear" and that should "such a man as he, and ninety-nine more like him . . . be on the floors of Congress their influence would soon be felt in the country."¹³⁷ Saxton thereafter took the opportunity to help make his wish a reality, contributing his time, effort, and vote to the Free Soil–Democratic Party coalition in Massachusetts that elected Sumner to the Senate. And as such, when Saxton first went inside the Senate chamber and saw "our own Charles Sumner" along with John P. Hale—another Free Soil senator—the view gratified him so much that he "wanted to jump down and throw [his] arms about their necks."¹³⁸ Yet, as much as Saxton's introduction to national politics in Washington would bring music and politics together in his mind, it would also sow the seeds that drove them apart later on.

Saxton's residency in Washington taught him not to expect personal satisfaction from political participation. First, Saxton found that prospects for advancement in a town like Washington were few for an unconnected individual like himself. "In Washington," Saxton claimed, "everything is done by favor"—favors that an unemployed print compositor had little capacity to contemplate receiving or returning. "Had I friends in Congress whose influence I could bring to bear upon me, I *might*, (& might not) find some office open for me," Saxton explained, "but it requires more boldness, more '*brass*,' than I've got to push myself into their notice, & to *beg* favors of them."¹³⁹ Second, once the Boston Printer's Union blacklisting stripped Saxton of any chance of procuring decent work at his trade in Washington, his friends assured him that a visit to Charles Sumner's office would resolve matters in his favor.¹⁴⁰ But for all Saxton had invested in Sumner as a candidate, there was little Sumner was able or prepared to do for him in return. "My visit to Charles Sumner this morning, farther than the gratification of the interview, & shaking hands with him, was of no avail, and I am as much in the dark as ever," Saxton reported to his diary after summoning up the courage to meet with his political hero. "If I could have had farther talk with him, & gone into explanations more, & perhaps carried a letter of introduction to him, it would have resulted differently, but he could be of no assistance to me in this case," Saxton concluded.¹⁴¹ The contrast between having an audience with Sumner and being in the audience of the Hutchinson Family Singers was night and day. Whereas Sumner left Saxton feeling "as dark as ever," the Hutchinsons later that same night made him forget that he was ever feeling dark in the first place.

Although the politician in this scenario possessed more traditional power than the musicians, it was the latter who proved capable and willing to be of real help to Saxton. Material and spiritual generosity was something Saxton felt he could legitimately expect from one of the Hutchinsons—because he could always, as he put it, "remind them gently of one song they sing, 'Do a good turn when you can.'"[142] By contrast, Saxton saw that he could not expect similar generosity from the country's political elites. Of course, any comparison between Sumner and the Hutchinson Family Singers is not a fair one. Politicians can hardly be expected to solve the personal problems of all their constituents, and even if musicians cannot be expected to either, they are nonetheless equipped with more appropriate tools for making it feel like they have. But whether the comparison is fair or logical is beside the point. At this stage in Saxton's life, he understood the purpose of musical artists like the Hutchinsons and politicians like Charles Sumner to be one and the same. Both agitated for the same causes, as far as Saxton was concerned, and both warranted respect, in his view, because their pure and exemplary characters were a model for all those individuals like Saxton who similarly sought to better themselves and help the nation along its path toward progress. Saxton supported the Hutchinsons' music *and* Sumner's candidacy because he believed, in both cases, that by doing so he might be able to make himself and others "happy."

In this moment, then, music and politics occupied a remarkably similar space in Saxton's political imagination. In theory, the kind of truth Saxton believed music to convey would always imbue his musical appreciation with a political resonance. But in practice, for Saxton, the purpose of music and politics would not overlap to the same degree forever.

The Estrangement of Music from Politics in Saxton's Political Imagination

At the end of March 1852, Saxton retreated to Boston, reporting "[I have] learned me many things that is well for me to know."[143] Music, he still believed, was not only an enjoyable and improving influence to be shared and appreciated but also one that could have real-world effects equal to any strictly political endeavor. As such, music would continue to occupy a space on a par with politics in Saxton's political imagination for at least the next four years. During this time, appreciating music and participating in politics represented two different but equally effective alternatives for achieving the same ends because they both served to define and express the ways in which Saxton thought he and his nation should progress.

Between 1852 and 1856, Saxton spent most of his time traveling in the West, trying to earn enough money to settle his debts. And while doing so, Saxton's politics and his musical interests remained the two most important planks of his identity. Both connected Saxton to his home region and helped provide him with a sense of self-worth despite remaining single and underemployed. However, by 1857, three factors converged to gradually pull the roles of music and politics apart in Saxton's mind: the kinds of music Saxton most frequently listened to became generally identified more with entertainment than with social purpose; the politics of slavery, with which Saxton remained deeply concerned, would become increasingly volatile; and as Saxton approached thirty years of age, he would grow increasingly embarrassed by his financial struggles and, once married, would consciously attempt to focus less on a "temptation" like music and more on cultivating new business endeavors and employment situations that could directly aid his family's situation.[144]

Before going West, however, Saxton would first take advantage of Boston's 1852–53 winter concert season. By day, he worked as an assistant foreman of a print office, where he was given "principal charge" of producing John S. Dwight's *Journal of Music*, and by night, he worked as an usher variously for "all the Societies who have given concerts in Boston."[145] Under this arrangement, Saxton got to see practically every musical performance of note and afterward could tally up his attendance at sixty-three "concerts," thirteen "theatrical performances," thirteen "operas," and three "Chinese artist" performances, on top of working at rehearsals of the "Germanians" every Wednesday afternoon and many Saturdays for several months.[146] Saxton earned $75 from ushering over the course of the season, but from his perspective, the "pecuniary aid" was only a small part of the value he derived from the work. "Scarcely a week has passed that I have not 'passed in' more or less of my friends, who have not only enjoyed it themselves, but made the enjoyment more than double for myself," Saxton explained.[147] The winter of 1852, as Saxton summarized it, served as "a musical engraving upon the 'tablet of my memory.'" "Its tones will ring through my soul in years to come," Saxton continued, "& light up many an hour of darkness & doubt."[148] To be sure, all this activity did leave Saxton feeling "wearied out & hardly fit to discharge the duties of [his] position with satisfaction." His supervisor at the print shop routinely criticized him for being distracted at work, until it appears that Saxton's solution was to quit, storm out of the office, and firm up plans for heading West.[149]

Once out of Boston, Saxton continued to define himself through the musical and political interests he had developed there. On a canal boat between Logansport and Delphi, Indiana, Saxton reacted almost as if he had stumbled upon Charles Sumner himself when he came across a man who was associated with the Massachusetts Free Soil Party: "I [was] much surprised to find such a man here," Saxton exclaimed; "'twas like meeting with an oasis, or a cool spring of water in a hot day in a deep woods."[150] Similarly, a few days later, when a new issue of *Dwight's Journal of Music* was first put into his hand, Saxton said that he "clasped it like a dear friend."[151] Music and politics here both clearly tapped into that same universal flow of pure feelings and pleasant associations that Saxton felt would eventually bind humanity together in a brotherhood of fellow feeling.

However, when in the West, Saxton also began to realize that his higher feelings were only engaged by a particular variety of political beliefs and musical performances. Certainly, the quality of entertainment that satisfied western folk did little for Saxton, who felt he had become used to the better fare available in Boston. In July 1853, for example, Saxton attended a "performance of a traveling theatre, consisting of farces, burlesques, songs, a female dancer, &c.," in Logansport, Indiana, but found that "it was so dull": "I was so disgusted I left before 'twas half out. My memory of *good things* is too fresh to allow me to enjoy anything quite so stupid."[152] Equally, he considered some of the attempts of local women to get up a parlor tune downright laughable. One especially excruciating musical experience occurred in Delphi, Indiana, not long after Saxton's arrival there to work as an engineer on the Lake Erie, Wabash, and St. Louis Railroad. Saxton relayed a detailed version of the episode into his diary as an example of the entertainments he was subject to in "Hoosierdom":

> Was ushered into the handsomely furnished parlor by the fair and smiling Josephine. Found two ladies present, & one gentleman. One lady was asked to play, & seemed not at all backward in complying. Crowding herself hard upon the piano, she struck into "Roory O'Moore," or something of that sort, Yankee Doodle side ways, I should think, & hammered it through in a most distressing manner. That being finished, the other lady, who seemed to be a sister, came to her assistance, & they labored through something they called a duett. If one was distressing, two were most *distressingest*. Whatever their object might be, to entertain or not, they certainly deserve credit for their perseverance, for no sooner was that piece finished than they attempted to *sing* a duett. O! ye shades of Beethoven, Mozart, Handel & all, forgive them! Such voices & such *harmony*! I've not heard the like in Hoosierdom, and O fates preserve me from the penalty of another hearing. I hope they did not feel as bad as I, but however uncomfortable my seat, & intense my sufferings, I think I bore it like

a martyr, & without an audible groan. What a feeling of relief to see them at last retire from the poor piano, worthy of better treatment.[153]

Saxton's dismissal of Delphi's local music talent was a bit rich, coming, as it did, from someone who would soon find himself so ill suited to his job as an engineer that his brother Edward—a drunkard no less—felt obliged to fire him lest his favoritism begin to show too obviously.[154] Yet Saxton's professional ineptness was itself part of the reason why music retained such a draw to him while he was away from home. He may have been failing at work, but he believed that he recognized good music when he heard it; and the value of appreciating good music was not something Saxton was prone to underestimate.

While in Indiana, Saxton filled his diary with reports of attending singing schools and choir meetings, serenading with young people about town, organizing and attending local balls, transcribing newspaper reports of Fugitive Slave Law controversies back in Boston, and having "hot" political discussions about the Nebraska controversy.[155] When it came to music, Saxton maintained that none he had in Delphi much satisfied him: "my famished senses cry for some *good* music," Saxton concluded in May 1854. "Such a thing I've not heard in Delphi. I have heard 'a heap' of *poor* music, & a few *good* pieces shockingly murdered."[156] Saxton did appreciate that some of the women had some musical potential, even if his own "poor voice" was of "very little assistance" to their efforts to improve.[157] Similarly, when it came to politics, the types of discourses Saxton desired were of a higher taste and content than he claimed to find in Indiana. A speech delivered by John L. Swifts at the New York Free Soil ratification meeting, for instance, which Saxton read among a packet of newspapers that a Boston friend had sent him, was so "full of classic eloquence, & high-toned Anti-Slavery sentiment" that to read it gave Saxton a "new strength & faith in mankind" that he felt at risk of losing in the West.[158]

Soon after leaving Delphi, Saxton saw the Boston-based abolitionist preacher Theodore Parker deliver an address in Cincinnati, and his description of the experience helps articulate just how close a space music and politics had come to occupy in his political imagination. "I have seen & heard Mr. Parker once more," Saxton reported, "& the tones of his voice fell like sweet, soothing music upon my ear, music that I have not heard for many a long month, but which my soul has longed for, & sometimes fainted, grown sad & weary without." As with the Hutchinsons a few years earlier, Saxton "wanted to seize hold of" Parker "& grasp that hand & tell him what happiness

"The Singing Girl" (New York: J. Wrigley, ca. 1840–80). Comic Valentine Collection, the Library Company of Philadelphia, www.librarycompany.org.

it was to meet him again." Saxton claimed that he could barely resist jumping out of his seat as Parker walked past on his way to speak but that he managed to avoid "committing any indecorum." Once Parker spoke, Saxton continued, "I sat & feasted my eyes, & drank in the words that fell from his lips, so natural, so eloquent. I could easily fancy myself once more in the Music Hall" where Saxton had often seen Parker speak in Boston. "But waking from my dream, & looking around, meeting no responsive, familiar & friendly glances, the delusion fled, & I was in Greenwood Hall, Mechanics Institute, Cincinnati: but I was listening to Mr. Parker of the Music Hall, that good, strong, fearless, progressive, eloquent man. He was the same, little, if any changed; would that I had changed as little."[159] By contrast, even Saxton's praise of an Anti-Nebraska meeting in Delphi—a political movement close in sentiment, if not always in practice, to Saxton's Free Soil principles—was decidedly more muted: "goodly number present," Saxton reported, "& some fair speeches."[160] To Saxton, hearing the cadence of a particular variety of Free Soil politics was practically akin to the musical experiences he had learned to appreciate so deeply: both spoke to the same part of Saxton's political imagination; both gave him a glimpse of "the good time coming"; and both gave him reason to hope for its imminent arrival. And religious experience, in this way, presented an evocative—and morally conservative—canvass on which the intellectual connections between music and politics came together in Saxton's mind.

Having traveled to Cincinnati after losing his engineering job, Saxton was quick to make the most of its higher-quality musical fare. In Cincinnati, Saxton could pick from a range of reputable musical concerts, operas, and minstrel performances over the winter of 1854–55—many of which he could talk his way into seeing for free.[161] Plus, a quick visit to the reading room of the Young Men's Mercantile Library Association made news from Boston readily available.[162] Nonetheless, within a few months, Saxton was enticed to move south by the offer of a twenty-dollars-per-week position as foreman of the *Memphis Eagle & Enquirer*. It was a decision he soon regretted. "I sometimes think it is most too much of a sacrifice for twenty dollars a week," Saxton complained of his life in Memphis:

> Living in a country where every thing is so different, where so many of the customs are even repulsive, & contrary to my views of right & justice, where I must keep my mouth shut, or suffer the consequences of expressing such "incendiary," "fanatical" sentiments as I cherish in my inmost soul. . . . I've attended slave auctions, & seen stout men,

made like ourselves in the image of God, but cursed with a black skin, with intelligence beaming from their eyes, & manliness in their face & bearing, standing upon the block to be sold to the highest bidder. They were examined like cattle. . . . And this is the land of liberty, where *all men* are created free & equal, with an inalienable right to the pursuit of life, liberty & happiness.

To make matters worse, Saxton also found Memphis barren of any opportunity for personal improvement: in Memphis "what chance is there for mental or spiritual culture? Scarcely none," Saxton answered himself, "& I feel sometimes that I am losing what little of spiritual goodness I ever possessed." Of "social advantages," Saxton protested, in Memphis, "I have none, which is no small item to one of my disposition."[163]

Despite his complaints, music in Memphis was still a refuge for Saxton amid what seemed an otherwise unfamiliar and disagreeable society. In a place where Saxton struggled to cope with the sight of blacks "most brutally beat" in the street, where he was the "only person" in his office who was happy to hear news of antislavery victories in the North, and where the only card he received on Valentine's Day was a "villainous one" with a "picture of an 'abolitionist'" on it, the preciousness of time stolen away in a musical realm came to feel all the more important.[164] "Indeed, I speak truth in saying that the happiest hours I've had in Memphis have been since I made the acquaintance of Mrs. [Hattie] Bernard," an older married actress with whom he would often "chat upon many subjects," before "she sang many of her best songs, which were a feast" to him.[165] As Saxton prepared to move back east eight months later, he declared, "I feel better for having heard . . . those *favorite* songs" that Bernard had played him, for, he continued, "music has more power over me than anything else, unless it be a *pretty woman*."[166] Even though Saxton was obviously smitten with Bernard, the continued value he placed on music in this situation is instructive.

In Memphis, by losing himself in music — be it in parlors with Mrs. Bernard, in concerts halls, or by resuming his secondary trade as an usher — Saxton was able to reconnect with the kind of values, character traits, and ultimately the political and moral beliefs that he felt had defined his character all along. Outside of music, Saxton felt he had no way to safely express what he believed in a slave state. In Memphis, as Saxton alleged, "I am more of a slave than the blacks around me," and "I feel ashamed that I keep my tongue so bridled, & that I choke down my indignation when looking at the wrong existing all about me"; "my spirit rebels against it."[167] The direct parallel that Saxton draws between his position and black enslavement can appear unfortunate and derives from the fact that American Fourierists had adopted the metaphor of slavery to critique Northern industrial labor relations and class conflict long before Southern proslavery polemicists like George Fitzhugh would do the same.[168] For Saxton, his time in Memphis made it clear that the supposedly universal current of good feeling that music gave him access to had always been a more politicized space than he had been apt to realize.

In June 1856, when Saxton finally returned to Boston, his experiences of slavery in the South encouraged him to take a special interest in that year's presidential election. "It has never happened before that there was only one issue before the people, and that that issue was slavery," Saxton explained of the election's unprecedented national significance.[169] Affronted by the South's approval of Preston Brooks's caning of Charles Sumner in Congress and fresh from his time in Tennessee, Saxton became a firm supporter of the Republican candidate, John C. Frémont, the "young, and gallant Pathfinder" whom he believed was "destined to be our leader in these dark times."[170] Whereas James Buchanan and the Democratic Party had "arranged themselves on the pro-slavery side," Saxton was "proud" to take on the label of a Black Republican and "march under the banner Free Men, Free Speech, and Frémont."[171] Soon he was busy donating his time and skills to local Frémont Clubs, printing up circulars and regularly attending their meetings and conventions.[172] Music remained an ongoing interest, but Saxton's more explicit participation in the political process helped separate his political convictions from his musical passions.

This shift, however, had less to do with Saxton fundamentally changing the way he thought about music or politics than it did with his own evolving approach to political engagement. By this point, following political news and formally participating in the political process had long been an important outlet for Saxton's beliefs. The difference now was that music and politics had become to him theoretically and practically distinct endeavors: Saxton was a "Black Republican" and a Frémont man, and to Saxton's mind at least, his taste for music had little to do with it. Music, if anything, only made it harder for Saxton to accurately distinguish between the right party and the wrong one, as became clear when he and a friend mistakenly joined up with a Democratic chorus parading through Boston on the assumption that they were Republicans.[173]

Accordingly, Saxton's accounts of concerts and political conventions became more rhetorically distinct. In writing about a Mass Convention held in

Deerfield, Massachusetts, for example, Saxton implied that it would ultimately be the political movement itself—the Frémont-led Republican Party—that would soon "purify" an "unhappy land": with Frémont, he said, "we shall be delivered from the darkness and doubt that now hangs over our country, and all shall be brightness and joy, and the sun of freedom shall shed its purifying and genial rays over the land, even into Kansas, right shall triumph over wrong, truth over falsehood, and peace and prosperity prevail where now 'grim visaged war' carries death and terror to our brothers and sisters in that unhappy land."[174] Concerts, by contrast, remained "good to hear" and would leave Saxton and his friends "well pleased" and "delighted" to have attended, but his descriptions of them no longer involved the transcendental qualities that they used to and that political events apparently still did.[175] Even a concert from the Hutchinsons provoked a comparatively tepid response. On hearing them perform in 1856, Saxton could only muster enough excitement to note that he had "listened with pleasure to the Hutchinsons' songs." Saxton showed more interest in his conversations after the performance, in which he learned of the whereabouts of mutual friends with whom he had lost touch, than in the concert itself.[176] Indeed, nostalgia would soon become one of the primary drivers of Saxton's musical interest, further separating its utility from his politics.[177]

However, Buchanan's victory over Frémont in the 1856 presidential election—an outcome that Saxton confessed he had "not calculated upon"—shook his faith in the political process. The electoral triumph of Southern proslavery forces, as Saxton interpreted it, tempered his conviction that salvation would necessarily come about directly through political means. "I am not one who believes that the election of this man or that man is going to dissolve the Union, for we are not governed by a President alone, nor by the laws that a Congress makes," Saxton rationalized. "God rules over us all, and has laws to be obeyed, and certain works to be accomplished, and certain purposes for everything in his universe, whether they agree with our own or not, and so I trust in Providence, and not worry."[178] A divine plan may have been at work, but Saxton saw little order to the reality of the nation's political situation; and for the time being, his personal circumstances—unmarried and still buried in debt—did not give much cause for optimism. Over the next few years, Saxton would value music less for its political potential than for its capacity to distract him from his troubles.

The shifts in how Saxton chose to incorporate music into his political life were not obvious. Music retained an important and enjoyable influence over Saxton, and one could easily interpret his ongoing patronage of concert halls

Music and the Making of a Conservative Radical

and parlor performances as a continuation of the same love for music he had begun to cultivate a decade earlier. In January 1858, for example, on getting to hear the German bass singer Karl Formes perform in Joseph Haydn's *The Creation*, Saxton would write that the sound of his voice "was enough to carry one 'up' to hear 'a new created world.'"[179] Or, in November 1857, Saxton professed, "Nothing so fits one to enter into the spirit of devotional exercises as good music. . . . Without it I am sometimes half insensible to good influences."[180] But even in these instances, Saxton's musical appreciation was moving inward. A loose clipping that Saxton added to his diary in February 1857 gives a fair representation of the newly personal dimension of musical pleasure that Saxton begins to experience: "MUSIC. What is more deeply interwoven with the sympathies of human nature than music? What will more touchingly express the feelings of joy or sorrow, hope or melancholy? Melancholy forgets to sigh or weep as aeolian chords sweep gently over its sea of troubles. What joy is complete without its all-enlivening strains? What warrior nerved without its thrilling blast? What church so lowly, and what service so devout, as that where the swelling chord and the organ peal mingle."[181] Here music's value lies in connecting more deeply with one's self, not in enabling an audience to unify in common cause and harmonious feeling; it is about coming to grips with one's own existence and using music to heighten individual experience and emotion—whether that be by rendering a warrior fearless or a churchgoer devout. Meanwhile, music also became a more distinctly nostalgic activity for Saxton. "It is pleasant to attend a concert in the old time-honored hall," Saxton wrote of a philharmonic concert led by Carl Zerrahn at Boston's Melodeon hall; "it carries one back to times crowded with sacred recollections, and aside from the music, there is a charm in sitting in the old place, for the sake of old memories."[182]

The more music became a more personal experience, the more Saxton came to see it as an amusement: one that he enjoyed precisely because it allowed him to forget the realities of his life. In describing a trip to visit his family in the countryside, Saxton emphasized music's contribution to the almost dream-like state of mind he attained while away from the city: "I had been living on love, and music, in the peaceful country," Saxton explained, "with good friends, a dear sister, and beautiful cousin, floating on the top wave of happiness, each day floating farther away from this sphere, oblivious to the practical, working-day notions of this earth."[183] Later, in June 1859, Saxton justified time he spent at the opera without even considering how doing so might have involved something deeper than entertainment. "It does look a little like dissipation, going to the opera every night, but it is a pleasure that is rare," Saxton insisted, "& I cannot resist the temptation when it costs me so little."[184] By June 1860, Saxton figured that his opera addiction might not have been having an entirely positive effect on him and was relieved to see the season close: "When opera is here, I want to go," Saxton confessed, "but I'd rather not have the temptation now."[185] The shift in Saxton's understanding of music may have been subtle, but it was clear—to argue for the importance of musical appreciation on the basis of music's ability to connect listeners with universal truths would have been a nostalgic throwback to his past self. Instead, by the start of the Civil War, Saxton saw his love for music to be contributing to his problems as much as it was alleviating their effects.

Oddly enough, there is no better evidence for the diminishing influence of music over Saxton's mind than the person he chose to marry. Saxton married Mary Grant in January 1861, and one of the most remarkable things about her, in this context, is that she was not particularly musical at all. Throughout his life, Saxton had used his diary to dream about the qualities he ideally wanted in a future wife, and musicality had unfailingly been among them.[186] When it came to Mary, however, the most praise he could give her in relation to music was of her respectful company at concerts: "Mary, tho' perhaps not appreciating so fully, has the merit of being an attentive listener," and "I like a companion who will not talk when there's music."[187] Probably more important at this point was that Mary proved herself to be "quite an enthusiastic Republican" who would go "home in ecstasies" after hearing Charles Sumner deliver a speech on Lafayette.[188] Either way, Mary herself probably articulated better than Saxton could why he fell for her. In a letter she sent to Saxton while he was away in South Carolina during the war, Mary explained how their love for each other showed that there were "sweeter" tones than music: "Funny you should take poor Mary Grant, *after all the girls you fancied*. You thought your wife must be musical; *but there are strings of the heart which love can play on, that make sweeter music than the ear ever listened to*. I have a heart full of love; *such as it is*, I give it all to you."[189] Music was still important to Saxton, and so were his political beliefs; but they no longer served the same purpose in his political imagination.

Part of the reason for Saxton's changing conception of music's public role had to do with a broader shift in the way urban Americans viewed the type of music he was most interested in at the time. After Saxton's return to Boston in 1856, the most common musical events he attended were operas, and opera at this stage, as Karen Ahlquist has argued, "could no longer be accepted as inherently elevating."[190] Popular opera styles in the 1850s—especially

Italian composers like Verdi—often spoke not to sentimental or comedic themes but to intractable moral dilemmas and tragedy. And this complicated the idea that music had intrinsically civilizing effects. Because now audiences were being hooked more often by the excitement of a moral problem than edified by the revelation of a moral lesson. Music lovers like Saxton, in turn, felt they needed to either clearly justify time spent in the concert hall or admit that certain shows had little to do with spiritual nourishment. Minstrel performances, for example, no longer held the appeal to Saxton that they once had: "at night went to hear the Campbell minstrels," Saxton noted in January 1856. "Enjoyed some parts of it,—much of it was as insipid [as] all such performances are to me."[191] By contrast, if Saxton enjoyed a concert, he had to do more than allude to music's intrinsic value to adequately explain his positive reaction. Of a concert by the piano virtuoso Sigismond Thalberg, Saxton explained that "the enjoyment is not entirely in the music, or its execution." Instead, "the appearance" and bearing of the artist is what "helps to give one that feeling of deep satisfaction," along with the seemingly important fact that Thalberg "stepped aside from the usual custom of answering an encore by playing such pieces as 'Lilly Dale,' with variations, and other once popular melodies": "It is encouraging a low taste, and I believe Thalberg is too true an artist to ever do anything of the kind."[192] Even a performance of the highest tone risked devolving into a frivolous affair if proper precautions were not taken and strict standards of taste not adhered to.

Meanwhile, the trajectory of American politics during the 1850s was also contributing to the separation of music from politics in Saxton's mind. Beginning his diary, as Saxton did, in a utopian community had encouraged him to interpret the world in the context of its progress toward the realization of an emancipatory future; at Brook Farm, Saxton had believed that distinctions of all kinds—class, race, gender, and nation—were destined to be dismantled by the "good time coming." Political developments of the 1850s, however, particularly the debates over slavery, tested this faith. Saxton had been a pacifist, predicting that nations will soon have no need for warships. But by September 1856, he declared himself "determined to shoulder a musket" and join "any number that are willing to go and fight for freedom and truth" over the question of popular sovereignty in Kansas.[193] The South, and later the Confederacy's insistence on fighting to perpetuate slavery, undermined Saxton's earlier Associationalist belief that Americans, and all of humanity for that matter, were united by the same set of fundamental truths. According to Saxton, the Civil War was a conflict that pitted "wrong on the one side" against "liberty & the right on the other," and as such, it was a question of when, not if, "the latter will prevail."[194] If there ever was to be a worldwide recognition of humanity's fundamental unity, then it would have to be brought about by force, not suggested into being by musical harmony.

In a practical sense, too, by the start of the Civil War, Saxton's personal circumstances did not leave much scope for music. In March 1860, as Saxton and his fiancée contemplated plans for their future life together, he could not help but worry about the lack of resources he had managed to accumulate over the years. "Thirty years old, & in no better circumstances than when I commenced learning my trade, nearly sixteen years ago!" Saxton calculated. "I ought to blush for it."[195] A week later, when Saxton opened a joint savings account with Mary, he only had three dollars to his name to contribute to it.[196] By contrast, in April 1862, his brother Rufus, who had chosen to attend West Point instead of going to Brook Farm, was taking in a brigadier general's salary in the order of $4,000 a year.[197] Saxton did not hold others accountable for his failures to succeed in business—at least not in his diary—but neither did he figure it was due to any lack of effort on his part: "I don't think I am to blame for my want of business tact, never having had a business education, nor entirely for my lack of shrewdness & energy that makes many succeed, that never having been born with me. To be sure they are talents that can be cultivated, & I confess to a lack of foresight & energy in now seeing it was for my good to do different. I confess to not being *smart*, & for my own sake as well as Mary's, I feel ashamed that my prospects are no more encouraging."[198] With a partner to support, Saxton threw himself into moneymaking endeavors. And in doing so, Saxton was at times forced to let his political preferences take a back seat to financial imperatives. Finding himself out of work during the 1860 presidential election, Saxton would sign up to canvass for voters on behalf of any political party that would hire him—"not particularly agreeable work," Saxton remarked of canvassing for the Bell-Everett ticket, "but pays well."[199] Once Saxton threw himself into an attempt to establish his own shop, selling newspapers, almanacs, magazines, and candy, spare moments to indulge in music were few and represented, as Saxton put it, "a pleasant change from ordinary life."[200]

STRANGELY, PERHAPS, the American Civil War was one of the most profitable events of Saxton's life. In February 1862, Saxton sold out of his failing newspaper shop and left for Port Royal, South Carolina, where his brother Rufus was serving as a captain and quartermaster under General Thomas W. Sherman. Within two weeks, Rufus had set up his brother with a ninety-dollars-a-month salary to work as his junior clerk, and before long, he would be assisting Rufus to organize the Union army's first black regiment.[201] Rufus Saxton would soon be promoted to military governor of the Department of the South and in turn cultivate a reputation as the foremost proponent of a wartime reconstruction policy that would have given land from abandoned plantations back to the freedpeople who had worked it.[202] Indeed, Rufus was personally responsible for executing General William T. Sherman's Special Field Order No. 15, which did—for a time—authorize the confiscation of four hundred thousand acres of Southern land so that it could be given to freed families to settle on without condition. Following the war, Rufus was a commissioner for the Freedman's Bureau, and Willard would follow his brother there too, taking on a civilian position at the bureau for five years before transferring to the Treasury Office in Washington, DC, where he would work in various administrative and clerical capacities until he retired five decades later. Professionally, at least, the Civil War was a boon for Willard Saxton.

But the Civil War probably struck Saxton as more of an ideological success than a professional one. Victory for the Northern states not only saved the Union but also dismantled the legal institution of American slavery—a development that Saxton had actively supported for decades. At a meeting of the African-American Second Baptist Church in Savannah, Georgia—held a month after Rufus Saxton had executed Special Field Order No. 15—Willard Saxton took obvious pride in the course of events: "The Gen. Saxton [Rufus] made one of his best speeches, & explained the Order, No. 15. It was such talk as had not long been tolerated in Savannah, & is not now palatable to the majority of the citizens. One old man got too full to hold in, rushed forward to Gen. S., knelt down, took his hand, & said for thirty-five years he had lived a slave, & he thanked 'du Lord he lib to see dis day.'" The depth of what Saxton saw the Union to have achieved moved him deeply. And he went on to describe the black congregation's ensuing rendition of the "Old Hundred" hymn in language that fifteen years earlier could only have applied to the likes of Jenny Lind. "The effect of" the congregation's final song, "was grand & thrilling, & I never listened to a chorus in an oratorio that sounded more sublime," Saxton explained. "It seemed as if the angels were present, & the spirit of God, had entered into each one of the two thousand hearts present filling it with a joy never experienced before, & opening their eyes to a clearer view of the glorious day of freedom just dawning upon them."[203] Music may have become less of a priority for Saxton over the years, but he still believed that its best strains spoke to his vision of a better world.

Of course, Saxton did not consider the freedpeople in this scene the radical instigators of their own freedom. Instead, what Saxton saw in their musical celebrations—two months before Lee would surrender at Appomattox—was the consummation of a victory that he had toiled for, on their behalf, for much of his adult life. In this moment, music still felt like an agent of political reform and moral uplift; it was still the harbinger of a more civilized society and a more evolved political culture. Music here still showed that it could educate its listeners to be better people. Although music had initially helped politicize Saxton, it gradually became a less potent practical force in his life once he found that its power, for him, came to reside in the realm of the ideal—in its intellectual construction of how social relations could be—rather than in its capacity to realize those conditions on its own. Music, in this way, enabled Saxton to judge society as it was but also made his utopian vision of what it should become a paean to order and respectability. The art of appreciating music was itself an act of Saxton's political imagination—one that cast the prospect of radical change into a bulwark of conservative civility.

Epilogue

> By the blood which cries to Heaven!
> Crimson upon our sod!
> Stand, Southrons! stand and conquer!
> In the name of the Mighty God!
> —ELLEN KEY BLUNT, "The Southern Cross," 1862

In October 1862, newspapers across the Confederacy began publishing the "beautiful soul-stirring lines" of a new "patriotic song from across the water."[1] The tune had freshly arrived from Paris, where its author—Ellen Key Blunt, a Maryland native and daughter of the late Francis Scott Key—had recently removed to pursue a career on the stage.[2] Confederates, having sworn off the old patriotic songs of the Union, were in need of original anthems, and Blunt's contribution to the cause—"The Southern Cross"—would be promoted as the inimitable product of a unique pedigree.[3] Yet the debt that Blunt's composition owed to "The Star-Spangled Banner" went beyond the genealogical. Blunt titled her song, like its predecessor, by the name of the flag that represented her cause, wrote lyrics that glorified the defense of her nation's rights from the threat of a "trampling army," and when published as a broadside, placed its verses below a handsome illustration of George Washington, whose patriotic vision, she suggested, Yankees had failed to uphold and Confederates sought to protect. Indeed, beneath its fervor for the Confederate cause, "The Southern Cross" was also an elaborate tribute to the same combination of unifying patriotism and self-interested nationalism that had defined the patriotic songwriting tradition in which her father's work had originally traded. In the Union, "They are singing our song of triumph, / Which *was* made to make us free," Blunt's verses complained. "While they are breaking away the heart-strings / Of our nation's harmony."[4] For Blunt, the Union's invasion of the South was a betrayal of the nation's most cherished patriotic principles, and, like her father during the War of 1812, she knew exactly which parties and sections of the nation were at fault for refusing to act in the common interest of the other.

At the same time as Blunt was writing "The Southern Cross," her nephew Frank Key Howard was being held by Union authorities in Baltimore for having published seditious material in his newspaper, the *Baltimore Exchange*.[5] Back in September 1861, Union officers had arrested Howard without a warrant, taken him from his home in the middle of the night, and sent him to occupy a cell at Fort McHenry indefinitely without trial. Neither the irony nor the injustice of the situation was lost on Francis Scott Key's grandson: "As I stood upon the very scene" where Francis Scott Key had watched the Battle of Fort McHenry forty-seven years earlier, "the flag which he had then so proudly hailed, I saw waving, at the same place, over the victims of as vulgar and brutal a despotism as modern times have witnessed."[6] For Howard, his status as a "political prisoner" seemed evidence enough of the Union's treacherous trajectory, and within a few months, a music publisher, Henry McCaffrey, would also take up residence at Fort McHenry upon his arrest for circulating rebel music.[7] Had Howard not already transferred to another prison, it would not have been difficult to imagine the wry exchanges that he and McCaffrey might have shared over the manner and location of their incarceration.[8]

CIVIL WAR RAISED the stakes of American patriotic music. Political parties engaging in figurative battles over the ballot box were hardly the equivalent of combatant parties engaged in a prolonged and devastating military conflict. Recognition of this distinction led to an assortment of local regulations in border towns and Union-occupied Confederate cities that outlawed any kind of language, material, or act that might reasonably be considered seditious — regulations that in many cases were interpreted to elevate the performance or sale of Confederate music into an act of treason. In March 1863, for example, an order issued to suppress Confederate songs in Baltimore (under which Henry McCaffrey was arrested) explained that "the publication or sale of secession music is considered by the commanding general and the Department at Washington an evil, incendiary, and not for the public good."[9] Legally speaking, such language suddenly transformed the prewar respectability of patriotic singing into an immoral, subversive, and alarmingly accessible weapon of war.

The existence of military laws that criminalized Confederate music nominally made it easier for rebel populations to express dissent through song. But the situation was not black and white. Illegality also made it extremely difficult for Confederate individuals to sing Confederate songs without jeopardizing their social standing in the process. Certainly, status-sensitive Confederate sympathizers hardly felt ladylike or gentlemanly when locked away in military prison, regardless of the fact that their crime may have simply been to sing a Confederate song. One wealthy New Orleans woman, Julia Le Grand, could barely contain her indignation when she realized that the patriotic tunes sung by neighboring women and children could now lead to their arrest under martial law, remarking in her diary that the world had never before seen "such nonsense and such a want of pride and dignity."[10] Importantly, though, Le Grand's frustration did not stem from being denied a new form of political influence; it came from a perception that she and her friends were *losing* access to a form of public expression they had long already felt entitled to use. Confederate music, in this sense—even when outlawed— betrayed evidence of a remarkable continuation of peacetime political practice for Confederate women and their families who were otherwise forced to operate within a set of thoroughly exceptional circumstances.[11]

Elsewhere inside Union territory, the threat inferred from Confederate music had far less purchase. In 1864, rebel songs were so far from being taboo in New York City that George P. Putnam, one of the city's most prominent publishers, could produce an entire anthology of them for the benefit of Union readers while the war was still being fought. As its editor explained, the purpose of *Rebel Rhymes and Rhapsodies* was not to mock Southerners but rather to "present as full a selection of the Songs and Ballads of the Southern people as will illustrate the spirit which actuates them in their Rebellion against the Government and Laws of the United States."[12] Recent Union battlefield advances and New York's significant Peace Democrat faction no doubt helped the collection meet with little serious criticism on its release; however, its appeal thereafter proved strong enough to warrant a second edition.[13] For purchasers of *Rebel Rhymes*, there was little risk that their consumption of Confederate songs might imply support for the Confederate cause.

Of course, by 1864, publishing the music of the rebellion in New York City was as much a statement of strength as respect: it showed that citizens of the Union could rise above even the most grievous sectional animosities not just to tolerate the creative expressions of their adversaries but also to appreciate the spirit that produced them. After Appomattox, Abraham Lincoln would articulate a similar sentiment when he reclaimed "Dixie" for the Union as "our lawful prize," noting separately that he thought it would be "good to show the rebels that," with the Union in power, "they will be free to hear it again."[14] The Union's postwar appropriation of Confederate music was a revealing demonstration of its magnanimity if only because it so clearly illustrates the lure of music's political power to those who seek to harmonize society from a position of strength. In the war's immediate aftermath, an orchestrated reconciliation of the nation's music would give Unionists a way to attest to both the righteousness of their cause and the organic unity of the reconstituted nation at the same time.

RIGHT THROUGH TO the conclusion of the Civil War, then, ideas about musical power and its effects encouraged Americans of all sorts to harness harmony—though not always for the reasons we might typically expect. Combinations of music and politics often ended up supporting the thoroughly conservative objectives of Americans who valued order and unity at a time of expanding democracy and deepening sectional tensions. And since much of music's political value was seen to reside in its capacity to smooth divisions and ameliorate conflict, its effects tended to serve to the interests of power as much as, or more so than, its challengers. Such an insight may seem counterintuitive to those of us versed in modern theories or assumptions about music's democratizing potential, but it could be frustratingly obvious to certain individuals at the time.[15] As one participant in the fleetingly popular Workingmen's movement protested, "the lawyers, office-seekers, petty magistrates, and speculators seem resolved that we shall shout only when they shout, or sing patriotic airs only when they are pleased to give them out," before adding, "We must take care not to be ridden by such patriots."[16] From the Workingmen's perspective, the very suggestion that Americans could only be at their best when acting in concert merely confirmed the self-interested designs they saw to be at the heart of American democracy—that sovereign power was wielded by a privileged elite who cared more about shaping the will of their constituents than following it.

The Workingmen were not alone. Federalists in the early national period may have set a precedent for the top-down use of music in American politics, but in the case of "Hail Columbia," Jeffersonian Republicans immediately claimed to see through the Federalist veneer of Joseph Hopkinson's ode to unanimity. When Republicans later sought to block a charter of incorporation for the Musical Fund Society of Philadelphia or when Jacksonian Democrats resisted the Boston Academy of Music's campaign to introduce music instruction into public schools, they did so on the grounds that substantive principles were at stake. These organizations represented not only an increased interest in the promotion of musical taste but also significant concentrations of socioeconomic power and cultural capital—the influence of which Republicans were determined to contain. Again, during the 1840 presidential election, while Whigs waxed lyrical about how their campaign music cast a refining influence over the conduct of their partisan activities—or that it imbued their politics with an air of respectability—Democrats charged that Whigs were *forced* to rely on songs because they would rather tell their supporters what to sing than respect what they had to say. Finally, as the Civil War loomed, S. Willard Saxton—a dedicated utopian, music lover, and abolitionist—found in music not merely a refuge from disorder but also a medium through which to fashion his most radical desires for change into conservative calls for the restoration of a more morally respectable union.

Uniquely, the particular combination of wartime circumstances surrounding Francis Scott Key's composition of "The Star-Spangled Banner" enabled this example of a conservative Federalist musical tradition to transcend partisan and sectional boundaries to legendary effect. Though often dismissed as curmudgeons who made little effort to understand the appeal of popular democracy, Federalists in fact thought deeply about how music could help fashion American values into the shape of their elite ideals. Francis Scott Key, Joseph Hopkinson, Francis Hopkinson, and John Adams all latched onto a belief that the power of music could persuade Americans to see the wisdom of deferring to the political judgments of their betters. And, as such, music presented to Federalist leaders an enticing means of social control—one that could convince Americans to rise above partisanship and unite instead around an elite Federalist point of view. Accordingly, songs like "Hail Columbia" and "The Star-Spangled Banner" were both written by young Federalist lawyers motivated by a desire to educate the nation in their own values, to espouse the importance of national unity over individual liberty, and to engender respect for an elite class of leaders.

The lure of this top-down approach to music, power, and politics in the United States did not fade with the demise of the Federalist Party. From the political ambitions of early elite musical organizations to Whig Party campaign songs and individuals like Saxton, a Federalist-inspired approach to the public utility of music in politics instead endured remarkably well over time. This is not to suggest that there was anything neat about nineteenth-century partisan realignments. Federalist ideas—like many of the actual people who held them—had the propensity to go anywhere. John K. Kane, for instance, one of the foremost Federalist founders of the Musical Fund Society of Philadelphia, went on to become not a Whig but instead a Jacksonian Democrat.[17] By the 1850s, a staunch old Democratic federal judge like Kane and a rabid young abolitionist like Saxton shared little common ground except, it turns out, for a mutual belief that music could help save the nation from the influence of its least respectable elements.

In 1858, a brief newspaper article published in the *Brooklyn Daily Times* declared, "A taste for music, when widely distributed among a people, is one of the surest indications of their moral purity, amiability, and refinement." Music, according to the column's author, not only "promotes sociality" but also "represses the grosser manifestations of the passions" and "substitutes in their place all that is beautiful and artistic." Walt Whitman, who penned the piece, was one of the few Democratic-leaning literary luminaries to spare much thought for the sociopolitical overtones of music before the Civil War. But his vision of a nation redeemed by the virtues of its musical taste illustrates just how easily a conservative elite musical tradition could be tailored to suit the needs of nationalists of all stripes. Whitman surely valued the qualities of the American "Common Man" higher than most of the individuals who have featured in these pages did, but, like them, he too harbored a fear that the basest instincts of the American people threatened the well-being of the nation. And, like them, he too held out hope that music could help lift Americans back into the realm of their truest principles and highest ideals.[18]

From the start, however, this musical ideal was subject to contestation and compromise. Claims that music's influence would refine and elevate the conduct of American politics formed part of a broader reaction to the perceived dangers of a rapidly expanding popular democracy. Under these circumstances, cultural exchanges *were* political exchanges, and the persistence of a Federalist musical tradition stretching well beyond the bounds of the Federalist era exemplified the extent to which cultural power constituted a legitimate extension of socioeconomic and political power.[19] Americans of all political persuasions believed music could shape the world they lived in. But conservative individuals—from Francis Scott Key to Ellen Key Blunt—drew on the ideal of a harmonious republic to promote a far less democratic vision of American society than is usually supposed. Accounting for their efforts speaks to the influence of elite values over popular politics. And it reminds us that harnessing harmony could also mean preserving privilege.

Notes

Abbreviations

AAS	American Antiquarian Society
APS	American Philosophical Society
CHM	Chicago History Museum Research Center
FO	Founders Online, National Archives
GHS	Georgia Historical Society
HSP	Historical Society of Pennsylvania
HUA	Harvard University Archives
JRPC	John Rowe Parker Correspondence, Kislak Center for Special Collections, University of Pennsylvania
LC	Library of Congress, Manuscripts Division
LCP	Library Company of Philadelphia
LLSMC	Lester S. Levy Sheet Music Collection, Sheridan Libraries Special Collections, Johns Hopkins University
Mason/Yale	Lowell Mason Papers, Irving S. Gilmore Music Library, Yale University
MdHS	Maryland Historical Society
MFSR	Musical Fund Society of Philadelphia Records, Kislak Center for Special Collections, University of Pennsylvania
MFSSR	Musical Fund Society of Philadelphia Supplementary Records, Kislak Center for Special Collections, University of Pennsylvania
MHS	Massachusetts Historical Society
NNV	A New Nation Votes: American Election Returns, 1787–1825, Tufts Digital Collections and Archives
OR	US War Department, *The War of the Rebellion: A Compilation of the Official Records of the Union and Confederate Armies*
PTJ	Thomas Jefferson, *Papers of Thomas Jefferson Digital Edition*
SWSJ	S. Willard Saxton Journal, Rufus and S. Willard Saxton Papers, Manuscripts and Archives Division, Sterling Memorial Library, Yale University
VHS	Virginia Historical Society

Introduction

1. *Daily Advertiser* (New York, NY), 30 July 1798.
2. *Daily Advertiser*, 31 July 1798.
3. *Daily Advertiser*, 31 July 1798. For an account of this incident emphasizing the lengths to which Republicans went to challenge Federalist power and policies,

including their "efforts to control the music of the country," see Bradburn, *Citizenship Revolution*, 179–80.

4. *Bee* (New London, CT), 8 August 1798.

5. On early African American musical culture, see White and White, *Sounds of Slavery*; Levine, *Black Culture and Black Consciousness*; Epstein, *Sinful Tunes*. Profiles of African American musicians, female composers, and hardscrabble white composers suffuse the literature in conscious distinction to the traditional tendency to memorialize white men; see, for instance, Jones, *Francis Johnson*; O'Connell, *Ballad of Blind Tom*; Tick, *American Women Composers*; Bailey, *Music and the Southern Belle*; Crist, "Ye Sons of Harmony."

6. "Rights of Women," *New York Weekly Museum*, 25 April 1795, quoted in S. Newman, *Parades and the Politics of the Street*, 178. In addition, on Native American music and resistance in early America, see Goodman, "But They Differ from Us in Sound."

7. The political history of the United States has been mined too deeply to adequately summarize here. However, I have most directly been informed by scholars associated with the so-called newest political history, which over the past fifteen years has leveraged the resources of the cultural turn to recover the history of the People as opposed to elites. While my approach to political history shares much with the "newest" political historians, my conclusions differ. The emblematic mission statement of the "newest political history" is Waldstreicher, Pasley, and Robertson's introduction to *Beyond the Founders*. On civil society, see Neem, *Nation of Joiners*; McCarthy, *American Creed*; Kelley, *Learning to Stand and Speak*. The foundational musicological treatment of early America is Sonneck's *Early Concert-Life*, though the best broader, more illustrative study is Crawford's *America's Musical Life*. For histories of sound in the early American context, see M. Smith, *Listening to Nineteenth-Century America*; Rath, *How Early America Sounded*; Goodman, "But They Differ from Us in Sound."

8. Slauter, *State as a Work of Art*; Kelly, *Republic of Taste*; Bechtold, "Revolutionary Soundscape"; Wood, "'Join with Heart and Soul and Voice'"; Riordan, "O Dear What Can the Matter Be?" My approach similarly resonates with work on early American cultures of oratory and performance; see Eastman, *Nation of Speechifiers*; Fliegelman, *Declaring Independence*.

9. On sensibility, see Knott, *Sensibility and the American Revolution*, esp. 198–201, 222; Eustace, *Passion Is the Gale*, esp. 483–84; Waldstreicher, *Perpetual Fetes*, esp. 74–79, 85–87; Wood, "Join with Heart and Soul and Voice," 1095–96; Bushman, *Refinement of America*, 81–83; Shields, *Civil Tongues and Polite Letters*; Blauvelt, *Work of the Heart*.

10. *Public Ledger* (Philadelphia, PA), 11 October 1837.

11. The shift from sensibility to sentimentalism is often conceived as a literary trend, but historians increasingly recognize its broader political and cultural impact as well. See, for instance, Good, *Founding Friendships*, 190, 248n6; Hessinger, *Seduced, Abandoned, and Reborn*, 42; Burstein, *Sentimental Democracy*, 307–24. On the emotional dimensions of antebellum political conflict more broadly, see Woods, *Emotional and Sectional Conflict*; Freeman, *Field of Blood*; A. Smith, *Stormy Present*. Fears that sincerity could be faked arguably increased over time but transcended both cultures of sensibility and sentimentality, and concern for the public's susceptibility to deception fueled political opposition to music (and the arts in general) across both emotional re-

gimes. For the centrality of sincerity to midcentury American cultural and social values and experience, see Halttunen, *Confidence Men and Painted Women*. Similar concerns can be observed in an earlier era as well; see Waldstreicher, *Perpetual Fetes*, esp. 77–85; Bellion, *Citizen Spectator*, esp. chap. 1.

12. My claims regarding the regularity with which nineteenth-century American diarists and letter writers commented on music are not unique; see also McWhirter, *Battle Hymns*, esp. 1–2; Cavicchi, *Listening and Longing*.

13. The elitism at issue in my argument requires some definition. I use the term "elite" primarily to refer to a minority of individuals whose social influence, wealth, or access to political power distinguished them from the rest of the population. Beyond this broad-based foundation, my use of the term borrows from both materialist and cultural approaches to its study. Elite identities here are *perceived* either internally via a process of self-construction or externally via the adoption of genteel behaviors and attitudes. Yet such perceptions must also be predicated on an individual's plausible connection to tangible sources of social, economic, or political power—even if only by association. Elites in this book, then, are individuals who thought themselves superior to their neighbors but who also—in one way or another—possessed credible means for demonstrating distinction through socioeconomic, political, associational, or occupationally derived influence. See Schocket, "Thinking about Elites"; Kornblith et al., "Symposium on Class in the Early Republic"; Cutterham, *Gentleman Revolutionaries*.

14. On the popularity and profits of the sheet-music business, see Crawford, *America's Musical Life*, chap. 12; Dichter and Shapiro, *Early American Sheet Music*; Epstein, introduction to *Complete Catalogue of Sheet Music*.

15. On the supposed impossibility of reconstructing private musical experiences from the nineteenth century, see Butsch, *Making of American Audiences*, vii. For a detailed overview of the pitfalls and opportunities of this archival method with regard to music, see Cavicchi, *Listening and Longing*, esp. 8–12. However, the broad approach to historical evidence adopted here was pioneered most notably by Ginzburg, *Cheese and the Worms*; Darnton, *Great Cat Massacre*. While a commentary approach to music and history is not common among early American political historians, scholarly variants of it can increasingly be found further afield. See Lidtke, *Alternative Culture*, esp. chaps. 2, 4, 5; Pasler, *Composing the Citizen*; and Körner, "Verdi and the Historians." Moreover, it is no longer the case that commentary-based approaches to music and history are entirely absent from the historical literature of early America or the nineteenth-century United States either. Inspired by musicology's turn to reception studies and history's turn to cultural life, historically based accounts of music's role in various aspects of nineteenth-century American society have helped show the applicability of musical evidence to histories of gender, immigration, consumerism, class, and social life. See Cavicchi, *Listening and Longing*; McWhirter, *Battle Hymns*, Broyles, *Music of the Highest Class*; Gac, *Singing for Freedom*; Roberts, *Blackface Nation*. Crist's "Ye Sons of Harmony" is the best instance of an early American historian using music to better understand issues of gender. A recent trend worth noting is the rise of song "biographies" that trace the uses and associations of particular American patriotic songs as they evolved over time. See, for instance, Stauffer and Soskis, *Battle Hymn of the Republic*; Ferris, *Star-Spangled Banner*; Davis, *Maryland, My Maryland*.

16. For an overview of creative literature and politics, see O'Donnell, "Literature and Politics in the Early Republic." Work on parades and festive culture is both significant and voluminous; see Waldstreicher, *Perpetual Fetes*; S. Newman, *Parades and the Politics of the Street*; Travers, *Celebrating the Fourth*; White, "It Was a Proud Day." On clothing and the material culture of nationalism more generally, see esp. Irvin, *Clothed in Robes of Sovereignty*. For the mammoth ball of cheese, see Pasley, "Cheese and the Words." It is worth noting that a significant literature concerned specifically with illuminating the process of how Old World melodies were reappropriated with different lyrics into early American contexts already exists, the fruits of which help inform this study. See, for instance, Goodman, "Transatlantic Contrafacta"; Gray, "Musical Politics in French Philadelphia"; Leavenworth, Marini, and Pappas, "Music and Meaning in Early America."

17. Wood, "Join with Heart and Soul and Voice," 1099–1102.

18. Goodman, "Transatlantic Contrafacta," esp. 395.

19. On understanding the performing arts as part of a larger early American "sporting culture," see K. Cohen, *They Will Have Their Game*.

20. "Grand Musical Performances," *Mirror of Taste and Dramatic Censor*, 1:5 (May 1810), 428. For further discussion of this quote, see Potter, *Food for Apollo*, 130. Similar perceptions persisted throughout the period of this study: in 1852, for example, the *Musical Times* remarked on how "music, in various form, greets you at every corner of the street. Organ music—Negro melodies—amateur glee clubs—amateur quartettes—infant drummers—sacred music societies—these abound in our midst. And as the increase of political parties multiplies the number of great men, so the creation of musical organizations wonderfully augments the multitude of song and solo singers." See "Correspondence: Boston, Feb. 2, 1852," *Musical Times* (New York, NY), 7 February 1852.

21. The emblematic representation of Federalism's relationship with popular politics is Fischer's *Revolution of American Conservatism*. However, this conception has lately given way to interpretations more apt to recognize the dynamism of Federalism as a larger political culture, see Ben-Atar and Oberg, eds., *Federalists Reconsidered*; Foletta, *Coming to Terms with Democracy*.

22. On the peculiarly emotive quality of the War of 1812, see esp. Eustace, *1812*. On the Federalist presence in civil society, see Koschnik, *Common Interest*; Neem, *Nation of Joiners*; Foletta, *Coming to Terms with Democracy*.

23. Typically, the purpose of music in antebellum electoral politics has been consumed by arguments over the so-called golden age of political participation. A selection of key contributions to this literature includes Altschuler and Blumin, *Rude Republic*; Silbey, *American Political Nation*; W. Gienapp, "Politics Seem to Enter into Everything."

24. For broader works that help shed light on the role of conservatism in antebellum politics, see Lynn, *Preserving the White Man's Republic*; A. Smith, *Stormy Present*; M. Mason, *Apostle of Union*; Varon, *Disunion!*; and, in particular, Higham, "From Boundlessness to Consolidation," delivered as a Commonwealth Fund Lecture at the University of London in 1968 and reprinted with an introductory note by Stuart McConnell in Higham, *Hanging Together*.

25. "Political Music," *Musical World and Times* (New York, NY), 15 July 1852; "Music in Congress," *Musical World and Times*, 22 January 1853. The precise editorial arrangements for the *Musical World* are difficult to ascertain. Dyer and Willis appear to have jointly held editorship of the paper until 2 October 1852, when both men are cited as publishers and Willis assumed the position of sole editor. Willis is commonly credited for the majority of *Musical World*'s editorial positions and policies. See Day, introduction to *New York Musical World*, ix. The title of this publication changes often over time but for consistency is referred to here as the *Musical World and Times*. For an additional example, see also I. B. Woodbury's approving note in the *Musical Pioneer* about the "fine effect" produced by members of the Maine legislature who were reported to have begun a practice of singing together before taking their seats; see "Musical Legislators," *Musical Pioneer and Chorister's Budget* (New York, NY), April 1858.

26. "Music in Congress," *Musical World and Times*, 29 January 1853.

Prologue

1. Quoted verses and commentary from "Extract of a Letter from Trenton, dated April 21," *Pennsylvania Packet* (Philadelphia), 1 May 1789. On Washington's inaugural and presidential "tours," see Breen, *Washington's Journey*; Moats, *Celebrating the Republic*; Washington, *Diaries of George Washington*, 5:445–97, 6:96–169; Henderson, *Washington's Southern Tour*. On Washington's presidential journeys as exercises in sentimentality, see in particular Waldstreicher, *Perpetual Fetes*, 117–26; Kelly, *Republic of Taste*, 214–19.

2. On harmony as a source of unification in the early American republic, see Wood, "Join with Heart and Soul and Voice." For evidence of the broad influence that news of this scene had, see an account of its replication on a North Carolina plantation in 1791 in Henderson's *Washington's Southern Tour*, 119.

3. For a recent study of the divisiveness and uncertainty inherent in the new nation's constitutional settlement, see J. Gienapp, *Second Creation*.

4. To avoid confusion, "Federalists" in the 1780s were chiefly defined by their support of the Constitution, which their "Anti-Federalist" opponents resisted. However, the party groupings at the heart of this book date principally to the 1790s instead, when "Federalists" were defined principally by their support for George Washington's administration. Many Federalists from the 1780s were also Federalists in the 1790s; but not all made this transition, and the two groups remain distinct.

5. George Washington, "Farewell Address," 19 September 1796, Washington Papers, LC, https://www.loc.gov/item/mgw2.024/.

6. A particularly useful account of the economic and regional dimensions of early national partisanship is Murphy, *Building the Empire State*, esp. chap. 3. But see also McCoy, *Elusive Republic*; Appleby, *Capitalism and a New Social Order*.

7. Washington, "Farewell Address," 19 September 1796, Washington Papers, LC.

8. Taylor, "From Fathers to Friends of the People."

9. [Jonathan Jackson], *Thoughts upon the Political Situation*, 49.

10. Ames, "American Literature," in *Works of Fisher Ames*, 472.

11. John Adams to James Sullivan, 26 May 1776, FO, https://founders.archives.gov/documents/Adams/06-04-02-0091.

12. On the Federalists' willingness to support the "informal" political contributions of women more than their Republican opponents were, see Zagarri, "Gender and the First Party System," quote on 119. For discussion of particular instances wherein Federalist ideology and political exigency combined in ways that led them to also favor more inclusive electorates than Republicans did, see Robertson, "Jeffersonian Parties, Politics, and Participation"; Gronningsater, "Expressly Recognized by Our Election Laws."

13. Benjamin Tallmadge quoted from 1793 in Hall, *Benjamin Tallmadge*, 167; Tallmadge, 1 March 1802, quoted in US Congress, *Annals of Congress*, 947–48.

14. *Annals of Congress*, 947–48.

15. An American [Noah Webster], *Revolution in France*, 34.

16. The most sympathetic account of Federalist fears of violence in the context of the French Revolution remains Cleves, *Reign of Terror*. On the French Revolution's influence on the "problem" of American democracy, see Hale, "Regenerating the World."

17. See Clark, *American Idea of England*; Yokota, *Unbecoming British*; Haynes, *Unfinished Revolution*.

18. Ames, "Danger of American Liberty," quoted in Fischer, *Revolution of American Conservatism*, 27.

19. See, for example, Parish, *Excellence of the Gospel*; Cleves, *Reign of Terror*, chap. 1.

20. Thomas Jefferson to William Short, 3 January 1793, FO, https://founders.archives.gov/documents/Jefferson/01-25-02-0016.

21. On American celebrations of the French Revolution as a "distinctly partisan affair," see S. Newman, *Parades and Politics of the Street*, esp. chap. 4. Jordan E. Taylor explains the persistence of positive interpretations of the French Revolution in the United States, even after it turned violent, as the result of distinctive, often partisan-based, news and information networks; see J. Taylor, "Reign of Error." For the impact of French émigrés, like Genêt, throughout early national American society and politics more broadly, see Furstenberg, *When the United States Spoke French*.

22. On early American political parties as a "cultural stance," see Pasley, *First Presidential Contest*, 6–7.

23. For a recent collection focused on the timing and shape of early American party development, see Peart and Smith, *Practicing Democracy*. The classic treatment remains Chambers and Burnham, *American Party Systems*, but for an extension of the "party system" approach deeper into the nineteenth century, see also Silbey, *American Political Nation*.

24. On cockades and other partisan symbols, see S. Newman, *Parades and Politics of the Street*, chap. 5. Attempts to identify the social composition of early American political parties remain difficult to do with precision. General patterns based on wealth, location, or economic interest are discernible, but exceptions often appear to undermine their utility. For a discussion of the nuances, see Fischer, *Revolution of American Conservatism*, 201–26.

25. See, in particular, Branson, *Frenchified Dames*; Haulman, *Politics of Fashion*.

26. The populist Republican critique of Federalists as aristocratic elitists did not deter elites themselves from joining their ranks. Elites and elitism traversed both par-

ties, but while leading Republican men may have styled themselves as friends of people as opposed to fathers, there was no reason for their friendship to beget equality. A focus on equality of opportunity gave plenty of latitude for elite Republicans to rationalize their own superior wealth and influence as a fair reflection of their merits, in contrast to Federalists, who appeared to claim that their higher status had more to do with who they were than what they could do. See, for example, Mitchell, *Oration*; Appleby, *Capitalism and a New Social Order*.

27. See, for example, Yokota, *Unbecoming British*; Clark, *American Idea of England*; Gould, *Among the Powers of the Earth*; Van Horn, *Power of Objects*, esp. chap. 6; Furstenberg and Waldstreicher, "Republican Court"; Shields and Teute, "Republican Court."

28. This more radical musical tradition resonated through the popularity of blackface minstrelsy in the antebellum period, even if its melodies were also adopted by midcentury middle-class reformers. The literature on minstrelsy is large, but for detail on this specific trajectory, see Roberts, *Blackface Nation*, esp. chaps. 2 and 3.

29. Silverman, *Cultural History of the American Revolution*, 33.

30. *Pennsylvania Gazette* (Philadelphia), 1 December 1763. Historical value of the pound converted based on calculations available from Williamson, "Five Ways to Compute."

31. Silverman, *Cultural History of the American Revolution*, 32.

32. *Whole Booke of Psalmes*; Crawford, *America's Musical Life*, 23–25. On the Bay Psalm Book and hymn singing as part of a broader "communal tradition," see Roberts, *Blackface Nation*, 51.

33. On the shift to the Old Way of singing, see Broyles, *Music of the Highest Class*, 35–37; Temperley, "Old Way of Singing."

34. Crawford, *America's Musical Life*, 25. See also Daniels, *Puritans at Play*, chap. 3. For a critic's argument, see *Pacificatory Letter*, quotation on 2.

35. See Bechtold, "Revolutionary Soundscape," esp. 425.

36. This interpretation of Billings is drawn from Bechtold, esp. 427–35. Billings prefaced his popular *New England Psalm-Singer* with an "Essay on the Nature and Properties of Sound" authored by an anonymous "Gentleman" (who may have been the physician Charles Stockbridge), which states, "Music being nothing but particular Sounds, variously modified, and adapted to please the Ear" can only be accurately understood in reference to the particles of air that carry it. "When," he explained, "the Parts of an elastic Body by Percussion, are put into a tremulous, vibrating Motion . . . those tremulous Motions, communicate correspondent Vibrations." And "the more frequent the Vibrations of two Musical Chords coincide, the more perfect the Concord, and the more agreeable to the Ear." As for why some combinations produce "Concord" and others produce "discord," the essay concludes that this can only be explained as a consequence of "Divine Will." Billings, *New-England Psalm-Singer*, quotes on 2, 3, 8.

37. Two important iterations of this argument include Bechtold, "Revolutionary Soundscape"; and Wood, "Join with Heart and Soul and Voice."

38. A substantial and growing literature surrounds the intersection of early national creative culture and its relationship to larger contests over power and authority in the new nation. Bushman's *Refinement of America* and Waldstreicher's *Perpetual Fetes*

represent foundational studies on the material culture and popular practices of early American nationalism, respectively. But debates persist, particularly over the extent to which Americans sought to emulate Europeans, especially the British—a process that John Murrin termed "Anglicization"—or instead transformed Old World examples into distinctively American alternatives. Collectively, cultural historians have approached questions of culture and power from a wide range of perspectives, spanning material history and popular political culture to theater history, literature, clothing, sport, and art history. An illustrative sampling includes Kelly, *Republic of Taste*; Nathans, *Early American Theatre*; K. Cohen, *They Will Have Their Game*; Irvin, *Clothed in Robes of Sovereignty*; Jaffee, *New Nation of Goods*; Anishanslin, *Portrait of a Woman in Silk*; M. Walsh, *Portrait and the Book*, esp. chap. 3; Bellion, *Citizen Spectator*; Slauter, *State as a Work of Art*. Debates over the dangers and presence of luxurious consumption in the new republic were critical to these discussions; see Brekke, "Scourge of Fashion"; J. Cohen, *Luxurious Citizens*. On "Anglicization," see Shankman, "Synthesis Useful and Compelling"; Murrin, *Rethinking America*.

Chapter One

1. National Park Service, "Annual Park Recreation Visitation."
2. WBAL-TV 11 Baltimore, "New Visitors Center Ready."
3. For an account of "The Star-Spangled Banner" in American society beyond the immediate circumstances of its composition, including its official adoption as the United States' national anthem in 1931, see Ferris, *Star-Spangled Banner*. Contemporary political debate over "The Star-Spangled Banner" following the election of President Donald J. Trump continues to demonstrate both that its original intent has purchase and the degree to which perceptions of its success have subsequently provoked contestation. See Robin, "Colin Kaepernick."
4. The identification of a Federalist musical tradition is not meant to imply that Republicans did not also use music regularly and often in their attempts to influence national affairs or that the Federalist approach to music's political use was the only way early Americans approached the subject. It does, however, imply that historians have missed something about the cultural politics of Federalism. While Jeffersonian Republicans have a well-deserved reputation for exploiting popular culture for political effect, Federalists' use of popular politics is typically explained as a last-ditch, hypocritical move that they were forced into only after their defeat in the electoral arena. This chapter, however, reveals that it required no great intellectual leap of Federalists to make use of a popular repertoire like music for political purposes, so long as doing so broadly supported their hierarchical view of the American polity. The single work most illustrative of the typical trajectory of the Federalists' relationship with popular political tactics is Fischer's *Revolution of American Conservatism*. The interpretation of Federalism adopted here is inspired by that collectively proposed in Ben-Atar and Oberg, *Federalists Reconsidered*. Republican songs were ubiquitous, and examples of them are suffused through existing scholarship on early American popular politics; see esp. S. Newman, *Parades and the Politics of the Street*, 177–81; Waldstreicher, *Perpetual Fetes*, esp. 204–5. Songs written outside of any strict connection to what I have termed a Fed-

eralist conception of music have garnered particular attention of late, especially in the context of the War of 1812; see Eustace, *1812*, 50–56, 81–85, 233–34; J. Clark, *American Idea of England*, 100–108; Waldstreicher, "Minstrelization and Nationhood." For an important overview of music and politics in the early republic that focuses on the shared belief that musical harmony had the power to produce political harmony, see Wood, "Join with Heart and Soul and Voice."

5. The three most rigorous accounts of the circumstances surrounding the composition and initial distribution of "The Star-Spangled Banner" are Sonneck, *Report on "The Star-Spangled Banner"*; Filby and Howard, *Star Spangled Books*; and Ashton, "Patriotic Sublime," chap. 1. The most useful popular accounts of the events that inspired "The Star-Spangled Banner" are contained within biographical treatments of Key; see Dubovoy, *Lost World of Francis Scott Key*; Molotsky, *Flag, the Poet, and the Song*; Delaplaine, *Francis Scott Key*. A brief but authoritative account of "The Star-Spangled Banner" is also located in Picker, "1814, September 13–14."

6. Attali, *Noise*, esp. 6–9.

7. A vast literature principally concerned with the emancipatory role of music in social movements has emerged since the 1960s. Some of the most important examples include Love, *Musical Democracy*; Eyerman and Jamison, *Music and Social Movements*; Mattern, *Acting in Concert*. A usefully balanced survey text is Street, *Music and Politics*. For a recent study that distinguishes the ability of music itself to generate a sense of shared understanding from the political actions of those seeking to exploit this power, see Shank, *Political Force of Musical Beauty*.

8. Surprisingly, perhaps, research into the Federalist Party itself has been in the vanguard of such historiographical developments. Landmark studies of Federalism by David Hackett Fischer, James M. Banner, and Linda K. Kerber all expressed, in one way or another, that Federalism is best understood more as a culture than as a political party; see Fischer, *Revolution of American Conservatism*; Banner, *To the Hartford Convention*; Kerber, *Federalists in Dissent*. More recent work has generally adopted a similar approach; see Foletta, *Coming to Terms with Democracy*. The most important exception to this interpretive trend is Stanley Elkins and Eric McKitrick, who emphasize the primacy of practical and personal disagreements on policy to explain the emergence of early American partisan differences. See Elkins and McKitrick, *Age of Federalism*.

9. Dowling, *Literary Federalism*, quote on xii. See also Simpson, "Federalism and the Crisis of Literary Order." The conclusions of this literary scholarship dovetail with the current attempts of some early American political historians to consider the impact of partisanship in the absence of recognizably organized party structures; see Pasley, *First Presidential Contest*; Estes, *Jay Treaty Debate*. Todd Estes argues that Federalists became operationally more democratic over the course of the 1790s despite their elitist ideology; however, evidence from this chapter suggests that this claim may overstate the extent to which their popular appeals possessed genuine democratic intent.

10. To borrow Andrew M. Schocket's phrase, the type of elitism I am concerned with here is "elitism of the mind or heart rather than the pocketbook or law." Schocket, "Thinking about Elites," 553.

11. On early national elite political culture, see Freeman, *Affairs of Honor*, esp. xv; Cutterham, *Gentleman Revolutionaries*.

12. Amphion, a character from Greek mythology, was joint king of Thebes with his twin brother, Zethus, and is said to have been so convincing a leader that he could assemble the fabled stone wall of Thebes by the sound of his harp (often referred to as his lyre). See Pliny, *Natural History of Pliny*, 2:230–31; Tripp, *Meridian Handbook of Classical Mythology*, 43–44.

13. John Adams to Charles Adams, 13 March 1796, Seymour Collection, MHS.

14. John Adams to Charles Adams, 13 March 1796; John Adams to Abigail Adams, 13 March 1796, Adams Papers (microfilm), reel 381, MHS. For detail on Pope's "Ode on St. Cecilia's Day," see Husk, *Account of the Musical Celebrations on St. Cecilia's Day*; Owen and Johnston, *New and General Biographical Dictionary*, 228; Pope, *Poetical Works of Alexander Pope*, 182n35.

15. John Adams to Charles Adams, 13 March 1796.

16. John Adams to Abigail Adams, 13 March 1796.

17. It is often noted that John Adams is far from representative of mainstream Federalism, but in this case, Adams's ideas are largely in keeping with how literary scholars have interpreted Federalist readings of Alexander Pope's poetry more broadly; see Simpson, *Federalist Literary Mind*, 37–40; Tennenhouse, *Importance of Feeling English*, 36–40. On the Jay Treaty, see Elkins and McKitrick, *Age of Federalism*, chap. 9; Estes, *Jay Treaty Debate*.

18. John Adams to Abigail Adams, 13 March 1796; John Adams to Charles Adams, 13 March 1796.

19. Diary of John Adams, vol. 1, 14 August 1769, Adams Family Papers: An Electronic Archive, MHS.

20. For an overview of American Revolutionary songs and their authors, see Schrader, "Songs to Cultivate the Sensations of Freedom"; Schlesinger Sr., "Note on Songs as Patriot Propaganda."

21. The belief in the westward progress of civilization is embodied in the concept of *translatio studii*; see Simpson, *Federalist Literary Mind*, 33–34; J. Ellis, *After the Revolution*, 5. For detail on eighteenth-century British musical debates, see Semi, *Music as a Science of Mankind*.

22. F. Hopkinson, *Seven Songs*. The work was first advertised on 29 November 1788 in the *Federal Gazette* (Philadelphia, PA). See Sonneck, *Francis Hopkinson*, 113. The volume itself is undated but includes a dedication to Washington by Hopkinson dated 20 November 1788. That Hopkinson had finished composing the work for publication at least five weeks before writing to Washington is derived from a letter written from Hopkinson to Jefferson on 23 October 1788, which mentions that a selection of his "Songs for the Harpsichord" were then being engraved. Despite its title, the finished collection actually contains eight songs. See Joseph Hopkinson to Thomas Jefferson, 23 October 1788, FO, https://founders.archives.gov/documents/Jefferson/01-14-02-0027.

23. On the accoutrements of early American elite political culture and debates concerning them, see, for example, Freeman, *Affairs of Honor*, 38–48. On the centrality of

monarchy to the making of the Constitution and the American presidency, see Nelson, *Royalist Revolution*.

24. F. Hopkinson, *Seven Songs*, n.p.

25. George Washington to Francis Hopkinson, 5 February 1789, FO, https://founders.archives.gov/documents/Washington/05-01-02-0208.

26. See, for instance, Comotti, *Music in Greek and Roman Culture*, 5–6.

27. Washington to F. Hopkinson, 5 February 1789.

28. On Anglophone music histories written in the context of the Enlightenment, see Semi, *Music as a Science of Mankind*, esp. chap. 4. For another elite American using music to compare the ancient and modern worlds, see John Quincy Adams, Diary, 8 April 1787, The Diaries of John Quincy Adams: A Digital Collection, MHS. Although the following authors do not emphasize music per se, on the resonance of antiquity in the new republic, see Richard, *Founders and the Classics*; Winterer, *Culture of Classicism*; Onuf and Cole, *Thomas Jefferson, the Classical World, and Early America*. American attention to the ancient world derived in large part from British fascination with classicism, and on this, see Ayres, *Classical Culture*. Kirsten E. Wood's essay on music in the early republic notes this specific exchange between Hopkinson and Washington but dismisses its invocations of classical literature as wordplay; see Wood, "Join with Heart and Soul and Voice," 1097. Another account emphasizing the broader significance of their exchange is Bechtold, "Revolutionary Soundscape."

29. Washington to F. Hopkinson, 5 February 1789.

30. On Burney and Hawkins's relationship, see Semi, *Music as a Science of Mankind*, esp. 144–51; Stevenson, "Rivals." The two best biographical treatments of Burney remain Grant, *Dr. Charles Burney*; Lonsdale, *Dr. Charles Burney*.

31. Francis Hopkinson to Thomas Jefferson, 12 March 1784, FO, https://founders.archives.gov/documents/Jefferson/01-07-02-0022.

32. [Lyon], *Lawfulness, Excellency, and Advantage of Instrumental Music*, quotes from 6, 13, and 15. Although the authorship of this anonymous pamphlet is subject to speculation, Hopkinson's support for its position on the use of instrumental music in public worship is not. See Sonneck, *Francis Hopkinson*, 81, 131–32. The pamphlet's popularity in Philadelphia was high enough to inspire a satirical "second edition" that is routinely, if speculatively, also attributed to Hopkinson. See [F. Hopkinson], *Second Edition of the Lawfulness . . . of Instrumental Music*.

33. F. Hopkinson, *Seven Songs*, n.p.

34. Francis Hopkinson to George Washington, 1 December 1788, FO, https://founders.archives.gov/documents/Washington/05-01-02-0110.

35. Francis Hopkinson to Thomas Jefferson, 23 October 1788, FO, https://founders.archives.gov/documents/Jefferson/01-14-02-0027, emphasis added.

36. Francis Hopkinson to Thomas Jefferson, 1 December 1788, FO, https://founders.archives.gov/documents/Jefferson/01-14-02-0106.

37. See, for example, Francis Hopkinson, *Account of the Grand Procession*; F. Hopkinson, "A New Roof," *Pennsylvania Packet* (Philadelphia), 29 December 1787; F. Hopkinson, "The Raising: A New Song for Federal Mechanics," *Pennsylvania Gazette* (Philadelphia), 6 February 1788.

38. F. Hopkinson to Jefferson, 1 December 1788.

39. Thomas Jefferson to Francis Hopkinson, 13 March 1789, FO, https://founders.archives.gov/documents/Jefferson/01-14-02-0402.

40. F. Hopkinson to Jefferson, 1 December 1788.

41. On the significance of family and fatherhood to elite leaders in the early republic, see Glover, *Founders as Fathers*.

42. This interpretation of Jefferson's relationship to music and politics gels with the work of scholars who have similarly characterized Jefferson's use of dinners to broker political outcomes or exert influence. See Allgor, *Parlor Politics*, esp. chap. 1; J. Ellis, *Founding Brothers*, esp. chap. 2. See also Gordon-Reed and Onuf, *Most Blessed of the Patriarchs*, chap. 7. For an important analysis of Jefferson's relationship to music with respect to race, slavery, and settler-colonial nation-building, see Gordon, "What Mr. Jefferson Didn't Hear."

43. Joseph Hopkinson to George Washington, 9 May 1798, FO, https://founders.archives.gov/documents/Washington/06-02-02-0191. All spellings appear as in original. Biographical literature on Joseph Hopkinson is not well developed. The standard text is Konkle, *Joseph Hopkinson*. See also M. Keith Siskin's brief but informative overview of Hopkinson's legal career, "Joseph Hopkinson."

44. For detail on the XYZ Affair, see Elkins and McKitrick, *Age of Federalism*, 549–641.

45. Joseph Hopkinson, "History of the Song of Hail Columbia in the handwriting of the author," 24 August 1840, Hopkinson Family Papers, HSP.

46. On the participatory nature of Federalist politics in the late 1790s, see Estes, *Jay Treaty Debate*, esp. chap. 6; Owen, "Legitimacy, Localism, and the First Party System."

47. The best detail on the partisan appropriation of foreign melodies is Goodman, "Transatlantic Contrafacta"; and Riordan, "O Dear What Can the Matter Be?," esp. 207–20. On the connection between popular politics and foreign cultural signifiers more generally, see S. Newman, *Parades and the Politics of the Street*, chap. 5.

48. "Serenading," *Aurora General Advertiser* (Philadelphia, PA), 9 May 1798; "Theatre," *Aurora General Advertiser*, 27 April 1798. On Federalist mobs attacking Bache, see Pasley, *Tyranny of the Printers*, 98; Waldstreicher, *Perpetual Fetes*, 163.

49. Joseph Hopkinson to George Washington, 9 May 1798, FO, https://founders.archives.gov/documents/Washington/06-02-02-0191.

50. On the Federalist associations of "The President's March," see S. Newman, *Parades and the Politics of the Street*, 181.

51. "Theatre," *Aurora General Advertiser*, 27 April 1798.

52. "Philadelphia–August 1.," *Aurora General Advertiser*, 1 August 1798.

53. "Philadelphia–Saturday, May 5.," *Aurora General Advertiser*, 5 May 1798; reprinted in the *Bee* (New London, CT), 16 May 1798.

54. Thomas Jefferson, "Notes on Presidential Appointments," 3 May 1798, *PTJ*, http://rotunda.upress.virginia.edu/founders/TSJN-01-30-02-0223. Hopkinson was twenty-seven years old at the time of writing "Hail Columbia," not twenty-two or twenty-three, as Jefferson supposes.

55. "Extract of Lying," *Gazette of the United States* (Philadelphia, PA), 27 April 1798.

56. "Bache and Callender," *Porcupine's Gazette* (Philadelphia, PA), 27 April 1798.

57. Joseph Hopkinson, "Hail Columbia, the Favorite New Federal Song." For a more detailed musicological analysis of "Hail Columbia" that also highlights its Federalism, see Gray, "Partisan National Song."

58. "The Managers," *Gazette of the United States*, 2 May 1798.

59. Helen Cripe comes to a similar conclusion on the paucity of material Jefferson actually wrote about music. See Cripe, *Thomas Jefferson and Music*, 10. The key primary source attesting to Jefferson's interest in music is Thomas Jefferson to Giovanni Fabbroni, 8 June 1778, FO, https://founders.archives.gov/documents/Jefferson/01-02-02-0066, in which he states that music is "the favorite passion" of his soul. But while Jefferson did have significant interest in music, there is no evidence to show that he directly considered the implications of its use outside of domestic settings. The general claim that Republicans' popular political tactics were sometimes inspired by Federalist tactics is not unique to musical politics. See, for instance, Pasley, *First Presidential Contest*, 11; Foletta, *Coming to Terms with Democracy*, 23, 25.

60. Michael Fortune to Thomas Jefferson, 23 June 1801, FO, https://founders.archives.gov/documents/Jefferson/01-34-02-0333.

61. Louis Dubois to James Madison, 5 March 1809, FO, https://founders.archives.gov/documents/Madison/03-01-02-0020.

62. "Jefferson and Liberty," *Philadelphia Gazette*, 23 June 1801.

63. Jefferson, *Jefferson's Scrapbooks*, 19–20, 467. Anonymous authors were not necessarily anonymous to readers at the time. It is speculated that Peter S. Du Ponceau may have authored this version of "Jefferson and Liberty," since Charles Willson Peale implied Du Ponceau's authorship in a letter to Jefferson dated 8 March 1801. See Jefferson, *Papers of Thomas Jefferson*, 33:96–99.

64. Jefferson, *Jefferson's Scrapbooks*, 24–25, 28–29, 32.

65. Jefferson, *Jefferson's Scrapbooks*, 116–17. On Elihu Doty's profession as a shipmaster, see "Loss of Ship Hope," *Farmer's Weekly Museum* (Walpole, NH), 3 November 1800; "For Bristol," *Commercial Advertiser* (New York, NY), 15 September 1801. Doty served as secretary for the New Bedford Democratic-Republican Committee; see "New-Bedford Dissent," *Weekly Eastern Argus* (Portland, ME), 15 September 1808; "The Spirit of '76," *Albany Register* (NY), 16 September 1808. This Elihu Doty is not to be confused with the American Chinese missionary of the same name (b. 1809). See Doty, *Doty-Doten Family*, 108–11.

66. Jefferson, *Jefferson's Scrapbooks*, 59–60; William Ray to Thomas Jefferson, 7 March 1809, FO, https://founders.archives.gov/documents/Jefferson/03-01-02-0020. No reply was forthcoming from Jefferson. Jefferson's previous letter to Ray, expressing satisfaction with a volume of his poetry, is dated 14 December 1808.

67. My analysis of Jefferson's scrapbooks, the full contents of which are listed in appendix 2 of Jefferson, *Jefferson's Scrapbooks*, found that the identity of five Federalist songwriters and four Republican songwriters were readily traceable. This tally is restricted to contributors from the United States whose political identities could have been determined relatively easily at the time and to entries that could be specifically identified as songs—not poems—by way of a suggested melody or tune, an indicated chorus section, or some other clearly stated directive (such as if the title of the piece

includes the word "song"). Federalist songwriters named in Jefferson's scrapbooks include R[obert]. T[reat]. Paine Jr. ("Song for July 4th, 1805"), T[homas] G[reen] Fessenden ("Soldier's Song"), Henry Mellen ("The Embargo.–A Song"), Mr. Blauvelt ("An Ode . . ."), and Jack Ratline, the penname of Lemuel Hopkins ("A Tickler for Timothy! A New Song"). Republican songwriters include Elihu Doty ("Ode to Liberty"), William Ray ("Patriotic Song"), C[harles] P[inckney] Sumner ("Mid Tears Which Freedom Loves to Shed"), and Benjamin Gleason ("Ode"). Jefferson also included a song by Thomas Paine ("The Land of Love and Liberty"), which was originally published back in 1776. Robert Treat Paine Jr.'s earlier composition "Adams and Liberty" is also included in Jefferson's scrapbook, but Paine's name is not attributed to it. See Jefferson, *Jefferson's Scrapbooks*, appendix 2. On Sumner's transition into an outspoken supporter of Jeffersonian Republicans, see Anne-Marie Taylor, *Young Charles Sumner*, 21–22. On Gleason's partisan affiliation, see Resch, *Suffering Soldiers*, 69. On the partisan affiliation of Mr. Blauvelt, see *Centinel of Freedom* (Newark, NJ), 18 November 1800.

68. This characterization of Jefferson's relationship to music resonates with Annette Gordon-Reed and Peter S. Onuf's conclusion that "Jefferson's passion for music, song, poetry, and language itself took a profound, democratic, vernacular turn, enabling him to imagine the nation in affective and sensual terms." See Gordon-Reed and Onuf, *Most Blessed of the Patriarchs*, 233.

69. Isaiah Thomas, signed cover page of the Isaiah Thomas Broadside Ballads Project, AAS. Quote reproduced in Schrader, "Broadside Ballads of Boston," 70. For a digitized version, see https://www.americanantiquarian.org/proceedings/44539422.pdf.

70. "The People's Friend," LLSMC. For evidence of Rembrandt Peale's authorship of the lyrics, see Charles Willson Peale to Thomas Jefferson, 8 March 1801, FO, https://founders.archives.gov/documents/Jefferson/01-33-02-0178; "Jefferson's March," LLSMC. On Peter S. Du Ponceau's authorship, see Philippe De Létombe to Thomas Jefferson, 28 February 1801, FO, https://founders.archives.gov/documents/Jefferson/01-33-02-0085; Peale to Jefferson, 8 March 1801.

71. Jeffersonian Republicans had a comparably greater trust in American citizens to operate sensibly in a democracy than Federalists did. Jefferson himself did believe in the existence of a "natural aristocracy" distinguishable by "virtue and talent" rather than "wealth and birth," but he also believed American citizens could tell the difference on their own and would cast their votes accordingly. See Thomas Jefferson to John Adams, 28 October 1813, FO, https://founders.archives.gov/documents/Jefferson/03-06-02-0446.

72. "Symptoms of Derangement," *Berkshire Reporter* (Pittsfield, MA), 25 April 1807.

73. Francis Scott Key to John Randolph, 14 May 1813, John Eager Howard Papers, MdHS.

74. Francis Scott Key to John Randolph, 26 February 1814, John Eager Howard Papers, MdHS.

75. Key to Randolph, 14 May 1813. For detail on Key's support for the War of 1812, see Dubovoy, *Lost World of Francis Scott Key*, chap. 6.

76. Francis Scott Key to John Randolph, 13 November 1814, John Eager Howard Papers, MdHS.

77. Key to Randolph, 13 November 1814. On the experience of southern Federalists during the War of 1812, see Broussard, *Southern Federalists*, 139–73.

78. [Key], "Star-Spangled Banner."

79. [Robert Treat Paine Jr.], "Adams and Liberty," 211–18.

80. "Jefferson and Liberty," in [Duane], *American Republican Harmonist*, 30; "Jefferson's Election," in J. Wilson, *National Song Book*, 88. For Fourth of July odes using "To Anacreon in Heaven," see "New Song sung at the celebration of the 4th of July, at Saratoga and Waterford, N.Y. By William Foster" and "Song [for the Fourth of July, 1803]," in [Duane], *American Republican Harmonist*, 7; "For the Fourth of July" and "The Fourth of July," in J. Wilson, *National Song-Book*, 86–87. A noncomprehensive list of songs published to the tune of "To Anacreon in Heaven" in the United States before 1814 can be found in Sonneck, *Star-Spangled Banner*, 25–26.

81. For an analysis of the partisan application of similar melodies (or parodies of entire songs), see Wood, "Join with Heart and Soul and Voice," 1107–13; Goodman, "Transatlantic Contrafacta."

82. [Key], "Star Spangled Banner."

83. Tevis, "Julia Anne Hieronymus Tevis," 76–77.

84. Key's presidential appointment was initially reported in the *Daily National Intelligencer* (Washington, DC) and widely copied thereafter; see, for example, "Yazoo Claims," *Boston Commercial Gazette*, 2 February 1815.

85. On the Federalist response to the Baltimore Massacre, see Broussard, *Southern Federalists*, 156–57. For Francis Scott Key's personal denunciation of the "party spirit" that had fueled the Baltimore anti-Federalist riots, see Dubovoy, *Lost World of Francis Scott Key*, 160. On John Hopper Nicholson's role in the initial distribution of "The Star-Spangled Banner," see Muller, *Star-Spangled Banner*, 25; Filby and Howard, *Star Spangled Books*, 18–19.

86. [Key], *Defence of Fort McHenry*. On the first printing of "The Star-Spangled Banner" to name Key as its author, see Filby and Howard, *Star Spangled Books*, 113–14.

87. For two useful discussions relating to the Republican use of songs during the War of 1812, see Eustace, *1812*, 50–56, 81–85, 233–34; Clark, *American Idea of England*, 100–108.

88. Whitman, *Address*, 19–20.

89. This is not to suggest that "The Star-Spangled Banner" is now or has always been interpreted as a straightforwardly patriotic and unifying anthem. For an account of how meanings of the song evolved over time, see Ferris, *Star-Spangled Banner*.

90. Key, *Poems of the Late Francis S. Key*, 198. The date and location of this speech is unspecified. Dubovoy's investigations suggest it took place in 1834 in Frederick, Maryland, and that the report of the event published by Taney was sourced from a now lost edition of the *Political Examiner and Public Advertiser* (Frederick-Town, MD). See Dubovoy, *Lost World of Francis Scott Key*, 575.

Chapter Two

1. Joel B. Sutherland to John K. Kane, 15 December 1822, MFSSR; Daniel Groves to John K. Kane, 22 December 1822, MFSSR.

2. *Philadelphia Democratic Press* copied in the *Alexandria Herald* (VA), 1 January 1823.

3. "Music," *National Advocate* (New York, NY), 27 December 1822.

4. William Lehman to John K. Kane, 9 December 1822, MFSSR.

5. Daniel Groves to John K. Kane, 14 December 1822, MFSSR.

6. Examples of this literature include Butterfield, *Tocqueville's America*; Roney, *Governed by a Spirit of Opposition*; Haulman, "Rods and Reels"; Shields, *Civil Tongues and Polite Letters*; Koschnik, *Common Interest*; Neem, *Nation of Joiners*; P. Hall, *Organization of American Culture*; Schreiber, "Bluebloods and Local Societies"; Foletta, *Coming to Terms with Democracy*; Crow, "Age of Promise." Levine's *Highbrow/Lowbrow* makes the most detailed use of musical organizations but unlike the other sources just referenced is only tangentially interested in the politicization of civic life. His claim that a bifurcation of high and low culture occurred in the United States during the nineteenth century is largely attested to in this chapter, as are the numerous critiques of his work demonstrating that a high/low culture divide began to take shape earlier than Levine's narrative tends to suggest. See, for example, Neem, *Nation of Joiners*, 225n1; Broyles, *Music of the Highest Class*, 2–3.

7. See, for instance, Broyles, *Music of the Highest Class*; Dimaggio, "Cultural Entrepreneurship"; Preston, *Opera on the Road*; Spitzer, *American Orchestras in the Nineteenth Century*; Butler, *Votaries of Apollo*; N. Newman, *Good Music for a Free People*; Ahlquist, *Democracy at the Opera*; Cavicchi, *Listening and Longing*; Potter, *Food for Apollo*.

8. The civic aspirations of early American artistic organizations working in media other than music are comparatively well recognized. On visual art, for example, see Lyons, *William Dunlap and the Construction of an American Art History*; Rebora, "American Academy of the Fine Arts"; Bellion, *Citizen Spectator*, esp. chap. 3; Miller, *Patrons and Patriotism*; Schreiber, "Philadelphia Elite"; Schreiber, "Academy"; Lovell, *Art in a Season of Revolution*; Harris, *Artist in American Society*; Brigham, *Public Culture in the Early Republic*. On theater, see Nathans, *Early American Theatre*; Nathans, "Forging a Powerful Engine." On sporting clubs and theater associations, see K. Cohen, *They Will Have Their Game*, esp. chap. 3. On literary clubs and culture, see Shields, *Civil Tongues and Polite Letters*; Roche, "Uranian Society"; Koschnik, *Common Interest*, chap. 4; Yankaskas, "Borrowing Culture"; McHenry, *Forgotten Readers*, chap. 1; Kelley, *Learning to Stand and Speak*, chap. 4; Dowling, *Literary Federalism*. An important musicological study that places the roots of the moral-uplift component of musical education far earlier than the nineteenth century is Goodman, "Tears I Shed."

9. "Musical Societies," *Euterpeiad, or Musical Intelligencer* (Boston, MA), 22 June 1822.

10. "Prospectus of the Euterpeiad," *Weekly Visitor, and Ladies Museum* (Boston, MA), 27 May 1820.

11. "Musical Information.–Musical Societies," *Lyre, or New-York Musical Journal* (New York, NY), 1 June 1824.

12. Even though individual music publications did tend to suffer from low patronage and often succumbed to short life spans as a result, American music journalism flourished over the course of the antebellum period in aggregate terms: between 1820 and 1860 a total of twenty-nine publications specializing in music were published in

the United States. See Hooker, "Creation of American Music Culture," 109. Notably, editors of musical publications often championed the unifying cross-sectional appeal of their work. For example, in a printed reply to a North Carolinian postmaster who had claimed not to be offended by antislavery music published in Boston's *Musical Visitor*, its editor, H. W. Day, explained that even though it is not the paper's "object to discuss . . . the question of Slavery, *pro or con*," he hoped all Southern readers would similarly judge music on its merits as opposed to its politics; see [Day], "No Offence," *Musical Visitor* (Boston, MA), 14 September 1843.

13. *New York American*, 24 February 1825, quoted in Lawrence, *Resonances*, xlii.

14. A useful overview of some of the key individuals and organizations from this chapter considered, more typically, from the perspective of early American music education history is Mark and Gary, *History of American Music Education*, 62–161.

15. See P. Clark, *British Clubs and Societies*, 2.

16. P. Clark, 62, 78–80, 121–22, quote on 118.

17. See Butler, *Votaries of Apollo*, 17–37, 44. Various subscription concert series occurred during the colonial period in urban centers all along the East Coast. For two particularly notable examples of these in Philadelphia, see Gualdo, "To the Philadelphia Merchants"; *Pennsylvania Gazette* (Philadelphia), 12 January 1764 (James Bremner's concert advertisement). Colonial newspaper advertisements constitute most of what is known of these early subscription concerts, and a useful compilation of them is reproduced in Tick and Beaudoin, *Music in the USA*, 41–46.

18. See Krauss, "Influence of the Edinburgh Musical Society," 259–74, esp. 270.

19. Tawa, *Psalm to Symphony*, 26, 28–29. On the Society for Promoting Regular Singing as an organized reform effort, see Chase, *America's Music*, 31–32.

20. See Tawa, *Psalm to Symphony*, 26–27; Byrnside, *Music in Eighteenth Century Georgia*, esp. 59–60; Wilentz, "Shape-Note Singing."

21. On the porousness of religion, entertainment, and politics specifically in relation to early nineteenth-century musical experiences, see Cavicchi, *Listening and Longing*, 61–68. On the continued relevance of singing schools to musical life during the Civil War, see Davis, *Music Along the Rapidan*, 197–98.

22. Peter Oliver quoted in Broyles, *Mavericks and Other Traditions*, 33.

23. The British ancestry of American psalm singing is regularly acknowledged; see Keene, *History of Music Education*, 31–34; Crawford, "Massachusetts Musicians," 583–629.

24. Crawford, *America's Musical Life*, 34.

25. To describe this phenomenon, David S. Shields uses the term "projecting societies," which he borrowed from Daniel DeFoe. See Shields, *Civil Tongues and Polite Letters*, xvi–xvii, 182.

26. Writing schools were public schools that focused on teaching reading, writing, and arithmetic, unlike grammar schools, which focused more on teaching Latin and Greek languages. Colonial Boston had five public schools—three writing schools and two grammar schools. See Seybolt, *Public Schools of Colonial Boston*.

27. Evidence of Webb's life is fragmentary. Despite serving as a selectman, an assessor, and a member of the General Court, there is little to document the notoriety gained from these exploits. Webb's obituary, after listing the preceding achievements

and noting his beginnings as a teacher, claimed, "His conversation was rich with reminiscences of the times of Hancock and Adams and their compeers." See "The Venerable Nathan Webb," *Boston Evening Transcript*, 1 March 1853. On his term in the Legislature, see Commonwealth of Massachusetts, *Resolves of the General Court*, 4. A portrait cameo of Nathan Webb cut by Peter Stephenson (1823–ca. 1860) is owned by the AAS, which provides a short biography of Webb based on his obituary. See "Nathan Webb (1767–1853), c. 1847," Portraits at the American Antiquarian Society, AAS, http://www.americanantiquarian.org/Inventories/Portraits/139.htm.

28. Nathan Webb, Diary, 20 November 1788, MHS.

29. Webb, Diary, 10 December 1788.

30. In the seven-week period between 10 November and 28 December 1788, Webb references his participation in these two music-related activities eleven times, which equates to a substantially greater number than had previously been the case. See Webb, Diary, 10 November to 28 December 1788.

31. Webb, Diary, 27 January 1789.

32. Webb, Diary, 12 February 1789, 27 February 1789.

33. Webb, Diary, 24 March 1789.

34. Webb, Diary, 10 March 1789, 24 March 1789, 30 March 1789, 31 March 1789.

35. Webb, Diary, 4 July 1789.

36. "Ode to Columbia's Favourite Son," *Massachusetts Magazine* (Boston, MA), October 1789.

37. "For Public Ornament: This Day," *Boston Gazette* (MA), 26 October 1789. The Stone Chapel in Boston was also known as the King's Chapel.

38. Newspaper reports from the next day do not mention exactly which pieces were played at the concert. See "Boston, Wednesday, Oct 28, 1789," *Massachusetts Centinel*, 28 October 1789, quoted in Smither, *Oratorio in the Classical Era*, 237.

39. The Savannah Musical Society operated ca. 1809–10; see "Savannah Musical Society," *Savannah Republican* (GA), 16 September 1809; "Musical Society," *Savannah Republican*, 1 February 1810. And from 1794, Charleston, South Carolina, could boast of two high-class concert associations once the St. Cecilia Society was joined by the Harmonic Society, which was reputed to put on European-quality performances of Haydn, Mozart, and Gluck, among others. See Ogasapian, *Music of the Colonial and Revolutionary Era*, 168.

40. Contemporary source quoted in Kromkowski, *Recreating the American Republic*, 362. By 1823, the number of musical societies in New Hampshire had purportedly risen to thirty-five; see Farmer and Moore, *Gazetteer of the State of New-Hampshire*, 40. By January 1825, New Hampshire had incorporated at least three more musical societies: the Martin Luther Sacred Music Society, the Northfield Sacred Music Society, and the Wentworth Instrumental Music Band, see "Incorporated Musical Societies," *Western Recorder* (Utica, NY), 25 January 1825.

41. "Musical Society," *Genius of Liberty* (Morristown, NJ), 5 February 1801.

42. Whitman, *Address*, 6.

43. "Communication," *Dartmouth Gazette* (Hanover, NH), 22 August 1810; "Musical Exhibition," *New Hampshire Patriot and State Gazette* (Concord, NH), 25 September 1810.

44. See, for instance, Musical Society at the Castle-Tavern in Pater-Noster Row, *Bylaws*; and [Royal Society of Musicians], *Laws for the Management and Appropriation of the Fund*. On similarities of the rules, constitutions, and structures adopted by all variety of associations in the early republic, see Butterfield, *Tocqueville's America*, 103–10. For evidence of a model constitution and bylaws shared to facilitate the creation of more sacred-music organizations, see [H. W. Day], "Formation of Musical Societies," *Musical Visitor*, 1 March 1843.

45. Early American textbooks and schooling, which similarly aimed to create a better public by shaping better orators and audiences, offer a fruitful comparison to musical organizations engaged in this process of republican refinement. See Eastman, *Nation of Speechifiers*; Cmiel, *Democratic Eloquence*; Fliegelman, *Declaring Independence*.

46. Solomon Livermore, *Practice of Music*, 11. Livermore was himself a Harvard-educated Federalist lawyer, noted for arguing in support of the need for Federalists to engage in partisan contests; see Fischer, *Revolution of American Conservatism*, 235–36.

47. Solomon Livermore, *Practice of Music*, 12.

48. Emerson, *Discourse on Music*, 11–12.

49. "Communication," *City Gazette* (Charleston, SC), 5 April 1819; Farmer, *Address*, 4.

50. Farmer, *Address*, 9.

51. "Extracts from an Address Delivered before the Psallonian Society," *Euterpeiad, or Musical Intelligencer*, 11 May 1822.

52. *Cincinnati Daily Gazette*, 28 April 1835; "Mr. Hammond," *Cincinnati Daily Gazette*, 19 May 1835.

53. "Hallowell Musical Institute," *Maine Cultivator and Hallowell Gazette*, 16 December 1848.

54. Worcester Mozart Society Constitution, [Worcester] Mozart Society Records of Secretary and Treasurer, 1850–56, with constitution, bylaws, membership lists, minutes of meetings, Worcester Choral Union Records, Octavo Vol. 3, AAS.

55. "On Our Musical Societies," *American Musical Journal* (New York, NY), April 1835.

56. "Musical Societies," *Western Recorder* (Utica, NY), 9 May 1826.

57. Eliot, unaddressed manuscript letter, n.d., Samuel A. Eliot Papers, Box 1, Folder 2, HUA.

58. Handel and Haydn Society, *Constitution*, 4.

59. Handel and Haydn Society, 3.

60. *Columbian Centinel*, 19 April 1816, quoted in Perkins, *History of the Handel and Haydn Society*, 39. According to Michael Broyles, the article quoted, signed "Public Good," was in all likelihood written by a founding member of the Handel and Haydn Society, making it "the most authentic and detailed statement of purpose that we have from the original meeting." See Broyles, *Music of the Highest Class*, 145. Initially, nine Boston congregations supplied singers to the Handel and Haydn Society: Brattle Street, Old South, Trinity, Hanover Street, Hollis Street, Federal Street, West Church, Chauncey Street, and Park Street. See Perkins, *History of the Handel and Haydn Society*, 39n2.

61. Perkins, *History of the Handel and Haydn Society*, 40.

62. See Broyles, *Music of the Highest Class*, 141, 351n48; Johnson, *Hallelujah, Amen!*, 34. The elevated self-perception of the society is also revealed by its attempt to commission Ludwig van Beethoven to compose an oratorio for it in 1823. Beethoven considered the request and thought it a flattering indication of his global reputation; but it is unclear if an agreement was ever reached, and the piece was never produced. See Johnson, *Hallelujah, Amen!*, 47–48.

63. For one example of a fledging musical society in Wilmington, Delaware, choosing to use the Handel and Haydn Society's collection, see Phoebe George Bradford, Diary, 19 February 1834, Phoebe George Bradford Diaries, MdHS.

64. See Broyles, *Music of the Highest Class*, 167, 329; Gac, *Singing for Freedom*, 88. For contemporary currency-value conversion, see Williamson, "Seven Ways to Compute."

65. Lowell Mason to John Rowe Parker, 20 June 1821, Mason/Yale.

66. Lowell Mason to W. W. Killip, 9 December 1861, Mason/Yale.

67. For a similar account of Federalist influence over civic association, see Neem, *Nation of Joiners*, esp. 117; Koschnik, *Common Interest*; Foletta, *Coming to Terms with Democracy*, esp. chap. 6.

68. "Act to Incorporate Musical Fund Society of Philadelphia," in [Musical Fund Society of Philadelphia], *Charter and By-Laws*, 5.

69. See [Royal Society of Musicians], *Laws for the Management and Appropriation of the Fund*; "Advertisement" in [New Musical Fund], *Songs, Chorusses, &c.*

70. Musical Fund Society of Philadelphia, *Constitution*, 13–14. An annotated copy, which indicates an intention to change the title of this document from "Constitution" to "By-Laws" can be found in Box 1, MFSR. On the decision to annually elect two physicians to the board, see Joint Board of Officers, special meeting, 19 April 1820, Box 3, MFSR.

71. Musical Fund Society of Philadelphia, *Constitution*, 7, quote on 13. Although both professional and amateur members were charged the same five-dollar annual fee, it was possible for professional members to purchase lifetime memberships for fifty dollars whereas amateur member lifetime memberships only cost twenty-five dollars.

72. Four of the six Federalist delegates in this race were Musical Fund Society members: William Lehman (elected a member of the Musical Fund on 7 May 1821), John M. Read (elected a member of the Musical Fund on 15 November 1820), John K. Kane (elected a member of the Musical Fund on 29 February 1820), and William M. Meredith (elected a member of the Musical Fund on 5 June 1820). See "Pennsylvania 1824 State Assembly, Philadelphia County, Philadelphia City," NNV, http://elections.lib.tufts.edu/catalog/tufts:pa.assembly.philadelphiacity.1824; [Musical Fund Society of Philadelphia], *Act of Incorporation*, 31–35; *National Gazette* (Philadelphia, PA), 12 October 1824.

73. *National Gazette*, 12 October 1824.

74. Schreiber, "Bluebloods and Local Societies," esp. 266.

75. For an investigation into the Federalist leanings of this group of civic associations in Philadelphia, the place of the Musical Fund Society of Philadelphia within it, and the social interconnectedness of its leadership, see Schreiber, "Bluebloods and Local Societies," esp. 265–66. On the Federalist influence over these types of early American civic associations more broadly in Philadelphia, see Koschnik, *Common Interest*, esp. chap. 5.

76. See Koschnik, *Common Interest*, 186–88.

77. Kane, *Autobiography*, 64.

78. Kane, 64–65.

79. Robert M. Patterson [for John K. Kane], n.d. and incomplete, Robert M. (Maskell) Patterson Papers, APS.

80. Patterson was the second president of the Musical Fund and held this position from 1838 to 1853. He was founding vice president from 1820 to 1829 and elected to this office again in 1836–38. See [Musical Fund Society of Philadelphia], *Charter and By-Laws*, 25.

81. Robert M. Patterson [for John K. Kane], n.d., Robert M. (Maskell) Patterson Papers, APS.

82. Kane, *Autobiography*, 63.

83. Other leading Philadelphia musicians appointed as founding managers or directors of music include Raynor Taylor, P. Gilles, and George Schetky. See Musical Fund Society of Philadelphia Minutes, special meeting, 29 February 1820, MFSR. Raynor Taylor's first name is often spelled "Rayner."

84. Benjamin Carr to John Rowe Parker, 7 December 1821, JRPC. Carr was also generally sympathetic to Federalist ideals; see Riordan, "Oh Dear What Can the Matter Be?," 207, 220, 227.

85. Quotes from Benjamin Carr to John Rowe Parker, 4 October 1821, JRPC. See also Benjamin Carr to John Rowe Parker, 7 December 1821, JRPC.

86. "Musical Fund Society of Philadelphia," *Euterpeiad, or Musical Intelligencer*, 5 January 1821 [1822]. The issue is mistakenly dated 1821 but was actually the first number to be published in January 1822.

87. Neem, *Nation of Joiners*, 4.

88. Pennsylvania General Assembly, *Act*. For discussion surrounding Pennsylvania's general incorporation act, see Butterfield, *Tocqueville's America*, 70, 80–85.

89. For an overview of the *Dartmouth* decision specifically as it relates to early national civic associations, see Neem, *Nation of Joiners*, 68–80.

90. See Neem, 78.

91. "Music," *National Advocate*, 20 February 1823. At this time, to charter an organization, one had to prove specifically that its objects were of public utility in order to justify the special privileges of incorporation. See Neem, *Nation of Joiners*, esp. 18–20.

92. See esp. "Music," *National Advocate*, 27 December 1822.

93. Joel B. Sutherland to John K. Kane, 15 December 1822, MFSSR.

94. Quote from Kane, *Autobiography*, 63.

95. Nineteenth-century contemporary quoted in Broyles, "Bourgeois Appropriation of Music," 233.

96. P. Clark, *British Clubs and Societies*, 11, 121.

97. P. Clark, 11.

98. Boston Academy of Music, *First Annual Report*, 5.

99. Broyles, *Music of the Highest Class*, 186.

100. The names of these nine members were Joseph Brown, Abel W. Bruce, Jonas Chickering, L. S. Cragen, Bela Hunting, Lowell Mason, George Pollock, George James Webb, and Increase S. Withington. See Broyles, 190, 355n17.

101. Boston Academy of Music, *Second Annual Report*, 3.
102. Boston Academy of Music, 4–5.
103. Boston Academy of Music, 14–15.
104. Boston Academy of Music, 16–17.
105. Mason, *Manual of the Boston Academy of Music*. The German work that Mason drew from was Kubler, *Anleitung zum Gesang-Unterrichte in Schulen* [Guide to the study of singing in schools]. See Ellis, "Lowell Mason"; Pemberton, "Manual of the Boston Academy of Music."
106. "Act to Incorporate the Boston Academy of Music," in Commonwealth of Massachusetts, *General Laws Passed by the General Court of Massachusetts*, 812.
107. Broyles, *Music of the Highest Class*, 174, 187–88.
108. Eliot's European tour took place around 1821–24. A brief selection of cities visited includes Paris, Rome, London, and Dresden. Letters from his tour are in the Samuel A. Eliot Papers, HUA. Broyles's consultation of these letters similarly found no mention of music in them; see Broyles, *Music of the Highest Class*, 188.
109. In 1846, Eliot's net wealth was reported to be $300,000, whereas 1847 tax records indicate that Mason's combined net wealth in 1847 was $41,000. By comparison, the third-wealthiest musician in Boston in 1847, George J. Webb, had a net wealth of $5,500. See Broyles, *Music of the Highest Class*, 186, 189.
110. Two $100 donations came from companies rather than individuals. See Broyles, 188–90.
111. See Broyles, 174–76, 190; Broyles, "Music and Class Structure," esp. 462–65.
112. Broyles, "Music and Class Structure," 464.
113. The signatories were Harrison Gray Otis, Nathan Appleton, Josiah Quincy, William H. Eliot, William H. Prescott, William Sullivan, John C. Warren, Patrick Tracy Jackson, and Israel Thorndike Jr.; see Broyles, 462n36. All these individuals were either prominent Federalists, part of the loosely organized set of elite investors known as the Boston Associates, or both: Otis and Sullivan were especially well-known Federalists and were chosen as commissioners to report the proposals of the Hartford Convention to the federal government; Quincy was a five-term Federalist mayor of Boston; Israel Thorndike ran as a Federalist candidate for the Massachusetts Senate in 1809 and had family connections to Boston Associates, as Appleton and Jackson did; William H. Prescott was a historian and prominent New England Federalist intellectual. See Peart, *Era of Experimentation*, chap. 1; J. Banner, *To the Hartford Convention*, 316–47; Foletta, *Coming to Terms with Democracy*, 47; "Massachusetts 1809 State Senate, Essex County, 1809," NNV, http://elections.lib.tufts.edu/catalog/tufts:ma.senator.essex.1809; Dalzell, *Enterprising Elite*, esp. chaps. 5 and 6.
114. Broyles, *Music of the Highest Class*, 190.
115. "Circular" (1826) quoted in Broyles, "Music and Class Structure," 462.
116. Broyles, *Music of the Highest Class*, 190.
117. See Livermore, *Twilight of Federalism*.
118. See Neem, *Nation of Joiners*, 81–85; Ryan, *Cradle of the Middle Class*, chap. 3; Blumin, *Emergence of the Middle Class*, 192–206, esp. 195.
119. Neem, *Nation of Joiners*.

120. "Eliot, Samuel Atkins (1798-1862)," in US Congress, *Biographical Dictionary of the United States Congress*.

121. For evidence of Eliot's partisan transition, see his National Republican-sponsored nomination for alderman in 1833, followed by his direction of a Whig Party Fourth of July celebration in 1834. "City Election," *Boston Traveler*, 13 December 1833; "Fourth of July," *Boston Traveler*, 8 July 1834. This was a typical transition for a New England Federalist; see Howe, *What Hath God Wrought*, 275-76.

122. [Eliot], "Annual Reports," 325-26. This article was published anonymously but drafts of it in Eliot's hand are located in the Samuel A. Eliot Papers, HUA. See Broyles, *Music of the Highest Class*, 204.

123. [Eliot], "Annual Reports," 325-26.

124. [Eliot], 326.

125. [Eliot], 330.

126. See Howe, "Evangelical Movement"; L. Banner, "Religious Benevolence," 23-41, esp. 31-34.

127. Broyles, "Music and Class Structure," 467-68.

128. See B. Wilson, "Documentary History," 1:60-63.

129. A copy of the full report can be found in B. Wilson, 2:109-29. Excerpts of the report as well as a sense of its continuing significance can be found via its inclusion in Tick and Beaudoin, *Music in the USA*, 139-44. Contemporary newspapers also reprinted direct excerpts from the report; see "Music in Our Public Schools," *Public Ledger* (Philadelphia, PA), 2 October 1837; "Music in Our Public Schools," *Hampshire Gazette* (Northampton, MA), 13 September 1837. The wide dissemination of the report was no accident: the School Committee initially tabled the report until three hundred copies of it could be printed. See B. Wilson, 1:66.

130. See "Excerpts from minutes of a meeting of the School Committee, 19 September 1837," in B. Wilson, "Documentary History," 2:129-30.

131. "Excerpts from minutes of a meeting of the Board of Aldermen, 25 September 1837," in B. Wilson, 2:130; "Excerpts from minutes of a meeting of the Board of Aldermen, 9 October 1837," in B. Wilson, 2:131. See also "Municipal," *Saturday Morning Transcript* (Boston, MA), 23 September 1837.

132. See "Excerpts from minutes of a meeting of the Board of Aldermen, 9 October 1837," in B. Wilson, "Documentary History," 2:131.

133. *Daily Advertiser and Patriot* (Boston, MA), 3 October 1837, in B. Wilson, 2:209-10.

134. Hale's criticism elicited five direct responses, all of which opposed his point of view (two of which Hale published himself). See *Daily Advertiser and Patriot*, 4 October 1837, in B. Wilson, 2:211-12; Alcott, "Music in Common Schools," 521-22; *Daily Evening Transcript* (Boston, MA), 15 November 1837 in B. Wilson, 2:213; *Daily Advertiser and Patriot*, 16 November 1837, in B. Wilson, 2:213-14; "Music in Schools," *American Annals of Education and Instruction*, Vol. 8, 1838, 32-34, in B. Wilson, 2:215-16. Hale's original criticism from the *Daily Advertiser* was reprinted two days later in "Music in Common Schools," *Weekly Messenger* (Boston, MA), 5 October 1837. More broadly, however, exhaustive keyword searches of Readex's American Historical Newspapers

database return not a single article that takes serious issue with the idea of introducing music into public schools, the closest being a satirical piece that sends up the "earnestness" with which Bostonians discussed the topic: *New York Gazette* (original), reprinted in "Yankee Doodle," *Gloucester Telegraph* (MA), 14 October 1837. By contrast, a multiplicity of articles expressed support for the teaching of music in public schools in general or in Boston's public schools in particular: "Music in Our Public Schools," *Public Ledger*, 2 October 1837; "Music in Our Public Schools," *Hampshire Gazette*, 13 September 1837; "Music in Schools," *Hampshire Gazette*, 21 November 1838; "Vocal Music," *Portland Weekly Advertiser* (ME), 18 September 1838; "Vocal Music in Schools," *Portland Weekly Advertiser*, 14 November 1837; "Facts for the Consideration of the Citizens of Cincinnati," *Cincinnati Daily Gazette*, 21 February 1837; "Report on Music," *Portsmouth Journal of Literature and Politics* (NH), 7 October 1837; "Columbia College," *Evening Post* (New York, NY), 29 December 1837; "Our Public Schools," *New-Bedford Mercury* (MA), 6 Jan. 1837; "Vocal Music in Schools," *Nantucket Inquirer* (MA), 12 September 1838.

135. For examples of such interpretations, see B. Wilson, "Documentary History," 1:67; Pemberton, "Critical Days," 69–82.

136. In colonial and early national America, prejudice against music in church and in public life was indeed prevalent. And though this position was largely outdated by the late 1830s, the period of its ascendancy would have been within the living memory of many people. As Hale's position suggests, its legacy was still influential. For a discussion of American debates over sacred music reform in colonial and Federal periods, see Broyles, *Music of the Highest Class*, chap. 2.

137. "Excerpt from minutes of a meeting of the Board of Aldermen, 9 October 1837," in B. Wilson, "Documentary History," 2:131.

138. Between 1822 (when the city of Boston was incorporated) and 1827, the city government in Boston spent an average of $68,343.36 per annum on its public schools, and these figures gradually increased to reach an average expenditure of $153,690.55 between 1840 and 1845; see [Eliot], "Public and Private Charities," 137. On the amount requested for the academy's experiment to put music in public schools, consider too that a similar request made in 1838 asked for "not more than $120 per annum for every school into which it [music] may be introduced." See "Excerpts from minutes of a meeting of the School Committee, 28 August 1838," in B. Wilson, "Documentary History," 2:139.

139. See "Excerpt from minutes of the quarterly meeting of the School Committee, 14 November 1837," in B. Wilson, "Documentary History," 2:131–32; Pemberton, "Critical Days," 72–73.

140. See *Daily Advertiser and Patriot*, 16 November 1837, in B. Wilson, "Documentary History," 2:213–14; B. Wilson, 1:68–69.

141. "Excerpt from minutes of a meeting of the School Committee, 9 January 1838," in B. Wilson, 2:132.

142. See Kaestle and Vinovskis, *Education and Social Change*, esp. 210; Neem, *Nation of Joiners*, 136–37. For a more positive interpretation of antebellum education reformers more generally, see Neem, *Democracy's Schools*, esp. chaps. 3 and 5. On the broader relationship between schools, education, and politics in the early national

period, see Beadie, *Education and the Creation of Capital*, part 2. The foundational text on tax-supported "common schools" remains Kaestle's *Pillars of the Republic*.

143. Mann, "Report on Public Schools," *Springfield Republican* (MA), 20 January 1845.

144. See, for example, "Boston Academy of Music," *Boston Recorder*, 3 September 1846.

145. [Eliot], "Public and Private Charities," 155–56.

146. [Eliot], 155.

147. [Eliot], 136, 154.

Chapter Three

1. George Templeton Strong, Diary, 12 March 1840, in Lawrence, *Resonances*, 68.

2. "Grand Vocal Concert" and "Concert at Niblo's," *Commercial Advertiser* (New York, NY), 10 March 1840. There are two mentions of Russell's intention to sing the Great National Whig Song at the 12 March show at Niblo's in this paper: the first is in an editorial note on page 2, and the second appears to be a paid advertisement on page 3. A further advertisement in the *Commercial Advertiser* on 12 March includes a full print of the show's intended program, which indicates that "The National Whig Song" would close part 1 of the two-part show. See also "Concert at Niblo's," *Spectator* (New York, NY), 12 March 1840. The title of the song varied and can be found referred to in a range of slightly different permutations. One of the earlier printings of the tune simply referred to it as a "Whig Song" to the tune of "Fine Old English Gentleman" by William Hayden, Esq., "sung at a meeting of the Roxbury Whig Association, on New Year's Day. See "Poetry," *National Aegis* (Worcester, MA), 12 February 1840.

3. Strong, Diary, 12 March 1840, in Lawrence, *Resonances*, 68–69. It may be possible to misread the final line of this transcription as an attempt at blackface dialect. However, this is more likely the phonetic depiction of a melody line that Strong could not remember the words to. The melody Russell used to sing this song was "The Marseillaise," even though it was more common for other performers to sing it to the tune to which its composer, William Hayden, originally prescribed it: "A Fine English Gentleman." Both tunes were already popular staples of Russell's regular repertoire. See esp. *Connecticut Courant* (Hartford), 7 March 1840. See also "National Whig Song," in *The Log Cabin and Hard Cider Melodies*, 37–38; "Mr. H. Russell," *Commercial Advertiser*, 12 March 1840; Lawrence, *Resonances*, 28–29, 67–69.

4. "Triumph of Locofocoism," *Newark Daily Advertiser* (NJ), 19 March 1840, with copy attributed to the *New York Courier and Enquirer*; "Postponement of Mr. Russell's Concert," *Commercial Advertiser*, 18 March 1840. On Russell in the United States and his repertoire, much of which was popular sentimental fare of his own composition, see Stevens, "Henry Russell in America."

5. *New York Evening Post*, 19 March 1840.

6. See "Postponement of Mr. Russell's Concert," *Commercial Advertiser*, 18 March 1840; "Triumph of Locofocoism," *Newark Daily Advertiser*, 19 March 1840, with copy attributed to the *New York Courier and Enquirer*; *New York Evening Post*, 19 March 1840; Lawrence, *Resonances*, 69.

7. "Triumph of Locofocoism," *Newark Daily Advertiser*, 19 March 1840, with copy attributed to the *New York Courier and Enquirer*.

8. *New York Evening Post*, 19 March 1840.

9. *Alexandria Gazette* (VA), 19 March 1840.

10. "Items," *North American* (Philadelphia, PA), 16 March 1840.

11. "The National Whig Song and Mr. Russell," *Ohio State Journal* (Columbus, OH), 25 March 1840, with copy attributed to the *New York Express*.

12. *Connecticut Courant*, 7 March 1840.

13. "Russell's Whig Concert," *Gloucester Telegraph* (MA), 18 November 1840, with copy attributed to the *Boston Transcript*.

14. [H. Theodore Hach], "Concerts," *Musical Magazine* (Boston, MA), 21 November 1840.

15. Emblematic contributions to this literature include Altschuler and Blumin, *Rude Republic*; Silbey, *American Political Nation*; W. Gienapp, "Politics Seem to Enter into Everything"; Baker, *Affairs of Party*; Neely, *Boundaries of American Political Culture*; Altschuler and Blumin et al., "Political Engagement and Disengagement." Helpful recent additions include Grinspan's *Virgin Vote*; and Cheathem's *Coming of Democracy*. Scholarship specifically on the 1840 election tends to pivot on the question of whether its outcome was a result of hoopla or the electorate's engagement with policy; see esp. Formisano, "New Political History"; Holt, "Election of 1840."

16. On this point, I diverge from Mark Cheathem's recent overview of presidential campaigning between 1828 and 1840, which emphasizes the role of cultural politics in helping political parties win elections specifically through attempts "to lure voters to their side." See Cheathem, *Coming of Democracy*, 2.

17. This interpretation accords with recent arguments that the so-called rise of a popular democracy in the United States was neither neat nor linear and in many localities took place earlier than previously assumed. See Robertson, "Jeffersonian Parties, Politics, and Participation"; Ratcliffe, "Right to Vote"; Pasley, *First Presidential Contest*. For a neater and generally more positive interpretation of democracy's expansion during this period, see Wilentz, *Rise of American Democracy*.

18. Russell, *Popular Music in England*, 18.

19. Russell, 24–26. On how the English experience of music and political culture drew from Continental exchange, see Manz, "Joseph Mainzer." The German musical community during this period was an important exporter of the idea that art music had public utility and that, in turn, the cultivation of public taste was a public good; see Gramit, *Cultivating Music*; Pasler, *Composing the Citizen*, esp. 85. On the circulation of such ideas between the Continent, Britain, and the United States, see Saloman, *Beethoven's Symphonies*. On the Chartist Movement as a transatlantic phenomenon, see Boston, *British Chartists in America*.

20. Russell, *Popular Music in England*, 18. On music in the context of class and reform in Europe more broadly, see Weber, *Music and the Middle Class*. For an account of music as part of the temperance movement in the United States as well as its relatively slower adoption into the antislavery movement, see Gac, *Singing for Freedom*.

21. Carwardine, *Evangelicals and Politics*, 55; Formisano, *Birth of Mass Political Parties*, 133.

22. See, for example, Schoening and Kasper, *Don't Stop Thinking about the Music*, 44–49.

23. Such an explanation similarly tends to overplay the extent to which participatory politics in the Jacksonian era was quantitatively different from what it had been during the Jeffersonian period. See Robertson, "Jeffersonian Parties, Politics, and Participation."

24. Sanjek, *American Popular Music and Its Business*, 39; Kornblith, "Craftsman as Industrialist."

25. See Bushman, *Refinement of America*, chap. 12; Halttunen, *Confidence Men and Painted Women*.

26. This interpretation chimes with recent scholarship concerning the rhetoric and existence of "separate spheres" between public and private life in the Jacksonian and antebellum period. Clear distinctions between public and private may not have existed, but contemporary ideals about their separation did; and this allowed for deliberate and politicized injections of private life into the public and vice versa. See Shire, "Sentimental Racism and Sympathetic Paternalism"; Lasser and Robertson, *Antebellum Women*; Hershberger, "Mobilizing Women, Anticipating Abolition"; Portnoy, *Their Right to Speak*. Older scholarship emphasizing that public and private were gendered concepts, not historical reality, include Kerber, "Separate Spheres"; C. Davidson, "No More Separate Spheres!"; and Kaplan, "Manifest Domesticity."

27. *Baltimore Republican*, 11 December 1839, quoted in Gunderson, *Log Cabin Campaign*, 74–77. See also Holt, *Rise and Fall of the American Whig Party*, 105–21.

28. *Delaware State Journal* (Dover), 17 December 1839, quoted in Bushman, *Refinement of America*, 428.

29. See, for example, Holt, *Rise and Fall of the American Whig Party*, 106.

30. For a good primary-source summation of the Whigs' interpretation of log cabins, hard cider, and champagne, see "Just Definitions," *Nantucket Inquirer* (MA), 15 August 1840, with copy attributed to the *Philadelphia Inquirer*.

31. See, for example, "General Harrison," *Norwich Courier* (CT), 19 February 1840, which favorably attests that "Gen. Harrison is a scholar and a gentlemen—as well as a soldier and statesmen. Few men in the U.S. are better versed in military science and history." See also Bushman, *Refinement of America*, 428.

32. Bushman, *Refinement of America*, 432.

33. On women's participation in the 1840 election more generally, see Zboray and Zboray, "Whig Women, Politics, and Culture in the Campaign of 1840." On the influence of women from the perspective of a music periodical, see "Women's Influence," *Musical Visitor* (Boston, MA), 12 October 1840.

34. Marini, "Hymnody and History," 145.

35. See Carwardine, *Evangelicals and Politics*, chap. 2, esp. 53, 453.

36. This insight builds on research into the sensations and science of music and sound in early America. See esp. Bechtold, "Revolutionary Soundscape"; Wood, "Join with Heart and Soul and Voice."

37. Miles, *Songs, Odes, Glees and Ballads*, 1–9. Similarly, Danny O. Crew's catalogue of presidential sheet music lists 144 pieces of music published with reference to William Henry Harrison, as opposed to just eighteen for Martin Van Buren. Crew's tally

for Van Buren also includes just one songster issued specifically in connection to the 1840 election alongside seven songs related to his 1848 presidential campaign as the nominee of the Free Soil Party. The rest of the pieces listed either relate to his 1836 presidential campaign or could have been broadly intended to celebrate Van Buren outside of a campaigning context (the specific year of publication is not always indicated). The larger tally for Harrison is lessened only by four pieces printed before the 1840 campaign began (in celebration of earlier military exploits), five funeral marches marking his death in office, eight pieces commemorating Harrison's 1840 campaign produced nostalgically in subsequent decades, plus one tune that is clearly a pro-Democrat parody. See Crew, *Presidential Sheet Music*, 424–26, 542–57. Democrats did expand their efforts later but never enough to produce close to an equal amount of campaign songs to the Whigs: in 1844, Democrats published eight songsters to the Whigs' twenty-nine (and one for the Liberty Party); in 1848, Democrats published one to the Whigs' eleven (while three appear for the Free Soil Party). See Miles, *Songs, Odes, Glees and Ballads*, 9–27. These figures underplay the sheer scale of campaign music available at the time, but the partisan ratios they speak to are instructive.

38. Poore, *Reminiscences*, 232. See also Norton, *Great Revolution of 1840*.

39. See, for example, the Democratic *O.K. Songster*, in which the majority of songs—in one way or another—are parodies of Whig singing, such as two separate Democratic versions of "Old Tippecanoe" as well as "Hurrah for Old Tippecanoe" and "The Hero of Tippecanoe"; *The O.K. Songster*, LCP. A characteristic anecdote in this vein involves a Democratic Methodist preacher, John Mathews, who was overheard singing the first line of a Clay song to a child on his lap instead of its "bastardised Democratic version" before deciding to sing a revival tune instead. Mathews's actions were reported, perhaps mistakenly, to his presiding elder, who reprimanded him for having sung a Whig song. See Carwardine, *Evangelicals and Politics*, 119.

40. *Ohio Statesman* (Columbus), 22 April 1840.

41. "Sing-Sing Party," *Albany Argus* (NY), 5 June 1840, copied with attribution from the *New York Evening Post*; "New Auxiliary in the Electioneering Field," *New York Morning Herald*, 20 March 1840. For further references to the newness of music in the 1840 campaign, see "Our Prospects," *Albany Argus*, 26 June 1840, copied with attribution from the *Baltimore Republican*; "New Mode of Disseminating Federal Principles," *Ohio Statesman*, 24 June 1840.

42. "Sing-Sing Party," *Albany Argus*, 5 June 1840. A diapason is a perfect octave interval in Pythagorean tuning.

43. "New Auxiliary in the Electioneering Field," *New York Morning Herald*, 20 March 1840.

44. "Sing-Sing Party," *Albany Argus*, 5 June 1840.

45. "Tippecanoe Minstrelsy," *Madisonian* (Washington, DC), 28 August 1840.

46. Plutarch, *Plutarch's Lives*, 161–62; "Tippecanoe Minstrelsy," *Madisonian*, 28 August 1840. A version of this Plutarch quote appears in the *Madisonian*. It is not word for word, but the similarity is close enough to show that the writer of the column clearly had this particular passage in mind. The quote, as it appears in the paper as far as can be deciphered, is as follows: "The songs of the Spartans, Plutarch tells us 'had a spirit, which could [illegible] the soul and impel it in an enthusiastic manner [illeg-

ible]. They consisted chiefly of the praises of heroes that had died for Sparta, or else of expressions of detestation for such wretches as had declined the glorious opportunity.'"

47. Plutarch, *Plutarch's Lives*, 134.

48. "A New Auxiliary in the Electioneering Field," *New York Morning Herald*, 20 March 1840; "Tippecanoe Minstrelsy," *Madisonian*, 28 August 1840.

49. "Anecdote of the Times," *Centinel of Freedom* (Newark, NJ), 10 November 1840, as attributed to the Pittsburg[h] *Daily American*. Also published in "Anecdote of the Times," *Newark Daily Advertiser*, 5 November 1840. A similar story about a shoemaker being persuaded to support Harrison on account of Whig singing, printed initially in the *Troy Whig*, can be found in "An Incident," *Bellows Falls Gazette* (VT), 27 June 1840. The shoemaker story is disparaged by Democrats in "Going for a Mere Song," *Rhode-Island Republican* (Newport), 24 June 1840.

50. "Political Songs," *Cleveland Daily Herald*, 2 March 1840.

51. "Electioneering Cabinet," *Daily National Intelligencer* (Washington, DC), 26 September 1840.

52. "Electioneering Cabinet," *Daily National Intelligencer*, 26 September 1840; *Albany Evening Journal* (NY), 16 April 1840.

53. *Log Cabin Minstrel*, iii–iv.

54. *Harrison Melodies*, 4.

55. *Harrison Log Cabin Song Book*, n.p.

56. *Log Cabin Minstrel*, iii.

57. *Log Cabin and Hard Cider Melodies*, n.p.

58. *Songs for the People*, 5–6.

59. "Songs for the People," *Centinel of Freedom*, 21 July 1840.

60. "Harrison Melodies," *Nantucket Inquirer*, 22 May 1840.

61. "Popular Whig Music," *Ohio State Journal*, 3 June 1840.

62. It was a common trope for Democrats to complain that their electoral fortunes were the result of "savvy Whig electioneering." See Haynes, *Unfinished Revolution*, esp. 122–26.

63. For detail on Thurlow Weed and Whig Party campaign organization, see Gunderson, "Thurlow Weed's Network."

64. The personal papers of men associated with political campaign management before the end of the Civil War generally do not give any indication that they considered campaign music part of their professional remit. Searches of the Greeley Papers at the Library of Congress and the Greeley Papers at the New York Public Library found no mentions of music beyond sending an assistant to purchase a piece of sheet music; see Horace Greeley to Cassius M. Morey, n.d. [ca. 1862], Horace Greeley Papers, LC. Later, in 1864, there is also no evidence that Lincoln's campaign manager, David Davis, had any hand in musical organization either; see David Davis Papers, CHM.

65. For evidence of both Weed's anti-campaign-music reputation and his denial of it, see Weed, *Life of Thurlow Weed*, 467.

66. Gunderson, *Log Cabin Campaign*, 123.

67. Weed, *Life of Thurlow Weed*, 467; Seitz, *Horace Greeley*, 61.

68. "Log Cabin Song Book," *Log Cabin* (New York, NY), 23 May 1840.

69. Robert Gray Gunderson highlighted one particularly evocative manuscript quote from a letter that Greeley supposedly wrote to Thurlow Weed, stating, "Our songs are doing more good than anything else. . . . Really, I think every song is good for five hundred new subscribers." The quote is in most cases ultimately sourced back to Seitz, *Horace Greeley*, 61, where the quote is given undated and without attribution or reference to its source. It is likely that Seitz sourced the quote from Francis Zabriskie, who also gives no citation for its provenance; see Zabriskie, *Horace Greeley*, 73. When read in the context of the *Log Cabin* itself and Weed's autobiography, the quote reads true enough, though the context surrounding the quote may help show whether it serves to exaggerate Greeley's political investment in the effects of Whig campaign music. For uses of this quote in modern scholarship, see Gunderson, *Log Cabin Campaign*, 123; Miles, *Songs, Odes, Glees and Ballads*, xxvi; Williams, *Horace Greeley*, 53.

70. Howe, *Political Culture of the American Whigs*.

71. Howe, 11–42, esp. 21.

72. See Galbreath, *Alexander Coffman Ross*, 7, 8–9, 13–15. Quotation on 15.

73. Galbreath, 20.

74. For notice of the "Harrison Song by Thomas Power, esq.," see *Harrison Melodies*, 42–43; *Gloucester Telegraph*, 9 May 1840; *New Hampshire Sentinel* (Keene), 22 April 1840; "Whig Harmony," *Nantucket Inquirer*, 25 March 1840; "New Music," *Commercial Advertiser*, 3 April 1840. On Power in Massachusetts masonry, see Gardner and Titus, *Proceedings of the Grand Lodge*, 63. Power is also credited with writing a tune called "Arouse ye, gay comrades," which was dedicated to the officers and members of the Tiger Boat Club; see *Boston Traveler*, 24 January 1840. Reaction to Power's Fourth of July address predictably split along partisan lines. See "Glorious Fourth," *Boston Traveler*, 7 July 1840; "Power's Oration," *Boston Traveler*, 7 August 1840; "Thomas Power, Esq.," *Boston Post* (MA), 4 September 1840.

75. "To the Friends of Harrison," *New-Bedford Mercury*, 6 November 1840.

76. *Tippecanoe Songbook*, 91–92. For notice of the song's use in the young men's Whig Fourth of July service, see "Fourth of July," *Commercial Advertiser*, 2 July 1840; "Obituary," *Philadelphia Inquirer*, 3 June 1881; Wilson and Fiske, *Appleton's Cyclopaedia*, 718.

77. *Harrison Melodies*, 40–41; *Log Cabin and Hard Cider Melodies*, 17–19; *Bellows Falls Gazette*, 25 April 1840; "Whigs—Attention!," *Boston Evening Transcript*, 25 October 1844; "Meeting of the Water Union of Ward 4," 5 September 1845; "Orrin D'Wolf," *Liberator* (Boston, MA), 22 August 1845.

78. For attributions to club members, see *Harrison Melodies*, 22; *Log Cabin Minstrel*, 43, 44.

79. Daniel Mulford to Levi Mulford, 28 January 1809, Daniel Mulford Papers, GHS.

80. Daniel Mulford to Levi Mulford, 6 July 1809, Daniel Mulford Papers, GHS.

81. See *Songs for the People*, 67–68; Griffith, *History of the Town of Carver Massachusetts*, 285–88, 305.

82. See, for example, "For the Telescope," *Christian Telescope and Universalist Miscellany* (Providence, RI), 14 April 1827; "Agents," *Christian Telescope and Universalist Miscellany*, 23 February 1828; "Agents," *Barre Gazette* (MA), 26 August 1836.

83. "Erection of the Log Cabin," *New-Bedford Mercury*, 22 May 1840. See also "Whigs of Carver," *New-Bedford Mercury*, 12 June 1840.

84. Griffith, *History of the Town of Carver Massachusetts*, 305.

85. Notices and proceedings of various Tippecanoe Clubs detailing resolutions, officeholders, and meeting times are easily found in Whig-affiliated newspapers published during the 1840 election. Some illustrative examples include "Tippecanoe Club in Louisa, [VA]," *Richmond Whig* (VA), 24 July 1840 (see also "Richmond Tippecanoe Club" in the same issue); "Tippecanoe Club," *Auburn Journal and Advertiser* (NY), 22 April 1840; "Tippecanoe Club," *Daily National Intelligencer*, 14 September 1840; "Preamble and Constitution of the First Tippecanoe Club of Columbus, Ohio," *Ohio State Journal*, 13 March 1840.

86. See, for example, "Tippecanoe Club," *Hartford Daily Courant* (CT), 1 August 1840.

87. *Six Patriotic Ballads*. The high material quality of the collection was noticed by its proponents at the time; see "Tippecanoe Songs," *Log Cabin*, 29 August 1840. The location of the Fifth Ward Club mentioned is not specified. It is easy to assume, because of its place of publication, that the club in question was New York City's Fifth Ward Club. Yet Albany, New York, also had an active Fifth Ward Tippecanoe Club, and there is at least one notice of the collection that associates it with the Philadelphia Fifth Ward Club. See "Six Patriotic Ballads," *Auburn Journal and Advertiser*, 7 October 1840; *Commercial Advertiser*, 26 August 1840; "Fifth Ward Tippecanoe Club," *Albany Evening Journal*, 8 April 1840.

88. "Tippecanoe Songs," *Log Cabin*, 29 August 1840.

89. Geffen, "Joseph Sill and His Diary," 276–77.

90. Joseph Sill quoted in Geffen, 277–78; [Musical Fund Society of Philadelphia], *Charter and By-Laws*, 25, 32, 36. Sully was, in fact, a founding member of the Musical Fund Society and later served as its vice president, from 1860 to 1873.

91. Geffen, "Joseph Sill and His Diary," 283–84.

92. For more background on Sill, see Geffen.

93. Joseph Sill, Diaries, 12 February 1837, HSP.

94. Sill, Diaries, 19 January 1832.

95. Sill, Diaries, 22 January 1837.

96. See, for example Sill, Diaries, 19 January 1832, 9 November 1840, 11 November 1840, 11 April 1844.

97. Sill, Diaries, 9 October 1840.

98. *New Orleans Bulletin*, 12 October 1842, quoted in Grimsted, *American Mobbing*, 198.

99. On antebellum rioting, see Grimsted; K. Smith, *Dominion of Voice*, 51–86. In Philadelphia esp., see Feldberg, *Philadelphia Riots of 1844*; Heath, *In Union There Is Strength*, esp. 18–24.

100. Sill, Diaries, 26 October 1835.

101. Fear of riots and descriptions of riots are replete throughout Sill's diary. See, for example, his observation of an Election Day riot in 1840: Sill, Diaries, 30 October 1840. See also his descriptions of public events leading up to Election Day: 9–30 October 1840.

102. Sill, Diaries, 12 October 1840.

103. Sill, Diaries, 1 October 1844.

104. On Lee's interest in politics and Whig affiliation, see, for example, a series of diary entries spanning 7–10 June 1848 in James Kendall Lee, Diary, VHS.

105. Lee, Diary, 7 November 1848.

106. Lee, Diary, loose insertion between pages 80 and 81, circa diary entries dated 5–10 November 1848.

107. Nathan Beekley, Diary, 6 October 1849, AAS. More detailed descriptions of Beekley and his concert attendance can be found in Cavicchi, *Listening and Longing*, 75–76, 132, 135, 170, 182. Transcriptions of the diary and editorial commentary are also available online via Clerk and the City, AAS.

108. Beekley, Diary, 9 October 1849.

109. Beekley, Diary, 9 and 10 October 1849.

110. "Songs and Cider," *Hartford Times* (CT), 8 August 1840.

111. "Let Religion and the Charities of the Day be free from Politics," *Albany Argus*, 27 November 1840.

112. *Norfolk Democrat* (Dedham, MA), 21 May 1841. Whigs did sing a version of this verse at the end of a song titled "Specie Law" that Democrats satirized during the election as well as after; see "Harrison Meeting at Hadley," *Hampshire Gazette* (Northampton, MA), 18 March 1840; "General Harrison's Thinking Committee," *Albany Argus*, 10 April 1840. The *Argus* credits notice of the verse to a recent edition of the *Madisonian*.

113. "The 'Blue Light' Federalism of 1812–The 'Cider' Federalism of 1840," *Pittsfield Sun*, 14 May 1840.

114. "The Way to Make a Military Hero, and . . . Elect a President," *Ohio Statesman*, 22 July 1840; "Character of Federalism," *Albany Argus*, 15 May 1840.

115. *Newark Daily Advertiser*, 1 February 1841; "Songs and Cider," *Hartford Times*, 8 August 1840.

116. "Songs and Cider," *Hartford Times*, 8 August 1840.

117. The best discussion of the 1840 election in the context of Anglophobia is in Haynes, *Unfinished Revolution*, esp. 122–26.

118. "New Mode of Disseminating Federal Principles," *Ohio Statesman*, 24 June 1840.

119. "'Sing Sing' Party," *Albany Argus*, 26 June 1840.

120. "Sing-Sing Party," *Albany Argus*, 5 June 1840, copied with attribution from the *New York Evening Post*. "Di tanti palpili" is an aria by Gioachino Rossini, which appears in the first act of his opera *Tancredi* (1813).

121. "Blasphemous Whig Songs," *New Hampshire Patriot and State Gazette* (Concord, NH), 5 October 1840, with copy attributed to the *Worcester Palladium*.

122. *National Clay Minstrel*, v–vi.

123. *Free Soil Minstrel*, iii. See also "Music and Politics," *Weekly Eagle* (Brattleboro, VT), 18 September 1848.

124. "Campaign Scott and Graham Songster," *Albany Evening Journal*, 27 September 1852.

125. "Jesse Songster," *Cleveland Leader*, 26 September 1856.

126. Burleigh, *Republican Campaign Songster*, iii–iv.

127. Burleigh, iii.

128. "Campaign Music," *Western Musical World* (Cleveland, OH), August 1868, with copy attributed to the *Song Messenger of the Northwest* (Chicago, IL).

129. "Music as a Moral Force," *Song Messenger of the Northwest*, March 1866.

Chapter Four

1. SWSJ, 16 May 1848.

2. This interpretation of Saxton's relationship with music takes inspiration from Josh Kun's concept of "audiotopias," which conceives of music as a space in which listeners can inhabit their perception of a more just world. Unlike Kun, however, I place greater emphasis on the extent to which the nature of music's emancipatory or utopic possibilities can also be conditioned by elite cultural ideals. See Kun, *Audiotopia*, 2, 22-28. On the "prophetic" power of music, see also Attali, *Noise*, esp. 11-12.

3. The best example of this literature remains Broyles, *Music of the Highest Class*. But see also Saloman, *Beethoven's Symphonies*; Potter, *Food for Apollo*. Recent works that focus more on various facets of music's place in the lived experience of mid-nineteenth-century life include Cavicchi, *Listening and Longing*; McWhirter, *Battle Hymns*; Gac, *Singing for Freedom*; and, Davis, *Music along the Rapidan*.

4. Despite the rise of bottom-up histories, sustained biographical treatments of early Americans still tend to gravitate toward individuals of prominence or celebrity. On this issue, see Gordon-Reed, "Writing Early American Lives as Biography." The key exception to this trend is Ulrich, *Midwife's Tale*. Coincidentally, perhaps, Ulrich's approach has directly inspired significant work into the lives of urban clerks who shared roughly analogous lifestyles to Saxton during the mid-nineteenth century. See esp. Augst, *Clerk's Tale*; Luskey, *On the Make*. On writing history through individuals, see Lepore, "Historians Who Love Too Much." Regarding the comparison between clerks and printers, see Wilentz, *Chants Democratic*, 10, 110, 130-31. Being a print worker required strong English literacy skills, and this made printers generally more educated and better paid than their colleagues in other crafts, even though print shops were highly mechanized and working in them involved significant physical labor.

5. In recent years, scholarship on conservatism and the sectional crisis has flourished. Michael F. Conlin and Adam I. P. Smith adopt a nonessentialist approach to its study, perceiving conservatism as a set of values spanning the importance of moderation, compromise, and faith in institutions that transcended attachments to one political party or another. Joshua A. Lynn, by contrast, makes the case that Democrats subscribed to a unique, more populist, conservatism of their own. This study, through Saxton's particular experiences, emphasizes the legacy of Federalist conservatism on antebellum antislavery radicalism and, in this sense, builds on earlier insights from Rachel Hope Cleves. It also highlights the importance of recognizing the significance of conservative ideals and self-identification even to antebellum Americans whose actions were otherwise radical. See Conlin, "Dangerous *Isms* and Fanatical *Ists*"; A. Smith, *Stormy Present*; Lynn, *Preserving the White Man's Republic*; Cleves, *Reign of Terror*.

6. For quote, see SWSJ, 25 May 1853; for a tally of Saxton's attendance at musical performances during the 1852–53 winter season, see SWSJ, 19 May 1853.

7. See, for example, SWSJ, 11 October 1849.

8. SWSJ, 25 June 1848.

9. SWSJ, 18 November 1850.

10. The result is an intimidating 174 volumes of material, 136 of which survive, including all volumes from the first twenty years of his journalizing that fall within the bounds of this chapter. One large gap between 1901 and 1913 accounts for twenty-four of the thirty-eight missing volumes, seven of which were recently donated to Yale University in 2012 and opened for research in 2013. Saxton does, however, destroy particular sections of his journal between 1847 and 1866, which while not an uncommon practice for antebellum diarists, does speak to the consciously constructed nature of the source and his expectation that it would be read by others.

11. SWSJ, 16 June 1847.

12. SWSJ, 31 January 1850.

13. SWSJ, 25 May 1853; quotes from SWSJ, 16 November 1866. On the writing and interpretation of diaries in the United States during this period, see Augst, *Clerk's Tale*, esp. chap. 1; Motz, "Folk Expression of Time and Place"; Stowe, *Keep the Days*, esp. preface and chaps. 1 and 2. On the use of diaries in historical scholarship more generally, see Rendall, "On Diaries"; Bunkers and Huff, *Inscribing the Daily*.

14. For an illustrative example of Saxton's criticism of his own diary writing, see SWSJ, 24 March 1851. Other instances of this are numerous, but see 1 September 1849, 23 March 1851, 1 November 1860.

15. SWSJ, 10 May 1854. For evidence of sharing his journal with friends, see 23 and 24 March 1851; for evidence of an expectation that his wife will read his diary, see 22 April 1861.

16. On the "biographical mania" of many nineteenth-century Americans, see Casper, *Constructing American Lives*, quote on 2.

17. J. A. Saxton to his father, 3 March 1845, Saxton Family Papers, Henry N. Flynt Library, Historic Deerfield, quoted in McFeely, *Yankee Stepfather*, 51.

18. SWSJ, 27 April 1860, 30 May 1860.

19. On joining the army, see SWSJ, 8 August 1861. Saxton starts considering going to Port Royal instead in February 1862.

20. Previous uses of Saxton's journal focus almost exclusively on mining it for insight into the Union's "Rehearsal for Reconstruction" at Port Royal or the politics of administrating the Freedmen's Bureau thereafter. However, little of significance has been attributed to these parts of the journal, which largely reflects that his involvement in Reconstruction occurred at a time when he was newly married, gainfully employed, and less interested in confiding as much of his life to paper as he used to be. See, for example, Foner, *Reconstruction*, 72; Golay, *Ruined Land*, 362; Fraser, *History of Hope*, 94, 316; Cimbala, *Under the Guardianship of the Nation*, 22–23, 64, 246, 276; Ochiai, *Harvesting Freedom*, 172. The term "Rehearsal for Reconstruction" is borrowed from Rose, *Rehearsal for Reconstruction*.

21. SWSJ, 23 November 1849. Saxton's wages here and throughout usually amount to totals that were typical of print-worker earnings at the time. The six-dollar

relief wage offered by the Print Worker's Union was broadly equivalent to a good average wage for someone—like Saxton—who was working on small-time print jobs. That said, in 1850, the printer's union would decry the average six-dollar-per-week wage earned by its members as "literally less than laborers' wages." During this period, it was also normal for print workers like Saxton to work "sub" jobs in lieu of attaining full-time positions at a more prominent periodical or book press, which could offer as much as sixteen dollars per week to the "best" compositors. See Wilentz, *Chants Democratic*, 131.

22. SWSJ, 24 November 1849.

23. SWSJ, 10 July 1850. See also 30 March 1848.

24. On the oratorio ticket, see SWSJ, 5 March 1848. Between June 1845 and October 1847, while the *Harbinger* was published out of Brook Farm, Dwight contributed more than ninety music columns to it. Saxton arrived to join the community as a print compositor for the *Harbinger* in April 1845; see Delano, *Brook Farm*, 235–36.

25. On working for *Dwight's Journal of Music*, see SWSJ, 1 April 1852. For Saxton celebrating Dwight's wedding, see SWSJ, 11 and 12 February 1851. For another mention of Dwight giving Saxton concert tickets on 30 October 1852, see SWSJ entry for 19 May 1853. Dwight was on the executive council at Brook Farm and in charge of its education program. Reflections made later and at the time suggest that Brook Farm's young people generally thought highly of Dwight, though little detail is known of the musical instruction he provided them.

26. On reading *Dwight's Journal of Music* in the West, see SWSJ, 13 July 1853.

27. Dwight has come to hold two distinct positions within the historiography: either as the preeminent innovator of early American music criticism or as a second-rate transcendentalist and apostle of Fourierist Associationalism. Scholars who are primarily interested in American music tend to treat Dwight's leadership role at Brook Farm as a quirk of his early life, a flight of fancy indulged in before finding his true calling. By contrast, scholars who are focused on American antebellum utopianism instead tend to mark Dwight's musical interests as the quirk of his personality. Despite that Dwight wrote much of his early music columns in the *Harbinger* right alongside pieces of his own that advocated more generally in support of the principles of Fourierist Associationalism, scholars disagree over the extent to which these two interests were interlinked. Michael Broyles, for instance, claims that even though "Dwight was very much under the sway of the Brook Farm experiment with its philosophy of utopian socialism, there is little of the social reformist element in his vision of music." However, as Ora F. Saloman argues, it is clear that Dwight's writing about music in the 1840s *was* in fact very much connected to his belief in the American Fourierist enterprise. Broyles, *Music of the Highest Class*, 257; Saloman, *Beethoven's Symphonies*, esp. chap. 8. A similar assessment of this debate is offered in Barnes, "Rhetoric of Democracy in American Musical Discourse," 98–112. For a recent study that links Dwight's Fourierist emphasis on "unity" to his later musical elitism, see M. Davidson, "John Dwight and the Harvard Musical Association Orchestra," esp. 251–57. Douglas W. Shadle questions whether the influence of Dwight's opinions was as large as scholars tend to suggest; see Shadle, *Orchestrating the Nation*, esp. 270–71. That said, scholars like Shadle, focused on questions surrounding nineteenth-century ideals of

American national music, have also done much to integrate the supposed ironies of Dwight's Fourierist transcendentalism with his otherwise snobbish reputation; see Shadle; Chmaj, "Fry versus Dwight."

28. See Guarneri, *Utopian Alternative*, 15–20, quotation on 18. On Charles Fourier and his ideas more generally, see Beecher, *Charles Fourier*.

29. The best discussion of Fourierism crossing the Atlantic is Guarneri, *Utopian Alternative*, chap. 1. But see also Delano, *"Harbinger" and New England Transcendentalism*. On the cultural contexts of these economic conditions, see Lepler, *Many Panics of 1837*.

30. Charles Fourier quoted in Beecher, *Charles Fourier*, 266. See also Jones and Patterson, introduction to *Charles Fourier*, xix.

31. Brisbane, *Albert Brisbane*, 229–31. This text, though confusingly credited, was actually authored by Albert. His wife, Redelia, contributes a character study that prefaces the work.

32. John S. Dwight, "Musical Review," *Harbinger* (Boston, MA), 14 June 1845.

33. Dwight.

34. Dwight.

35. Dwight.

36. Dwight.

37. See also, for example, Dwight's "Musical Review" columns in the *Harbinger*, 28 June 1845, 16 August 1845, 17 January 1846. For a nuanced study locating Dwight's utopian musical universalism as part of a larger transatlantic diplomatic and nation-building movement that stretched into the twentieth century, see Gienow-Hecht, *Sound Diplomacy*, esp. chap. 2.

38. John S. Dwight, "Musical Review," *Harbinger*, 30 January 1847. Dwight's review of the German composer Franz Lachner's (1803–90) *Sinfonia Passionata* was based on a performance of the work conducted under the auspices of the Boston Academy of Music on 16 January 1847.

39. SWSJ, 24 July 1847.

40. SWSJ, 21 July 1847.

41. SWSJ, 7 April 1851.

42. SWSJ, 7 April 1859.

43. On Anna Bishop (1810–84), see Preston, *Opera on the Road*, 230–37.

44. SWSJ, 2 January 1851.

45. SWSJ, 11 January 1851.

46. SWSJ, 3 June 1850.

47. SWSJ, 10 April 1858.

48. Jenny Lind (1820–87) was a Swedish-born vocalist who enjoyed significant success in Berlin and London before choosing to retire early from the operatic stage. Lind thereafter accepted an invitation from P. T. Barnum to undertake a legendarily popular concert tour of the United States. The best treatments of Lind's American tour are in Cavicchi, *Listening and Longing*, chap. 1; Lawrence, *Reverberations*, 36–64; Buckley, "To the Opera House," chap. 6. On the marketing aspects of Lind's tour, see Samples, "Humbug and the Nightingale"; Ware and Lockard, *P. T. Barnum Presents Jenny Lind*. For a gendered approach to reading the Lind phenomena, see Linkon, "Reading Lind Mania." And for an overview of Lind's career more generally, see Rogers, "Jenny

Lind." On the significance of the prima donna in nineteenth-century Western society, see Rutherford, *Prima Donna and Opera*.

49. SWSJ, 17 September 1850.

50. SWSJ, 13, 17, 23, and 25 September 1850.

51. SWSJ, 26 and 23 September 1850.

52. SWSJ, 26, 28, and 29 September 1850; 5, 8, 10, and 11 October 1850; 27 June 1851.

53. See, for example, SWSJ, 26 September 1850, 11 October 1850.

54. SWSJ, 10, 11, and 12 October 1850.

55. SWSJ, 10 and 13 October 1850.

56. For details of this performance, see Ware and Lockard, *P. T. Barnum Presents Jenny Lind*, 38–40. For one particularly evocative report of mob behavior at a Jenny Lind concert, written by an upper-class Bostonian woman, see Caroline Wells Healey Dall Journal, 30 October 1850, quoted in Cavicchi, *Listening and Longing*, 167.

57. SWSJ, 12 October 1850.

58. SWSJ, 17 October 1850.

59. See, for example, "Jenny Lind," *Harbinger*, 18 April 1846; "Jenny Lind," *Harbinger*, 4 July 1846.

60. "Jenny Lind's Songs," *Harbinger*, 28 August 1847.

61. SWSJ, 23 September 1850.

62. SWSJ, 31 May 1852.

63. "Farewell Concert," *Dwight's Journal of Music* (Boston, MA), 29 May 1852.

64. SWSJ, 25 June 1851.

65. Mrs. Joel J. Baily Diaries, 3 September 1850, HSP. On her husband's business, see Luskey, *On the Make*, 78.

66. "Jenny Lind Martyr," *Boston Evening Transcript*, 7 October 1850.

67. "Extravagant Expectations Disappointed," *Boston Evening Transcript*, 21 December 1850.

68. See Ware and Lockard, *P. T. Barnum Presents Jenny Lind*, 12. On Barnum's "branding" of Lind and his "advertising puffery," see Samples, "Humbug and the Nightingale."

69. SWSJ, 6 November 1848.

70. SWSJ, 11 January 1851.

71. SWSJ, 31 January, 8 and 9 February, 5 and 13 May 1848 (concerts); SWSJ, 10 February and 14 March 1848 (lectures); SWSJ, 15 February 1848 (Associationalists); SWSJ, 17 February and 1 May 1848 (temperance); SWSJ, 12 April 1848 (French Revolution); SWSJ, 25 April 1848 (antislavery).

72. SWSJ, 21 May 1848.

73. SWSJ, 6 November 1848.

74. SWSJ, 9 February 1848, 20 July 1848.

75. On the antiwar stance of Brook Farmers, see Guarneri, *Utopian Alternative*, 258–61.

76. See SWSJ, 20 July 1848.

77. Buckley, "To the Opera House," 472.

78. SWSJ, 28 September 1850.

79. SWSJ, 29 September 1850.

80. SWSJ, 3 October 1850.
81. SWSJ, 27 September 1850.
82. SWSJ, 12 October 1850.
83. SWSJ, 25 June 1851.
84. SWSJ, 25 June 1851.
85. SWSJ, 23 June 1851.
86. William R. Dempster (1809–71) was a British-born vocalist who enjoyed significant popularity in the United States, where his performances were consistently received more favorably than in Europe. Musically, his stock-in-trade—like compatriot Henry Russell—was the sentimental parlor tune. Specialist biographical material on Dempster is not well developed, but see Tawa, "Dempster, William Richardson."
87. SWSJ, 30 November 1850.
88. SWSJ, 31 October 1851.
89. SWSJ, 21 June 1851.
90. SWSJ, 5 January 1850.
91. SWSJ, 25 June 1851.
92. SWSJ, 13 September 1850.
93. SWSJ, 10 October 1850.
94. SWSJ, 13 September 1850.
95. SWSJ, 7 October 1850.
96. Saxton's journal performs his relationship with Louise Kleinstrup with extreme care. While Saxton was "surprised" by a kiss from her at one point, he was careful never to suggest that any impropriety took place between them, despite their relationship being a source of gossip among their friends. Saxton in his journal was at pains to deny these rumors even while clearly relishing in the attention it directed toward him. See SWSJ, 29 October 1848, 20 May 1848, and 18 June 1850.
97. SWSJ, 31 July 1850. For quotes see SWSJ, 1 August 1850.
98. SWSJ, 23 October 1850. The intermittent frequency of letters that Peter Kleinstrup sent home to his family in Boston regularly led them to fear the worst, and ultimately, he passed away on the Pacific coast without striking it rich. See Swift, *Brook Farm*, 126.
99. SWSJ, 12 October 1850.
100. SWSJ, 16 October 1850.
101. SWSJ, 13 October 1850.
102. SWSJ, 4 March 1852.
103. SWSJ, 22 April 1852. Incidentally, Webster was reported to have drunkenly interrupted one of Jenny Lind's performances; see Remini, *Daniel Webster*, 693–94.
104. SWSJ, 17 October 1850, 11 November 1850.
105. SWSJ, 11 November 1850, 13 November 1850.
106. See, for instance SWSJ, 8 and 17 January 1851. On antislavery third parties and their coalition tactics, see Brooks, *Liberty Power*, 171–79.
107. SWSJ, 17 January 1851.
108. SWSJ, 3 October 1850. On the conservative self-image of Bostonians and others who resisted the Fugitive Slave Law, see A. Smith, *Stormy Present*, chap. 2. On "revolutionary" antislavery agitation more broadly, see Sinha, *Slave's Cause*, chap. 15.

109. SWSJ, 14 October 1850, 5 October 1850.

110. SWSJ, 10 November 1851.

111. SWSJ, 6 July 1852.

112. For tallies of Saxton's concert attendance, see SWSJ, 19 May 1853.

113. SWSJ, 10 November 1851. A piece called "The Spirit Waltz" was published in Boston around 1850 by George P. Reed, but its authorship was wrongly attributed to Beethoven. The piece was popular enough to inspire poetry, but its true provenance is unknown. See Lawrence, *Resonances*, 360–61; Block, *Amy Beach*, 10. For a poem published on the effect of Beethoven's "Spirit Waltz," see "Beethoven's Spirit Waltz," *Littell's Living Age* (Boston, MA), 21 July 1849.

114. SWSJ, 10 November 1851. George Ripley and Charles Dana had both moved on from Brook Farm to establish themselves as prominent newspapermen in New York, and Saxton was hopeful they would assist him to find a situation there.

115. SWSJ, 10 January 1852.

116. SWSJ, 15, 20, 26, and 27 December 1851. Richard Hoffman (1831–1901) was an English-born New York pianist who performed with Jenny Lind during her American tour. He specialized in performing a German-orientated repertoire of J. S. Bach, Beethoven, and Mendelssohn and composed piano pieces in the genteel salon tradition. See Hoffman, *Some Musical Recollections*. Catherine Hayes (1818–61) was an Irish opera singer best known for her interpretations of Italian opera; see Walsh, *Catherine Hayes*. On concert culture in mid-nineteenth-century New York City, particularly with regard to its gendered aspects, see Block, "Matinee Mania." Much has been made of the fact that white abolitionists like Saxton were drawn to minstrel music and melodies. Saxton's experiences attest to the wealth of scholarship that draws on this trend to upend supposedly clear distinctions between highbrow and lowbrow culture before the Civil War and to highlight the appropriation of so-called black music by white working- and middle-class people. However, Saxton's journals also evince the extent to which antebellum Americans did, nonetheless, find value in making distinctions between what they perceived to be refined and unrefined music and between types of music they felt had the capacity to improve or endanger the nation's moral and political trajectory. See Roberts, *Blackface Nation*; Gac, *Singing for Freedom*; Cavicchi, *Listening and Longing*; Mahar, *Behind the Burnt Cork Mask*; Lott, *Love and Theft*; Levine, *Highbrow/Lowbrow*.

117. For the quote, see SWSJ, 25 November 1851.

118. SWSJ, 12 January 1852.

119. See Gac, *Singing for Freedom*, 174–83. "Get Off the Track!" features the minstrel melody from "Old Dan Tucker."

120. When Jenny Lind arrived at New York in 1850, members of the Hutchinson Family Singers met with her in an unsuccessful attempt to convince the Swedish singer to publicly disavow American slavery. Lind refused to comment on the slavery issue until after she had finished touring the Southern states. On returning to the North, she finally alluded to the issue in public by noting that the recent publication of Harriet Beecher Stowe's *Uncle Tom's Cabin* had helped to aid "the welfare of our black *brethren*." Antislavery advocates had already utilized Lind's image to promote their cause regardless. See Gac, *Singing for Freedom*, 8–9.

121. SWSJ, 21 December 1851.
122. See Gac, *Singing for Freedom*, 184–86.
123. SWSJ, 31 January 1848.
124. SWSJ, 9 February 1848.
125. Frederick Douglass quoted in Gac, *Singing for Freedom*, 227.
126. On the Hutchinsons' earnings and quarrelling during this period, see Gac, 225–35.
127. SWSJ, 4 January 1852.
128. SWSJ, 13 January 1852, 4 January 1852.
129. SWSJ, 12 January 1852.
130. SWSJ, 21 January 1852.
131. SWSJ, 6 March 1852.
132. SWSJ, 22 March 1852.
133. SWSJ, 5 March 1852.
134. SWSJ, 9 March 1852.
135. SWSJ, 11 March 1852.
136. SWSJ, 18 March 1852.
137. SWSJ, 6 November 1850.
138. SWSJ, 21 January 1852.
139. SWSJ, 21 March 1852.
140. SWSJ, 10 March 1852.
141. SWSJ, 11 March 1852.
142. SWSJ, 11 March 1852.
143. SWSJ, 22 March 1852.
144. SWSJ, 1 June 1859, 17 June 1860.
145. SWSJ, 25 May 1853, 19 May 1853.
146. SWSJ, 19 May 1853, 25 May 1853. The "Germanians" was the colloquial name given to the Germania Musical Society, a classical music ensemble made up of German immigrants who received a particularly warm reception in Boston. See N. Newman, *Good Music for a Free People*.
147. SWSJ, 25 May 1853.
148. SWSJ, 19 May 1853.
149. SWSJ, 25 May 1853.
150. SWSJ, 4 July 1853.
151. SWSJ, 13 July 1853.
152. SWSJ, 25 July 1853.
153. SWSJ, 22 September 1853.
154. SWSJ, 29 June 1854.
155. On singing school and choir participation, see SWSJ, 15 and 26 November 1853, 6 and 24 December 1853. On serenading, see 31 October 1853, 6 and 15 November 1853. On Saxton's attendance at balls and helping to organize one, see 29 December 1853, 18 January 1854. On transcribing the controversy over the Fugitive Slave Law in Boston, specifically the high-profile case of Anthony Burns, see 6 June 1854. On discussing the Anti-Nebraska movement, see 12 March 1854, 8 July 1854.

The best recent accounts of the politics driving these controversies are in Brooks, *Liberty Power*, chap. 7; A. Smith, *Stormy Present*, chap. 2 and 3.

156. SWSJ, 15 May 1854.

157. SWSJ, 2 December 1853.

158. SWSJ, 29 October 1853.

159. SWSJ, 16 October 1854.

160. SWSJ, 8 July 1854. In Indiana, nativist Know Nothings held sway over the otherwise Free Soil–driven Anti-Nebraska movement. See Brooks, *Liberty Power*, 197; Holt, *Rise and Fall of the American Whig Party*, 859–66.

161. SWSJ, 16, 18, 22, and 26 November 1854; 25 December 1854 (on this occasion Saxton was let in for free but ejected by the performer's agent, against whom Saxton had recently testified in court on a separate matter); 3 February 1855.

162. SWSJ, 14 September 1854.

163. SWSJ, 22 April 1855.

164. SWSJ, 28 August 1855, 3 February 1856, 14 February 1856.

165. SWSJ, 29 April 1855.

166. SWSJ, 30 December 1855.

167. SWSJ, 22 April 1855.

168. See Guarneri, *Utopian Alternative*, 375–81.

169. SWSJ, 21 July 1856.

170. SWSJ, 7 June 1856 (on Sumner's caning); quote in SWSJ, 21 July 1856.

171. SWSJ, 21 July 1856, 5 August 1856.

172. SWSJ, 27 August 1856, 8 September 1856, 18 September 1856, 29 September 1856.

173. SWSJ, 3 November 1857.

174. SWSJ, 18 September 1856.

175. SWSJ, 9 September 1856.

176. SWSJ, 19 September 1856.

177. See, for example, SWSJ, 24 January 1857.

178. SWSJ, 16 November 1856.

179. SWSJ, 24 January 1858. This was not a solo performance, but for Saxton, "Formes was the central point of interest," a perspective mirrored in contemporary reviews of the event. See "Oratorios," *Boston Evening Transcript*, 25 January 1858. Formes (1815–86) was a renowned German opera singer who found success first in Vienna and then in London before making regular tours to the United States, the first of which was in 1857. See Formes, *My Memoirs*.

180. SWSJ, 8 November 1857.

181. SWSJ, loose clipping, n.d. [ca. February 1857]. In 1856, a Portland, Maine, journal of literature and news attributed a version of this quote to an "A. Clarke" but is possible that the clipping was inserted later or retrospectively into the journal. In 1874, a San Francisco journal published a similar but different version attributed to a songwriter named "B. Shrafl." See "What Is Said of Music," *Portland Transcript* (ME), 25 October 1856; "The Influence of Music," *Common Sense* (San Francisco, CA), 28 November 1874. Neither of these two later examples match the clipping in Saxton's journal exactly,

which does not credit the quote to anyone and, like many of the other clippings in this volume of the journal, was probably sourced from the *Boston Evening Transcript*.

182. SWSJ, 24 January 1857. Carl Zerrahn (1826–1909) was a German-born American musician who immigrated to the United States in 1848 with the Germania Musical Society and who chose to remain in the United States after the group disbanded in 1854. He was a prolific musical personality in Boston, serving as the conductor of the Handel and Haydn Society (1854–98), the Orchestral Union (1854–68), the Philharmonic (1857–63), and the Harvard Musical Association Orchestra (1865–82). See N. Newman, *Good Music for a Free People*, esp. 254.

183. SWSJ, 18 August 1857.

184. SWSJ, 1 June 1859.

185. SWSJ, 17 June 1860.

186. See esp. SWSJ, 6 September 1849.

187. SWSJ, 12 November 1859.

188. SWSJ, 5 November 1860, 1 October 1860.

189. Mary Grant (née Saxton) to S. Willard Saxton, quoted in SWSJ, 3 May 1862. Emphasis is as appears in the journal.

190. Ahlquist, *Democracy at the Opera*, 160.

191. SWSJ, 18 January 1856.

192. SWSJ, 3 January 1857. Sigismond Thalberg (1812–71) was a German or Austrian musician born near Geneva, Switzerland (the precise circumstances of his birth are contested), who gained fame in Europe as one of the foremost virtuoso pianists of his age. Contemporary European commentators had trouble agreeing on whether to prefer Thalberg or his virtuoso contemporary Franz Liszt. See Hominick, "Sigismund Thalberg."

193. SWSJ, 4 September 1856.

194. SWSJ, 15 April 1861. For similar language, see also 13 April 1861.

195. SWSJ, 5 March 1860.

196. SWSJ, 13 March 1860.

197. SWSJ, 30 March 1862.

198. SWSJ, 5 December 1860.

199. SWSJ, 23 October 1860. The next day, Saxton was "very glad" for the chance to change employers and began canvassing for the Republican Party instead; see 24 October 1860. Saxton considered canvassing tiring work but explained that it paid better than printing; see 2 November 1860. Once the election was over and Saxton was again out of work, he and a friend started up a short-lived "experiment" involving the production of photographic likenesses of politicians for sale; see 13–17 November 1860.

200. SWSJ, 2 October 1861. On Saxton opening and running a storefront, see 7 December 1860–March 1862. Notably, Saxton's personal trajectory away from musical idealism tracks with a more broadly felt shift detailed in Barnes, "Rhetoric of Democracy in American Musical Discourse," esp. 203–6.

201. SWSJ, 17 March 1862. See also Westwood, "Generals David Hunter and Rufus Saxton and Black Soldiers."

202. See Ochiai, "Port Royal Experiment Revisited."

203. SWSJ, 2 February 1865.

Epilogue

1. Quotes from "Patriotic Song from Across the Water," *Charleston Courier* (SC), 28 October 1862, with attribution for the song's original appearance in the *Richmond Enquirer*. For examples of other contemporaneous newspaper printings of "The Southern Cross," see "The Southern Cross," *Charleston Mercury* (SC), 3 October 1862; "Patriotic Song," *Mobile Register* (AL), 2 November 1862. The song was also published in Moore, *Rebel Rhymes*, 287–89; and earlier, presumably, as a broadside under the titles "God and Liberty" and "The Southern Cross"; see [Blunt], "God and Liberty!"; [Blunt], "Southern Cross."

2. For notices of Blunt's theatrical movements in Europe, see, for example, "Of Mrs. Ellen Key Blunt," *Boston Daily Advertiser*, 31 July 1861 (in London); *Newark Daily Advertiser* (NJ), 27 May 1862 (in Paris); *Alexandria Gazette* (VA), 21 May 1862 (in Paris); *Richmond Examiner* (VA), 11 June 1862 (in Paris); "Americans in Paris," *Baltimore Sun*, 23 July 1863 (still in Paris).

3. On the Confederacy's search for an anthem and its rejection of existing patriotic songs popular in the Union, see McWhirter, *Battle Hymns*, chap. 3. For newspapers boosting Blunt's "Southern Cross" on the grounds that her father had written "The Star-Spangled Banner," see "Patriotic Song from Across the Water," *Charleston Courier*, 28 October 1862; "The Southern Cross," *Charleston Mercury*, 3 October 1862; and "Patriotic Song," *Mobile Register*, 2 November 1862.

4. Lyrics quoted are from the broadside version of "The Southern Cross"; see [Blunt], "Southern Cross."

5. See Howard, *Fourteen Months*. Howard and other political prisoners with him had, by this time, been offered release but on principle had refused to accept the conditions of the parole that accompanied it; see Howard, esp. 76–80.

6. Howard, 9.

7. See Frank Key Howard to Edwin M. Stanton, 3 March 1862, in Howard, 76; *Alexandria Gazette*, 25 July 1862; *Evening Star* (Washington, DC), 24 July 1862. McCaffrey remained at Fort McHenry for at least two weeks before agreeing to be released on parole; see *Alexandria Gazette*, 13 August 1862.

8. Howard only actually spent the best part of a day in Fort McHenry before being moved to spend time incarcerated at Fortress Monroe, Fort Lafayette, and Fort Warren; see Howard, *Fourteen Months*.

9. "A New Military Order," *Baltimore Sun*, 10 March 1863; "The Music Publishers Have More Trouble," *Baltimore Daily Gazette*, 12 March 1863; John. A. Dix to George B. McClellan, 4 September 1861, *OR*, Ser. 2, Vol. 1, 591–92. A manuscript duplicate of Schenck's order that Baltimore's music publishers also hand over their plates can be found enclosed in Gen. R. C. Schenck to J. I. Clark Hare, 11 March 1863, Item no. 234, Series II, Hare-Willing Family Papers, APS. For evidence of military orders in other places that banned either the performance or distribution of Confederate songs, see "Arrest of Balmer & Weber, Music Dealers," *Daily Missouri Republican* (St. Louis), 28 June 1862; Order of the Provost Marshal, St. Louis, No. 834, 14 June 1862, reprinted under the headline "Disloyal Females" in *Daily Missouri Republican*, 15 June 1862.

10. Le Grand, *Journal*, 233.

11. For more detail on the legality and significance of Confederate music in the American Civil War, see Coleman, "Confederate Music and the Politics of Treason."

12. Moore, *Rebel Rhymes*, n.p.

13. "Books and the War," *Boston Evening Transcript*, 23 May 1864; *New York Evening Post*, 23 January 1864; *New York Tribune*, 14, 15, and 16 April 1864.

14. Abraham Lincoln quoted in McWhirter, *Battle Hymns*, 174. On music and reconciliation at the conclusion of the Civil War, see McWhirter, 171–76. For detail on postwar reconciliation and its political and racial implications, see Blight, *Race and Reunion*.

15. See, for example, Love, *Musical Democracy*; Eyerman and Jamison, *Music and Social Movements*; Mattern, *Acting in Concert*; Rosenthal and Flacks, *Playing for Change*.

16. "A workingman" quoted in Huston, "What We Talk about When We Talk about Democracy." On the Workingmen's movement, see Wilentz, *Chants Democratic*, esp. chap. 5.

17. The best work to illuminate Kane's family is Grow, *Liberty to the Downtrodden*.

18. [Whitman], "What Is Music Then?," *Brooklyn Daily Times*, 28 July 1858, reprinted in Holloway and Schwarz, *I Sit and Look Out*, 173–74. For further evidence of a Federalist upbringing exerting influence over a radical democrat's approach to musical power, see Roosevelt, *Science of Government*, 50. On Whitman and music, see Reynolds, *Walt Whitman*, esp. chap. 3; Faner, *Walt Whitman and Music*. Josh Kun positions Whitman, via his 1860 poem "I Hear America Singing," as having "unwittingly created" a monocultural approach to hearing American nationalism through the "frequencies of cultural consensus." I suggest a longer history was also at play. See Kun, *Audiotopia*, chap. 1, quotations in note on 31 and 30 respectively.

19. For more on the legacies of Federalist conservatism, including its contribution to radical antislavery, see esp. Cleves, *Reign of Terror*, chap. 6; Grow, *Liberty to the Downtrodden*.

Bibliography

Manuscript Archives and Digital Collections

American Antiquarian Society (Worcester, MA)
   Clerk and the City, https://clerkandthecity.wordpress.com/
   Isaiah Thomas Broadside Ballads Project: Verses in Vogue with the Vulgar,
      https://www.americanantiquarian.org/thomasballads/
   Nathan Beekley Diary
   Portraits at the American Antiquarian Society, https://www.americanantiquarian
      .org/Inventories/Portraits/
   Worcester Choral Union Records
American Philosophical Society (Philadelphia, PA)
   Hare-Willing Family Papers
   Robert M. (Maskell) Patterson Papers
Chicago History Museum Research Center (Chicago, IL)
   David Davis Papers
Georgia Historical Society (Savannah, GA)
   Daniel Mulford Papers
Harvard University Archives (Boston, MA)
   Samuel A. Eliot Papers
Historical Society of Pennsylvania (Philadelphia, PA)
   Hopkinson Family Papers
   Joseph Sill Diaries
   Mrs. Joel J. Baily Diaries
Irving S. Gilmore Music Library, Yale University (New Haven, CT)
   Lowell Mason Papers
Johns Hopkins University (Baltimore, MD)
   Lester S. Levy Sheet Music Collection, Sheridan Libraries
      Special Collections
Kislak Center for Special Collections, University of Pennsylvania
      (Philadelphia, PA)
   John Rowe Parker Correspondence
   Musical Fund Society of Philadelphia Records
   Musical Fund Society of Philadelphia Supplementary Records
Library of Congress (Washington, DC)
   George Washington Papers, Series 2, Letterbooks 1754–1799, https://www.loc
      .gov/collections/george-washington-papers/about-this-collection/
   Horace Greeley Papers, Manuscripts Division

Maryland Historical Society (Baltimore, MD)
    John Eager Howard Papers
    Phoebe George Bradford Diaries
Massachusetts Historical Society (Boston, MA)
    Adams Family Papers (microfilm)
    Adams Family Papers: An Electronic Archive, https://www.masshist.org
        /digitaladams/archive/
    The Diaries of John Quincy Adams: A Digital Collection, http://www.masshist
        .org/jqadiaries/php/
    Nathan Webb Diary
    Seymour Collection
National Archives (Washington, DC)
    Founders Online, National Historic Publications and Records Commission,
        https://founders.archives.gov/
New York Public Library (New York, NY)
    Horace Greeley Papers
Rotunda, University of Virginia Press, "American Founding Era Collection,"
        https://www.upress.virginia.edu/founding-era
    The Papers of Thomas Jefferson Digital Edition
Sterling Memorial Library, Manuscripts and Archives, Yale University (New Haven, CT)
    Rufus and S. Willard Saxton Papers
Tufts Digital Collections and Archives (Boston, MA)
    A New Nation Votes: American Election Returns 1787–1825, http://elections.lib
        .tufts.edu/catalog/tufts
Virginia Historical Society (Richmond, VA)
    James Kendall Lee Diary

Newspapers and Other Periodicals

Alabama
    Mobile Register
California
    Common Sense (San Francisco)
Connecticut
    Bee (New London)
    Connecticut Courant (Hartford)
    Hartford Daily Courant
    Hartford Times
    Norwich Courier
Georgia
    Macon Telegraph
    Savannah Republican
Illinois
    Song Messenger of the Northwest
        (Chicago)
Maine
    Maine Cultivator and Hallowell Gazette
    Portland Weekly Advertiser
    Portland Transcript
    Weekly Eastern Argus (Portland)
Maryland
    Baltimore Sun
Massachusetts
    Barre Gazette
    Berkshire Reporter (Pittsfield)
    Boston Commercial Gazette
    Boston Daily Advertiser
    Boston Evening Transcript
    Boston Gazette
    Boston Post
    Boston Recorder

Boston Traveler
Daily Advertiser and Patriot (Boston)
Dwight's Journal of Music (Boston)
Euterpeiad, or Musical Intelligencer (Boston)
Gloucester Telegraph
Hampshire Gazette (Northampton)
Harbinger (Boston)
Liberator (Boston)
Littell's Living Age (Boston)
Massachusetts Magazine (Boston)
Musical Magazine (Boston)
Musical Visitor (Boston)
Nantucket Inquirer
National Aegis (Worcester)
New-Bedford Mercury
Norfolk Democrat (Dedham)
Saturday Morning Transcript (Boston)
Springfield Republican
Pittsfield Sun
Weekly Messenger (Boston)
Weekly Visitor, and Ladies Museum (Boston)

Missouri
Daily Missouri Republican (St. Louis)

New Hampshire
Dartmouth Gazette (Hanover)
Farmer's Weekly Museum (Walpole)
New Hampshire Patriot and State Gazette (Concord)
New Hampshire Sentinel (Keene)
Portsmouth Journal of Literature and Politics

New Jersey
Centinel of Freedom (Newark)
Genius of Liberty (Morristown)
Newark Daily Advertiser

New York
Albany Argus
Albany Evening Journal
Albany Register
American Musical Journal (New York)
Auburn Journal and Advertiser
Commercial Advertiser (New York)
Daily Advertiser (New York)

Log Cabin (New York)
Lyre, or New-York Musical Journal (New York)
Musical Pioneer and Chorister's Budget (New York)
Musical Times (New York)
Musical World and Times (New York)
National Advocate (New York)
New York Evening Post
New York Morning Herald
New York Tribune
Spectator (New York)
Western Recorder (Utica)

Ohio
Cincinnati Daily Gazette
Cleveland Daily Herald
Cleveland Leader
Ohio State Journal (Columbus)
Ohio Statesman (Columbus)
Western Musical World (Cleveland)

Pennsylvania
Aurora General Advertiser (Philadelphia)
Federal Gazette (Philadelphia)
Gazette of the United States (Philadelphia)
National Gazette (Philadelphia)
North American (Philadelphia)
Pennsylvania Gazette (Philadelphia)
Pennsylvania Packet (Philadelphia)
Philadelphia Gazette
Philadelphia Inquirer
Porcupine's Gazette (Philadelphia)
Public Ledger (Philadelphia)

Rhode Island
Christian Telescope and Universalist Miscellany (Providence)
Rhode-Island Republican (Newport)

South Carolina
Charleston Courier
Charleston Mercury
City Gazette (Charleston)

Vermont
Bellows Falls Gazette
Weekly Eagle (Brattleboro)

Virginia
  Alexandria Gazette
  Alexandria Herald
  Richmond Examiner
  Richmond Whig

Washington, DC
  Daily National Intelligencer
  Evening Star
  Madisonian

Published Sources

Ahlquist, Karen. *Democracy at the Opera: Music, Theatre, and Culture in New York City, 1815–60*. Urbana: University of Illinois Press, 1997.

Alcott, William A., ed. "Music in Common Schools." In *American Annals of Education and Instruction*, vol. 7. Boston: Otis, Broaders, 1837.

———. "Music in Schools." In *American Annals of Education and Instruction*, vol. 8. Boston: Otis, Broaders, 1838.

Allgor, Catherine. *Parlor Politics: In Which the Ladies of Washington Help Build a City and a Government*. Charlottesville: University of Virginia Press, 2000.

Altschuler, Glenn C., and Stuart M. Blumin. *Rude Republic: Americans and Their Politics in the Nineteenth Century*. Princeton, NJ: Princeton University Press, 2000.

Altschuler, Glenn C., Stuart M. Blumin, Harry L. Watson, Jean Harvey Baker, and Norma Basch. "Political Engagement and Disengagement in Antebellum America: A Round Table." *Journal of American History* 84, no. 3 (December 1997): 855–909.

Ames, Fisher. *Works of Fisher Ames, Compiled by a Number of His Friends*. Boston: T. B. Wait, 1809.

An American [Noah Webster]. *The Revolution in France, Considered in Respect to Its Progress and Effects*. New York: George Bunce, 1794.

Anishanslin, Zara. *Portrait of a Woman in Silk: Hidden Histories of the British Atlantic World*. New Haven, CT: Yale University Press, 2016.

Appleby, Joyce. *Capitalism and a New Social Order: The Republican Vision of the 1790s*. New York: NYU Press, 1984.

———, ed. *Recollections of the Early Republic: Selected Autobiographies*. Boston: Northeastern University Press, 1997.

Ashton, James Jackson. "Patriotic Sublime: Music and the Nation in America, 1790–1848." PhD diss., Johns Hopkins University, 2015.

Attali, Jacques. *Noise: The Political Economy of Music*. Translated by Brian Massumi. Minneapolis: University of Minnesota Press, 1985.

Augst, Thomas. *The Clerk's Tale: Young Men and Moral Life in Nineteenth-Century America*. Chicago: University of Chicago Press, 2003.

Ayres, Philip. *Classical Culture and the Idea of Rome in Eighteenth-Century England*. Cambridge: Cambridge University Press, 1997.

Bailey, Candace. *Music and the Southern Belle: From Accomplished Lady to Confederate Composer*. Carbondale: Southern Illinois University Press, 2010.

Baker, Jean H. *Affairs of Party: The Political Culture of the Northern Democrats in the Mid-Nineteenth Century*. Ithaca, NY: Cornell University Press, 1983.

Banner, James M., Jr. *To the Hartford Convention: The Federalists and the Origins of Party Politics in Massachusetts, 1789–1815*. New York: Knopf, 1970.

Banner, Lois W. "Religious Benevolence as Social Control: A Critique of an Interpretation." *Journal of American History* 60, no. 1 (June 1973): 23–41.

Barnes, Molly Leeanna. "The Rhetoric of Democracy in American Musical Discourse, 1842–1861." PhD diss., University of North Carolina at Chapel Hill, 2016.

Beadie, Nancy. *Education and the Creation of Capital in the Early American Republic.* Cambridge: Cambridge University Press, 2010.

Bechtold, Rebeccah. "A Revolutionary Soundscape: Musical Reform and the Science of Sound in Early America, 1760–1840." *Journal of the Early Republic* 35, no. 3 (Fall 2015): 419–50.

Beecher, Jonathan. *Charles Fourier: The Visionary and His World.* Berkeley: University of California Press, 1986.

Bellion, Wendy. *Citizen Spectator: Art, Illusion, and Visual Perception in Early National America.* Chapel Hill: Omohundro Institute and University of North Carolina Press, 2011.

Ben-Atar, Doron, and Barbara B. Oberg, eds. *Federalists Reconsidered.* Charlottesville: University of Virginia Press, 1998.

Billings, William. *The New-England Psalm-Singer; or, American Chorister. Containing a Number of Psalm-Tunes, Anthems and Canons. In Four and Five Parts.* Boston: Edes and Gill, 1770.

Blauvelt, Martha Tomhave. *The Work of the Heart: Young Women and Emotion, 1780–1830.* Charlottesville: University of Virginia Press, 2007.

Blight, David W. *Race and Reunion: The Civil War in American Memory.* Cambridge, MA: Harvard University Press, 2001.

Block, Adrienne Fried. *Amy Beach, Passionate Victorian.* New York: Oxford University Press, 1998.

———. "Matinee Mania, or the Regendering of Nineteenth-Century Audiences in New York City." *19th-Century Music* 31, no. 3 (2008): 193–216.

Blumin, Stuart M. *The Emergence of the Middle Class: Social Experience in the American City, 1760–1900.* Cambridge: Cambridge University Press, 1989.

[Blunt, Ellen Key]. "God and Liberty!" Broadside. Confederate States of America, n.d.

———. "The Southern Cross." Broadside. Confederate States of America, n.d.

Boston, Ray. *British Chartists in America, 1839–1900.* Manchester: Manchester University Press, 1971.

Boston Academy of Music. *First Annual Report of the Boston Academy of Music.* Boston: Perkins, Marvin, 1833.

———. *Second Annual Report of the Boston Academy of Music.* Boston: Perkins, Marvin, 1834.

Bradburn, Douglas. *The Citizenship Revolution: Politics and the Creation of the American Union, 1774–1804.* Charlottesville: University of Virginia Press, 2009.

Branson, Susan. *These Fiery Frenchified Dames: Women and Political Culture in Early National Philadelphia.* Philadelphia: University of Pennsylvania Press, 2001.

Breen, T. H. *George Washington's Journey: The President Forges a New Nation.* New York: Simon and Schuster, 2016.

Brekke, Linzy A. "The 'Scourge of Fashion': Political Economy and the Politics of Consumption in the Early Republic." *Early American Studies* 3, no. 1 (Spring 2005): 111–39.

Brigham, David. *Public Culture in the Early Republic: Peale's Museum and Its Audience*. Washington, DC: Smithsonian Institution Press, 1995.

Brisbane, Redelia. *Albert Brisbane: A Mental Biography*. Boston: Arena, 1893.

Brooks, Corey M. *Liberty Power: Antislavery Third Parties and the Transformation of American Politics*. Chicago: Chicago University Press, 2016.

Broussard, James H. *The Southern Federalists, 1800–1816*. Baton Rouge: Louisiana State University Press, 1978.

Broyles, Michael. "Bourgeois Appropriation of Music: Challenging Ethnicity, Class, and Gender." In *The American Bourgeoisie: Distinction and Identity in the Nineteenth Century*, edited by Sven Beckert and Julia B. Rosenbaum, 233–46. New York: Palgrave Macmillan, 2010.

———. *Mavericks and Other Traditions in American Music*. New Haven, CT: Yale University Press, 2004.

———. "Music and Class Structure in Antebellum Boston." *Journal of the American Musicological Society* 44, no. 3 (Autumn 1991): 451–93.

———. *"Music of the Highest Class": Elitism and Populism in Antebellum Boston*. New Haven, CT: Yale University Press, 1992.

Buckley, Peter George. "To the Opera House: Culture and Society in New York City, 1820–1860." PhD diss., State University of New York at Stony Brook, 1984.

Bunkers, Suzanne L., and Cynthia A. Huff, eds. *Inscribing the Daily: Critical Essays on Women's Diaries*. Amherst: University of Massachusetts Press, 1996.

Burleigh, William H., ed. *The Republican Campaign Songster*. New York: H. Dayton, 1860.

Burney, Charles. *A General History of Music, from the Earliest Ages to the Present Period*. 5 vols. London: Printed for the author and sold by Payne and Son; Robson and Clark; and G.G.J. and J. Robinson, 1776[–89].

Burstein, Andrew. *Sentimental Democracy: The Evolution of America's Romantic Self-Image*. New York: Hill and Wang, 1999.

Bushman, Richard L. *The Refinement of America: Persons, Houses, Cities*. New York: Knopf, 1992.

Butler, Michael. *Votaries of Apollo: The St. Cecilia Society and the Patronage of Concert Music in Charleston, South Carolina, 1766–1820*. Columbia: University of South Carolina Press, 2007.

Butsch, Richard. *The Making of American Audiences: From Stage to Television, 1750–1999*. Cambridge: Cambridge University Press, 2000.

Butterfield, Kevin. *The Making of Tocqueville's America: Law and Association in the Early United States*. Chicago: University of Chicago Press, 2015.

Byrnside, Ronald L. *Music in Eighteenth-Century Georgia*. Athens: University of Georgia Press, 1997.

Carwardine, Richard. *Evangelicals and Politics in Antebellum America*. New Haven, CT: Yale University Press, 1993.

Casper, Scott E. *Constructing American Lives: Biography and Culture in Nineteenth-Century America*. Chapel Hill: University of North Carolina Press, 1999.

Cavicchi, Daniel. *Listening and Longing: Music Lovers in the Age of Barnum*. Middletown, CT: Wesleyan University Press, 2011.
Chambers, William Nisbet, and Walter Dean Burnham, eds. *The American Party Systems: Stages of Political Development*. New York: Oxford University Press, 1967.
Chase, Gilbert. *America's Music: From the Pilgrims to the Present*. 3rd ed. Urbana: University of Illinois Press, 1987.
Cheathem, Mark R. *The Coming of Democracy: Presidential Campaigning in the Age of Jackson*. Baltimore: Johns Hopkins University Press, 2018.
Chmaj, Betty E. "Fry versus Dwight: American Music's Debate over Nationality." *American Music* 3, no. 1 (1985): 63–84.
Cimbala, Paul A. *Under the Guardianship of the Nation: The Freedmen's Bureau and the Reconstruction of Georgia, 1865–1870*. Athens: University of Georgia Press, 1997.
Clark, Jennifer. *The American Idea of England, 1776–1840*. Farnham, UK: Ashgate, 2013.
Clark, Peter. *British Clubs and Societies, 1580–1800: The Origins of an Associational World*. New York: Oxford University Press, 2000.
Cleves, Rachel Hope. *The Reign of Terror in America: Visions of Violence from Anti-Jacobinism to Antislavery*. Cambridge: Cambridge University Press, 2009.
Cmiel, Kenneth. *Democratic Eloquence: The Fight over Popular Speech in Nineteenth-Century America*. Berkeley: University of California Press, 1990.
Cohen, Joanna. *Luxurious Citizens: The Politics of Consumption in Nineteenth-Century America*. Philadelphia: University of Pennsylvania Press, 2017.
Cohen, Kenneth. *They Will Have Their Game: Sporting Culture and the Making of the Early American Republic*. Ithaca, NY: Cornell University Press, 2017.
Coleman, Billy. "Confederate Music and the Politics of Treason and Disloyalty in the American Civil War." *Journal of Southern History* 86, no. 1 (February 2020): 75–116.
Commonwealth of Massachusetts. *General Laws Passed by the General Court of Massachusetts*. Boston: Secretary of the Commonwealth, 1833.
———. *Resolves of the General Court of the Commonwealth of Massachusetts*. Boston: Adams, Rhoades, 1810.
Comotti, Giovanni. *Music in Greek and Roman Culture*. Translated by Rosaria V. Munson. Baltimore: Johns Hopkins University Press, 1979.
Conlin, Michael F. "The Dangerous *Isms* and Fanatical *Ists*: Antebellum Conservatives in the South and the North Confront the Modernity Conspiracy." *Journal of the Civil War Era* 4, no. 3 (June 2014): 205–33.
Crawford, Richard. *America's Musical Life: A History*. New York: Norton, 2005.
———. "Massachusetts Musicians and the Core Repertory of Early American Psalmody.'" In *Music in Colonial Massachusetts, 1630–1820*, vol. 2, *Music in Homes and Churches*, edited by Barbara Lambert, 583–629. Boston: Colonial Society of Massachusetts, 1985.
Crew, Danny O. *Presidential Sheet Music: An Illustrated Catalogue of Published Music Associated with the American Presidency and Those Who Sought the Office*. Jefferson, NC: McFarland, 2001.
Cripe, Helen. *Thomas Jefferson and Music*. Rev. ed. Charlottesville, VA: Thomas Jefferson Foundation and University of North Carolina Press, 2009.

Crist, Elizabeth B. "'Ye Sons of Harmony': Politics, Masculinity, and the Music of William Billings in Revolutionary Boston." *William and Mary Quarterly* 60, no. 2 (April 2003): 333–54.

Crow, Frank Warren. "The Age of Promise: Societies for Social and Economic Improvement in the United States, 1783–1815." PhD diss., University of Wisconsin-Madison, 1952.

Cutterham, Tom. *Gentleman Revolutionaries: Power and Justice in the New American Republic*. Princeton, NJ: Princeton University Press, 2017.

Dalzell, Robert F. *Enterprising Elite: The Boston Associates and the World They Made*. Cambridge, MA: Harvard University Press, 1987.

Daniels, Bruce C. *Puritans at Play: Leisure and Recreation in Colonial New England*. New York: St. Martin's, 1995.

Darnton, Robert. *The Great Cat Massacre: And Other Episodes in French Cultural History*. New York: Basic Books, 1984.

Davidson, Cathy N. "Preface: No More Separate Spheres!" *American Literature* 70, no. 3 (September 1998): 443–63.

Davidson, Mary Wallace. "John Sullivan Dwight and the Harvard Musical Association Orchestra: A Help or a Hindrance?" In *American Orchestras in the Nineteenth Century*, edited by John Spitzer 247–68. Chicago: Chicago University Press, 2012.

Davis, James A. *Maryland, My Maryland: Music and Patriotism during the American Civil War*. Lincoln: University of Nebraska Press, 2019.

———. *Music Along the Rapidan: Civil War Soldiers, Music, and Community during Winter Quarters, Virginia*. Lincoln: University of Nebraska Press, 2014.

Day, David A. Introduction to *The New York Musical World, 1852–1860*, ix–xiv. Ann Arbor, MI: UMI, 1993.

Delano, Sterling F. *Brook Farm: The Dark Side of Utopia*. Cambridge, MA: Harvard University Press, 2004.

———. *"The Harbinger" and New England Transcendentalism: A Portrait of Associationalism in America*. Cranbury, NJ: Associated University Presses, 1983.

Delaplaine, Edward S. *Francis Scott Key: Life and Times*. New York: Biography Press, 1937.

Dichter, Harry, and Elliot Shapiro. *Handbook of Early American Sheet Music, 1768–1889*. New York: Dover, 1977.

Dimaggio, Paul. "Cultural Entrepreneurship in Nineteenth-Century Boston: The Creation of an Organizational Base for High Culture in America." *Media, Culture and Society* 4, no. 1 (January 1982): 33–50.

Doty, Ethan Allen. *The Doty-Doten Family in America: Descendants of Edward Doty, an Emigrant by the Mayflower, 1620*. Brooklyn, NY, 1897.

Dowling, William C. *Literary Federalism in the Age of Jefferson: Joseph Dennie and The Port-Folio, 1801–1812*. Columbia: University of South Carolina Press, 1999.

[Duane, William], ed. *The American Republican Harmonist; or, A Collection of Songs and Odes: Written in America, on American Subjects and Principles: A Great Number of Them Never before Published*. Philadelphia: William Duane, 1803.

Dubovoy, Sina. *The Lost World of Francis Scott Key*. Bloomington, IN: WestBow, 2014.

Eastman, Carolyn. *A Nation of Speechifiers: Making the American Republic after the Revolution*. Chicago: University of Chicago Press, 2009.

[Eliot, Samuel A.]. "Annual Reports of the Boston Academy of Music, from 1833 to 1840 Inclusive . . ." *North American Review* 52, no. 111 (April 1841): 320–38.

———. "Public and Private Charities in Boston." *North American Review* 61, no. 128 (July 1845): 135–59.

Elkins, Stanley, and Eric McKitrick. *The Age of Federalism: The Early American Republic, 1788-1800*. New York: Oxford University Press, 1995.

Ellis, Howard. "Lowell Mason and the 'Manual of the Boston Academy of Music,'" *Journal of Research in Music Education* 3 (Spring 1955): 3–10.

Ellis, Joseph J. *After the Revolution: Profiles of Early American Culture*. New York: Norton, 1979.

———. *Founding Brothers: The Revolutionary Generation*. New York: Vintage Books, 2002.

Emerson, Caleb. *A Discourse on Music, Pronounced at Amherst, N.H., before the Handellian Musical Society*. Amherst, NH: Joseph Cushing, 1808.

Epstein, Dena J. Introduction to *Complete Catalogue of Sheet Music and Musical Works Published by the Board of Trade of the United States of America, 1870*, edited by Board of Music Trade of the United States of America, v–xxvi. New York: Da Capo, 1973.

———. *Sinful Tunes: Black Folk Music to the Civil War*. Urbana: University of Illinois Press, 1977.

Estes, Todd. *The Jay Treaty Debate, Public Opinion, and the Evolution of Early American Political Culture*. Amherst: University of Massachusetts Press, 2006.

Eustace, Nicole. *1812: War and the Passions of Patriotism*. Philadelphia: University of Pennsylvania Press, 2012.

———. *Passion Is the Gale: Emotion, Power, and the Coming of the American Revolution*. Chapel Hill: Omohundro Institute and University of North Carolina Press, 2008.

Eyerman, Ron, and Andrew Jamison. *Music and Social Movements: Mobilizing Traditions in the Twentieth Century*. Boston: South End, 1998.

Faner, Robert D. *Walt Whitman and Music*. Carbondale: Southern Illinois University Press, 1951.

Farmer, Henry T. *An Address Pronounced before the Union Harmonic Society of Charleston, S.C.* Charleston, SC: T. B. Stephens, 1821.

Farmer, John, and Jacob B. Moore. *Gazetteer of the State of New-Hampshire*. Concord, NH: Jacob B. Moore, 1823.

Feldberg, Michael. *The Philadelphia Riots of 1844: A Study of Ethnic Conflict*. Westport, CT: Greenwood, 1975.

Ferris, Marc. *Star-Spangled Banner: The Unlikely Story of America's National Anthem*. Baltimore: Johns Hopkins University Press, 2014.

Filby, P. W., and Edward G. Howard, eds. *Star Spangled Books: Books, Sheet Music, Newspapers, Manuscripts, and Persons Associated with "The Star-Spangled Banner."* Baltimore: Maryland Historical Society, 1972.

Fischer, David Hackett. *The Revolution of American Conservatism: The Federalist Party in the Era of Jeffersonian Democracy*. New York: Harper and Row, 1965.

Fliegelman, Jay. *Declaring Independence: Jefferson, Natural Language, and the Culture of Performance*. Stanford, CA: Stanford University Press, 1993.

Foletta, Marshall. *Coming to Terms with Democracy: Federalist Intellectuals and the Shaping of an American Culture*. Charlottesville: University of Virginia Press, 2001.

Foner, Eric. *Reconstruction: America's Unfinished Revolution, 1863–1877*. New York: Harper & Row, 1988. Reprint, New York: Perennial Classics, 2002.

Formes, Karl. *My Memoirs: Autobiography of Karl Formes*. San Francisco: James H. Barry, 1891.

Formisano, Ronald P. *The Birth of Mass Political Parties: Michigan, 1827–1861*. Princeton, NJ: Princeton University Press, 1971.

———. "The New Political History and the Election of 1840." In *Politics and Political Change: A "Journal of Interdisciplinary History" Reader*, edited by Robert I. Rotbery, 161–82. Cambridge, MA: MIT Press, 2001.

Fraser, James W., *A History of Hope: When Americans Have Dared to Dream of a Better Future*. New York: Palgrave, 2002.

Freeman, Joanne B. *Affairs of Honor: National Politics in the New Republic*. New Haven, CT: Yale University Press, 2001.

———. *The Field of Blood: Violence in Congress and the Road to Civil War*. New York: Farrar, Straus and Giroux, 2018.

Free Soil Minstrel, The. New York: Martin and Ely, 1848.

Furstenberg, François. *When the United States Spoke French: Five Refugees Who Shaped a Nation*. New York: Penguin, 2014.

Furstenberg, François, and David Waldstreicher, eds. "The Republican Court." Special issue, *Journal of the Early Republic* 35, no. 2 (Summer 2015).

Gac, Scott. *Singing for Freedom: The Hutchinson Family Singers and the Nineteenth-Century Culture of Reform*. New Haven, CT: Yale University Press, 2007.

Galbreath, Charles Burleigh. *Alexander Coffman Ross: Author of "Tippecanoe and Tyler, Too."* Columbus, OH: Fred. J. Heer, 1905.

Gardner, William Sewall, and Charles H. Titus. *Proceedings of the Grand Lodge of the Most Ancient and Honorable Fraternity of Free and Accepted Masons of the Commonwealth of Massachusetts*. Boston: Rockwell and Churchill, 1872.

Geffen, Elizabeth M. "Joseph Sill and His Diary." *Pennsylvania Magazine of History of Biography* 84, no. 3 (July 1970): 275–330.

Gienapp, Jonathan. *The Second Creation: Fixing the American Constitution in the Founding Era*. Cambridge, MA: Harvard University Press, 2018.

Gienapp, William E. "'Politics Seem to Enter into Everything': Political Culture in the North, 1840–1860.'" In *Essays on American Antebellum Politics, 1840–1860*, edited by Stephen E. Maizlish and John J. Kushma, 14–69. College Station: Texas A&M University Press, 1982.

Gienow-Hecht, Jessica C. E. *Sound Diplomacy: Music and Emotions in Transatlantic Relations, 1850–1920*. Chicago: University of Chicago Press, 2009.

Ginzburg, Carlo. *The Cheese and the Worms: The Cosmos of a Sixteenth-Century Miller*. Translated by John Tedeschi and Anne Tedeschi. Baltimore: Johns Hopkins University Press, 1976.

Glover, Lori. *Founders as Fathers: The Private Lives and Politics of the American Revolutionaries*. New Haven, CT: Yale University Press, 2014.

Golay, Michael. *A Ruined Land: The End of the Civil War*. New York: Wiley, 1999.

Good, Cassandra. *Founding Friendships: Friendships Between Men and Women in the Early American Republic*. New York: Oxford University Press, 2015.

Goodman, Glenda. "'But They Differ from Us in Sound': Indian Psalmody and the Soundscape of Colonialism, 1651–75." *William and Mary Quarterly*, 69, no. 4 (Fall 2012): 793–822.

———. "'The Tears I Shed at the Songs of Thy Church': Seventeenth-Century Musical Piety in the English Atlantic World." *Journal of the American Musicological Society* 65, no. 3 (Fall 2012): 691–725.

———. "Transatlantic Contrafacta, Musical Formats, and the Creation of Political Culture in Revolutionary America." *Journal of the Society for American Music* 11, no. 4 (November 2017): 392–419.

Gordon, Bonnie. "What Mr. Jefferson Didn't Hear." In *Rethinking Difference in Music Scholarship*, edited by Olivia Bloechl, Melanie Lowe, and Jeffrey Kallberg, 108–32. Cambridge: Cambridge University Press, 2015.

Gordon-Reed, Annette. "Writing Early American Lives as Biography." *William and Mary Quarterly* 71, no. 4 (October 2014): 491–516.

Gordon-Reed, Annette, and Peter S. Onuf. *"Most Blessed of the Patriarchs": Thomas Jefferson and the Empire of Imagination*. New York: Liveright, 2016.

Gould, Eliga H. *Among the Powers of the Earth: The American Revolution and the Making of a New World Empire*. Cambridge, MA: Harvard University Press, 2012.

Gramit, David. *Cultivating Music: The Aspirations, Interests, and Limits of German Musical Culture, 1770–1848*. Berkeley: University of California Press, 2002.

Grant, Kerry S. *Dr. Charles Burney as Critic and Historian of Music*. Ann Arbor, MI: UMI Research Press, 1983.

Gray, Myron. "Musical Politics in French Philadelphia, 1781–1801." PhD diss., University of Pennsylvania, 2014.

———. "A Partisan National Song: The Politics of 'Hail Columbia' Reconsidered." *Music and Politics* 11, no. 2 (Summer 2017). http://dx.doi.org/10.3998/mp.9460447.0011.201.

Griffith, Henry S. *History of the Town of Carver Massachusetts: Historical Review, 1637 to 1910*. New Bedford, MA: E. Anthony, 1913.

Grimsted, David. *American Mobbing, 1828–1861: Toward Civil War*. New York: Oxford University Press, 1998.

Grinspan, Jon. *The Virgin Vote: How Young Americans Made Democracy Social, Politics Personal, and Voting Popular in the Nineteenth Century*. Chapel Hill: University of North Carolina Press, 2016.

Gronningsater, Sarah L. H. "'Expressly Recognized by Our Election Laws': Certificates of Freedom and the Multiple Fates of Black Citizenship in the Early Republic." *William and Mary Quarterly* 75, no. 3 (July 2018): 465–506.

Grow, Matthew J. *"Liberty to the Downtrodden": Thomas L. Kane, Romantic Reformer*. New Haven, CT: Yale University Press, 2009.

Gualdo, John. "To the Philadelphia Merchants, and Others." Broadside. Library Company of Philadelphia, 1769.

Guarneri, Carl J. *The Utopian Alternative: Fourierism in Nineteenth-Century America*. Ithaca, NY: Cornell University Press, 1991.

Gunderson, Robert Gray. *The Log Cabin Campaign*. Lexington: University Press of Kentucky, 1957.

———. "Thurlow Weed's Network: Whig Party Organization in 1840." *Indiana Magazine of History* 48, no. 2 (June 1952): 107–18.

Hale, Matthew Rainbow. "Regenerating the World: The French Revolution, Civic Festivals, and the Forging of Modern American Democracy, 1793–1795." *Journal of American History* 103, no. 4 (March 2017): 891–920.

Hall, Charles Swain. *Benjamin Tallmadge, Revolutionary Soldier and American Businessman*. New York: Columbia University Press, 1943.

Hall, Peter Dobkin. *The Organization of American Culture, 1700–1900: Private Institutions, Elites, and the Origins of America Nationality*. New York: NYU Press, 1984.

Halttunen, Karen. *Confidence Men and Painted Women: A Study of Middle-Class Culture in America, 1830–1870*. New Haven, CT: Yale University Press, 1982.

Handel and Haydn Society. *Constitution of the Handel and Haydn Society. Instituted April, 1815*. Boston: Stebbins, 1815.

Harris, Neil. *The Artist in American Society: The Formative Years: 1790–1860*. New York: G. Braziller, 1966.

Harrison Log Cabin Song Book, The. Columbus, OH: I. N. Whiting, 1840.

Harrison Melodies. Boston: Weeks, Jordan, 1840.

Haulman, Kate. *The Politics of Fashion in Eighteenth-Century America*. Chapel Hill: University of North Carolina Press, 2011.

———. "Rods and Reels: Social Clubs and Political Culture in Early Pennsylvania." *Early American Studies* 12, no. 1 (Winter 2014): 143–73.

Hawkins, John. *A General History of the Science and Practice of Music*. London: Novello, Ewer, 1776.

Haynes, Sam W. *Unfinished Revolution: The Early American Republic in a British World*. Charlottesville: University of Virginia Press, 2010.

Heath, Andrew. *In Union There Is Strength: Philadelphia in the Age of Urban Consolidation*. Philadelphia: University of Pennsylvania Press, 2019.

Henderson, Archibald. *George Washington's Southern Tour, 1791*. Boston: Houghton Mifflin, 1923.

Hershberger, Mary. "Mobilizing Women, Anticipating Abolition: The Struggle against Indian Removal in the 1830s." *Journal of American History* 86, no. 1 (June 1999): 15–40.

Hessinger, Rodney. *Seduced, Abandoned, and Reborn: Visions of Youth in Middle-Class America, 1780–1850*. Philadelphia: University of Pennsylvania Press, 2005.

Higham, John. "From Boundlessness to Consolidation: The Transformation of American Culture, 1848–1860." In *Hanging Together: Unity and Diversity in American Culture*, edited by Carl J. Guarneri, 149–65. New Haven, CT: Yale University Press, 2001.

Hoffman, Richard. *Some Musical Recollections of Fifty Years*. New York: C. Scribner's Sons, 1910.

Holloway, Emory, and Vernolian Schwarz, eds. *I Sit and Look Out: Editorials from the "Brooklyn Daily Times."* New York: Columbia University Press, 1932.

Holt, Michael F. "The Election of 1840, Voter Mobilization, and the Emergence of Jacksonian Voting Behavior." In *A Master's Due: Essays in Honor of David Herbert Donald*, edited by William J. Cooper, Michael F. Holt, and John McCardell, 16–58. Baton Rouge: Louisiana State University Press, 1985.

———. *The Rise and Fall of the American Whig Party: Jacksonian Politics and the Onset of the Civil War*. New York: Oxford University Press, 1999.

Hominick, Ian G. "Sigismund Thalberg (1812–1871), Forgotten Piano Virtuoso: His Career and Musical Contributions." DMA diss., Ohio State University, 1991.

Hooker, Richard. "The Invention of American Musical Culture: Meaning, Criticism, and Musical Acculturation in Antebellum America." In *Keeping Score: Music, Disciplinarity, Culture*, edited by David Schwarz, Anahid Kassabian, and Lawrence Siegel, 107–26. Charlottesville: University of Virginia Press, 1997.

[Hopkinson, Francis]. *A Second Edition of the Lawfulness, Excellency and Advantage of Instrumental Music in the Public Worship of God, but Chiefly of Organs*. Philadelphia: Andrew Steuart, 1763.

———. *Seven Songs for Harpsichord or Forte Piano*. Philadelphia, n.d.

———. *An Account of the Grand Procession. Performed at Philadelphia on Friday the 4th of July 1788. To Which Is Added, a Letter on the Same Subject*. Philadelphia: Hall and Sellers, 1788.

———. "Hail Columbia, the Favorite New Federal Song Adapted to the President's March." [Philadelphia]: [B. Carr], 1798.

Howard, Frank Key. *Fourteen Months in American Bastiles*. Baltimore: Kelly, Hedian and Piet, 1863.

Howe, Daniel Walker. "The Evangelical Movement and Political Culture in the North during the Second Party System." *Journal of American History* 77, no. 4 (March 1991): 1216–39.

———. *The Political Culture of the American Whigs*. Chicago: University of Chicago Press, 1979.

———. *What Hath God Wrought: The Transformation of America, 1815–1848*. New York: Oxford University Press, 2007.

Husk, William Henry. *An Account of the Musical Celebrations on St. Cecilia's Day*. London: Bell and Daldy, 1857.

Huston, Reeve. "What We Talk about When We Talk about Democracy: Reengaging the American Democratic Tradition." *Common-Place* 9, no. 1 (October 2008). http://commonplace.online/article/talk-talk-democracy/.

Irvin, Benjamin H. *Clothed in Robes of Sovereignty: The Continental Congress and the People Out of Doors*. New York: Oxford University Press, 2011.

[Jackson, Jonathan]. *Thoughts upon the Political Situation in the United States of America*. Worcester, MA: Isaiah Thomas, 1788.

Jaffee, David. *A New Nation of Goods: The Material Culture of Early America*. Philadelphia: University of Pennsylvania Press, 2010.

Jefferson, Thomas. *The Papers of Thomas Jefferson*. Edited by Barbara B. Oberg et al. Vol. 33. Princeton, NJ: Princeton University Press, 2006.

———. *Thomas Jefferson's Scrapbooks: Poems of a Nation, Family, and Romantic Love Collected by America's Third President*. Edited by Jonathan Gross. Hanover, NH: Steerforth, 2006.

Jefferson's March, Performed at the Grand Procession at Philadelphia on the 4th of March 1801. Philadelphia: John Aitken, 1801.

Johnson, H. Earle. *Hallelujah, Amen! The Story of the Handel and Haydn Society of Boston*. New York: Da Capo, 1965.

Jones, Charles K. *Francis Johnson (1792–1844): Chronicle of a Black Musician in Early Nineteenth-Century Philadelphia*. Cranbury, NJ: Rosemont, 2006.

Jones, Gareth Stedman, and Ian Patterson. Introduction to *The Theory of the Four Movements*, by Charles Fourier, vii–xxvi. Cambridge: Cambridge University Press, 1996.

Kaestle, Carl F. *Pillars of the Republic: Common School and American Society, 1730–1860*. New York: Hill and Wang, 1983.

Kaestle, Carl F., and Maris A. Vinovskis. *Education and Social Change in Nineteenth-Century Massachusetts*. Cambridge: Cambridge University Press, 1980.

Kane, John K. *Autobiography of the Honorable John K. Kane, 1785–1858, Judge of the District Court of the United States for the Eastern District of Pennsylvania*. Philadelphia: privately printed, 1949.

Kaplan, Amy. "Manifest Domesticity." *American Literature* 70, no. 3 (September 1998): 443–63.

Keene, James A. *A History of Music Education in the United States*. Centennial, CO: Glenbridge, 1982.

Kelley, Mary. *Learning to Stand and Speak: Women, Education, and Public Life in America's Republic*. Chapel Hill: Omohundro Institute and University of North Carolina Press, 2006.

Kelly, Catherine E. *Republic of Taste: Art, Politics, and Everyday Life in Early America*. Philadelphia: University of Pennsylvania Press, 2016.

Kerber, Linda K. *Federalists in Dissent: Imagery and Ideology in Jeffersonian America*. Ithaca, NY: Cornell University Press, 1970.

———. "Separate Spheres, Female Worlds, Woman's Place: The Rhetoric of Women's History." *Journal of American History* 75, no. 1 (June 1988): 9–39.

[Key, Francis Scott]. *Defence of Fort McHenry*. Broadside. Baltimore, 1814. Maryland Historical Society.

———. *Poems of the Late Francis S. Key, Author of the Star-Spangled Banner*. Edited by Roger B. Taney. New York: Carter and Brothers, 1857.

———. "The Star-Spangled Banner: A Patriotic Song." Baltimore: [Thomas] Carr, 1814. Maryland Historical Society.

Knott, Sarah. *Sensibility and the American Revolution*. Chapel Hill: Omohundro Institute and University of North Carolina Press, 2009.

Konkle, Burton Alva. *Joseph Hopkinson, 1770–1842, Jurist-Scholar-Inspirer of the Arts: Author of Hail Columbia*. Philadelphia: University of Pennsylvania Press, 1931.

Kornblith, Gary J. "The Craftsman as Industrialist: Jonas Chickering and the Transformation of American Piano Making." *Business History Review* 59, no. 2 (Autumn 1985): 349–68.

Kornblith, Gary J., Seth Rockman, Jennifer L. Goloboy, Andrew M. Schocket, and Christopher Clark. "Symposium on Class in the Early Republic." Special issue, *Journal of the Early Republic* 25, no. 4 (Winter 2005).
Körner, Axel. "Verdi and the Historians: Politics, Passion, and New Mezzi Di Lavoro." *Journal of Modern Italian Studies* 20, no. 1 (January 2015): 127-37.
Koschnik, Albrecht. *"Let a Common Interest Bind Us Together": Associations, Partisanship, and Culture in Philadelphia, 1775-1840*. Charlottesville: University of Virginia Press, 2007.
Krauss, Anne McClenny. "James Bremner, Alexander Reinagle and the Influence of the Edinburgh Musical Society on Philadelphia." In *Scotland and America in the Age of Enlightenment*, edited by Richard B. Sher and Jeffrey R. Smitten, 259-74. Edinburgh: Edinburgh University Press, 1990.
Kromkowski, Charles A. *Recreating the American Republic: Rules of Appointment, Constitutional Change, and American Political Development, 1700-1870*. Cambridge: Cambridge University Press, 2002.
Kubler, G. F. *Anleitung zum Gesang-Unterrichte in Schulen* [Guide to the study of singing in schools]. Stuttgart: J. B. Metzler'schen Buchhandlung, 1826.
Kun, Josh. *Audiotopia: Music, Race, and America*. Berkeley: University of California Press, 2005.
Lasser, Carol, and Stacey Robertson. *Antebellum Women: Public, Private, Partisan*. Lanham, MD: Rowman and Littlefield, 2010.
Lawrence, Vera Brodsky. *Resonances, 1836-1850*. Vol. 1 of *Strong on Music: The New York Music Scene in the Days of George Templeton Strong*. Chicago: University of Chicago Press, 1988.
———. *Reverberations, 1850-1856*. Vol. 2 of *Strong on Music: The New York Music Scene in the Days of George Templeton Strong*. Chicago: University of Chicago Press, 1995.
Leavenworth, Peter S., Stephen A. Marini, and Nikos Pappas, eds. "Music and Meaning in Early America." Special issue, *Common-Place* 13, no. 2 (Winter 2013).
Le Grand, Julia. *The Journal of Julia Le Grand, New Orleans, 1862-1863*. Edited by Kate Rowland and Angus E. Croxall. Richmond, VA: Everett Waddey, 1911.
Lepler, Jessica M. *The Many Panics of 1837: People, Politics, and the Creation of a Transatlantic Financial Crisis*. New York: Cambridge University Press, 2013.
Lepore, Jill. "Historians Who Love Too Much: Reflections on Microhistory and Biography." *Journal of American History* 88, no. 1 (June 2001): 129-44.
Levine, Lawrence. *Black Culture and Black Consciousness: Afro-American Folk Thought from Slavery to Freedom*. New York: Oxford University Press, 1977.
———. *Highbrow/Lowbrow: The Emergence of Cultural Hierarchy in America*. Cambridge, MA: Harvard University Press, 1990.
Lidtke, Vernon. *The Alternative Culture: Socialist Labor in Imperial Germany*. New York: Oxford University Press, 1985.
Linkon, Sherry Lee. "Reading Lind Mania: Print Culture and the Construction of Nineteenth-Century Audiences." *Book History* 1 (1998): 94-106.
Livermore, Shaw. *The Twilight of Federalism: The Disintegration of the Federalist Party, 1815-1830*. Princeton, NJ: Princeton University Press, 1962.

Livermore, Solomon Kidder. *On the Practice of Music: A Discourse Pronounced at Pepperell, Massachusetts, May 17th, 1809, before the Middlesex Musical Society*. Amherst, NH: Joseph Cushing, 1809.

Log Cabin and Hard Cider Melodies, The: A Collection of Popular and Patriotic Songs. Boston: Charles Adams, 1840.

Log Cabin Minstrel, The; or, Tippecanoe Songster. Roxbury, MA: Patriot and Democrat Office, 1840.

Lonsdale, Roger H. *Dr. Charles Burney: A Literary Biography*. Oxford, UK: Clarendon, 1965.

Lott, Eric. *Love and Theft: Blackface Minstrelsy and the American Working Class*. New York: Oxford University Press, 1993.

Love, Nancy S. *Musical Democracy*. Albany: SUNY Press, 2006.

Lovell, Margaretta. *Art in a Season of Revolution: Painters, Artisans, and Patrons in Early America*. Philadelphia: University of Pennsylvania Press, 2005.

Luskey, Brian P. *On the Make: Clerks and the Quest for Capital in Nineteenth-Century America*. New York: NYU Press, 2010.

Lynn, Joshua A. *Preserving the White Man's Republic: Jacksonian Democracy, Race, and the Transformation of American Conservatism*. Charlottesville: University of Virginia Press, 2019.

[Lyon, James]. *The Lawfulness, Excellency, and Advantage of Instrumental Music in the Public Worship of God*. Philadelphia: William Dunlap, 1763.

Lyons, Maura. *William Dunlap and the Construction of an American Art History*. Amherst: University of Massachusetts Press, 2005.

Mahar, William. *Behind the Burnt Cork Mask: Early Blackface Minstrelsy and Antebellum American Popular Culture*. Urbana: University of Illinois Press, 1999.

Manz, Stefan. "Joseph Mainzer (1801–1851) and the Popularisation of Choral Singing in Britain." *Immigrants and Minorities* 30, nos. 2–3 (July–November): 152–70.

Marini, Stephen A. "Hymnody and History: Early American Evangelical Hymns as Sacred Music." In *Music in American Religious Experience*, edited by Philip Vilas Bohlman, Edith L. Blumhofer, and Maria M. Chow, 123–54. New York: Oxford University Press, 2006.

Mark, Michael L., and Charles L. Gary. *A History of American Music Education*. 3rd ed. New York: Schirmer Books, 1992.

Mason, Lowell. *Manual of the Boston Academy of Music, for Instruction in the Elements of Vocal Music on the System of Pestalozzi*. Boston: Carter, Hendee, 1834.

Mason, Matthew. *Apostle of Union: A Political Biography of Edward Everett*. Chapel Hill: University of North Carolina Press, 2016.

Mattern, Mark. *Acting in Concert: Music, Community, and Political Action*. New Brunswick, NJ: Rutgers University Press, 1998.

McCarthy, Kathleen D. *American Creed: Philanthropy and the Rise of Civil Society, 1700–1865*. Chicago: University of Chicago Press, 2003.

McCoy, Drew R. *The Elusive Republic: Political Economy in Jeffersonian America*. Chapel Hill: Omohundro Institute and University of North Carolina Press, 1980.

McFeely, William S. *Yankee Stepfather: General O. O. Howard and the Freedmen*. New York: Norton, 1964.
McHenry, Elizabeth. *Forgotten Readers: Recovering the Lost History of African American Literary Societies*. Durham, NC: Duke University Press, 2002.
McWhirter, Christian. *Battle Hymns: The Power and Popularity of Music in the Civil War*. Chapel Hill: University of North Carolina Press, 2012.
Miles, William. *Songs, Odes, Glees, and Ballads: A Bibliography of American Presidential Campaign Songsters*. New York: Greenwood, 1990.
Miller, Lillian B. *Patrons and Patriotism: The Encouragement of the Fine Arts in the United States, 1790–1860*. Chicago: University of Chicago Press, 1966.
Mitchell, Samuel Latham. *An Oration, Pronounced before the Society of Black Friars*. New York: Friar M'Lean, 1793.
Moats, Sandra. *Celebrating the Republic: Presidential Ceremony and Popular Sovereignty*. DeKalb: Northern Illinois University Press, 2010.
Molotsky, Irvin. *The Flag, the Poet, and the Song: The Story of the Star-Spangled Banner*. New York: Dutton, 2001.
Moore, Frank, ed. *Rebel Rhymes and Rhapsodies*. New York: George P. Putnam, 1864.
Motz, Marilyn Ferris. "Folk Expression of Time and Place: 19th-Century Midwestern Rural Diaries." *Journal of American Folklore* 100, no. 396 (June 1987): 131–47.
Muller, Joseph. *The Star-Spangled Banner: Words and Music Issued between 1814–1864*. New York: G. A. Baker, 1935.
Murphy, Brian Phillips. *Building the Empire State: Political Economy in the Early Republic*. Philadelphia: University of Pennsylvania Press, 2015.
Murrin, John M. *Rethinking America: From Empire to Republic*. New York: Oxford University Press, 2018.
[Musical Fund Society of Philadelphia]. *Act of Incorporation, Approved February 22, 1823; Amendment Thereof Approved April 28, 1857, and By-Laws as Revised and Amended May 7, 1912, Together with a List of Officers and Members, Historical Data, and List of Portraits*. Philadelphia, 1930.
———. *Charter and By-Laws of the Musical Fund Society of Philadelphia and List of Officers and Members*. Philadelphia, 1930.
———. *Constitution of the Musical Fund Society of Philadelphia*. Philadelphia: Thomas H. Palmer, 1822.
Musical Society at the Castle-Tavern in Pater-Noster Row. *Bylaws of the Musical Society at the Castle-Tavern in Pater-Noster Row*. London, 1731.
Nathans, Heather S. *Early American Theatre from the Revolution to Thomas Jefferson: Into the Hands of the People*. Cambridge: Cambridge University Press, 2003.
———. "Forging a Powerful Engine: Building Theatres and Elites in Post-Revolutionary Boston and Philadelphia." *Pennsylvania History* 66, special supplemental issue (1999): 113–43.
National Clay Minstrel and True Whig's Companion for the Presidential Canvass of 1844, The. Philadelphia: George Hood, 1843.
National Park Service. "Annual Park Recreation Visitation (1904–Last Calendar Year): Fort McHenry NM & HS." https://irma.nps.gov/Stats/SSRSReports/Park

Specific Reports/Annual Park Recreation Visitation (1904 - Last Calendar Year)?Park=FOMC.

Neely, Mark E., Jr. *The Boundaries of American Political Culture in the Civil War Era*. Chapel Hill: University of North Carolina Press, 2005.

Neem, Johann N. *Creating a Nation of Joiners: Democracy and Civil Society in Early National Massachusetts*. Cambridge, MA: Harvard University Press, 2008.

———. *Democracy's Schools: The Rise of Public Education in America*. Baltimore: Johns Hopkins University Press, 2017.

Nelson, Eric. *The Royalist Revolution: Monarchy and the American Founding*. Cambridge, MA: Harvard University Press, 2014.

Newman, Nancy. *Good Music for a Free People: The Germania Musical Society in Nineteenth-Century America*. Rochester, NY: University of Rochester Press, 2010.

Newman, Simon P. *Parades and the Politics of the Street: Festive Culture in the Early American Republic*. Philadelphia: University of Pennsylvania Press, 1997.

[New Musical Fund]. *Songs, Chorusses, &c. Performed at the King's Theatre, Haymarket, on Thursday, the 6th of March, 1794, for the Benefit of the New Musical Fund, Established April 16th, 1786. To Which Are Added, a List of the Subscribers*. London: A. Grant, 1794.

Norton, A. B. *The Great Revolution of 1840: Reminiscences of the Log Cabin and Hard Cider Campaign*. Mount Vernon, OH: A. B. Norton, 1888.

Ochiai, Akiko. *Harvesting Freedom: African American Agrarianism in Civil War Era South Carolina*. Westport, CT: Praeger, 2004.

———. "The Port Royal Experiment Revisited: Northern Visions of Reconstruction and the Land Question." *New England Quarterly* 74, no. 1 (March 2001): 94–117.

O'Connell, Deirdre. *The Ballad of Blind Tom, Slave Pianist: America's Lost Musical Genius*. New York: Overlook, 2009.

O'Donnell, Catherine. "Literature and Politics in the Early Republic: Views from the Bridge." *Journal of the Early Republic* 30, no. 2 (Summer 2010): 279–92.

Ogasapian, John. *Music of the Colonial and Revolutionary Era*. Westport, CT: Greenwood, 2004.

O.K. Songster. [S.l.: s.n., 1840].

Onuf, Peter S., and Nicholas Cole, eds. *Thomas Jefferson, the Classical World, and Early America*. Charlottesville: University of Virginia Press, 2011.

Owen, Kenneth. "Legitimacy, Localism, and the First Party System." In *Practicing Democracy: Popular Politics in the United States from the Constitution to the Civil War*, edited by Daniel Peart and Adam I. P. Smith, 173–95. Charlottesville: University of Virginia Press, 2015.

Owen, William, and William Johnston, eds. *A New and General Biographical Dictionary, Vol. VI*. London: n.p., 1784.

Pacificatory Letter about Psalmody or Singing of Psalms, Dated December 23, 1723. Boston: J. Franklin for Benjamin Eliot, 1724.

[Paine, Robert Treat, Jr.]. "Adams and Liberty." In *The American Musical Miscellany*, 211–18. Northampton, MA: D. Wright, 1798.

Parish, Elijah. *The Excellence of the Gospel Visible in the Wretchedness of Paganism. A Discourse Delivered December 20, 1797, Being the Tenth Anniversary of His Ordination*. Newburyport, MA: A. March, 1798.

Pasler, Jann. *Composing the Citizen: Music as Public Utility in Third Republic France.* Berkeley: University of California Press, 2009.

Pasley, Jeffrey L. "The Cheese and the Words: Popular Political Culture and Participatory Democracy in the Early American Republic." In *Beyond the Founders: New Approaches to the Political History of the Early American Republic*, edited by Jeffrey L. Pasley, Andrew W. Robertson, and David Waldstreicher, 31–56. Chapel Hill: Omohundro Institute and University of North Carolina Press, 2004.

———. *The First Presidential Contest: 1796 and the Founding of American Democracy.* Lawrence: University Press of Kansas, 2013.

———. *Tyranny of the Printers: Newspaper Politics in the Early American Republic.* Charlottesville: University of Virginia Press, 2000.

Pasley, Jeffrey L., Andrew W. Robertson, and David Waldstreicher, eds. *Beyond the Founders: New Approaches to the Political History of the Early American Republic.* Chapel Hill: Omohundro Institute and University of North Carolina Press, 2004.

Peart, Daniel. *Era of Experimentation: American Political Practices in the Early Republic.* Charlottesville: University of Virginia Press, 2014.

Peart, Daniel, and Adam I. P. Smith, eds. *Practicing Democracy: Popular Politics in the United States from the Constitution to the Civil War.* Charlottesville: University of Virginia Press, 2015.

Pemberton, Carol A. "Critical Days for Music in American Schools." *Journal of Research in Music Education* 36, no. 2 (Summer 1988): 69–82.

———. "'The Manual of the Boston Academy of Music,' 1834: A Remarkable Book from a Remarkable Era." *Bulletin of Historical Research in Music Education* 7, no. 2 (July 1986): 41–54.

Pennsylvania General Assembly. *An Act to Confer on Certain Associations of the Citizens of This Commonwealth the Powers and Immunities of Corporations, or Bodies Politic in Law, April 6, 1791.* 6 April 1791. https://en.wikisource.org/wiki/Act_Approved_April_6,_1791.

People's Friend, The: Written & Composed for the Celebration of the 4th of March 1801, Words by A Citizen [Rembrandt Peale], music by John L. Hawkins. Philadelphia: G. Willig, 1801.

Perkins, Charles C. *History of the Handel and Haydn Society of Boston Massachusetts.* Vol. 1. Boston: Alfred Mudge and Son, 1883.

Picker, John. "Late 1740s; 1814, September 13–14: Two National Anthems." In *A New Literary History of America*, edited by Greil Marcus and Werner Sollors, 84–88. Cambridge, MA: Harvard University Press, 2009.

Pliny. *The Natural History of Pliny.* Edited and translated by John Bostock and H. T. Riley. Vol. 2. London: G. Bell, 1890.

Plutarch. *Plutarch's Lives, Translated from the Original Greek; with Notes, Critical and Historical; and a Life of Plutarch, Vol. 1.* Edited by John Langhorne and William Langhorne. London: Richards, 1823.

Poore, Perley. *Reminiscences of Sixty Years in the National Metropolis.* Vol. 1. Philadelphia: Hubbard Brothers, 1886.

Pope, Alexander. *The Poetical Works of Alexander Pope.* Vol. 1. London: William Pickering, 1835.

Portnoy, Alisse. *Their Right to Speak: Women's Activism in the Indian and Slave Debates.* Cambridge, MA: Harvard University Press, 2005.

Potter, Dorothy T. *"Food for Apollo": Cultivated Music in Antebellum Philadelphia.* Lanham, MD: Rowman and Littlefield and Lehigh University Press, 2011.

Preston, Katherine K. *Opera on the Road: Traveling Opera Troupes in the United States, 1825-60.* Urbana: University of Illinois Press, 1993.

Ratcliffe, Donald. "The Right to Vote and the Rise of Democracy, 1787-1828." *Journal of the Early Republic* 33, no. 2 (Summer 2013): 219-54.

Rath, Richard Cullen. *How Early America Sounded.* Ithaca, NY: Cornell University Press, 2003.

Rebora, Carrie J. "The American Academy of the Fine Arts, New York, 1802-1842, Volumes I & II." PhD diss., City University of New York, 1990.

Remini, Robert V. *Daniel Webster: The Man and His Time.* New York: Norton, 1997.

Rendall, Steven. "On Diaries." *Diacritics* 16, no. 3 (Autumn 1986): 56-65.

Resch, John P. *Suffering Soldiers: Revolutionary War, Veterans, Moral Sentiment, and Political Culture in the Early Republic.* Amherst: University of Massachusetts Press, 1999.

Reynolds, David S. *Walt Whitman.* New York: Oxford University Press, 2005.

Richard, Carl J. *The Founders and the Classics: Greece, Rome, and the American Enlightenment.* Cambridge, MA: Harvard University Press, 1994.

Riordan, Liam. "'O Dear What Can the Matter Be?': The Urban Early Republic and the Politics of Popular Song in Benjamin Carr's Federal Overture." *Journal of the Early Republic* 31, no. 2 (Summer 2011): 179-227.

Roberts, Brian. *Blackface Nation: Race, Reform, and Identity in American Popular Music, 1812-1925.* Chicago: University of Chicago Press, 2017.

Robertson, Andrew W. "Jeffersonian Parties, Politics, and Participation: The Tortuous Trajectory of American Democracy." In *Practicing Democracy: Popular Politics in the United States from the Constitution to the Civil War*, edited by Daniel Peart and Adam I. P. Smith, 99-122. Charlottesville: University of Virginia Press, 2015.

Robin, William. "Colin Kaepernick and the Radical Uses of 'The Star-Spangled Banner.'" *New Yorker*, 29 August 2016. https://www.newyorker.com/culture/culture-desk/colin-kaepernick-and-the-radical-uses-of-the-star-spangled-banner.

Roche, John F. "The Uranian Society: Gentleman and Scholars in Federal New York." *New York History* 52, no. 2 (April 1971): 121-32.

Rogers, Francis. "Jenny Lind." *Musical Quarterly* 32, no. 3 (July 1946): 437-48.

Roney, Jessica Choppin. *Governed by a Spirit of Opposition: The Origins of American Political Practice in Colonial Philadelphia.* Baltimore: Johns Hopkins University Press, 2014.

Roosevelt, Clinton. *The Science of Government, Founded on Natural Law.* New York: Dean and Trevett, 1841.

Rose, Willie Lee. *Rehearsal for Reconstruction: The Port Royal Experiment.* Indianapolis: Bobbs-Merrill, 1964.

Rosenthal, Rob, and Richard Flacks. *Playing for Change: Music and Musicians in the Service of Social Movements.* New York: Routledge, 2011.

[Royal Society of Musicians]. *Laws for the Management and Appropriation of the Fund for the Support of Decayed Musicians, Members of the Royal Society of Musicians, and Their Families*. London, 1790.

Russell, Dave. *Popular Music in England, 1840–1914: A Social History*. Manchester: Manchester University Press, 1987.

Rutherford, Susan. *The Prima Donna and Opera, 1815–1930*. Cambridge: Cambridge University Press, 2006.

Ryan, Mary P. *Cradle of the Middle Class: The Family in Oneida County, New York, 1790–1865*. Cambridge: Cambridge University Press, 1981.

Saloman, Ora Frishberg. *Beethoven's Symphonies and J. S. Dwight: The Birth of American Music Criticism*. Boston: Northeastern University Press, 1995.

Samples, Mark C. "The Humbug and the Nightingale: P. T. Barnum, Jenny Lind, and the Branding of a Star Singer for American Reception." *Musical Quarterly* 99, nos. 3–4 (Fall-Winter 2016): 286–320.

Sanjek, Russell. *American Popular Music and Its Business: The First Four Hundred Years*. Vol. 2. New York: Oxford University Press, 1988.

Schlesinger, Arthur M., Sr. "A Note on Songs as Patriot Propaganda, 1765–1776." *William and Mary Quarterly* 11, no. 1 (January 1954): 78–88.

Schocket, Andrew M. "Thinking about Elites in the Early Republic." *Journal of the Early Republic* 25, no. 4 (Winter 2005): 547–55.

Schoening, Benjamin S., and Eric T. Kasper. *Don't Stop Thinking about the Music: The Politics of Songs and Musicians in Presidential Campaigns*. Lanham, MD: Lexington Books, 2012.

Schrader, Arthur F. "Broadside Ballads of Boston, 1813: The Isaiah Thomas Collection." *Proceedings of the American Antiquarian Society* 98 (April 1988): 69–111. https://www.americanantiquarian.org/proceedings/44539422.pdf.

———. "Songs to Cultivate the Sensations of Freedom." In *Music in Colonial Massachusetts, 1630–1820*, vol. 1, *Music in Public Spaces*, edited by Barbara Lambert, 105–56. Boston: Colonial Society of Massachusetts, 1980.

Schreiber, Lee L. "The Academy: School for Artists or Private Art Club." *Pennsylvania History* 47, no. 4 (October 1980): 331–50.

———. "Bluebloods and Local Societies: A Philadelphia Microcosm." *Pennsylvania History* 48, no. 3 (July 1981): 251–66.

———. "The Philadelphia Elite in the Development of the Pennsylvania Academy of Fine Arts, 1805–1842." PhD diss., Temple University, 1977.

Seitz, Don C. *Horace Greeley: Founder of the "New York Tribune."* Indianapolis: Bobbs-Merrill, 1926.

Semi, Maria. *Music as a Science of Mankind in Eighteenth-Century Britain*. Translated by Timothy Keats. Farnham, UK: Ashgate, 2012.

Seybolt, Robert Francis. *The Public Schools of Colonial Boston*. Cambridge, MA: Harvard University Press, 1935.

Shadle, Douglas W. *Orchestrating the Nation: The Nineteenth-Century American Symphonic Enterprise*. New York: Oxford University Press, 2016.

Shank, Barry. *The Political Force of Musical Beauty*. Durham, NC: Duke University Press, 2014.

Shankman, Andrew. "A Synthesis Useful and Compelling: Anglicization and the Achievement of John M. Murrin." In *Anglicizing America: Empire, Revolution, Republic*, edited by Ignacio Gallup-Diaz, Andrew Shankman, and David J. Silverman, 20–56. Philadelphia: University of Pennsylvania Press, 2015.

Shields, David S. *Civil Tongues and Polite Letters in British America*. Chapel Hill: Omohundro Institute and University of North Carolina Press, 1997.

Shields, David S., and Fredrika J. Teute. "The Republican Court and the Historiography of a Woman's Domain in the Public Sphere." *Journal of the Early Republic* 35, no. 2 (July 2015): 169–83.

Shire, Laurel Clark. "Sentimental Racism and Sympathetic Paternalism: Feeling like a Jacksonian." *Journal of the Early Republic* 39, no. 1 (Spring 2019): 111–22.

Silbey, Joel H. *The American Political Nation, 1838–1893*. Stanford, CA: Stanford University Press, 1991.

Silverman, Kenneth. *A Cultural History of the American Revolution: Painting, Music, Literature, and the Theatre in the Colonies and the United States from the Treaty of Paris to the Inauguration of George Washington, 1763–1789*. New York: Thomas Y. Crowell, 1976.

Simpson, Lewis P. "Federalism and the Crisis of Literary Order." *American Literature* 32, no. 3 (November 1960): 253–66.

———. *The Federalist Literary Mind: Selections from the Monthly Anthology and Boston Review, 1803–1811*. Baton Rouge: Louisiana State University Press, 1962.

Sinha, Manisha. *The Slave's Cause: A History of Abolition*. New Haven, CT: Yale University Press, 2016.

Siskin, M. Keith. "Joseph Hopkinson (1770–1842)." In *Great American Lawyers: An Encyclopedia*, vol. 1, edited by John R. Vile, 365–72. Santa Barbara, CA: ABC-CLIO, 2001.

Six Patriotic Ballads Respectfully Dedicated to the Tippecanoe Associations, Partly Written and Arranged by a Member of the Fifth Ward Club. New York: Thomas Birch, 1840.

Slauter, Eric. *The State as a Work of Art: The Cultural Origins of the Constitution*. Chicago: University of Chicago Press, 2009.

Smith, Adam I. P. *The Stormy Present: Conservatism and the Problem of Slavery in Northern Politics, 1846–1865*. Chapel Hill: University of North Carolina Press, 2017.

Smith, Kimberly K. *The Dominion of Voice: Riot, Reason, and Romance in Antebellum Politics*. Lawrence: University Press of Kansas, 1999.

Smith, Mark M. *Listening to Nineteenth-Century America*. Chapel Hill: University of North Carolina Press, 2001.

Smither, Howard E. *The Oratorio in the Classical Era*. Vol. 3 of *A History of the Oratorio*. Chapel Hill: University of North Carolina Press, 1987.

Songs for the People; or, Tippecanoe Melodies. New York: James P. Giffing, 1840.

Sonneck, O. G. *Early Concert-Life in America, 1731–1800*. Leipzig: Britkopf and Hartel, 1907.

———. *Francis Hopkinson: The First American Poet-Composer and James Lyon, Patriot, Preacher, Psalmodist, 1735–1794*. Washington, DC: H. L. McQueen, 1905.

———. *Report on "The Star-Spangled Banner," "Hail Columbia," and "Yankee Doodle."* Washington, DC: Government Printing Office, 1909.

———. *The Star-Spangled Banner*. Washington, DC: Government Printing Office, 1914.

Spitzer, John, ed. *American Orchestras in the Nineteenth Century*. Chicago: University of Chicago Press, 2012.

Stauffer, John, and Benjamin Soskis. *The Battle Hymn of the Republic: A Biography of the Song That Marches On*. New York: Oxford University Press, 2013.

Stevens, John Anthony. "Henry Russell in America: Chutzpah and Huzzah." DMA diss., University of Illinois at Urbana-Champaign, 1975.

Stevenson, Robert. "'The Rivals'—Hawkins, Burney, and Boswell." *Musical Quarterly* 36, no. 1 (January 1950): 67–82.

Stowe, Steven M. *Keep the Days: Reading the Civil War Diaries of Southern Women*. Chapel Hill: University of North Carolina Press, 2018.

Street, John. *Music and Politics*. Cambridge, UK: Polity, 2012.

Swift, Lindsay. *Brook Farm: Its Members, Scholars, and Visitors*. New York: Macmillan, 1900.

Tawa, Nicholas E. "Dempster, William Richardson." *Grove Music Online*. 1 July 2014. https://www.oxfordmusiconline.com/grovemusic/view/10.1093/gmo/9781561592630.001.0001/omo-9781561592630-e-1002262206.

———. *From Psalm to Symphony: A History of Music in New England*. Boston: Northeastern University Press, 2001.

Taylor, Alan. "From Fathers to Friends of the People: Political Personae in the Early Republic." In *Federalists Reconsidered*, edited by Doron Ben-Atar and Barbara B. Oberg, 225–45. Charlottesville: University of Virginia Press, 1998.

Taylor, Anne-Marie. *Young Charles Sumner and the Legacy of the American Enlightenment, 1811–1851*. Amherst: University of Massachusetts Press, 2001.

Taylor, Jordan E. "The Reign of Error: North American Information Politics and the French Revolution, 1789–1795," *Journal of the Early Republic* 39, no. 3 (Fall 2019): 437–66.

Temperley, Nicholas. "The Old Way of Singing: Its Origins and Development." *Journal of the American Musicological Society* 34, no. 3 (Autumn 1981): 511–44.

Tennenhouse, Leonard. *The Importance of Feeling English: American Literature and the British Diaspora, 1750–1850*. Princeton, NJ: Princeton University Press, 2007.

Tevis, Julia Anne Hieronymus. "Julia Anne Hieronymus Tevis, 1799–1879." In *Recollections of the Early Republic: Selected Autobiographies*, edited by Joyce Appleby, 68–102. Boston: Northeastern University Press, 1997.

Tick, Judith. *American Women Composers before 1870*. Rochester, NY: University of Rochester Press, 1995.

Tick, Judith, and Paul Beaudoin, eds. *Music in the USA: A Documentary Companion*. 2nd ed. New York: Oxford University Press, 2008.

Tippecanoe Songbook: A Collection of Log Cabin and Patriotic Melodies. Philadelphia: Marshall, Williams, and Butler, 1840.

Travers, Len. *Celebrating the Fourth: Independence Day and the Rites of Nationalism in the Early Republic*. Boston: University of Massachusetts Press, 1997.

Tripp, Edward. *The Meridian Handbook of Classical Mythology*. New York: New American Library, 1970.

Ulrich, Laurel Thatcher. *A Midwife's Tale: The Life of Martha Ballard, Based on Her Diary, 1785-1812*. New York: Knopf, 1990.

US Congress. *Annals of Congress*. House of Representatives, 7th Cong., 1st sess. 7 December 1801 to 3 May 1802.

———. *Biographical Dictionary of the United States Congress*. Washington, DC: Office of the Historian. http://bioguide.congress.gov/biosearch/biosearch.asp.

US War Department. *The War of the Rebellion: A Compilation of the Official Records of the Union and Confederate Armies*. Washington, DC: Government Printing Office, 1880-1901.

Van Horn, Jennifer. *The Power of Objects in Eighteenth-Century British America*. Chapel Hill: Omohundro Institute and University of North Carolina Press, 2017.

Varon, Elizabeth R. *Disunion! The Coming of the American Civil War, 1789-1859*. Chapel Hill: University of North Carolina Press, 2008.

Waldstreicher, David. *In the Midst of Perpetual Fetes: The Making of Modern American Nationalism, 1776-1820*. Chapel Hill: Omohundro Institute and the University of North Carolina Press, 1997.

———. "Minstrelization and Nationhood: 'Backside Albany,' Backlash, and the Wartime Origins of Blackface Minstrelsy." In *Warring for America, 1803-1818: Cultural Contests in the Era of 1812*, edited by Nicole Eustace, Robert Parkinson, and Fredrika J. Teute, 29-55. Chapel Hill: Omohundro Institute and University of North Carolina Press, 2017.

Waldstreicher, David, Jeffrey L. Pasley, and Andrew W. Robertson. Introduction to *Beyond the Founders: New Approaches to the Political History of the Early American Republic*, edited by Jeffrey L. Pasley, Andrew W. Robertson, and David Waldstreicher, 1-28. Chapel Hill: Omohundro Institute and University of North Carolina Press, 2004.

Walsh, Basil. *Catherine Hayes: The Hibernian Prima Donna*. Dublin: Irish Academic Press, 2000.

Walsh, Megan. *The Portrait and the Book: Illustration and Literary Culture in Early America*. Iowa City: University of Iowa Press, 2017.

Ware, W. Porter, and Thaddeus C. Lockard Jr. *P. T. Barnum Presents Jenny Lind: The American Tour of the Swedish Nightingale*. Baton Rouge: Louisiana State University Press, 1980.

Washington, George. *The Diaries of George Washington*. Edited by Donald Jackson and Dorothy Twohig. Vols. 5-6. Charlottesville: University of Virginia Press, 1976.

WBAL-TV 11 Baltimore. "New Visitors Center Ready for Star Spangled Celebration." YouTube, 2 March 2011. http://www.youtube.com/watch?v=J2lXRhDpHPc.

Weber, William. *Music and the Middle Class: The Social Structure of Concert Life in London, Paris and Vienna between 1830 and 1848*. 2nd ed. Aldershot, UK: Ashgate, 1975.

Weed, Thurlow. *Life of Thurlow Weed Including His Autobiography and Memoir*. Vol. 1. Edited by Harriet A. Weed. Boston: Houghton, Mifflin, 1884.

Westwood, Howard C. "Generals David Hunter and Rufus Saxton and Black Soldiers." *South Carolina Historical Magazine* 86, no. 3 (July 1985): 165–81.
White, Shane. "'It Was a Proud Day': African Americans, Festivals, and Parades in the North, 1741–1834." *Journal of American History* 81, no. 1 (June 1994): 13–50.
White, Shane, and Graham White. *The Sounds of Slavery: Discovering African American History through Songs, Sermons, and Speech*. Boston: Beacon, 2005.
Whitman, Z[ackariah]. G[ardner]. *An Address Delivered before the Harmonick Club, a Musical Society in Boston*. Boston: Joshua Cushing, 1809.
Whole Booke of Psalmes Faithfully Translated into English Metre, The. Cambridge, MA, 1640.
Wilentz, Sean. *Chants Democratic: New York City and the Rise of the American Working Class, 1788–1850*. New York: Oxford University Press, 1984.
———. *The Rise of American Democracy: Jefferson to Lincoln*. New York: Norton, 2005.
———. "1853: *The Sacred Harp*: Shape-Note Singing." In *A New Literary History of America*, edited by Greil Marcus and Werner Sollors, 225–30. Cambridge, MA: Harvard University Press, 2009.
Williams, Robert C. *Horace Greeley: Champion of American Freedom*. New York: NYU Press, 2006.
Williamson, Samuel H. "Seven Ways to Compute the Relative Value of a U.S. Dollar Amount, 1790 to Present." MeasuringWorth.com, http://www.measuringworth.com/uscompare/.
———. "Five Ways to Compute the Relative Value of a UK Pound Amount, 1270 to Present." MeasuringWorth.com, https://www.measuringworth.com/calculators/ukcompare/.
Wilson, Bruce Dunbar. "A Documentary History of Music in the Public Schools of the City of Boston, 1830–1850." 2 vols. PhD diss., University of Michigan, 1973.
Wilson, James Grant, and John Fiske, eds. *Appleton's Cyclopaedia of American Biography*. Vol. 5. New York: D. Appleton, 1900.
Wilson, James J. comp. *A National Song-Book, Being a Collection of Patriotic, Martial, and Naval Songs and Odes, Principally of American Composition*. Trenton, NJ: James J. Wilson, 1813.
Winterer, Caroline. *The Culture of Classicism: Ancient Greece and Rome in American Intellectual Life, 1780–1910*. Baltimore: Johns Hopkins University Press, 2002.
Wood, Kirsten E. "'Join with Heart and Soul and Voice': Music, Harmony, and Politics in the Early American Republic." *American Historical Review* 119, no. 4 (October 2014): 1083–116.
Woods, Michael E. *Emotional and Sectional Conflict in the Antebellum United States*. Cambridge: Cambridge University Press, 2014.
Yankaskas, Lynda K. "Borrowing Culture: Social Libraries and American Civil Life, 1731–1854." PhD diss., Brandeis University, 2009.
Yokota, Kariann Akemi. *Unbecoming British: How Revolutionary America Became a Postcolonial Nation*. New York: Oxford University Press, 2011.
Zabriskie, Francis Nicoll. *Horace Greeley: The Editor*. New York: Funk and Wagnalls, 1890.

Zagarri, Rosemary. "Gender and the First Party System." In *Federalists Reconsidered*, edited by Doron Ben-Atar and Barbara B. Oberg, 118–34. Charlottesville: University of Virginia Press, 1998.

Zboray, Ronald J., and Mary Saracino Zboray. "Whig Women, Politics, and Culture in the Campaign of 1840: Three Perspectives from Massachusetts." *Journal of the Early Republic* 17, no. 2 (Summer 1997): 277–315.

Index

Note: Italic page numbers refer to tables and illustrations.

abolitionism, 3, 10, 104, 135–37, 138, 162, 203n116. *See also* anti-slavery movement
Academy of Painting, 70
Academy of Vocal Music, 70
Adams, Abigail, 24–25
Adams, Charles, 24–26
Adams, Charles Francis, 136
Adams, John: Benjamin Franklin Bache on, 35; on democracy, 15–16; and Federalist musical ideal, 24–26, 32, 39, 46, 162, 174n17; Federalist support for, 1, 34; image on sheet music of "Hail Columbia," 37, *38*; and XYZ Affair, 33
Adams, Samuel, 52
"Adams and Liberty," 43
Ahlquist, Karen, 153
Albany Argus, 107, 109
Albany Evening Journal, 94, 110
Alexandria Gazette, 86
Alien and Sedition Acts, 1, 35
almanacs, publication of melodies in, 7
amateur literary culture, 99
American Academy of Sciences, 70
American diarists, on music, 5, 167n12
American elites: attitudes about American people, 64; conservative ideals about music, 9, 10, 11, 12, 56–61, 113; and cultivation of national culture, 23–24; cultural stewardship of, 62–64, 66–69; defining of, 167n13; diarists' reflections on music, 5, 6; harmony as goal of, 3–4, 15, 24, 163; and origins of popular politics, 22; political practices of, 5; power to control use of music, 3, 4; in Republican Party, 39–40, 170–71n26; on role of music, 9, 26; and salon concert culture, 51–52, 53; use of music as social control, 3; and will of the people, 14
American identity, development of, 18–19
American Musical Journal, 58–59
American nationalism, popular practices of, 172n38
American patriotic songs, uses and associations of, 167n15
American people: constitutional definition of, 14; Federalist elites' cultural stewardship of, 62–64, 66–69; judgment of common good, 81; relationship with leaders, 12, 14–17, 18, 20, 22, 24, 26, 39, 40–41, 42, 45, 178n71; will of, 14, 15
American Philosophical Society, 63
American political culture: and creation of popular republican democracy, 12, 87–88, 93, 107, 111, 162, 163, 190n17; early political parties' role in, 17–18, 120, 170n24; elitist ideals at origin of, 7, 9, 47; Federalist influence on, 9, 24; and Francis Hopkinson, 27; music's role in development of, 3, 4, 6, 8, 10, 27, 167n15; newspapers' role in conveying of, 7; and origins of popular politics, 22, 172–73n4; and partisan allegiance, 18; power and authority in, 4, 9; quality of engagement in, 1, 87, 88; role of partisanship in, 3, 10, 11, 12, 23, 173nn8, 9;

235

American political culture (cont.)
shifting emotional landscapes of, 4–5.
See also antebellum political music;
early American political music
American Revolution: Federalists
on, 15, 16, 24, 32–33, 36, 37, 42,
47; French contribution to, 70;
popular music of, 26; radical
elements of, 14
Ames, Fisher, 15, 17
Amphion's harp, 24–25, 174n12
Andrew, J. A., 99
Anglican revivalism, 41
antebellum electoral politics: and
establishment of two-party system,
89; as golden age of political participation, 168n23; and partisan mobs
and election riots, 104, 195n101;
popular nature of participation, 87,
190n15; quality of political engagement, 88; social and cultural connections of, 87
antebellum political music: as agent of
political change, 87; arguments over
use of, 88; and expansion of the
franchise, 89; as legitimate form of
political expression, 87; and partisanship, 84–87; precedents for, 92–93;
purpose of campaign songs, 87; as
respectable outlet for political
passions, 87, 88, 89, 105–7; role of, 10,
12, 84–87, 110–11, 168n23; Henry
Russell's performance of, 84–86;
significance of, 88–92
antislavery movement: and legacy of
Federalist conservatism, 197n5; role
of music in, 89; and S. Willard
Saxton, 10, 129, 135, 136, 140, 144,
146, 148–50, 154, 156, 162. *See also*
abolitionism
Appleton, Nathan, 186n113
art societies, 49
Attali, Jacques, 22–23
audiotopias, 197n2
Aurora, 35, 36

Bach, Johann Sebastian, 203n116
Bache, Benjamin Franklin, 34–36
Baily, Mrs. Joel J., 128
Baltimore Exchange, 159
Banner, James M., 173n8
Barnum, P. T., 131, 200n48
Battery, New York City, 1
Battle of New Orleans, 19
Battle of Tippecanoe, 90
"Bay Psalm Book," 19
Bee, 2
Beekley, Nathan, 105–7
Beethoven, Ludwig van, 64, 66, 124–25,
132, 137, 145, 184n62, 203nn113, 116
Ben-Atar, Doron, 172n4
Benevolent Empire, 77
Bennett, James Gordon, 92–93
Berkshire Reporter, 40–41
Bernard, Hattie, 149
Bible societies, 56
Billings, William, 20, 171n36
Birch, Thomas, 102
Bishop, Anna, 124
blackface dialect, 189n3
blackface minstrelsy, 154, 171n28,
203n116
Blunt, Ellen Key, 10, 158, 163
Boston, Massachusetts, public schools
of, 77–80, 82, 161, 181n26, 187n129,
187–88n134, 188n138
Boston Academy of Music: charter of,
71–72, 77; conservatism of, 76–77;
and Samuel Atkins Eliot, 72–81; and
elitism, 50, 59, 70, 72–74, 81,
186n113; and Federalism, 74,
186n113; founding of, 9, 50, 69, 70;
funding of, 72–73, 186n110; influence
on public culture, 82; and Lowell
Mason, 61, 70–71, 78–79, 81;
music-education program of, 70, 71,
72, 76, 77–80, 82, 161, 188n138;
national reputation of, 51; political
function of, 81–82; public concerts
of, 70, 71, 74, 81, 200n38; purpose
of, 70–71

236 *Index*

Boston Associates, 186n113
Boston Evening Transcript, 128
Boston Handel and Haydn Society, 59–60, 61, 69, 70–71, 183n60, 184n62
Boston Handel and Haydn Society Collection of Church Music, The, 60–61
Boston Harmonick Club, 45, 55
Boston Independent Musical Society, 53
Boston Mechanic's Fair, 130
Boston Musical Fund Society, 114, 126, 130
Boston Philharmonic Society, 132
Boston Printer's Protective Union, 118, 141, 142, 199n21
Boston School Committee, 77–79, 80, 187n129
Boston Telegraph, 114
Boutwell, George S., 135
Bremner, James, 19
Briggs, George N., 135
Brisbane, Albert, 119–21
Britain: as ally of the United States, 24, 33, 34, 35; and classicism, 175n28; cultural emulation of, 172n38; debates on musical power, 22, 26, 28–29; as model for American republic, 16; musical organizations of, 51–53, 56, 62, 63, 70; popular music in Victorian period, 88
broadsides, 7
Brook Farm: and antiwar sentiment, 130; John S. Dwight at, 119, 120, 123, 199nn24, 25, 27; S. Willard Saxton at, 117, 119, 123, 124, 129, 134, 138–39, 154, 155, 199n24, 203n114
Brooklyn Daily Times, 163
Brooks, Preston, 150
Brown, Joseph, 185n100
Broyles, Michael, 183n60, 186n108, 199n27
Bruce, Abel W., 185n100
Bryant, William C., 85–86
Buchanan, James, 150–51
"Buckeye Song," 102
Buckley, Peter, 130

Burleigh, William H., 110
Burney, Charles, 28–30
Bushman, Richard L., 90, 171–72n38

"Ça Ira," 1, 34
call-and-response style, of lining-out, 19
Carr, Benjamin, 67
Centinel of Freedom, 96
Channing, William Henry, 129
Chartist Movement, 88
Cheathem, Mark, 190n16
Chickering, Jonas, 185n100
Christy's Minstrels, 137–38
Chronotype, 134
citizenship, duties of, 24, 39, 42, 74
civil society: hierarchical vision of, 9, 41, 66, 75–76, 81, 82, 172n4; and musical organizations, 9, 50–51, 56, 67, 79, 81, 82, 83, 100; scale and variety of, 9; state's relationship with, 9, 14, 49, 72; and voluntary associations, 3, 48–49, 68, 180n6; and Whig Party's Tippecanoe Clubs, 100–101
Civil War, 153, 154–56, 159–61
Clark, James, 48
Clarke, Jennie, 124
class: and common man, 83, 88, 90, 163; and creation of political identity, 3; musical evidence in histories of, 167n15; music's leveling effect on, 2, 89, 166n5; and presidential election of 1840, 90. *See also* American elites; lower class; middle class; working class
Clay, Henry, 105, 192n39
Cleveland Daily Herald, 94
Cleves, Rachel Hope, 197n5
Cobbett, William, 36
colonial period, access to European music in, 19
Columbian Centinel, 60
Commercial Advertiser, 189n2
common man, 83, 88, 90, 163

Index 237

Confederacy: and Civil War, 154; songs in support of, 10, 158, 159–61
Congress, role of music in, 11, 169n25
Congreve, William, 30
Conlin, Michael F., 197n5
Connecticut Courant, 86
conservatism: of Boston Academy of Music, 76–77; of Federalist Party, 15–16, 197n5; of Francis Scott Key, 163; of musical organizations, 9, 10, 11, 12, 56–61, 62, 82–83, 162; of musical tradition of Whig Party, 19, 79–80, 81, 111; values of, 197n5
consumerism, 167n15
Cragen, L. S., 185n100
Crew, Danny O., 191–92n37
Cripe, Helen, 177n59
Crist, Elizabeth B., 167n15
Cross, Benjamin, 67
Currier, Nathaniel, 102

Daily National Intelligencer, 94
Dana, Charles, 203n114
Darnton, Robert, 167n15
Dartmouth v. Woodward (1819), 68
Davis, David, 193n64
Day, H. W., 181n12
deception, public's susceptibility to, 166–67n11
democracy: conservative reaction to expansion of, 87–88, 190n17; Samuel Atkins Eliot on, 75–76; and expansion of the franchise, 89, 93, 111, 161; Federalist Party on, 15–16, 40–41, 82; and intelligence required for universal suffrage, 61; popular democracy, 12, 87–88, 93, 107, 111, 162, 163, 190n17; Republican Party on, 16, 40, 178n71
Democratic Party: campaign songs of, 92, 94; conservatism of, 197n5; and Free Soil Party, 135–36, 142; mass political organizing techniques of, 88; and presidential election of 1840, 88; and presidential election of 1852, 11, 137; and presidential election of 1856, 150–51; on public education, 79, 80; rallies of, 103; songsters of, 192nn37, 39; on Whig Party's use of campaign songs, 10, 84, 85, 86, 92, 93, 95, 97, 107–10, 162, 192n39, 193n62, 196n112
Democratic-Republican clubs, 17
Dempster, William R., 131–32, 202n86
Dewey, Orville, 103
Dial, 120
Dickinson, John, 26
"Dixie," 160
Doty, Elihu, 40
Douglass, Frederick, 136, 139
Dowling, William C., 23
Dubois, Louis, 39
Du Ponceau, Peter S., 40, 64, 177n63
Dwight, John S.: at Brook Farm, 119, 120, 123, 199nn24, 25, 27; and early American music criticism, 120, 121–22, 123, 124–28, 132, 144, 199–200n27, 200n38; and Fourierist Associationalism, 119, 120, 121, 122–23, 131, 199–200n27; and S. Willard Saxton, 119, 124–27, 131, 132, 144, 145
Dwight, Mary, 127
Dyer, Oliver, 11, 169n25

early American political music: and American identity, 19; conservative potential of, 2, 8, 10, 11, 12; Federalist conception of, 8, 9, 10, 12, 22, 23, 24–32, 168n21; motivations in use of, 5, 6, 8, 21–22, 26; and musical organizations, 168n20; Old World melodies reappropriated in, 168n16; and partisanship, 1, 34, 36; political logic of use of, 6; politics of determining meaning of, 1–2, 7; purpose of, 4, 5, 6; respectability of, 2, 11–12; role in legitimating leaders, 13; sense of order and respectability projected by, 2, 11–12
Edinburgh Musical Society, 52

education: public music education, 70, 72, 77–80, 82, 187–88n134, 188n138; public schools, 61, 181n26; textbooks and schooling compared to musical organizations, 183n45
Eliot, Samuel Atkins, 59, 72–81, 186nn108, 109, 187n121
Eliot, William, 73–74, 186n113
elite identities: internal and external perception of, 167n13; and middle class, 89
elitism: and Boston Academy of Music, 50, 59, 70, 72–74, 81, 186n113; defining of, 23, 167n13, 173n10; in Federalist values, 9, 14, 15, 17, 18, 19, 22, 23–24, 40–41, 45, 46–47, 51, 56, 56–61, 62, 64, 74, 170–71n26, 173n9; and Musical Fund Society of Philadelphia, 50, 62, 81. *See also* American elites
Elkins, Stanley, 173n8
Emerson, Caleb, 57
Enlightenment, 28
enslaved people: agency expressed in music, 2; S. Willard Saxton on, 140; threats of revolt of, 17
Estes, Todd, 173n9
European cultural standards, American culture measured against, 18–19, 20, 172n38
European music: exclusive access to, 19; and musical associations, 51, 60, 70; patrons of, 27; and public education, 70
Euterpeiad, or Musical Intelligencer, 49, 67
evangelical religion: and musical organizations, 70, 74, 76–77, 81; role of music in, 89, 90–91; and Whig Party, 10, 90–91, 94, 109
Evangelical United Front, 77
Evening Post, 85, 92
Everett, Edward, 79

Fabbroni, Giovanni, 177n59
factional interests, 26

federal government, debates on role of, 14–15
Federalism: cultural politics of, 23, 46, 62–64, 66–69, 74, 98, 172n4, 173n8, 186n113; Democratic Party's linking Whig campaign music to, 108–9; ideology of, 23, 24, 51, 74, 83; legacy of, 46; as literary expression, 23; and Musical Fund Society of Philadelphia, 62–64, 66–69, 74, 162, 184n72; principles of, 9, 168n21
Federalist Party: black cockades worn by, 1, 18, 34, 35; Britain as model for American republic, 16; British values and traditions respected by, 16, 17, 42; changes from 1780s to 1790s, 169n4; conception of music in politics, 8, 9, 10, 12, 22, 23, 24–32, 39, 40–41, 43, 45, 46–47, 74, 168n21; conservatism of, 15–16, 197n5; on democracy, 15–16, 40–41, 82; electoral viability of, 9, 56, 62, 74–75, 83; elite values of, 9, 14, 15, 17, 18, 19, 22, 23–24, 40–41, 45, 46–47, 51, 56, 56–61, 62, 64, 74, 162, 170–71n26, 173n9; "Hail Columbia" as favorite of, 1–2, 34, 35, 36–37, 41, 44, 161, 162; hierarchical view of American polity, 41, 70, 74, 172n4; influence on civil society, 82; moral principles of, 18, 24; musical ideal of, 32–37, 39–41, 51, 162; music tradition of, 22–23, 30, 39, 40, 45, 88, 162, 163, 172–73n4, 177–78n67; on national identity, 18; and national unity, 15, 18, 26, 34–35, 36, 37, 41, 42–43; on natural rights, 16; as patriotic Friend of Order, 18; political collapse of, 75; popular politics used by, 22, 172n4; on relationship between American people and their leaders, 12, 14–17, 18, 20, 22, 24, 26, 40–41, 42, 45, 178n71; on social control, 17; and "The Star-Spangled Banner," 8–9, 23; strategies for manipulating public

Index 239

Federalist Party (cont.)
  opinion, 30; and top-down approach,
  9, 20, 22–23, 24, 26, 39, 41, 57, 161,
  162; and urban-centered fiscal-
  military state, 14, 15; and War of
  1812, 9, 42, 44; George Washington
  supported by, 169n4
"Federal Song–'Hail Columbia'," 1
Federal Street Theatre, Boston, 72
Fenno, John, 36
"Fine English Gentleman, A," 189n3
"Fine Old English Gentleman," 189
fire-prevention societies, 56, 100
Fischer, David Hackett, 168n21, 172n4,
  173n8
Fitzhugh, George, 150
Fletcher, Andrew (of Saltoun), 96
Formes, Karl, 152, 205n179
Fort McHenry, 21, 42–44, 46, 159
Fort McHenry National Monument and
  Historic Shrine, 21
Fortune, Michael, 39
Fourier, Charles, 119–20, 124, 131
Fourierist Associationalism, 117,
  119–24, 119–200n27, 129, 131, 134,
  150, 155
Fourth of July celebrations, 43, 54, 99
France: as ally of the United States, 24,
  34, 36, 70; French Revolution, 16,
  17, 34, 129, 170nn16, 21; United
  States Quasi-War against, 1; and
  XYZ Affair, 33
Frederick-Town Herald, 45
Freedmen's Bureau, 117, 156–57, 198n20
Free Soil Party, 109, 129, 135–37, 139,
  141–42, 144–46, 148, 192n37, 205n160
Frémont, Jessie Benton, 110
Frémont, John C., 110, 150–51
Frémont Clubs, 150
French Revolution, 16, 17, 34, 129,
  170nn16, 21
Fugitive Slave Law, 129, 135, 136, 146

Garrison, William Lloyd, 104
Gazette of the United States, 36, 37, 39

gender: and creation of political
  identity, 3; musical evidence in
  histories of, 167n15. *See also* women
"General Harrison's log cabin march and
  quick step," 91
Genêt, Edmond, 17
Germanians (Germania Musical
  Society), 144, 204n146, 206n182
Germany, 70, 190n19
"Get Off the Track!," 138
Gilles, P., 185n83
Ginzburg, Carlo, 167n15
Gleason, Benjamin, 40, 177n67
Gluck, Christoph Willibald, 182n39
"God Save the King," 2, 7, 34
"Good Hard Cider," 102
Gordon-Reed, Annette, 178n68
grammar schools, 181n26
Grant, Ulysses S., 110
Grant Clubs, 110
Great Awakening, 52
Greeley, Horace, 97–98, 102, 120,
  193n64, 194n69
Groves, Daniel, 48
Gunderson, Robert G., 97, 194n69

"Hail Columbia": John Adams's image on
  sheet music of, 37, 38; as Federalist
  song, 1–2, 34, 35, 36–37, 41, 44, 161,
  162; Joseph Hopkinson's composition
  of, 33, 34, 36–37, 176n54; popularity
  of, 34, 37, 44
Hale, John P., 142
Hale, Nathan, 78, 187n134, 188n136
Hallowell Musical Institute, 58
Hamilton, Alexander, 14–15
Handel, George Frideric, 54, 59, 145
Handellian Musical Society, 57
Handel Society of Dartmouth College, 55
Harbinger, 117, 119, 121, 122, 126,
  199nn24, 27
Harmonic Society, 182n39
harmony: and campaign songs, 95; as
  goal of American elites, 3–4, 15, 24,
  163; and harmonious sensations

produced by music, 20, 80, 130–31, 132; and role of early American political music, 4, 11, 13, 45; role of music in forging harmonious republic, 20, 25, 160–61; Joseph Sill on, 103
Harrison, William Henry: and campaign songs, 84, 91, 92–93, 94, 107–9, 192n39; man-of-the-people image, 90; as scholar, 90, 191n31; and songsters, 95, 191–92n37
Harrison Log Cabin Song Book, The, 95
Harrison Melodies, 95, 96
"Harrison Song," 96, 99
Hartford Convention, 9, 108, 186n113
Hartford Times, 107
Harvard Musical Association, 120
Hawkins, John, 28–29
Hayden, William, 99, 189nn2, 3
Haydn, Joseph, 54, 59, 64, 66, 152, 182n39
Hayes, Catherine, 138, 203n116
"Hero of Tippecanoe, The," 192n39
Historical Society of Pennsylvania, 63
Hoffman, Richard, 138, 203n116
Hopkinson, Francis, 26–32, 33, 39, 162, 174n22, 175nn28, 32
Hopkinson, Joseph, 33–37, 63, 161, 162
Howard, Edward D., 110
Howard, Frank Key, 158–59
Hoxie, Joseph, 108
"Hunters of Kentucky," 19
Hunting, Bela, 185n100
Hupfelt, Charles, 67
"Hurrah for Old Tippecanoe," 192n39
Hutchinson, Abby, 138–40
Hutchinson, Asa, 140
Hutchinson, John, 141
Hutchinson Family Singers, 138–43, 151, 203n120

ideology: and creation of political identity, 3; of Federalism, 23, 24, 51, 74, 83
immigration, 167n15

Independent Musical Society, 54–55
Institution for the Instruction of the Blind, 63

Jackson, Andrew, 79, 87, 88, 93
Jackson, Jonathan, 15
Jackson, Patrick Tracy, 186n113
Jacksonian period, 88, 191n26, 191nn23, 26
Jay Treaty, 24, 26, 33, 46
Jefferson, Maria, 31
Jefferson, Thomas: Michael Fortune's correspondence with, 39; Francis Hopkinson's correspondence with, 30–32, 174n22; on Joseph Hopkinson, 36, 176n54; on music and politics, 32, 39–40, 176n42, 177n59, 178n68; on natural aristocracy, 178n71; and Republican Party, 15, 17; scrapbooks of, 39–40, 177–78n67; on self-sufficient agrarian landholders, 14; on the United States Constitution, 31
"Jefferson and Liberty," 39–40, 43, 177n63
"Jefferson's Election," 43
"Jefferson's March," 40
Jessie Songster, 110
Journal of Music, Dwight's 119, 144, 145

Kane, John K., 48, 63–64, 66–67, 68, 162–63, 184n72
Kerber, Linda K., 173n8
Key, Francis Scott: composing of "The Star-Spangled Banner," 8–9, 21, 22, 24, 41–45, 46, 105, 158, 159, 162; connection to Federalist tradition, 22, 23, 24, 41, 42, 45, 46; conservatism of, 163; daughter extending patriotic songwriting tradition of, 10, 158; on partisanship, 24, 41–44, 45, 46; songwriting success of, 44–45
Kleinstrup, Louise, 112, 133–34, 141, 202nn96, 98
Kleinstrup, Peter, 202n98
Know Nothings, 205n160

Index 241

Kubler, G. F., 186n105
Kun, Josh, 197n2, 208n18

Lachner, Franz, 123, 200n38
Law Association of Philadelphia, 63
Lee, James Kendall, 105
Lee, Robert E., 157
Le Grand, Julia, 160
Lehman, William, 63, 184n72
Liberty Party, 192n37
"Liberty Song," 26
library societies, 56
Lincoln, Abraham, 160
Lincoln, Levi, Jr., 68
Lind, Jenny: and Boston Musical Fund Society, 126, 130; charitable giving of, 133–34; concert tours of the United States, 125–28, 127, 135, 136, 200n48; and Richard Hoffman, 203n116; political convictions of, 138, 203n120; and S. Willard Saxton, 125–36, 139, 140, 156; and Daniel Webster, 202n103
lining-out, 19, 52
Liszt, Franz, 206n192
literary societies, 49
"Little Pig's Tail," 107
Livermore, Solomon Kidder, 57, 183n46
Log Cabin, 97, 102, 194n69
"Log Cabin," 102
Log Cabin and Hard Cider Melodies, The, 96
Log Cabin Minstrel, The: or, Tippecanoe Songster, 95
Log Cabin Song Book, 97
lower class, 14
luxurious consumption, 172n38
Lynn, Joshua A., 197n5
Lyre, or New-York Musical Journal, 49–50

McCaffrey, Henry, 159
McKitrick, Eric, 173n8
Madison, James, 15, 39
Madisonian, 93, 192–93n46
Maine Cultivator and Hallowell Gazette, 58
Malcolm, Samuel, 1

Mann, Horace, 79–80
Manual of the Boston Academy of Music, 71
"Marseillaise, The," 17, 34, 189n3
Mason, Lowell, 60–61, 70–71, 72, 78–79, 81, 185n100, 186nn105, 109
Massachusetts Board of Education, 79–80
Massachusetts Centinel, 54
Mathews, John, 192n39
Maxim, John, 100
Memphis Eagle & Enquirer, 148
Mendelssohn, Felix, 125, 203n116
Meredith, William M., 184n72
Mexican-American War, 129–30
middle class: adoption of melodies of blackface minstrelsy, 171n28, 203n116; on democratic and egalitarian society, 14; and musical organizations, 59, 69, 70, 74, 76–77; and music as moral influence, 88; music's role in aspirations of, 89
Middlesex Musical Society of Massachusetts, 55, 57
minorities, 16
Mirror of Taste and Dramatic Censor, The, 8
modernity, debates on, 28
morality: music as moral corrective, 4, 11, 56, 59, 70, 74, 88, 163; in Whig Party's political culture, 98; in Whig Party's use of music, 90
Morey, Cassius M., 193n64
Motier, Gilbert du (Marquis de La Fayette), 153
Mozart, Wolfgang Amadeus, 64, 145, 182n39
Mulford, Daniel, 99
Mulford, Levi, 99
Murrin, John, 172n38
music: as adaptable tool, 8; American diarists on, 5, 167n12; and aspirations of middle class, 89; William Billings's theory of physical properties of sound, 20, 171n36; collective participation in, 4, 7, 8, 168n20; elite culture connected to, 19; emancipatory role in social movements, 173n7;

formats for circulation of lyrics and melodies, 7; forms of, 168n20; German views on public utility of art music, 190n19; ideals of American national music, 163, 199–200n27; and lack of sound recording, 4, 7; and leveling of class, 2, 89, 166n5; as moral corrective, 4, 11, 56, 59, 70, 74, 88, 163; as populist medium, 5; religion connected to, 19–20; respectable music, 60; sensations and science of music and sound, 91, 191n36; social effects of, 23; temperament moderated by, 9, 11, 25, 30, 112, 126, 127–28, 129, 131–32. *See also* antebellum political music; early American political music; patriotic music

Musical Fund Hall, 103

Musical Fund Society of Cincinnati, 58

Musical Fund Society of Philadelphia: constitution of, 66–67; and elitism, 50, 62, 81; and Federalism, 62–64, 66–69, 74, 162, 184n72; founding of, 9, 50, 64; incorporation of, 48, 68–69, 82, 161, 185n91; influence on public culture, 79, 82; membership of, 62–63, 67, 102, 184n71, 195n90; as model for precursor to the Boston Academy of Music, 73–74; national reputation of, 51; physicians on board of, 62, 184n70; sketch of members of, 65

musical literacy, in religious music, 20

musical organizations: of Britain, 51–53, 56, 62, 63, 70; and civil society, 9, 50–51, 56, 67, 79, 81, 82, 83, 100; and early American political music, 168n20; elitist conservatism in, 9, 10, 11, 12, 56–61, 62, 82–83, 162; and Federalist elite cultural stewardship, 62–64, 66–69, 74, 83, 186n113; and improvement of public life, 49, 55, 56–58, 62, 66, 67, 79, 81, 82–83; incorporation of, 48, 68; and middle class, 59, 69, 70, 74, 76–77; and music as public good, 49, 50–51, 53, 58, 59, 60, 61, 82, 183n60; and music press, 49–50, 60–61; origins of, 51–56; political debates surrounding, 56–57, 61; purpose of, 49, 50, 56, 57; and salon concert culture, 51–52, 53; and singing schools, 52–53, 54, 55, 56, 82; and singing societies, 53; structure of, 49, 55–56; and subscription concert series, 51–52, 181n17; textbooks and schooling compared to, 183n45; top-down approach of, 57–58, 82–83. *See also* Boston Academy of Music; Musical Fund Society of Philadelphia

Musical Pioneer, 169n25

musical power: in ancient world, 27–28; and development of popular American political culture, 3, 4; English debates on, 22, 26, 28–29; Francis Hopkinson on, 30; S. Willard Saxton on, 112, 113, 128, 131, 132, 139; George Washington on, 27–28, 29

Musical Times, 168n20

Musical Visitor, 181n12

Musical World and Times, 10–11, 169n25

musicians marching, 106

musicology: on antebellum music periodicals, 113; on early American music, 3, 166n7; and reception studies, 167n15

music press: and musical organizations, 49–50, 60–61; purpose of, 49–50; growth of, 180–81n12

mutual-protection societies, 56

Nantucket Inquirer, 96

National Clay Minstrel, The, 109

nationalism, 3, 20, 158, 172n38, 208n18

National Republicans, 75, 187n121

"National Whig Song, The," 84, 86, 96, 99, 189nn2, 3

Nebraska controversy, 146, 148, 205n160

Neem, Johann, 75

New England Psalm-Singer, 171n36
newest political history, 5, 166n7
New Hampshire, 55, 182n40
New Hampshire Patriot, 55
New Hampshire Patriot and State Gazette, 109
New Musical Fund in London, 62
New North Singing Society, 53, 54
newspapers: advertisements for subscription concert series, 181n17; and partisanship, 42, 44, 85–86; political songs published by, 11, 96, 97; on sounds and sensations of political gatherings, 7; on "The Star-Spangled Banner," 44. *See also specific newspapers*
Newton, Isaac, 119
New York Courier, 85
New York Daily Advertiser, 1
New York Evening Post, 92, 109
New York Express, 86
New York Philharmonic Society, 50
New York Tribune, 120
Niblo, William, 84–86, 138
Nicholson, Joseph Hopper, 44–45
Norfolk Democrat, 107
North American, 86
North American Review, 75, 107
North Writing School, Boston, 53

Oberg, Barbara B., 172n4
"Ode Inscribed to the 4th of July, 1805," 40
Odeon Theatre, Boston, 72, 73, 74
"Ode to Columbia's Favorite Son," 54
"Ode to Liberty," 40
Ohio State Journal, 86, 96
Ohio Statesman, 108–9
O. K. Songster, The, 192n39
"Old Tippecanoe," 192n39
Oneida peoples, 36
Onuf, Peter S., 178n68
Otis, Harrison Gray, 186n113

Paine, Robert Treat, Jr., 43, 178n67
Paine, Thomas, 178n67

Panic of 1837, 120
Parker, John Rowe, 61, 67
Parker, Theodore, 136, 146, 148
partisanship: and antebellum political music, 84–87; and early American political music, 1, 34, 36; Joseph Hopkinson on, 33–34; Thomas Jefferson on, 31; Francis Scott Key on, 24, 41–44, 45, 46; music as defense against, 11, 12, 26; and newspapers, 42, 44, 85–86; role in American political culture, 3, 10, 11, 12, 23, 173nn8, 9
Pasley, Jeffrey L., 166n7
patriotic music: and American identity, 19; and Civil War, 159; Thomas Jefferson's promotion of, 40; nationalizing capabilities of, 40; political basis of, 2, 8, 9, 24. *See also* "Hail Columbia"; "Star-Spangled Banner, The"
"Patriotic Song," 40
patriotism: and American Revolution, 32–33; Joseph Hopkinson on, 34; and musical organizations, 54, 55; music's contribution to, 4; and national unity, 42–43, 45; political tensions over, 3, 20, 43–44; timeless patriotism, 21; top-down patriotism, 24; of Whig campaign songs, 107, 109
Patterson, Robert M., 64, 66–67, 185n80
Patton, Ludlow, 139
Peace Democrats, 160
Peale, Charles Willson, 177n63
Peale, Rembrandt, 40
Pennsylvania Packet, 13
"People's Friend, The," 40
Philadelphia Academy of Fine Arts, 63
Philadelphia Democratic Press, 48
Phillips, Wendell, 136
Pierce, Franklin, 11
Pips, Sebastian, 128
Pittsburgh Daily American, 93–94
Pittsfield Sun, 107
Plutarch, 93, 192–93n46

political identities, factors contributing to creation of, 3, 17–18, 170–71n26
political participation: golden age of, 168n23; popular nature of, 87, 190n15; and S. Willard Saxton's ties to music, 125–37, 138, 139, 141–43, 157, 162; of women, 16, 90, 111, 160
Pollock, George, 185n100
Polybius, 93
Pope, Alexander, 25–26, 174n17
Porcupine's Gazette, 36
Power, Thomas, 99, 194n74
power: of campaign songs, 110; and early national creative culture, 171–72n38; established elite power, 5; Federalist Party's moral justification for, 18; links between intimate and institutional power, 4; and perceptions of elite identities, 167n13; top-down power, 5, 9–10, 20, 22–23, 24, 26, 39, 41, 75–76, 162. *See also* musical power
Prescott, William H., 186n113
presidential election of 1800, 39
presidential election of 1840: role of class and refinement in, 90; role of music in, 10, 84, 87, 88–92, 109, 111, 161–62, 189n2; and songsters, 191–92n37, 192n39
presidential election of 1844, 105
presidential election of 1848, 105, 109–10
presidential election of 1852, 10–11, 110, 137
presidential election of 1856, 150–51
presidential election of 1860, 110, 117
presidential election of 1868, 110
"President's March, The," 34–35
private sphere, 191n26
protest music, 2
Psallonian Society, 58
public sphere, 14, 191n26
Putnam, George P., 160

Quasi-War against France (1798), 1
Quincy, Josiah, 186n113

race, and creation of political identity, 3
Randolph, John, 42
Ray, William, 40, 178n67
Read, John M., 184n72
Rebel Rhymes and Rhapsodies, 160
Reconstruction, 156
Reed, George P., 203n113
reform movements: John S. Dwight on societal reform, 121; educational reform, 79; and musical organizations, 59, 69, 70, 74, 76–77; and music as moral influence, 88; role of music in, 89
Regular Singing, 20, 52
Reign of Terror, 16
religion: and devotional singing, 19–20; and instrumental music in church, 30, 40–41, 175n32, 188n136; and musical organizations, 54, 58, 60, 70, 71, 76–77; role of music in, 122–23; and S. Willard Saxton, 129, 148–49, 152, 156; and singing schools for improving psalm singing, 52–53. *See also* evangelical religion
Republican Campaign Songster, 110
Republican Party (Civil War Era): and presidential election of 1856, 150–51; Mary Grant Saxton's support of, 153; and music in presidential election of 1860, 110; and music in presidential election of 1868, 110; S. Willard Saxton canvassing for, 206n199
Republican Party (Jeffersonian): as agents of Jacobin terror, 18; on agrarian-based local control, 14, 15; on Britain representing monarchical tyranny, 16; conception of music in politics, 39–40, 45; on democracy, 16, 40, 178n71; elites of, 32, 39–40, 64, 170–71n26,; on equality of opportunity, 171n26; and France, 33, 34; on incorporation of voluntary organizations, 68; on music sung by Federalists, 1–2, 35–36, 37, 39; musical tradition of, 40, 43, 177n67;

Index   245

Republican Party (Jeffersonian) (cont.)
music used to influence national affairs, 32, 172n4; and national unity, 45; oppositional roots of, 32, 37; popular political tactics of, 177n59; public influence of, 67–68; on public sphere, 14; on relationship between American people and their leaders, 14–15, 39, 40, 178n71; Revolutionary ideals of, 16, 17; songsters of, 110; tricolored cockades of, 17, 18, 34

respectability: antebellum political music as outlet for political passions, 87, 88, 89, 105–7; and Nathan Beekley, 106–7; of early American political music, 2, 11–12; and Joseph Sill, 102, 103–4; of Whig Party's campaign songs, 88, 89, 90, 93, 95, 97, 102, 105–6, 109, 111, 162

"Rights of Women, The," 2

Ripley, George, 117, 120, 203n114

Robertson, Andrew W., 166n7

Ross, Alexander Coffman, 98, 100

Royal Society of Musicians, 62

Russell, Dave, 88

Russell, Henry, 84–86, *85*, 109, 202n86

Sacred Harp, 52

St. Cecilia Society, 51, 182n39

Salem Mozart Association, 68

Saloman, Ora F., 199n27

Saxton, Edward, 146

Saxton, Jonathan Ashley, 116–17

Saxton, Mary Grant, 117, 153, 155

Saxton, Rufus, 117, 135, 155–56

Saxton, S. Willard: aesthetic judgment of, 124, 125, 129, 131; and antislavery movement, 10, 129, 135, 136, 140, 144, 146, 148–50, 154, 156, 162; at Brook Farm, 117, 119, 123, 124, 129, 134, 138–39, 154, 155, 199n24, 203n114; canvassing for political parties, 117, 136–37, 155, 206n199; and Civil War, 154–56; and commercialized music culture, 112, 113–14; in debtor's prison, 117; and John S. Dwight, 119, 124–27, 131, 132, 144, 145; estrangement of music from politics, 143–46, 148–55; existential crisis in transition to urban life, 112–13, 197n4; family background of, 116–17; and financial imperatives, 155; foundations of musical appreciation, 118–25; and Fourierist Associationalism, 123–24, 129, 134, 150, 154; and Freedmen's Bureau, 117, 156–57, 198n20; and Hutchinson Family Singers, 138–43, 151; journal of, 113, 114, *115*, 116, 117, 118–19, 123–28, 129, 136, 139, 146, 152, 153, 155, 198nn10, 20, 202n96, 203n116, 205–6n181; and Jenny Lind, 125–36, 139, 140, 156; marriage of, 153, 155; and opera, 153–54; photograph of, *116*; political participation tied to music, 125–37, 138, 139, 141–43, 157, 162; and printing trade, 117, 118, 119, 137, 140, 141, 142, 144, 155, 197n4, 198–99n21, 203n114; and Reconstruction, 156; relationship to music, 10, 113–14, 116–17, 123, 124–25, 131–32, 137–38, 143, 144–46, 148–53, 156–57, 197n2; and religion, 129, 148–49, 152, 156; and Charles P. Sumner, 141–42, 143, 144, 150; on utopic qualities of music, 112–13, 125, 126, 157, 162–63, 197n2; in West, 143, 144–46, 148–50

Schenck, R. C., 207n9

Schetky, George, 185n83

Schocket, Andrew M., 173n10

Schreiber, Lee, 63

Scott, Winfield, 10

Scott and Graham Songster, 110

Seitz, Don C., 194n69

self-made man, 75

sensibility, culture of, 4, 166–67n11

sentimentalism, 4–5, 121, 166–67n11

September Massacres, 17

Shadle, Douglas W., 199–200n27

sheet-music industry, 5, *101*, 102

Sherman, Thomas W., 155
Sherman, William T., 156
Sill, Joseph, 102–5, 195n101
"Singing Girl, The," 147
"Six Patriotic Ballads," 101, 102, 195n87
slavery: and music press, 181n12; political tensions over, 3, 17; S. Willard Saxton's observations on, 140; South's views on expansion of, 14. *See also* antislavery movement
Smith, Adam I. P., 197n5
social life, musical evidence in histories of, 167n15
Society for Promoting Regular Singing in the Worship of God, 52
Song Messenger of the Northwest, 110
Songs for the People, 96, 100
songsters: of Democratic Party, 192nn37, 39; prefaces outlining purpose of, 6; and presidential election of 1840, 191–92n37, 192n39; publication of melodies in, 7; Whig songsters, 91, 95–97, 99, 101, 102, 109, 110, 191–92n37; Republican Party (Civil War Era) songsters, 110
South, 14. *See also* Confederacy
"Southern Cross, The" (Blunt), 158
Spear, Charles, 134
Spear, John M., 134
"Specie Law," 196n112
spoils system, 79, 84
sporting clubs, 49
"Star-Spangled Banner, The": and Ellen Key Blunt's "The Southern Cross," 158; contemporary political debate over, 172n3; evolution of meaning of, 179n89; and Federalist Party, 8–9, 23; Francis Scott Key's composing of, 8–9, 21, 22, 24, 41–45, 46, 105, 158, 159, 162; as a national anthem, 105; political context of, 8, 43–44, 46, 47; popularity of, 44; publication of, 44–45
state, civil society's relationship with, 9, 14, 49, 72
Stockbridge, Charles, 171n36

Street, Alfred B., 99
Strong, George Templeton, 84, 189n3
Sullivan, William, 186n113
Sully, Thomas, 102, 195n90
Sumner, Charles Pinckney, 40, 135–36, 141–43, 144, 150, 153, 178n67
Swifts, John L., 146
Swindells, James H., 50
Switzerland, 70

Tallmadge, Benjamin, 16
Taney, Roger B., 45–46
taste, cultural politics of: and John S. Dwight on music, 123; in German music and society, 190n19; in musical organizations, 49, 53, 56–62, 64, 66–67, 69, 73–74, 82, 161; in comparisons to European music, 18; and S. Willard Saxton, 125, 132, 146, 150, 154; and Joseph Sill on music, 103; in Whig campaign songs, 95, 96; and Walt Whitman on music, 163
Taylor, Alan, 15
Taylor, Jordan E., 170n21
Taylor, Raynor, 185n83
temperance reform, role of music in, 89, 138
Tevis, Julia Hieronymus, 44
Thalberg, Sigismond, 154, 206n192
theatrical associations, 49
Thomas, Isaiah, 40
Thorndike, Israel, Jr., 186n113
"Tippecanoe and Tyler, Too," 91–92, 98, 107
Tippecanoe Clubs, 99–100, 102, 195nn85, 87
Tippecanoe Songbook, 99
"Tip's Invitation to Loco," 102
"To Anacreon in Heaven," 40, 43
transcendentalism, 122, 199–200n27
Trump, Donald J., 172n3
Tyler, John, 138

Ulrich, Laurel Thatcher, 197n4
Union Harmonic Society, 58

Unitarianism, 77
United States Constitution: Federalist Party on, 16; the People defined in, 14; ratification of, 11, 22, 26, 31
United States Supreme Court, 68
University of Pennsylvania, 63
utopianism, 121, 122, 123, 199n27

Van Buren, Martin, 90, 94, 129, 191–92n37
Vaughan, John, 102
Verdi, Giuseppe, 154
voluntary associations: and civil society, 3, 48–49, 68, 180n6. *See also* musical organizations
voting rights, Federalists on, 15–16

Waldstreicher, David, 166n7, 171–72n38
War of 1812: and American political music, 22, 45, 172–73n4; and composition of "The Star-Spangled Banner," 8, 21, 41, 44–45, 46, 158; era of good feelings following, 62; and Federalist Party, 9, 42, 44; and "Hunters of Kentucky," 19
Warren, John C., 186n113
Washington, George: and association with monarchical privilege, 27; Charles Burney's work compared to sentiments of, 29, 29; and codification of federal framework, 13–14; Federalist support for, 169n4; goal of neutrality, 33; Francis Hopkinson's correspondence with, 26–31, 32, 174n22, 175n28; Joseph Hopkinson's correspondence with, 33, 34; illustration in published version of "The Southern Cross," 158; musical organizations honoring, 54; on musical power in ancient world, 27–28, 29; as president, 15, 27; principles of, 107; women of Trenton serenading, 13
Webb, George James, 72, 185n100, 186n109

Webb, Nathan, 53–55, 181–82n27, 182n30
Webster, Daniel, 135, 202n103
Webster, Noah, 16
Weed, Thurlow, 97, 194n69
Western Musical World, 110
Western Recorder, 59
Whig Party: authorship of campaign songs, 95–96, 97, 98–100, 102; campaign songs of, 10, 84–86, 88, 90–95, *91*, 96, 97, 98–100, 102, 110–11, 162, 193n49; connection of civil society to public life, 81–82; conservatism of musical tradition, 19, 79–80, 81, 111; and creation of Massachusetts Board of Education, 79; Democratic Party's response to campaign songs, 10, 84, 85, 86, 92, 93, 95, 97, 107–10, 162, 192n39, 193n62, 196n112; and educational reform, 79; and Samuel Atkins Eliot, 75–80, 81, 187n121; elite conservatives of, 75, 98; and evangelical religion, 10, 90–91, 94, 109; "Harrison and Reform" slogan, 89; justifications of campaign music, 102–7; and log cabin raisings, 88; patriotic antiwar sentiment of, 130; political culture of, 98; populist campaigning of, 88; and presidential election of 1840, 10, 97, 193n64; and presidential election of 1852, 137; rallies of, 88, 104–5; and respectability of political music, 88, 89, 90, 93, 95, 97, 102, 105–6, 109, 111, 162; and Henry Russell, 84; songsters of, 91, 95–97, 99, *101*, 102, 109, 110, 191–92n37
white men, political rights of, 15, 111
Whitman, Walt, 163, 208n18
Whitman, Zachariah Gardner, 45, 55
Whitting, Isaac N., 96
Willis, Richard Storrs, 11, 169n25
Winthrop, Robert C., 136
Withington, Increase S., 185n100

women: and Confederate music, 160; "informal" political participation of, 16; as members of musical organizations, 54; political agency expressed in music, 2, 160; role in presidential election of 1840, 90, 111; voting rights of, 15; George Washington serenaded by, 13
Wood, Kirsten E., 175n28
Woodbury, I. B., 169n25
Woodworth, Samuel, 19
Worcester Mozart Society, 58
working class: agency expressed in music, 1, 2; black music appropriated by, 203n116; musical organizations' prejudice against, 60; political practices of, 5; and popular music, 88
Workingmen's movement, 161
writing schools, 53, 181n26

XYZ Affair, 33

"Yankee Doodle," 18–19
Young Men's Mercantile Library Association, 148

Zabriskie, Francis, 194n69
Zanesville Tippecanoe Club, 98
Zerrahn, Carl, 152, 206n182

www.ingramcontent.com/pod-product-compliance
Lightning Source LLC
Chambersburg PA
CBHW031805220426
43662CB00007B/537